promote and grow their sport business from a competitive perspective and relative to the five prominent leagues based in the United States and those located in other nations.

In *Sports Capitalism*, the specific topics and subtopics selected and analyzed with respect to Major League Baseball, and the National Football League, National Basketball Association, National Hockey League and Major League Soccer represent the issues, opportunities, problems and/or threats that, in part, affect those leagues' current, and potentially their future international business strategies and environments. That is, the research performed for this book indicated that those topics and subtopics are likely the most consequential and important matters that will determine which, if any, of the professional sports leagues will be industry leaders worldwide and thus economically successful as global business organizations during the early to middle years of the 21st century.

Since it was formed during the early 1900s and before the other professional sports groups, Major League Baseball is the league featured in Chapter 1 of *Sports Capitalism*. Designated as the administrative parent of two entities, Major League Baseball includes the American League and National League and their respective divisions, teams and players. After introducing Major League Baseball's international subunit, which is responsible for the implementation and operation of all the baseball league's global activities, plans, programs and relationships, the chapter highlights and addresses the topics and subtopics that involve and relate to Major League Baseball's short- and long-term business and international strategies. In part, those are composed of the former and if any, future league expansions and team relocations abroad, the formation, development and demise of the Canadian Baseball League, league and team owners' decisions about whether and/or how to schedule a World Cup of Baseball tournament, manage a player drug test program and adopt an international player draft system, contract for the worldwide broadcasts and videos of regular season games, playoffs and World Series championship series, improve the living conditions at the teams' baseball academies in the nations of Latin America, measure the affects of foreign baseball players on teams' fans and markets, and collect facts about how much the sport of baseball is respected and played in America and foreign countries.

As Chapter 1 depicts for Major League Baseball and Chapters 2–5 for the other United States-based professional sports leagues, some business decisions and international strategies that involve global issues, opportunities, problems and threats are primarily concerned with intra-league or internal policies. Those, for example, relate to the league's number of games, revisions to and adoption of baseball rules, and to collective bargaining agreements, season schedules and teams' locations and rosters. Other matters, however, are specifically inter-league and involve external issues. That is, those concerns are related to foreign nations' cultures and institutions, and to their respective economic, social and political systems. In short, the intra- and inter-league matters are why business decisions and strategies about the global sports industry appear to be controversial and complex for the United States baseball league's commissioners and franchise owners, and also for the foreign governments, federations and officials who must determine whether America's professional sports leagues should be permitted to participate in international sports events, and to conduct business transactions with affiliated companies and citizens in their respective countries.

Since America's most prominent and longstanding football league was organized after Major League Baseball and before the National Basketball Association and Major League Soccer, and because it and the sport have always been more popular with United States sports fans than the National Hockey League and ice hockey, it is the globalization strategies of the National Football League that are represented and discussed in Chapter 2. Similar to Major League Soccer, the National Football League franchises have always been located in the United States. Nevertheless, the National Football League has indeed progressed to successfully promote and extend its brand name and logo worldwide, and to establish business relationships and operate global grassroots programs, activities and events in foreign nations.

As such, in Chapter 2 there are several topics explored that relate to and affect the National Football League's short- and long-term international business strategies. Listed in no specific order, the league's topics and subtopics in this chapter included the mission and accomplishments of the National Football League International, attendances at and results of National Football League exhibition and preseason games overseas, the league's global television rights, licensing contracts and vendor commitments, facts about the American Bowl series of games, investment in and development of the World League of American Football and later the National Football League Europe and its World championships, organization and purpose of NFL Enterprises, sponsorship of international Flag Football programs, formation and responsibilities of the league's offices in Canada, Mexico and Japan, business ventures in China, England and Spain, and partnerships with Spain's F.C. Barcelona and with such media agencies as Keith Prowse International and Visa International Service Association. Besides that array of interests, Chapter 2 also predicts whether the National Football League is expected to locate, before 2010, one or more of its teams or any new franchises outside of America's borders.

In contrast to the special topics and subtopics identified for Major League Baseball and the National Football League, the international business activities, alliances, events, programs and relationships established by the other three United States-based leagues are examined in Chapters 3–5, respectively. Chapter 3's focus, for example, is concentrated on the global strategies of the National Basketball Association. According to the league's Commissioner, David Stern, the National Basketball Association is the primary professional organization that represents basketball, which is the world's second most popular sport after outdoor soccer. Since he joined the league as its Commissioner during the early 1980s, Stern has ambitiously and astutely implemented the business' marketing strategies for profit, which in turn, have positioned the National Basketball Association to be a prominent international sport league that will thrive during the early to middle 2000s.

Based on Stern's vision and factors like Michael Jordan and the Dream Team's championship at the 1992 Olympic Games in Barcelona, Spain, Chapter 3 reveals, for example, where and how such foreign basketball players as Canada's Steve Nash, Germany's Dirk Nowitzski and China's Yao Ming are recruited and then persuaded to join franchises in the National Basketball Association, and why some of the league's teams and superstar players are idolized by basketball fans living in cities and rural areas throughout Croatia, Ireland, Italy, Mexico, the Philippines, Spain, Russia and Yugoslavia. The chapter also explains how the National Basketball Association has expanded its global empire as a business. That is, the league had to encourage and assist promoters to operate state-of-the-art basketball arenas in populated international markets, and it sponsored clinics and summer camps in Africa and grassroots programs elsewhere to benefit the youth who enjoy playing basketball games. Furthermore, the league arranged the television broadcast of regular season and playoff games, and championship series in 200 nations, and even distributed computer games and videos to retailers in numerous countries to be sold to consumers. After those topics are discussed, the chapter provides some interesting facts about the role of international players in the Women's National Basketball Association, which is the dominant professional basketball league for women in America and perhaps in the world. In short, those and other relevant professional basketball activities, events and programs are integrated into Chapter 3.

After the National Basketball Association's global operations have been presented in Chapter 3, the international business activities, events, relationships and other matters that relate to the National Hockey League are analyzed in Chapter 4, and then to Major League Soccer in Chapter 5. Besides describing the business goals, responsibilities and functions of the NHL International, and the domestic and global implications of the league's economic and financial conflicts with the National Hockey League Players Association, Chapter 4 also examines the following topics: how the 2004 World Cup of Hockey might affect professional ice hockey worldwide, why one or more of the National Hockey League's existing franchises will likely relocate from a city in Canada or the United States to a metropolitan area in Eastern or Western Europe before 2010, and whether the skating skills and performances of American, Canadian and European players are different during games and might conflict in the rink. To identify the developments and operations of other hockey organizations, Chapter 4 briefly explores the histories of the World Hockey Association and International Hockey League, and the formation of the Federal Hockey League in Canada. Lastly, the chapter predicts the anticipated affects, if any, of a Fall 2004 player strike and/or management lockout with respect to ice hockey fans and sports markets in North America and foreign nations.

Subsequent to the discussion of the National Hockey League in Chapter 4, Major League Soccer's domestic and international business environment, stature and short- and long-term viability are significant matters that were incorporated in Chapter 5. Those involved such topics as the league's formation, development and growth since 1996, and the potential for team relocations and league expansions beyond the United States borders during the early 2000s. Other issues included in the chapter are the league's interests to organize and establish stable minor league development and youth soccer programs in America; whether there will be new soccer stadiums built and financed by investors and/or owners of franchises; the league's progress toward establishing an international soccer player draft system and the successful negotiation of rights fees that are demanded by some national teams based in Europe and South America; expansion of television broadcasts and the league's soccer games into China and various Latin America and Middle Eastern countries; significance of the World Cup tournaments with respect to Major League Soccer teams and players; and how the league's operations might be influenced by world events and the elite soccer teams in Europe.

After Chapter 5 concludes, there is the Conclusion. It will summarize the topics and subtopics in Chapters 1–5 and then designate the current and future global strategies and business environments of the five eminent American professional team sports leagues. Those are, of course, Major League Baseball and the National Football League, National Basketball Association, National Hockey League and Major League Soccer. From an international perspective, each league's primary interests, opportunities, threats and relationships are highlighted and contrasted. Finally, after the Conclusion there is the Appendix, Glossary, Selected Bibliography and Index, which are the contents that complete *Sports Capitalism*.

Notes

1. For the well-researched books that focus on the business, economics and operations of the professional team sports industry, which essentially includes topics about franchise owners, leagues, players, teams and various organizations and institutions such as the sports media and players' unions, see Roger G. Noll, ed., *Government and the Sports Business* (Washington, D.C.: The Brookings Institution, 1974); James Quirk and Rodney D. Fort, *Pay Dirt: The Business of Professional Team Sports* (Princeton, N.J.: Princeton University Press, 1992); Roger G. Noll and Andrew Zimbalist, eds., *Sports, Jobs and Taxes: The Economic Impact of Sports Teams and Stadiums* (Washington, D.C.: Brookings Institution Press, 1997); Frank P. Jozsa, Jr. and John J. Guthrie, Jr., *Relocating Teams and Expanding Leagues in Professional Sports: How the Major Leagues Respond to Market Conditions* (Westport, CT: Quorum Books, 1999); Paul Downward and Alistair Dawson, *The Economics of Professional Team Sports* (London, England and New York, N.Y.: Routledge, 2000); Frank P. Jozsa, Jr., *American Sports Empire: How the Leagues Breed Success* (Westport, CT: Praeger Publishers, 2003); Douglas M. Turco, *The Wide World of Sport Programming* (Champaign, IL: Stipes Publishing L.L.C., 1996); James E. Thoma and Laurence Chalip, *Sport Governance in the Global Community* (Morgantown, WV: Fitness Information Technology, Inc., 1996); Trevor Slack, *Understanding Sport Organization* (Champaign, IL: Human Kinetics, 1997); Carlos Pestana Barros, Muradali Ibrahimo, and Stefan Szymanski, *Transatlantic Sport: The Comparative Economics of North American and European Sports* (Cheltenham, UK: Edward Elgar Publishing Limited, 2002). Besides those books, there are other titles that specifically relate to each league, that is, Major League Baseball and the National Football League, National Basketball Association, National Hockey League and Major League Soccer. The following are three entries per

league from this book's Selected Bibliography. See Marvin Miller, *A Whole Different Ballgame: The Sport and Business of Baseball* (New York, N.Y.: Birch Lane Press, 1991); Neil J. Sullivan, *The Dodgers Move West: The Transfer of the Brooklyn Baseball Franchise to Los Angeles* (New York, N.Y.: Oxford University Press, 1987); Harold Seymour, *Baseball: The Golden Age*, 2nd ed. (New York, N.Y.: Oxford University Press, 1989); *NFL International* (New York, N.Y.: National Football League, 2002); *NFL 2001 Record & Fact Book* (New York, N.Y.: National Football League, 2001); *Super Bowl XXXVIII Game Program* (Houston, TX: National Football League, 2004); Andrew D. Bernstein, *NBA Hoop Shots: Classic Moments From a Super Era* (San Francisco, CA: Woodford Press, 1996); Zander Hollander, ed., *The Modern Encyclopedia of Basketball* (Old Tappan, N.J.: Four Winds Press, 1969); Martin Tarango, *Basketball Biographies* (Jefferson, N.C. and London, England: McFarland & Company, 1991); M.R. Carroll, Andrew Podnieks, and Michael Harling, *The Concise Encyclopedia of Hockey* (Vancouver, Canada: Greystone Books, 2001); John Davidson and John Steinbreder, *Hockey For Dummies*, 2nd ed. (Foster City, CA: IDG Books Worldwide Inc., 2000); Patrick Houda and Joe Pelletier, *The World Cup of Hockey* (Toronto, Canada: Warwick Publishing, Inc., 2002); Roger Allaway, Jose Colin, and David Litterer, *The Encyclopedia of American Soccer History* (Lanham, MD: Scarecrow Press Inc., 2001); Keir Radnedge, *The Complete Encyclopedia of Soccer: The Bible of World Soccer* (London, England: Carlton, 2000); Dan Woog, *The Ultimate Soccer Encyclopedia* (Chicago, IL: Lowell House, 1999). To read about a specific topic such as baseball in Cuba, see Roberto Gonzalez Echevarria, *The Pride of Havana: A History of Cuban Baseball* (New York, N.Y.: Oxford University Press, 1999); Milton H. Jamail and Larry Dierker, *Full Count: Inside Cuban Baseball* (Carbondale, IL: Southern Illinois University Press, 2000); S.L. Price, *Pitching Around Fidel: A Journey Into the Heart of Cuban Sports* (Hopewell, N.J.: Ecco Press, 2000). Some articles about various aspects of professional sports leagues include Michael A. Flynn and Richard J. Gilbert, "The Analysis of Professional Sports Leagues as Joint Ventures," *Economic Journal* (February 2001), F27; D.W. Miller, "Scholars Call a Foul on Pro Sports Leagues," *The Chronicle of Higher Education* (13 October 2000), A28–29; James Quirk and Mohamed A. El-Hodiri, "An Economic Model of a Professional Sports League," *Journal of Political Economy 79* (March/April 1975), 1302–1319; John Vrooman, "A General Theory of Sports Leagues," *Southern Economic Journal* (1 April 1995), 971–990. To read about international business and globalization, see John D. Daniels, Lee H. Radebaugh, and Daniel P. Sullivan, *Globalization and Business* (Upper Saddle Road, N.J.: Prentice Hall, 2002); Moses N. Kiggundu, *Managing Globalization in Developing Countries and Transition Economies* (Westport, CT: Praeger Publishers, 2002); M. de Mooy, *Global Marketing and Advertising: Understanding Cultural Paradoxes* (Thousand Oaks, CA: Sage Publications, 1998); V. Terpstra and K. David, *The Cultural Environment of International Business*, 3rd ed. (Cincinnati, OH: South-Western, 1991); A.N. Wise and B.S Meyers, eds., *International Sports Law & Business* (Ardsley, N.Y.: Transnational Publishers, 2002). For a recent title about the historical relationship between business and sport, see Phil Schaaf, *Sports, Inc.: 100 Years of Sports Business* (Amherst, N.Y.: Prometheus Books, 2004). With respect to Schaaf's book, one sportswriter had said, "*Sports, Inc.* is a well-documented and entertaining chronicle of the long-standing and mutually beneficial commercial connections between sports and business. Its insightful perspectives warrant its inclusion in personal and public libraries." This comment is in Dean Bonham, "Book Takes a Look at the History of Sports as a Business," at <http://www.sportsbusinessnews.com> cited 2 March 2004.

2. See Kenneth L. Shropshire, "Thoughts on International Professional Sports Leagues and the Application of United States Antitrust Laws," *Denver University Law Review*, Vol. 67:2

(Winter 1990): 193–212. According to Shropshire, "The models are truly the author's guess today of how internationalization might best occur. Obviously, there are initial jurisdictional concerns in any extraterritorial application of U.S. laws. As those jurisdictional concerns are addressed, the potential to apply a foreign states' antitrust laws should be considered as well. An interpretation of antitrust issues, particularly the rule of reason, single entity defense and the labor exemption is quite complex in its own right. With the application of U.S. antitrust laws to the internationalization of professional sports leagues, the complexity only increases."

3.   Besides economists, historians and political scientists, there are professors in other academic disciplines that have authored books about amateur and professional sports. For example, see Allen Guttman, *Games and Empires: Modern Sports and Cultural Imperialism* (Chapel Hill, N.C.: Columbia University Press, 1994). The Publishers Weekly reviewed Professor Guttman's book in "Games and Empires: Modern Sports and Cultural Imperialism," at <http://www.amazon.com> cited 13 September 2003. For his other book, see Allen Guttman, *Sports Spectators* (New York, N.Y.: Columbia University Press, 1986).

4.   "If the small stock of American entrepreneurs fails to cultivate international publics, control over the distinctly American industry of major league sports could move abroad." To evaluate the author's predictions, see Eric M. Leifer, *Making the Majors: The Transformation of Team Sports in America* (Cambridge, MA: Harvard University Press, 1996). For a historical perspective, in Appendix A Leifer lists the major leagues in professional baseball, basketball, football and hockey. By sport, the earliest leagues were baseball's National Association in 1871–1875, basketball's American Basketball League in 1925–1931, football's National Football League in 1920–present, and hockey's National Hockey Association in 1910–1916. In Appendix A of Leifer's book, there were no listings of amateur or professional soccer leagues or associations. Accordingly, it is in a section titled 'A Strange New World' of Chapter 9 that describes the future organization of the professional sports leagues. Based on Leifer's forecasts, "The prospect of penetrating international markets is too alluring for any opportunity to be slighted." For his other global views, see Eric M. Leifer, "The Ultimate Expansion: Internationalizing Sports," *Across the Board* (June 1999), 20–24.

5.   Eric M. Leifer, personal letter, 1 June 2003.

6.   Rather than imperialism against anti-imperialism or civilization against civilization, the future international battles will revolve around capital versus culture. This clash was forecasted in Walter LaFeber, *Michael Jordan and the New Global Capitalism* (New York, N.Y. and London, England: W. W. Norton & Company, 1999). The spotlight reviews of LaFeber's book were headlined as 'Nike and Michael conquer the world,' 'Complex theory extremely simple for Jordan fans,' and 'Good enough.' For the specific reviews, see "Michael Jordan and the New Global Capitalism," at <http://www.amazon.com> cited 31 March 2003.

7.   See Mark S. Rosentraub, "Governing Sports in the Global Era: A Political Economy of Major League Baseball and Its Stakeholder," *Indiana Journal of Global Legal Studies*, Vol. 8:12 (Fall 2000), 121–144. According to Rosentraub, because of the involvement of more foreign-born players, there are incentives for the North American sports leagues, particularly Major League Baseball, to develop and perhaps locate franchises in other countries such as those in Asia and Latin America. For the author's research about how professional sports teams hold cities hostage to seek taxpayer's money for new facilities, see Mark S. Rosentraub, *Major League Losers: The Real Costs of Sports and Who's Paying For It* (New York, N.Y.: Basic Books, 1997).

8.   William B. Gould IV, "Baseball and Globalization: The Game Played and Heard and Watched 'Round the World,'" *Indiana Journal of Global Legal Studies*, Vol. 8:85 (Fall

2000), 85–120. Similar to Rosentraub's prognostications, Major League Baseball's search overseas for more revenues and players will continue to implicate U.S. and international antitrust and labor law issues. With respect to players and the globalization of professional sports, Gould concludes, "The movements of players into the United States from other countries inevitably portends internationalization, the playing of games abroad and ultimately a genuine World Series or World Cup. Baseball may no longer be the national pastime in this twenty-first century but much more than that."

9. Because of baseball's longstanding traditions and the sport's local support, continuity and stability in America, it is unrealistic that Major League Baseball will soon place franchises outside Canada and the United States. For more insights about this viewpoint, see Leonard Koppett, "The Globalization of Baseball: Reflections of a Sports Writer," *Indiana Journal of Global Legal Studies*, Vol. 8:8 (Fall 2000), 81–84. In summarizing his article, Koppett states, "To conclude, both the game and business of baseball will continue to spread worldwide, but this globalization will only serve to strengthen rather than weaken MLB hegemony over professional baseball on this planet." His book on the topic is *Sports Illusion, Sports Reality: A Reporter's View of Sports, Journalism, and Society*, 2nd ed. (Urbana and Chicago, IL: University of Illinois Press, 1994).

10. Despite the dollar-peso exchange rates and stadium problems, Major League Baseball had discussed and evaluated bids from Monterrey, Mexico and San Juan, Puerto Rico to host some Montreal Expos' home games in the 2003 and 2004 regular seasons. This matter was discussed in Mark Asher, "Viva, Monterrey, Mexico and Los Expos," at <http://www.sportsbusinessnews.com> cited 19 August 2003; Eric Fisher, "Hoping Les Becomes Los Expos 2004," at <http://www.sportsbusinessnews.com> cited 22 August 2003; "Its Offic-ial—Les/Los Expos Return For 2004," at <http://www.sportsbusinessnews.com> cited 11 December 2003; Mary Jordan, "Mexico and Les/Los Expos," at <http://www.sports-businessnews.com> cited 2 October 2003; David King, "How About Dueling Permanent Homes For Les/Los Expos," at <http://www.sportsbusinessnews.com> cited 17 December 2003; Stephanie Myles, "Los Expos Set to Return to San Juan," at <http://www.sportsbus-inessnews.com> cited 4 December 2003; Jerry Crasnick, "Baseball May [be] Headed to the Caribbean," at <http://www.sportsbusinessnews.com> cited 3 December 2002; Kevin Baxter, "Los Expos in Puerto Rico," at <http://www.sportsbusinessnews.com> cited 6 March 2003.

11. See Alan Bairner, *Sport, Nationalism, and Globalization: European and North American Perspectives* (Albany, N.Y.: State University of New York Press, 2001). To support Bairner's thesis, the book's Chapter Two, 'British Nationalism or Ulster Nationalism?' examines the relationships between politics, Protestants and sports in Northern Ireland. For a review of this title, see "Sport, Nationalism, and Globalization: European and North American Perspectives," at <http://www.amazon.com> cited 31 March 2003.

12. For a scholarly critique of globalization, see Toby Miller, Geoffrey Lawrence, Jim McKay, and David Rowe, *Globalization and Sport: Playing the World* (Thousand Oaks, CA: Sage Publications, 2001). In their conclusion, the authors contend that "Our message is, however, a cautionary one—before you buy the sneaker, or sign for the TV package, follow the life of the commodity sign through its history, keeping citizenship and labour at the forefront in your thoughts." A description of this title is in "Globalization and Sport: Playing the World," at <http://www.amazon.com> cited 31 March 2003. Besides those publications, globalization and sport were also discussed in such articles as Peter Donnelly, "The Local and the Global: Globalization in the Sociology of Sport," *Journal of Sport and Social Issues*, Vol. 20, No. 3 (1996), 239–257; Jean Harvey, Genevieve Rail, and Lucie Thibault, "Globalization and Sport: Sketching a Theoretical Model For Empirical Analysis," *Journal*

of Sport and Social Issues, Vol. 20, No. 3 (1996), 258–277; Brian Stoddart, "Convergence," *Journal of Sport and Social Issues*, Vol. 21, No. 1 (1997), 93–102; C. Roger Rees, "Race and Sport in Global Perspective," *Journal of Sport and Social Issues*, Vol. 20, No. 9 (1996), 22–32; Toby Miller, "How Founding the United Nations Professionalized Sport," *Journal of Sport and Social Issues*, Vol. 22, No. 2 (1998), 123–126; Deborah Stevenson, "Women, Sport, and Globalization: Competing Discourses of Sexuality and Nation," *Journal of Sport and Social Issues*, Vol. 26, No. 2 (2002), 209–225; Robert V. Bellamy, Jr., "Issues in the Internationalization of the U.S. Sports Media: The Emerging European Marketplace," *Journal of Sport and Social Issues*, Vol. 17, No. 3 (1993), 168–180.

13.   Regarding Wolff's book, several five-star customer reviews were written and appear in "Big Game, Small World: A Basketball Adventure," at <http://www.amazon.com> cited 10 July 2003. To agree with or dispute those reviews, read Alexander Wolff, *Big Game, Small World: A Basketball Adventure* (New York, N.Y.: Warner Books, 2002). For online articles that were authored by Wolff about professional basketball as an international sport, see Alexander Wolff, "A Truly Global Game," at <http://sportsillustrated.cnn.com> cited 26 June 2003; "Basketball in a Post-9/11 World," at <http://www.twbookmark.com> cited 25 June 2003; "Foreign Intrigue," at <http://cnnsi.printthis.clickability.com> cited 28 June 2003; "Expanding to Europe Could be in the Cards For the NBA," at <http://sports-illustrated.cnn.com> cited 26 June 2003; "International Basketball Association?" at <http://sportsillustrated.cnn.com> cited 26 June 2003; "The Decline of U.S. Dominance," at <http://sportsillustrated.cnn.com> 25 June 2003; "The Rest of the World Nearly Has Caught Up to the U.S.," at <http://sportsillustrated.cnn.com> cited 26 June 2003.

14.   See Han Westerbeek and Aaron Smith, *Sport Business in the Global Marketplace* (New York, N.Y.: Palgrave Macmillan, 2003). In a section titled 'Global Sport Scenarios: The Next 50 Years,' the authors provide the book's thesis. "We have argued that the drivers of change or globalisation will converge through the nexus of uncertainties that will determine the fate of the world and of sport." For a brief description of this title, see "Sports Business in the Global Marketplace," at <http://www.amazon.com> cited 31 March 2003.

15.   Are the living conditions in the baseball academies of Latin American countries, and the treatment of Latino baseball players by Major League Baseball, an abomination? For case studies and examples that report these issues, see Arturo J. Marcano and David P. Fidler, *Stealing Lives: The Globalization of Baseball and the Tragic Story of Alexis Quiroz* (Bloomington, IN: Indiana University Press, 2003). This topic is further described in Gary Marx, "An Expose on Baseball Training Facilities in Latin America," at <http://www.sportsbusinessnews.com> cited 19 August 2003, and in Jim Souhan, "Latin American Academies Becoming the Norm," at <http://www.sportsbusinessnews.com> cited 14 January 2003. For a contrary view, that is, why the globalization of sports integrates races and represents equal opportunity employment, see Tom Ferraro, "Globalization of Sports Can Enlighten Athletes," *Long Island Business News* (14 April 2000), 54A. Some customer reviews of this title are reported in "Stealing Lives: The Globalization of Baseball and the Tragic Story of Alexis Quiroz," at <http://www.amazon.com> cited 31 March 2003.

16.   For some academic references about the organizations and operations of global businesses, see three recent international business textbooks. These titles are Charles W. L. Hill, *International Business*, 3rd. ed. (New York, N.Y.: McGraw-Hill/Irwin, 2002); Ronald E. Seavoy, *Origins and Growth of the Global Economy* (Westport, CT: Praeger Publishers, 2003); Donald A. Ball, Wendell H. McCulloch, Jr., Paul L. Frantz, J. Michael Geringer, and Michael S. Minor, *International Business* (New York, N.Y.: McGraw-Hill/Irwin, 2004). As reflected in the Selected Bibliography of *Sports Capitalism*, the primary online source for daily news about the business and economics of sports was at <http://www.sportsbusiness-

news.com>. For a monthly fee of $10, the subscriber had access to articles about each of the five professional sports and the Olympic Games, ownership and media topics, and other sports such as badminton, cycling, indoor soccer, lacrosse, running and table tennis

17.   See Gerald Eskenazi, "Pro Leagues in America Eye the Globe," *The New York Times* (9 April 1989), 19, and Joe Gergen, "Is Global Expansion the Wave of the Future?" *The Sporting News* (28 August 1989), 9. Accordingly, both authors declared that global expansion was on the agenda of every North American sports league during the latter 1980s.

18.   To comprehend the U.S. professional sports leagues' revenue changes and strategy revisions in Europe since the early to middle 1990s, see A. Craig Copetas, "Europe is U.S. Sports' New Classroom," *Wall Street Journal* (29 November 1996), B7; Gordon Edes, "Making it Sound so Easy For MLB to Play Games in Europe," at <http://www.sports businessnews.com> cited 27 March 2003; Eric Fisher, "NFL Owners Will Keep NFL Europe Alive," at <http://www.sportsbusinessnews.com> cited 18 September 2003; Roger Mills, "Bucs Owners Expanding Their Horizons—Into European Soccer," <http://www. sportsbusinessnews.com> cited 6 March 2003; John Vinocur, "Baseball in Europe," at <http://www.sportsbusinessnews.com> cited 19 August 2003.

19.   Two publications are cited here. First, there is Chris Pursell, "Fields of Competition: American Pastimes Going For O'seas Gold," *Variety* (29 June 1998), 27–28. Second, there is Allison Wright, "Play Ball," *Business Mexico* (April 2000), 44–48.

20.   Excluding Major League Soccer, the United States professional sports leagues vigorously pursue consumers and sales abroad because foreign markets provide large amounts of economic potential. This strategy is described in Ichiro Suzuki, "Going Global: Major League Sports Poised to Expand to Overseas," *The Washington Times* (5 January 2003), A1. Moreover, MLB and the NFL, NBA and NHL each seek to expand their business in international markets. For more information about those strategies, see Kelly Grimes, "Global Access Sends Major League Baseball Overseas," *Business Wire* (30 April 1996), 43; Alexander Blenkinsopp, "Asian Invasion: Baseball's Ambassadors," *Harvard International Review* (Spring 2002), 12–13; Paul Dykewicz, "Spotlight: Baseball's All-Star Game Goes Global," *Satellite News* (21 July 2003), 1; Thomas Heath, "NFL Has Ambitions For China," *The Washington Post* (1 August 2002), D1; Lucian Kim, "Football's Drive to Gain Yardage in Europe," *The Christian Science Monitor* (17 May 1999), 1; Joe Mandese, "How Fox Deal Aids NFL Global Aim," *Advertising Age* (3 January 1994), 4–5; Luke Cyphers, "NBA Shoots Toward the Pacific Rim as Part of Global Marketing," *The Asian Wall Street Journal Weekly* (6 April 1992), 2; Peter Gwin, "Transatlantic: How Europe is Shaping US Basketball Hoops," *Europe* (June 1997), 33–35; Frank Lawlor, "NBA Czar Reaches Out to World," *International Herald Tribune* (4 February 1999), 17; Hillary Cassidy, "Power Play: NHL Nets Broadcast Partners For Overseas Promos," *Brandweek* (11 December 2000), 9; Larry Wigge, "Global Ice Rink," *The Sporting News* (14 February 2000), 42; Shimbun Yomiuri, "NHL Short Sighted in Drive For Global Expansion," *The Daily Yomiuri* (5 September 2000), 1. Besides those readings, some online articles on this topic include Richard Alm, "The Globalization of Sports," at <http://www.sports-businessnews.com> cited 25 November 2002; Barbara Barker, "The Internationalization of the NBA," at <http://www.sportsbusinessnews.com> cited 25 November 2002; Ken Belson, "NFL Continues to Market Itself in Japan," at <http: //www.sportsbusinessnews.com> cited 19 August 2003; Brendan M. Case, "The NFL Heads to Mexico," at <http://www. sportsbusinessnews.com> cited 3 December 2002; Joseph Coleman, "NBA Commissioner Sees More Globalization of Basketball," at <http://www.yahoo.com> cited 11 November 1999; Eric Fisher, "MLB Finally Taking Notice of Far East," at <http://www.sports-businessnews.com> cited 19 August 2003; Ashley McGeachy Fox, "NBA Continues to

Expand Horizons," at <http://www.sportsbusinessnews.com> cited 9 October 2003; Lynn Henning, "Challenges Faced From Baseball's Expanding International Horizons," at <http://www.sportsbusinessnews.com> cited 25 November 2002; Amy Shipley, "Baseball Looking to Internationalize," at <http://www.sportsbusinessnews.com> cited 19 August 2003; Sarah Talalay, "The Internationalization of the NBA Continues," at <http://www. sportsbusinessnews.com> cited 2 January 2004. Finally, a few articles about MLS and international business that appear in this book's Selected Bibliography are Eduardo Porter, "World Cup 2002: Si, Si!—Zeal of Hispanic-Americans For Soccer Finals," *Wall Street Journal* (6 May 2002), B1; Alex Yannis, "MetroStars Seek a Foreign Influence," *The New York Times* (12 June 1999), 5; Grahame L. Jones, "The Inside Track: Q & A with Don Garber," *The Los Angeles Times* (6 June 2003), D2; "MLS Set to Expand Their Horizons," at <http://www.sportsbusinessnews.com> cited 25 November 2002; "MLS Signs a Spanish Sponsorship Agreement With Yahoo," at <http://www.sportsbusinessnews.com> cited 19 August 2003; "MLS Signs Agreement With Fox Sports International," at <http://www. sportsbusinessnews.com> cited 3 April 2003.

Chapter 1

Major League Baseball

In America, professional baseball's National League of Professional Baseball Clubs (NL) and American League of Professional Baseball Clubs (AL) were established, respectively, in 1876 and 1901. Each league, which then consisted of eight teams, became the organizational entities that formed Major League Baseball (MLB) in 1903. That year, to arouse baseball fans and other sports enthusiasts in the United States (U.S.), the AL Boston Americans defeated the NL Pittsburgh Pirates in MLB's first World Series, which was played at Huntington Avenue Grounds in Boston and Exposition Park in Pittsburgh.

Until the late 1960s, MLB franchises remained located primarily in medium to large cities throughout the U.S. There were at least two eastern Canadian cities, however, that contained relatively large and diverse populations. As such, these cities were well-prepared places to host a NL and/or AL professional baseball team. Because of the revolutionary advancements and economic efficiencies that had occurred within North America's telecommunications and transportation networks, in 1969 MLB's existing franchise owners collectively approved a NL expansion team to be placed in Montreal, and in 1977 an AL expansion team in Toronto. Since 1977, however, there have been no MLB clubs to relocate or expand outside of the U.S. border. Apparently, MLB officials had jointly decided that, besides Montreal and Toronto in Canada, other foreign cities did not contain the ballparks, fan bases or economic and demographic characteristics to support a relocated team or a new professional baseball franchise. Nevertheless, despite the league's policy, from the late 1970s to the early 2000s MLB had continued to market, promote and internationalize its brand name and sport.[1]

Given the league's formation, history and tradition, this chapter analyzes why, when, where and how American-style professional baseball has gradually become a global sport, especially since the early 1990s. To highlight the status of baseball and the elements of MLB's international strategy, Chapter 1 focuses on the league's organizational structure and other professional baseball leagues in various countries, the presence and numerical growth of foreign players in MLB, and on other topics such as the league's investment in and supervision of baseball academies and other facilities that are located overseas. Furthermore, the chapter discusses the significance of MLB's policies abroad with respect to the drug test programs administered to Latin American players, the expected development of an international player draft system, a World Cup of Baseball tournament, and the creation and suspension of the Canadian Baseball League. After a table lists the non-North American cities that represent potential sites to locate a current or expansion MLB team, the chapter concludes with a brief history of women's baseball leagues. To a great extent, these elements and topics involve inter-country agreements and alliances, and sports events and business relationships that, in turn, influence and impact the game of professional baseball and MLB's fans, franchises, players and markets in America and elsewhere.

Reorganization Strategy

Between 1920 and 1945, nearly 50 foreign-born men who were primarily from the island of Cuba had played in either the NL or AL. Then, in the late 1940s groups of young and skilled baseball stars from various Latin American countries had emerged to willingly sign teams' contracts and, as their occupation and career, decided to join U.S. minor league and MLB rosters to play professional baseball. To avoid a lifetime of poverty and second, to hopefully earn a sizable income, those talented athletes had emigrated to America, in large part, from rural and urban communities in the Dominican Republic, Mexico, Puerto Rico and Venezuela. Thus, the number of Latino players in MLB has increased for almost 90 years. Besides Latinos, since the 1980s an increasing number of Japanese, Korean and Taiwanese athletes have become MLB players. Indeed, the import of foreign players and other factors such as the league's interest to expand, control and manage global partnerships, sponsorships and licensing agreements, and the league's opportunities to broadcast its teams' regular season, playoff and World Series games overseas, had compelled MLB to restructure and consolidate its international business activities into one organizational unit during the late 1980s. According to some experienced baseball officials, this corporate-wide reorganization was initiated by MLB, respectively, before the other U.S.-based professional sports leagues had formed similar units within their organizations.[2]

Based on the documents published by sports analysts, in 1989 the division of Major League Baseball International (MLBI) was established. When formed and as it currently exists, the division's mission has been to expand, promote and manage MLB's global business operations. That is, to develop and nurture various alliances, partnerships and sponsorships with foreign broadcast, marketing, media and industrial companies, and also, to provide and support baseball activities, grassroots programs and services abroad that result in more worldwide exposure, economic opportunities and free cash flows for the league and its member franchises. By the early 2000s, for example, in Australia, the Czech Republic and Holland, MLBI had created the Road Show, which was an interactive entertainment event that was marketed to baseball fans at community fairs and shopping malls in those countries. To simulate the sport's game conditions, the Show's visitor's batted baseballs ejected from pitching machines, threw baseballs at stationary targets and posed in uniforms to have their pictures displayed on baseball cards. Likewise, in Germany, Italy and South Africa, kids who were 8–12 years old participated in hitting, pitching and running contests while in some European nations an Envoy interactive program identified the whereabouts and performances of promising young baseball players. Because of those events and other popular programs, since 1989 MLBI has progressed to become a profitable organizational unit of MLB. To illustrate, from the late 1990s to early 2000s the unit's annual cash inflows exceeded $50 million. This income had reportedly earned each NL and AL team an additional profit of at least $1 million.[3]

As a result of MLBI's global business deals, commercial relationships and support of grassroots programs for baseball and other sports fans, more revenues have been forthcoming from such sources as broadcast rights fees, licensing and sponsorship agreements, and the sale of team-specific merchandise and memorabilia. Invariably, these business opportunities and contracts have further contributed value to the NL and AL, and their member teams' earnings. As evidence of MLBI's influence, five former moneymaking deals are summarized as follows. First, Global Access Telecommunications Services Inc., which then was located in Boston, Massachusetts transmitted eight hours of regular season MLB games each week to populations in such Asian countries as Taipei and Taiwan during 1996. Three years later, the World Series games between the best NL and AL teams were telecast to fans in 212 countries and in 2002, the World Series generated $50 million in revenues based on the broadcasts to 100 million people in 224 nations. Second, in 2003 MLB had signed lucrative five-year, $500 million licensing agreements with seven U.S.-based business partners. Collectively, these companies committed to promote, sell and distribute in international retail markets adult baseball apparel and headwear items that included caps, fleece, jerseys, t-shirts, turtlenecks and uniforms. Third, such sponsors as Adidas, Anheuser-Busch, Gillette, MasterCard, Nike and Pepsi-Cola agreed to provide specialized baseball products to consumers who lived in various Asian, European, and Central and South American countries. Fourth, each week approximately 40 of MLB's regular season games and the league's 2003 All-Star Game were beamed from U.S. ballparks into 200 countries by four Intelsat Ltd. satellites. Besides its telecommunications equipment in the U.S., Intelsat's terrestrial end-to-end infrastructure then included teleports in Germany and Hong Kong, and fiber-interconnected points of presence in England and Germany. Fifth, for baseball games that were not broadcast on television, MLB offered streaming video programs over the Internet to sports fans located throughout the world.[4]

As a consequence of the cash inflows from MLBI's operations during the 1990s and 2000s, there are two significant implications. One, MLB and its clubs will gradually become less dependent on U.S. and Canadian fans and markets in North America for their sales volumes, revenues and net profits. This means that, in the long-term, a smaller proportion of MLB's economic resources and money reserves will be allocated to support domestic marketing programs and to invest in other product development projects. Two, if necessary, the teams' franchise owners will demand more taxpayer subsidies from their respective local and/or state governments to pay the construction costs of a new and modern ballpark located at a site in the home city. Consequently, in the end MLB's business and globalization strategies may eventually result in social dislocations and disharmonious relationships between various NL and AL teams and their local, regional and national fan bases, and their communities and perhaps with government officials.

The previous paragraph concludes the analysis of MLB's reorganization strategy and MLBI's mission, organization and short- and long-term business matters. In the next portion of Chapter 1, the discussion focuses on the motivations and interests of baseball fans and other sports groups who reside in foreign countries. As a result of this section in the chapter, the reader learns where and why millions of kids and adults abroad adore American-style baseball and become fans of MLB.

Global Baseball Markets

For at least two decades, MLB has attempted to market and promote its brand, image and sport in nations across the globe. As a result, baseball spectators from Toronto in Canada to Miami in Florida flock to teams' regular season home games and fans from Madrid in Spain to Moscow in Russia view professional baseball programs on television and the Internet, and/or listen to sports announcers describe the drama of a nine-inning game on the radio. Meanwhile, children and teenagers enthusiastically compete in elementary and high school baseball games, and young and middle-age adults play on teams in local amateur and professional leagues. To determine why and how baseball has succeeded from an international perspective, the status of MLB is depicted as it exists within the sports environment of selected nations. Based on the research performed for *Sports Capitalism*, the countries that follow are listed according to how comprehensively baseball is ingrained in their cultures and how remote or connected the baseball fans in each nation are with respect to MLB. The first country highlighted is Japan and then Mexico, Puerto Rico, the Dominican Republic, Cuba, Venezuela, some nations in Europe and finally, China and Russia.

Japan

Introduced to the country in 1867 as a sport, baseball's history is represented by wa, which is a Japanese term for team unity. Indeed, prior to baseball Japan's sports culture had primarily stressed individual athletic endeavors such as judo and sumo wrestling. But, the societal emphasis on the group made baseball and team play a natural fit in the nation. The sport became more popular in 1934, when the New York Yankees home run player Babe Ruth had visited Japan. However, since the 1980s baseball has gradually eroded as a reflection of Japanese culture. Although the sport is extremely popular on the island, the old ways no longer necessarily apply, in part, because young people focus more on gadgets and individual activities. "It's [baseball] changed drastically. Now individualism has spread all over Japan. It's more like Americanized," said Akiri Ogi, a former manager of the Japanese Pacific League's Orix Blue Wave team. In the Land of the Rising Sun, there is a nationwide federation of officials and related groups that govern baseball events as performed by teams in Japan's high schools. Since 1915, a prestigious national baseball tournament, identified in Japanese as Koshien, has been scheduled each summer to determine a championship high school team. In the majority, Japanese athletes of all ages are devoted, disciplined and passionate baseball players. That is, they practice the sport daily and assume that hard work and concentration will better prepare themselves and their team for the national tournament. Frequently, skilled players are remembered for their achievements in games at the Koshien tournament, which perhaps will qualify them to be drafted by one or more of Japan's professional teams.[5]

Interestingly, various private sector corporations will generally sponsor and support the Japanese's semiprofessional and professional baseball league teams. Consequently, a team's previous and current performances are perceived to have a direct impact on the corporation's stock price. In 2003, for example, the performance-to-stock price correlation supposedly affected three Japanese companies. They were Hanshin Electric Railway, which is a transportation company, and Joshin Denki, an electronics retailer and Takara, a toy manufacturer. As such, this correlation suggests that if American professional baseball teams, in the future, attach themselves to large corporations or small to medium sized businesses rather than to cities as proposed by Eric M. Leifer in *Making the Majors*, the firms' stock market valuations would reflect, in part, the baseball statistics and performances of both players and teams such as batting averages, home runs, runs batted in, winning and slugging percentages, and the number of appearances and victories in an international World Series or World Cup of Baseball tournament.[6]

Based on the fanfare and hoopla about the AL New York Yankees' left fielder Hideki Matsui and the Seattle Mariners' right fielder Ichiro Suzuki, who are each a national hero and legend in Japan, perhaps MLB and its respective affiliated businesses, partners and sponsors that are located in the U.S. and abroad have mutually benefited. For example, because of Matsui and Suzuki hundreds of regular season games are currently broadcast on Japanese television networks. During 2003, the Japanese viewership of MLB games averaged 1.5 million television viewers, which was an increase from 983,000 in 2002 while 75 million Japanese watched the World Series. This interest in baseball motivated Yomiuri Shimbum Holdings, who owns the Yomiuri Giants, to promote the Chicago Cubs and New York Mets series in Tokyo during 2000 and the New York Yankees and Tampa Bay Devil Rays series during 2004. To acquire the series, Yomiuri had to pay MLBI a fee and MLB compensates its teams for all the gate and concession receipts they lose by ceding spring training and home dates. With respect to the Yankees-Devil Rays 2004 season-opening games in Tokyo, the managing director of MLB's Japan office Jim Small remarked, "Our goal is to eliminate the culture completely, or as much as possible, during the 2 1/2 hours they are on the field. We want those 2 1/2 hours to be exactly like if they are playing at Tropicana Field [Devil Rays' ballpark in Florida]. But outside those 2 1/2 hours we want them to experience and enjoy the culture." Furthermore, consumer prices have soared on baseball trading cards that feature Japanese players, and the retail food business booms at such sports restaurants as Tokyo's Dome Baseball Café. According to Paul Archey, who is MLBI's senior vice president, "It became clear we [MLB] really needed to have an anchor [a regional Tokyo office], a true presence in the Far East." In short, despite the alarm and resistance to sports globalization as portrayed by a portion of Japanese baseball officials, and by some academicians, politicians and a few sports franchise owners, MLB has succeeded to thrill baseball fans, penetrate the marketplace and thrive in Japan, where the national economy has remained relatively stagnate since the late 1980s.[7]

Mexico

Since the middle of the 1990s, various MLB teams have competed in exhibition and preseason games, and played regular season series in Mexico. Specific cities such as Hermosillo, Mexico City, Monterrey and Tijuana were and continue to be especially attractive places to conduct an American professional baseball event. Even so, in their decisions to schedule games and series in Mexico, MLB's Commissioner and franchise owners must consider several baseball-related economic, demographic and social realities. For example, Mexico's ballparks and other sports facilities are undersized and therefore are deficient with respect to such commercial amenities and services as adequate outdoor advertising and bill-board display areas, enough indoor clothing, merchandise and equipment outlets, an abundant and well-placed number of concessions and restrooms, well-protected and premium parking facilities, and modern clubhouses for players and press boxes for sports writers and television broadcasters. Furthermore, based on the cost-of-living standards in Canada and the U.S., Mexico's median household income is at the subsistence level. This means that MLB teams are compelled at games to maintain below average ticket prices and to charge customers at their ballparks no more than marginal costs for the purchases of apparel, beverages, food items, game-day programs, merchandise and other salable items. Moreover, whenever the Mexican peso was undervalued on currency markets, those prices and costs in dollars would be extremely high. To illustrate, some fans paid $150 per ticket to attend the Florida Marlins and Houston Astros game at Estadio Foro Sol in Mexico City during early 2004. When the score was tied after nine innings, the teams left the field and fans threw seat cushions, plastic cups and other debris to protest the decision. Regardless, Mexicans adore and respect the game of baseball. That is, they attend games, root for their favorite teams and spend money for products sold at the ballparks. Thus, MLB and its respective teams have earned higher profits by scheduling and playing exhibition, preseason and regular season games and series in Mexico.

To illustrate MLB's sources of profits, in 2000 the league received approximately $5 million from licensing deals with Mexican media giant Grupo Televisa SA, from television agreements with Entertainment Sports Program Network's (ESPN) Spanish channels that are owned by the Walt Disney Company, and from broadcasting contracts with the News Corporation's Fox network. Meanwhile, the NL Arizona Diamondbacks, a team that is located in Phoenix, Arizona and the NL San Diego Padres, a team that is headquartered in San Diego, California either broadcasted games in Spanish from Mexican ballparks and/or had played exhibition and/or preseason series in Mexico. In turn, those specific MLB events had international business implications. That is, the games played by the small-market

Diamondbacks and Padres stimulated spending by Mexico's sports fans. In retrospect, this had resulted in higher broadcast rights fees for the league and generated an increase in the teams' revenues from the sales of ballpark food, baseball equipment, merchandise and souvenirs, and from tickets and parking.[8]

During 2003, MLB evaluated the bids submitted by three U.S. cities and by Montreal in Canada, San Juan in Puerto Rico, and Monterrey in Mexico. Those six cities offered to host some or all of the Montreal Expos' 2004 regular season home games. In Monterrey, there were successful professional baseball games played at stadiums there in 1996 when 70,000 spectators attended a three-game regular season series between the Padres and NL New York Mets, and in 1999 when 27,100 fans watched the Padres and NL Colorado Rockies compete. Although Monterrey's 1.1 million in population appears to be about average in market density relative to U.S. MLB cities, its 26,000-seat Estadio [Stadium] ranks below league for the requirements in capacity. According to some newspaper reports, the league had initially decided that Montreal, and not San Juan or Monterrey, was the preferred city to play the Expos' 81 home games during the Summer of 2004. Then, in late 2003 MLB chose San Juan as the city to host 22 Expos games. This league decision was made when a dispute about the control of television rights was settled. That is, Puerto Rican promoter Antonio Munoz received the rights to broadcast the games from Hiram Bithorn Stadium while the Expos' 59 remaining home games were scheduled at Olympic Stadium in Montreal. Anyway, a few medium to large cities in Mexico seem to be reasonable places to locate a MLB franchise in 2005 or thereafter. Commissioner Bud Selig confirmed this concept when he said, "We've [MLB] always talked about Mexico City and Monterrey [as future team locations], but it's all very preliminary. But we have looked at it and continue to look at it."[9]

At an estimated price of $170 million, in 2003 Mexican-American billionaire Arturo Moreno had purchased the AL Anaheim Angels from the Walt Disney Corporation. Although Disney reported that the 2002 World Series champion Angels' had incurred operating losses of nearly $10 million per year during the early 2000s, Moreno seems determined to target his franchise's marketing campaigns at Southern California's Mexican-American sports fans who fluently speak English and Spanish. As such, he foresees unique business opportunities for baseball's Angels to attract and then exploit a sports market that primarily consists of U.S. Hispanic communities and Latin American populations.[10]

Puerto Rico

During April of 2003, a ten-game professional baseball series was played at 19,000-seat Hiram Bithorn Stadium in San Juan, Puerto Rico, whose mainland contains approximately 2.7 million residents. There, the NL Montreal Expos and its opponent teams drew nearly 143,000 spectators to their games. Although Puerto Rico's annual per capita income is relatively substandard at $10,000, the series sold out at the Stadium despite an average ticket price of $28. Before the series began, the City of San Juan had spent $2.5 million to renovate the ballpark's field, restrooms, clubhouses and press box. To impress MLB and for exposure, during game days a Baseball Festival was held near the Stadium. An estimated 45,000 people participated in the Festival, which featured player appearances and autograph sessions, and a variety of interactive baseball activities for fans, and especially events for kids and teenagers. Besides those games played at the Stadium, the series was also televised on the Deportes 13 channel in San Juan while Direct-TV broadcasted the competitions throughout Latin America.[11]

In Puerto Rico, baseball or *pelota* has deep cultural roots in society. That is, the sport represents nationalism and an expression of the people's self-identification and collective pride. Since 1942, 200 Puerto Rican players have spent regular seasons or portions of seasons on teams' rosters in the U.S. big leagues. Those athletes included the former NL Pittsburgh Pirates' superstar and Hall of Fame inductee Robert Clemente, who died in 1972 from an airplane crash, and the formidable AL Kansas City' slugger and all-star Juan Gonzalez. To open MLB's 2003 regular season, there were approximately 38 Puerto Ricans listed on team rosters. Clearly, those players were motivated to excel and become role models for baseball fans who lived in nations throughout Latin America.[12]

Besides Mexico City and Monterrey, MLB considers San Juan to be a viable site for a relocated team and/or new professional baseball franchise. At least one Puerto Rican investment group had developed a business plan to move the Expos from Montreal to San Juan in time to open the 2004, 2005 or 2006 regular season. Even though the island is threatened by criminal activities, poverty households, healthcare problems and occasional hurricanes, Puerto Rico's entertainment and tourist industry, and the nation's baseball fans would especially welcome MLB to locate a club in San Juan, which is the country's largest and most festive city.

Dominican Republic

Baseball arrived on this island during the early 1900s when refugees fled from Cuba to avoid political repression and the threat of a civil war. Since the sport of baseball was beloved by Cubans, it eventually became a passion for Dominicans who played on sports teams and/or watched games as spectators. Everywhere one looks on the island, children play baseball on grassy fields and actual baseball diamonds, and in the streets and parking lots. The kids without money for equipment play barehanded with broomsticks for bats, and use tennis balls or even dolls' heads in place of baseballs. Given the typical players' and fans' emotions about and dedication to the sport, it is a well-accepted belief of the island's poorest natives that baseball is associated with integrity, patriotism and star appeal. That is, baseball helps the people to forget and offers them hope. In short, it gives families a reason to smile and laugh while dancing to merengue in the streets.

This relatively small nation of eight million residents is commercially affiliated with, and economically dependent on the MLB for a sizable proportion of its citizens' compensation. According to a recent study completed in Santo Domingo, as of 2003 the U.S. professional baseball league was responsible for an estimated 1,200 direct, and 900 indirect jobs in the country. Annually, MLB spends approximately $15 million in the Republic to operate its baseball academies and injects another $76 million into the country as donations and gifts, and for the payments to baseball agents and players, and local scouts and coaches. In fact, the 79 Dominican players on MLB's 2003 rosters had earned about $210 million that year in salaries. Undoubtedly, a moderate to high percentage of that money was returned to the players' Dominican families and friends, and/or remitted to various businesses on the island.[13]

Because of the Republic's disproportionate supply of young and talented baseball players, and given the presence and significance of sports academies, MLB will likely continue to invest its money to improve the island's housing and infrastructure, and thus increase the country's economic growth. However, some reasonable yet enforceable government guidelines and rules are needed there to regulate the abusive conduct and inhumane practices of some professional baseball coaches, scouts and sports agents who, as reported, have consistently violated the human rights of Dominican players and their families. Accordingly, MLB should conscientiously terminate the employment of those individuals who are convicted of such infractions.

Cuba

During the middle to late 1800s, Cuban teams played their first organized baseball game on the island. By the early to middle 1900s, the sport had become the country's primary leisure pastime. As of 2003, there were two dominant Cuban leagues with eight teams each that played 90 games per season, which extends each year from November to April. The nation's largest ballpark has been 45,000-seat El Stadio in Havana, where most seats are priced at one to three pesos. During baseball games, an electronic scoreboard normally flashes players' batting averages. There is, however, no alcohol, food, merchandise, souvenirs, snacks or scorecards for sale at the stadium. Many Cuban sports fans are baseball addicts, and as games are played, they celebrate and create noise by blowing their horns and whistles. Occasionally, the hometown fans will fight in the bleachers and intimidate the teams that visit by throwing peanuts at their players in the outfield and those in the dugouts.[14]

During the MLB regular season, which is scheduled from April to September, Cubans try to read news reports and baseball statistics about the progress of the island's players who have defected to the U.S. such as the New York Yankees' pitcher Jose Contreras. Unsurprisingly, even President Fidel Castro, as a former baseball pitcher, is a passionate sports fan. To illustrate, he has seriously threatened and attempted to prevent American and foreign baseball agents and scouts from tampering with Cuban players. Yet, since 1991 approximately 35 Cuban baseball coaches and players have fled Castro's tyrannical government. Furthermore, as a political dictator he influences all sports events and business transactions in that country. According to *Sports Illustrated* senior writer S.L. Price, who wrote *Pitching Around Fidel: A Journey Into the Heart of Cuban Sports*, Castro's regime emphasizes Cuban athletes' achievements in global competitions to underscore the momentum and vitality of the 55 year old revolution.[15]

Interestingly, on the league's opening day in 2003 there were nine Cubans on MLB team rosters. One very productive, veteran Cuban player was the AL Texas Rangers' [in 2004 Baltimore Orioles] designated hitter Rafael Palmeiro. Because of his prodigious home run and runs batted in totals, and the mandatory waiting period of five years after retirement, Palmeiro will probably receive a unanimous vote on the first ballot and be inducted into the Baseball Hall of Fame, which is located in Cooperstown, Pennsylvania. Given the publicity of Palmeiro's achievements, if the Castro government collapses and/or the U.S. embargo were lifted, many Cuban athletes will be rewarded after they enter the international sports market, especially those players with experiences and superior skills in baseball and soccer.

Venezuela

According to published information, American oil workers introduced baseball to Venezuela during the 1920s. Since then, baseball has gradually replaced soccer to become the nation's most popular national sport. Venezuela's Professional Baseball League was founded in 1941. Sixty-two years later, the league consisted of four teams each in the Eastern and Western Divisions. The regular baseball season there begins each year in October and ends in January. When the regular season concludes, a tournament is played to determine the Venezuelan League's champion. To win the championship, teams have generally played a qualifier round, a round-robin series and a final series. The winning team then must compete in a Caribbean League series against the other championship clubs from the Dominican Republic, Mexico and Puerto Rico. Beside the winter season schedule, there is a Venezuelan Summer Minor League system that is subsidized by MLB.[16]

During baseball's celebrated and longstanding history in Venezuela, the Professional League's seasons were interrupted by a ballplayers' strike in 1959 and again in 1974. Because of security concerns and shortages of food and gasoline, however, in December of 2003 baseball team owners suspended the League's games to support the ongoing national strike, which was organized by the country's business and union leaders to oust Venezuelan President Hugo Chavez. Ironically, during the strike Chavez had opposed the powerful media companies that owned several of Venezuela's professional baseball teams.[17]

During 2003, 37 Venezuelans were listed on MLB team rosters. The NL included such star players as the San Francisco Giants' infielder Edgardo Alfonzo and Philadelphia Phillies' infielder Bobby Abreu, and in the AL, there was the Chicago White Sox' outfielder Magglio Ordonez and Seattle Mariners' pitcher Freddy Garcia. The four athletes, like those from Mexico, the Dominican Republic and Puerto Rico, had likely developed their big league skills while they performed on teams in their nation's baseball academies.

European Nations

Although baseball in many European countries was revitalized because of the 1992 Summer Olympic Games, for decades the sport has been popular in Holland and Italy. Moreover, baseball's acceptance as a game and its participation rates as a leisure activity have recently increased among sports fans in France, Greece and the United Kingdom. Indeed, to encourage the sport's growth in Germany and elsewhere, MLB conducts clinics and sponsors interactive programs that teach children and young adults how to play various team positions and learn the basics of American-style baseball games and competitive startegies.[18]

At a representative European baseball championship series that is scheduled each year, typically the teams' players are not overly obsessed with scoring runs and beating their opponents to win the tournament. Meanwhile, during games many spectators seem confused about the sport's rules and coaches' decisions to signal players to bunt, attempt hit and run plays, and adjust their defensive positions for certain batters. In comparison with other sports, therefore, professional baseball's player development system and fan interest in Europe lacks the status of games and leagues in basketball, American football and obviously, in ice hockey and outdoor soccer.

Nevertheless, the dismal European baseball environment has not discouraged or prevented MLB from pursuing its global strategies on the continent. Because of the Expos' 2002 and 2003 game attendances in San Juan, Puerto Rico and the Padres' previous competitions in Monterrey, Mexico, and the importation of numerous baseball players from the countries in Latin America, the league has studied whether to play some 2005 exhibition and regular season games in Europe' largest cosmopolitan cities such as London, Madrid, Munich, Paris and/or Rome, and in various cities of baseball friendly countries like the Czech Republic, Italy and the Netherlands. This decision, however, is somewhat dependent on whether the European media, and especially sports journalists, newspaper editors and television producers will tend to advertise and promote the games and programs of America's favorite pastime sport. Anyway, if one or more of these cities or countries are selected as future game sites, then the respective European sports stadiums will require extensive renovation and costly retrofitting to comply with MLB rules regarding a baseball fields' dimensions and the seat area of the facilities. For this investment to occur, however, the macroeconomic conditions must improve, part- icularly in France and Germany.[19]

China and Russia

According to MLBI's Jim Small, various medium to large cities in China and Russia are rated as high priority places to eventually stage professional baseball games. In China, the dominant sports played by millions of athletes are badminton, basketball, soccer and table tennis. In contrast, there are approximately 35,000 amateur baseball players in the nation who compete on teams. Nonetheless, a national Chinese baseball league exists. The league, in 2003, consisted of teams located in Beijing, Guangdong, Shanghai and Tianjin. Each city government's sports authority owned and controlled those teams, who each played a schedule of 24 games, which were held only during daylight hours. The teams' players are normally recruited from government sports schools, earn approximately 4,000 to 8,000 Chinese yuan per month, and are not allowed to be exchanged or traded between the clubs. Based on recent Chinese government statistics, the average attendance per baseball game is less than 3,000 spectators. Curiously, during baseball games some enthusiastic fans occasionally sing songs with heroic lyrics about the workers' revolution while teams' cheerleaders perform well-rehearsed dance routines. Because of the forthcoming 2008 Summer Olympic Games to be played in Beijing, the Chinese government vigorously supports the development of players and the growth of baseball throughout the country. Dynasty XX, which is a marketing firm operated by an American businessman, has signed contracts with some sponsors that include the U.S. baseball card company, Upper Deck. Also, the marketing firm plans to conduct baseball clinics and teach Chinese kids how to appreciate the sport's games as competition, fun and entertainment. For sure, if trends continue MLB teams will participate in exhibition and/or preseason baseball games and other events on mainland China before 2008. To illustrate their relationship, in late 2003 MLB and the China Baseball Association (CBA) signed a working agreement that involved funds, scouts and player development programs for the Chinese national baseball team. Basically, the deal allowed American professional and collegiate coaches to work in China with young prospects and likewise offered Chinese coaches the opportunity to do the same thing in the U.S. with MLB teams. Also, MLB will train Chinese umpires and begin to scout base-baseball players in China. With respect to the agreement, the CBA's secretary-general Shen Wei said, "We want to develop stars. Baseball in China could use its own Yao Ming [Chinese player on the NBA Houston Rockets]."[20]

In Russia, several leisure and sports activities are an integral part of the country's national culture although Russian children typically play on basketball, hockey and soccer clubs during those sports' annual seasons. But during the early 1990s, the Summer Olympic Games in Barcelona, Spain inspired some of Russia's athletes and sports enthusiasts to organize teams and play American-style baseball games. Invariably, the Olympic Games became the event that triggered the sport's growth in Russia during the middle to late 1990s. In Moscow, for example, there are leagues for nearly 30 baseball teams that seek to enroll boys who are 8–16 years old. Even more indicative of the sport's progress, for the third consecutive year a competitive baseball team of 10–12 year old players from Moscow performed well enough to win the 2003 European Little League Championship. Furthermore, the Russian Baseball Federation for the first time hosted the 2003 European Juvenile Baseball Championship tournament that was played at Moscow's Moskvich Stadium. Besides the Little League and Juvenile sports programs, in Russia there are 2,400 or more experienced players who compete on at least 40 adult baseball clubs. One passionate baseball fan is the press secretary of the Russian Olympic Committee, Aleksandr Ratner. He hopes that MLB will eventually allow its regular season games, and perhaps division playoffs and World Series to be broadcast for free to households on Russia's all-sports channel. Moreover, Ratner has proposed to employ MLB coaches at summer baseball camps held throughout

Russia to teach kids how to field, hit and pitch baseballs, and how to play offense and defense positions during game conditions.[21]

In other words, to further advance baseball in communities and thus generate more interest in the sport at the grassroots level in China and Russia, MLB has several options to consider. First, the league might decide to cooperate with local and national government officials to co-sponsor clinics and workshops that educate children and young adults about what basic skills are needed to successfully compete in baseball events, and teach how important teamwork, coordination and esprit de corps are to win games and tournaments; second, the league may provide Chinese and Russian youth leagues, and their respective clubs and players with such modern and proper baseball equipment as baseballs, bats and mitts, and also donate money for the purchase of bases, spiked shoes and uniforms; and third, the league might encourage baseball's union, which is titled the Major League Baseball Players Association (MLBPA), to contribute its organization's resources and therefore participate in baseball programs for athletes who live in rural and urban areas of China and Russia. In short, those efforts by MLB and the MLBPA are each long-term investments that will likely enhance the sport of baseball in the two countries.

Because of the game's global exposure and increasing popularity in numerous nations besides Canada and the U.S., American baseball is currently regarded as an entertainment activity and an international sport. When the youth from countries in Africa, Asia, Europe, Latin America and elsewhere practice together and join local teams to play games, some of those ambitious and talented athletes develop the skills necessary to become proficient baseball players as young adults and even the potential to qualify as professional prospects.

As a result, during the 1990s and early 2000s MLB experienced extraordinary growth in the employment of non-U.S. athletes who had played professional baseball for such big league teams as the NL Florida Marlins or AL Texas Rangers, and/or on a team in an American baseball minor league system in the U.S. or Canada. Beside the influx of international players, this employment growth also affected various North American and foreign global businesses, cities, government agencies and ministries, and sports federations and markets. In the next section of this chapter, MLB's growing use of and dependence on foreign baseball players is analyzed. In effect, this phenomenon has become a productive and efficient strategy for MLB to globally promote and expand the sport.

Foreign Players

Since the 1920s, MLB has experienced an irregular but positive inflow of well-prepared international-born players. Before the 1950s, the majority of those athletes were natives of Cuba. Later, the players primarily gravitated from Latin American countries while a portion of them had departed from Canada, Japan, Korea, Taiwan and other nations. Thus, because of various economic, political, social and sports-specific reasons, hundreds of moderate to highly skilled foreign-born baseball players migrated to the U.S., especially during the middle to late 1990s and early 2000s.

To be more specific, the proportion of MLB players who were born outside the U.S. has measurably increased since 1970. That year, the proportion was approximately 10 percent. Then, because of baseball's globalization and MLB strategies, the proportion rose to 19 percent in 1997, 24 percent in 2001, 26 percent in 2002, and eventually to 29 percent in 2003. Numerically, the latter percentage represents 230 players from 16 countries and Puerto Rico. Of those 230 players, 79 or 34 percent were born in the Dominican Republic, 38 or 17 percent in Puerto Rico, 37 or 16 percent in Venezuela, 17 or 7 percent in Mexico, and 10 or 4 percent each in Canada, Cuba or Japan. Based on MLB teams' rosters and disabled lists on the opening day of the 2003 season, there were at least 201 players from merely seven foreign countries. Why is the distribution of foreign players, when based on the respective countries' percentages, such an important statistic to MLB from an international business perspective? Since that question has several implications, it needs to be addressed next.[22]

During the early 2000s, there were at least four MLB teams that employed a relatively moderate to large number of foreign players. Those teams included the AL' Kansas City Royals and New York Yankees, and the NL' Montreal Expos and Philadelphia Phillies. To be competitive in their respective divisions, evidently the general managers of those and other professional baseball clubs had developed plans, adopted player policies, and approved risky investments that resulted in the recruitment and employment of numerous foreign-born athletes to play various team positions. In part, the managers' strategies succeeded for some MLB clubs but failed to affect the winning percentages and division standings of other NL and AL teams. As a result, the former franchises will likely continue to recruit and hire talented players who were born in nations besides the U.S., while the latter teams will reevaluate the quality and employment of their foreign-born athletes. Those decisions are illustrated in the paragraphs that follow.

After several regular seasons of dismal performances, during 2003 the small-market Royals had decided to diversify its roster and try to win a division title with eight players, and a coach, of Latin American heritage. According to reports, it was the Royals' president Dan Glass who had foresaw the benefits of adding Caribbean players to the team. That is, during the late 1990s he initiated some improvements of the club's baseball academy in the City of Salcedo in the Dominican Republic. As a result of Glass' decision, the academy expertly trained, strengthened and prepared some outstanding athletes who were ultimately promoted to the Royals' big-league roster in Kansas City. To measure those players' impact on performances, the team played outstanding baseball and led the AL Central Division for several weeks during the 2003 regular season. Due to injuries and a slump, however, the club did not qualify for the AL playoffs. The premier players on that team had included such Latinos as shortstop Angel Berroa, center fielder Carlos Beltran and left fielder Raul Ibanez. Meanwhile, because of his exuberant attitude and leadership efforts the Royals' Tony Pena received the AL Manager of the Year award by a large vote margin. Regarding his achievements, Pena said that, "Dominicans, and all Latinos, are showing that we can take on large responsibilities in baseball. We know how to do more than throw or hit well. We have to forget about the language. We have to forget about all the problems we have in the way and go forward."[23]

In 2003, there were 11 athletes from Japan on MLB's opening day rosters. The performances and skills of two Japanese-born players, however, were particularly applauded by baseball fans and the media, and thus deserve recognition in this section of the chapter. One player who excelled was Ichiro Suzuki, the AL Seattle Mariners' right fielder. In 2001, Suzuki led the Mariners to a West division title. For his achievements, he earned the AL Rookie of the Year award and more significantly, the AL Most Valuable Player trophy. Because of Suzuki's fielding and hitting abilities, and his contributions to baseball's image in Seattle, Washington and in the other AL cities, during 2001 the Mariners' 162 regular season games were broadcast live to sports fans in Japan while spectators at the club's ballpark in Seattle enjoyed Japanese cuisine. Besides the exposure of and financial return to the Mariners and other clubs in MLB, Suzuki's presence improved the communications and economic linkages between Japan and the U.S., which have been two countries with vastly different cultures, political systems and social values. As an aside, when Suzuki completed his three-year $14 million guaranteed contract in 2003, he became eligible for arbitration with the Mariners. After his third productive season as an outfielder, in late 2003 the Mariners decided to resign Suzuki to a four-year contract extension valued at $44 million. According to the deal, the club bought out Suzuki's first year of free agent eligibility although the contract makes Suzuki the highest paid player in the franchise's history.[24]

Because of his well-deserved fame, stature and superior baseball talent, Hideki Matsui is the second noteworthy Japanese-born player to be highlighted here. In 2003, he played left field for the large-market New York Yankees, which is an extremely wealthy franchise that has frequently won MLB's East division and AL titles, and occasionally succeeded in World Series championships. When Matsui, the former all-star center fielder for the Tokyo Yomiuri Giants had completed the minimum nine years of service as a player in Japan's professional baseball league, he officially filed for free agency in 2002 in order to negotiate a contract of employment with a MLB franchise. Despite a team payroll that exceeded $150 million in 2003, the Yankees' owner George Steinbrenner signed Matsui to a three-year $21 million contract. Besides his salary payments, Matsui's contract included three other significant benefits. Those were one, a no-trade clause; two, a provision that Matsui cannot be demoted to the minor leagues without his consent; and three, a mutual agreement that allowed him to become a free agent in 2005. Based on his performances as a Yankee thus far, Matsui is equitably compensated. In 2003, he batted .287, swatted 42 doubles and 19 home runs, batted in 106 runners, and placed second to the Royals' Angel Berroa for the AL Rookie-of-the-Year award. Furthermore, the Yankees won the East division and AL titles, but were defeated in six games by the underrated Florida Marlins in the 2003 World Series. As an aside, on opening day of the 2004 season the NL New York Mets' shortstop Kazuo Matsui totaled three hits including a lead-off home run and two doubles, walked twice and batted in three runs. As a seven-time all-star in Japan where he hit 39 home runs in 2002 and 33 in 2003 for the Seibu Lions, Katsui entertained the 50 or more Japanese media who had attended the game at [Ted] Turner Field in Atlanta, Georgia. About Kazuo Matsui's performance the Mets' manager Art Howe said, "The kid, he just looked to me like he was ready. It was time to start playing. He put his game face on. And I hope it's the same game face he wears every night." In short, it appears that another baseball player from Japan will excel in MLB.[25]

The exodus of such baseball legends as Suzuki and Matsui, and of other high caliber players from Japan to MLB has resulted in financial problems for the struggling professional teams in Japan's Central and Pacific Leagues. That is, those Leagues' weakest clubs are undercapitalized, inadequately subsidized by their respective Japanese corporate sponsors, and under publicized relative to their local and national television exposure. As such, if an increasing number of skilled players like Suzuki and Matsui decide to abandon their teams in one or both of Japan's professional leagues and then join a MLB club, eventually the Japanese baseball leagues, to survive, might be forced to merge. This consolidation, in turn, would likely force the Japanese leagues' to reduce total membership from 12 to perhaps six franchises, which means fewer players and less corporate sponsorships. Indeed, because of the drastic restructuring of businesses in Japan, the number of corporate baseball teams has declined from 237 in the early 1990s to about 80 in 2004. As a result, more than 100 former industrial league players have moved from Japan to the U.S. since the late 1990s. Although these players must adjust to a new culture, most of them will likely join American baseball farm clubs and independent league teams that perform below the level of MLB.

Consequently, a portion of Japan's sports fans are alienated and undoubtedly feel betrayed when their outstanding baseball players decide to forego their loyalties and traditions, and defect for a team in MLB. Those hostile attitudes, however, have gradually subsided and even reversed in recent years. That is, rather than blame the Japanese players or MLB for the defections, generally fans now believe the players' emigration signals that Japan's professional baseball leagues have matured in prestige and quality as sports organizations. As an aside, in conjunction with the increase of Japanese, Latinos and other nationalities on MLB teams' rosters, the proportion of African American players has dramatically declined. That proportion has decreased from 26 percent in 1975 to 19 percent in 1995, and finally to 10 percent in 2003. As concluded by the researchers of one study, although America's professional basketball and football leagues are attractive options for the U.S.' second largest minority group, for various economic and social reasons the minor and major league baseball organizations have lost their inspirational appeal as sports choices for many outstanding black high school and college amateur athletes.[26]

To better reveal the distribution of MLB players by country and position, Tables A.1 and A.2 were developed and placed in the Appendix. In Table A.1, a total of 959 players appeared on the rosters of the 30 teams during the Spring training period in March of 2004. With respect to those players' distribution, 700 or 73 percent were from America, 214 or 22 percent from Latin American nations, and 45 or 5 percent from such countries as Australia, Japan and South Korea. There were four teams with 29 Americans, one team with 12 Latinos and one team with six players from other nations. Furthermore, the fewest Americans played for the Los Angeles Dodgers and the minimum number of Latinos for the Milwaukee Brewers. Meanwhile, 6 or 20 percent of the teams employed only players from the U.S. and Latin American nations. However, before the 2004 regular season had begun in early April of 2004 a few of the rookies and/or veteran players might be cut from a squad, transferred to a minor league team or traded to another MLB club.

In turn, Table A.2 shows an allocation of the skill positions of 259 non-American players during the middle of March in 2004. Based on the table, the highest proportion of positions was pitchers at 46 percent, and then infielders at 25 percent, outfielders at 20 percent and catchers at 9 percent. Interestingly, the Los Angeles Dodgers and Minnesota Twins had the largest number of pitchers at eight while the San Francisco Giants had merely one. Moreover, according to the distribution the Florida Marlins had the most infielders at five, the Kansas City Royals and Los Angeles Dodgers four each outfielders, and the Anaheim Angels three catchers. For some reason, the teams with at least 15 foreign players were the Los Angeles and Baltimore Orioles while the Milwaukee Brewers and Toronto Blue Jays had fewer than six international athletes on their rosters. In short, there was a moderately wide range of non-U.S. players per team.

This discussion concludes the sections about MLBI, global baseball markets and foreign players in professional baseball. Thus far, this chapter's contents infer that MLB has moderately improved its market share as an international sport, and also has strategically prepared its organization to compete as a global sports business vis-à-vis the other U.S.-based professional leagues into the early to middle years of the 21st century. Nevertheless, other relevant short- and long-term events, issues and trends, presented as baseball topics, need to be addressed about MLB because they might influence whether people, who are located in rural and urban areas across the planet will be attracted to and support American-style baseball. Accordingly, a few of those topics are highlighted and analyzed in the next portion of Chapter 1.

Baseball Topics

The globalization strategies, worldwide activities and grassroots programs implemented by MLB, particularly since the late 1980s, have certainly rewarded numerous foreign-born baseball players and their families, provided jobs for coaches, general managers, ballpark employees and sports agents, and increased the revenues of sports-affiliated businesses and other organizations that are based in both modern and underdeveloped countries. Nonetheless, for MLB there are several precarious developments, opportunities and threats that have emerged, and which have been identified and studied. Besides being controversial and newsworthy, these baseball-related topics have worldwide consequences for the future of

America's professional sports leagues, teams and players since there are enormous economic and social benefits, costs and risks to be evaluated. From the research performed for *Sports Capitalism*, the following five topics directly involve the sport of baseball and/or MLB. Because of their uncertain domestic and global affects, those topics are scrutinized in the next few pages of this chapter.

Latin American Baseball Academies

To effectively discover, scout, recruit and train talented teenagers and young adults who have the potential to become professional baseball players and perhaps international superstars, several MLB franchises such as the NL's Chicago Cubs, Cincinnati Reds and Los Angeles Dodgers, and the AL's Chicago White Sox, Minnesota Twins and New York Yankees have purchased and/or leased properties in foreign countries. That is, those and other MLB clubs have invested in, constructed and renovated baseball academies and assorted facilities, for example, in Latin American countries. Because the majority of those structures are located in remote areas outside of North America, they reportedly have been exploited and unregulated throughout their existence. For example, in Latin America the nations' ballparks and practice fields, housing complexes and recreation buildings have been neglected and essentially ignored by MLB and the league's team owners. Especially apparent are the dilapidated apartments, dormitories and houses, which means that the living conditions are basically abominable. According to some inspectors' reports, most players' housing units were not air-conditioned, and on average contained uneven concrete floors, lacked sufficient floor space for dinning tables, bedrooms and closets, needed bathroom showers, tubs, sinks and toilets, smelled from unsanitary and leftover kitchen debris, and had roofs that often profusely leaked when it rained. Despite the filthy and unhealthy conditions, however, the foreign baseball academies and other facilities have served as the player development centers of the MLB teams who have a vested interest in, respectively, the junior, rookie and minor league baseball organizations in Latin America.[27]

Because of the pressures from international groups and also for self-interest purposes, during the early 2000s some NL and AL clubs had modestly renovated the structures, and thereby improved the living standards and/or ballpark specifications at their academies in Latin America and elsewhere. In 2001, for example, the Chicago Cubs invested nearly $180,000 when the club purchased a batting cage, erected new dugouts and installed an irrigation system at its ballpark in Santana, which is a city in the Dominican Republic. Yet, when MLB inspectors criticized the quality of the franchise's Latin American housing units, the Cubs decided to move its academy in the Dominican Republic from Santana to San Pedro de Macoris. At the latter location, the baseball stadium has such attractive amenities as manicured grass and a well-kept infield, extra pitching mounds and spacious locker rooms. To avoid bad publicity and future inspections, the Cubs had planned to eventually relocate its academy from San Pedro de Macoris to a new complex east of Santo Domingo. Meanwhile, for years the Cincinnati Reds and New York Yankees have shared a world-class complex in the Dominican

Republic. Each team has spent thousands of dollars per month for the use of several baseball fields and practice infields, weight and dormitory rooms, and for buildings to operate a barbershop, café and basketball court. Besides the Cubs, Reds and Yankees in the Dominican Republic, there are other MLB teams that have leased decent housing and training facilities to tenants in Puerto Rico and Venezuela. Even so, as of 2003 the vast majority of baseball's academies and other real estate properties in Latin America required better management and thus more money for additional maintenance, repairs and capital improvements.[28]

In a January 2003 memorandum to the MLB Commissioner's Office, the authors of *Stealing Lives: The Globalization of Baseball and the Tragic Story of Alexis Quiroz*, who were Arturo J. Marcano and David P. Fidler, critiqued a 7-page document entitled "MLB Academy Standards and Compliance Inspection Procedure." This document, which was drafted by MLB sometime during 2001–2002, listed several detailed provisions to rectify the absence of rules needed to regulate the baseball academies located in the Dominican Republic and Venezuela. In their memorandum to MLB, Marcano and Fidler related the league's standards to reform the academies as based on the principles of centralization, harmonization, implementation and specialization. To satisfy those principles, the authors listed at least four policies that Commissioner Bud Selig's Office should enact and enforce. First, the Office should make the standards binding as Major League Rules (MLR); second, the Office should make the standards consistent and uniform with the regulations and protections that exist in the MLRs; third, the Office should broaden and deepen the rules to specifically represent the Latin American baseball academies; and fourth, the Office should create inspection machinery so that the rules are enforced. According to Marcano and Fidler, if these four policies were adopted then the standards would be useful guidelines to apply and improve the treatment and support of Latin children and young men by the Commissioner's Office and MLB team owners. For sure, the document and memorandum outline some appropriate reforms and necessary requirements to qualitatively upgrade the structures and thus healthcare conditions of the players who are tenants within the teams' Latin American baseball academies.[29]

As the NL and AL clubs continue to search for baseball prospects in Latin America and in other emerging markets, MLB will be expected to willingly allocate its scarce resources and invest more time and money in such foreign players' human capital needs as education and healthcare, and in physical capital assets that include international ballparks and the infrastructures of the local cities. If those projects are invested in and successfully completed, in the short-term this strategy will enhance the living standards of the poorest athletes who are from communities in third world countries. Whereas in the long-term, the investments undertaken and completed will motivate foreign players to compete and win games for their clubs, and therefore increase the respective MLB teams' performances and the franchise owners' profits.

Drug Tests

According to plans that were designed for MLB's 2003 regular season, which began in April of that year and concluded in September, MLB and the MLBPA agreed to implement a multimillion-dollar program to test major and minor league baseball players for the illegal use of steroids. For each player, there were two unannounced tests. In total, if 5 percent or more of the athletes had tested positive for drug use, then further tests would be conducted until less than 2.5 percent of those tested had received positive results in two consecutive years. Obviously, the specific players sampled and the drug test results are confidential information that has not been provided to the public or reported in the media.[30]

To control the league's administrative costs but ensure the enforcement of its policies, MLB's initial drug test program excluded Dominican Republic and Venezuelan athletes who, in total, represented 34 percent of players with contracts. Unfortunately, during August of 2003 *The Washington Post* reported that a portion of the Dominican Republic's professional baseball prospects, which included those players with MLB contracts, had frequently injected animal steroids and dietary supplements in their bodies to boost performances in practices and games. What was MLB's reaction, if any, when the newspaper had published that information?

Because of the *Posts*'s report and criticism from respected academic sports authors such as Indiana University's professor of international law David P. Fidler, MLB decided to expand its program in 2004 and thereby issue drug tests to the minor league players who performed for teams in Latin America. According to NL and AL policies, those players will be randomly tested during three different time periods within a year. Although the test frequency differs between foreign minor leaguers and MLB players, the Hispanics Across America organization president Fernando Mateo declared, "Young players in the Dominican Republic and across Latin America will now enjoy the safeguards against dangerous steroids that they deserve."[31]

If there are serious consequences, that is, penalties for players who frequently fail their tests, then MLB's drug program will emit significant social benefits. Some drug test programs, however, are undoubtedly flawed and there are administrative costs and user fees for MLB to issue and process the tests. Furthermore, if any program errors should occur, then some big league players who may have tested positive will likely appeal their cases to the MLBPA and request that organization's support. So, if enough players complain about the program's results, the MLBPA may decide to challenge MLB and demand that the test standards be restudied, downgraded, or in the extreme, the MLBPA could threaten to strike the NL and/or AL. In the long-term, however, the development, management and strict enforcement of an international drug test program is a worthwhile policy for MLB to permanently adopt.

Global Player Draft System

To distribute the pool of relatively inexperienced but talented college baseball players more equitably so that the small-market clubs such as the NL Pittsburgh Pirates and AL Baltimore Orioles could then compete for division titles and World Series championships, MLB implemented a draft system in 1965. Eighteen years later, the system was amended. That is, all baseball high school players in America were subjected to the draft. Then, in 1989 and 1991, respectively, amateur baseball players from the U.S. territories and Canada were included in the draft. Despite those reforms, however, in 2002 the international major leaguers, who represented nearly 40 percent of the players on the 30 MLB clubs and on the minor league affiliates' rosters, were excluded from the draft. Consequently, MLB's medium to large market teams, which had benefited from abundant cash inflows and earnings from game attendances, local and regional television and radio broadcast agreements, and merchandise sales, had signed contracts with the majority of outstanding international players. During 2003, for example, the New York Yankees hired Japan's Hideki Matsui for $21 million and Cuba's Jose Contreras for $32 million. Obviously, those and other extravagant multimillion-dollar contract deals have created short- and long-run competitive imbalances between the wealthy and low-budget franchises in the NL and AL.[32]

The first proposal to adopt an international draft system attracted support in 1993. That year, a group of baseball's scouting directors and general managers unanimously voted for the proposal. Since then, there have been groups of representatives from MLB and the MLBPA that have informally offered, and during collective bargaining sessions formally negotiated, different types of global draft proposals. Nonetheless, although the league and union continue to debate proposals, they respectfully disagree on an international draft's coverage and its processes, procedures and rules.

Besides those specific concerns about an international draft system, there are other controversial issues about drafting players that require resolutions. First, the MLB teams that have well-established baseball contacts and academies in Latin America and/or Asia generally oppose a global draft. Those large-market clubs, such as the NL Atlanta Braves and AL Toronto Blue Jays have a vested interest in the current free agent system because of their experience, freedom and resourcefulness to locate, recruit, scout and sign to long-term contracts the highest skilled international baseball players. This means that, in order to compete, the small-market teams with a deficient amount of resources and below average cash inflows like the NL Milwaukee Brewers and AL Oakland Athletics must reinvest their earnings, if any, to lease or build and maintain academies and to establish scouting networks in Latin America and elsewhere. Second, a worldwide draft system must respond to and incorporate a variety of conditions. What special provisions, for example, would be required for the foreign players who are drafted from countries that host their own professional leagues such as in Australia, Japan, Korea, Mexico and Venezuela? Third, what, specific eligibility standards are there with respect to an international player's age, education and nationality? Fourth, the system will include how many rounds or series for the teams to draft players? While MLB negotiators prefer a high number of rounds, the MLBPA favors a low number of rounds. To illustrate those differences in rounds, during the Summer of 2002 MLB franchise owners proposed one 40-round draft that would include amateur players from every country except Cuba. Alternatively, the union preferred one eight-round draft for American amateur players and one eight-round draft for non-U.S. amateur players. According to management's lead labor lawyer Rob Manfred, the boundaries negotiated between MLB and the union had ranged from 20 to 38 rounds. Fifth, when might MLB teams trade their drafted players and what factors or forces will determine the market values of those players who were drafted? Sixth, the MLBPA philosophically opposes any draft system because there are explicit and implicit restraint-of-trade issues. The union, therefore, has not been eager to approve the suppression of bonuses granted to athletes who were drafted from foreign countries because those players' rights are controlled by one or a few of the league's elite baseball teams. Seventh, during the Summer of 2002 MLB owners and players agreed to implement a revenue sharing plan and also decided to adopt and enforce a luxury tax. The plan and tax were passed, respectively, to re-distribute revenues from large- to small-market clubs and to penalize the NL and AL teams who had annual payrolls that exceeded a designated amount. Essentially, those rules partially succeeded in the 2003 regular season when one of the four NL playoff teams was the small-market Florida Marlins. In the AL, beside the large-market Boston Red Sox and New York Yankees, the small-market Minnesota Twins and Oakland Athletics each had qualified for the playoffs. Furthermore, because of its $150 million payroll the Yankees paid an estimated $40 million in luxury taxes. In short, a committee of MLB owners and MLBPA officials meet periodically to reconcile their differences and perhaps implement an international draft system before 2006.[33]

World Cup of Baseball

The initial discussion of an international or World Cup competition in baseball began when MLB players expressed an interest to play on an American or foreign team in the 1992 Summer Olympic Games, which was held from July 25 to August 9 in Barcelona, Spain. Because of the interruptions in scheduled games that would have occurred during the U.S. professional baseball's regular season, it was not practical or realistic for MLB players to participate in those Olympic Games.

Nevertheless, since 1992 several MLB franchise owner groups and player committees and subcommittees have discussed the concept of a World Cup tournament. Given the availability of medium sized and large ballparks in the U.S., the enthusiastic support of American baseball fans, and extensive television and radio network coverage especially in North America, during 2002 former MLB president Paul Beeston proposed that an eight-team World Cup tournament be played in American at various sites in 2005. According to Beeston's proposal, eventually the tournament would be expanded to 12 teams. Those would include some competitive national clubs from Japan and European countries, and perhaps later from the best baseball programs in China and Russia. Meanwhile, in October of 2003 Cuba hosted a low-key World Cup of Baseball tournament that consisted of four teams each from Asia and Europe, and one team each from Australia and South Africa. Interestingly, the ten-team tournament coincided with a meeting of the General Congress of the International Baseball Federation that had convened in Cuba.[34]

While MLBI negotiated with the Japanese to open the 2004 regular season in Tokyo, and with other baseball officials to conduct Spring Training and play regular season games in Europe and Latin America, during the Summer of 2003 MLB president and chief operating officer Bob DuPuy had likewise proposed a schedule for a 2005 World Cup of Baseball. The tournament, as drafted by DuPuy, is to be held every fourth year. To be successful, Dupuy said the tournament's date, format and structure needed to consider such business and sports issues as the variety of media broadcasts, players' eligibility requirements and compensation levels, ballpark sites, the number and type of civic and corporate sponsorships, and MLB's coordination with and cooperation from the primary international baseball federations in each foreign country.[35]

Besides the Beeston and DuPuy proposals, in July 2003 MLB's senior vice president of international business operations Paul Archey presented his version of a World Cup of Baseball tournament to a marketing committee that was organized by MLB Commissioner Bud Selig. According to his plan, Archey preferred that 16 nations compete in the first World Cup tournament at sites in U.S. cities that have domed stadiums and warm climates. Based on opinions from baseball officials, a tournament's optimal time would be two weeks during March 2005. If approved, this time frame would require that MLB teams reduce their practice sessions and game schedules during Spring Training, which is the preseason period.[36]

Given that one or more of the aforementioned proposals are feasible and negotiable, it appears that MLB had temporarily distanced itself from the Summer Olympic Games in 2004, and possibly in 2008, in order to pursue its goal of establishing an international World Cup of Baseball tournament in 2005 or shortly thereafter. Based on estimated values, to participate in a Summer Olympics would cost each MLB club at least $2 million in foregone revenues as a result of postponing its regular season games. This opportunity cost is obviously unacceptable to Commissioner Selig and to baseball's NL and AL franchise owners and players. So, even though the Commissioner's Office and other MLB officials have continued to evaluate plans that permit major leaguers to play in an Olympic Games, there are vital regular season scheduling and economic problems that will likely prohibit MLB's participation before the 2012 Summer Olympic Games, which may take place in New York City, New York or Toronto, Canada. Essentially, until disputes about issues such as players' drug tests, teams' revenue proportions, game schedules and travel arrangements are resolved between MLB and the International Olympic Committee, to stage a 2005 or 2006 World Cup tournament is the U.S. professional baseball league's priority event.

Canadian Baseball League

The Vancouver-based CBL, which was Canada's first national, independent professional hardball confederation, was co-founded in 2002 by Tony Riviera and Charlton Lui. "Our concept," said Riviera, "is to create parity across the league." To accomplish that objective, the league had planned to restrict player salaries and control administrative expenses through a centralized budgeting system, and to promote a family atmosphere at games where fans and players could easily commingle and communicate in the ballpark. As the Canadian Press' Shi Davidi observed, "To succeed, the CBL will have to prevail over an indifference toward the game among Canadians by providing entertaining baseball while integrating themselves into the community."[37]

When the league was organized, there were four CBL-owned Canadian clubs in both the East and West Divisions, and each of the league's teams employed 25 former minor and major league professional baseball players who would compete to play during the 72-game schedule. To contain costs and maximize sales revenues, each of the teams' salaries were capped at $300,000 per year and season tickets for 36 home games ranged from $216 to $360. After the stadiums were leased and the negotiation of a regional television contract had concluded, the CBL commenced its inaugural season on 21 May 2003 in London, Ontario.[38]

Because of an ineffective leaguewide marketing campaign, the inferior quality of teams and games in each Division, poor weather conditions in eastern Canada, and apathetic fan support, on 25 July 2003 the CBL suspended its operations. To explain the league's failure, the average attendance was about 1,000 spectators per game, which was 50 percent below the teams' breakeven attendance. Furthermore, excessive rainfall during the Summer months of 2003 forced the East Division teams to cancel 25 percent of their games and thus, the league had earned zero income from advance ticket sales. Moreover, due to insufficient cash inflows the CBL's umpires were reportedly not compensated. As those events occurred, widespread rumors had circulated in the media that the league might collapse soon. When it did, the CBL commissioner and Canada's only member of the U.S. Baseball Hall of Fame, Ferguson Jenkins, declared that after the league reorganizes, he would continue to work towards creating a successful future for a professional baseball organization in Canada.[39]

Given the data, facts and other information about the history, organization and progress of MLB, which is the world's most prestigious and touted professional baseball league, and the league's international business strategies and relationships as presented in this chapter, Table 1.1 lists five foreign cities, arranged alphabetically, that are potential sites for at least one MLB relocated and/or new franchise to be established after 2004. Each city was chosen primarily based on its expected fan base and market support for a U.S. professional baseball team, and on its location, population and summer climate.

If the cities listed in Table 1.1 are ranked from the best to least attractive, the optimum site to place a MLB team after 2004 is in Mexico's wealthiest city, Monterrey, which is located approximately 100 miles southwest of the nearest Texas bo-

Table 1.1 Foreign MLB Cities, Post 2004

City	Country	Population	Area
Mexico City	Mexico	8.6	21.2
Monterrey	Mexico	1.1	3.5
Havana	Cuba	2.3	2.7
San Juan	Puerto Rico	.4	2.1
Santo Domingo	Dominican Republic	2.2	2.8

Note: Population is the city's 2003 population in millions. For each city, Area is the metropolitan area's 2003 population in millions. A metropolitan area comprises several urbanized areas that are economically linked to each other.

Source: "The World Gazetteer," at <http://www.world-gazetteer.com> cited 1 November 2003.

rder. In Monterrey, there is modern architecture everywhere and plenty of American restaurants and stores dispersed throughout the urban area. Besides the city of Monterrey's sports reputation as the home of the Mexican Baseball Hall of Fame, the Mexican League's Monterrey Sultans play there in a 27,000-seat stadium that could, if necessary, be expanded to 30,000. The Sultans' ballpark, which was built in 1990, is considered the best baseball facility in Latin America. Two wealthy entrepreneurs, Jose Maiz Garcia and Carlos Bremer Gutierrez, have presented a proposal to MLB and requested that the league permit the NL Expos to relocate from Montreal to Monterrey. Maiz had earned a fortune from his construction business and Bremer, the Chief Executive Officer of Value Grupo Financiero, had successfully managed investors' money for decades. Although not a dreamer or linguist, Bremer has stated to reporters that Montreal and Monterrey each translate into "royal" or "king's mountain." As reported in an article in the *Wall Street Journal*, "It's hard not to see the appeal of trading Canada for Latin America. The Monterrey market is convenient to a number of Texas cities and is even home to 1,500 Dallas Cowboy season ticket holders. Manifestly, Latin America has plenty of budding A-Rods and millions more baseball fans. Isn't it time to given them a real chance to root for the home team?"[40]

Following Monterrey, the second to fifth ranked cities for MLB to locate a franchise are, respectively, Mexico City, San Juan, Santo Domingo and Havana. Mexico City and its surrounding Area each have a huge population that support Mexican Baseball League teams while San Juan and Santo Domingo are cities that have thousands of avid baseball fans. However, because of President Fidel Castro's regime and the U.S. embargo of Cuba, at this time Havana is not a viable location for a big league team although it is the nearest of the listed cities to MLB's East, Midwest and Southeastern teams' sites. In short, when the decision to select an international location is approved, MLB owners will inevitably evaluate the economic benefits and costs of each city as a site and then decide which is the best place to relocate an existing club or locate an expansion franchise.

Chapter 1's analysis about MLB's international business strategies has revealed the key activities, interests, relationships and trends that involved the league and its member franchises. Rather than summarize the chapter's content, however, one topic remains to be discussed. That is, before the Summary and Notes appear, it is worthwhile to provide an overview of women's baseball organizations and their related events.

Women's Baseball

Since the late 1800s, millions of women in various nations have been ardent baseball fans. Yet, because of various economic, social, and sports-specific factors and traditions, the majority of the world's females have failed to play the sport as girls or as adults in groups. Thus, they did not join existing amateur, semiprofessional or professional men's teams, or establish competitive leagues that could be sustained beyond the short-term. Fortunately, those conditions changed when women's baseball leagues emerged in several countries, and especially in developed nations during the middle to late 1990s. As such, the following is an overview of women's baseball organizations and programs in America and Australia.

To enhance public awareness, provide an opportunity for female athletes to participate in the game of baseball, and promote the game's qualities and standards, American Justine Siegal formed the Women's Baseball League Inc. (WBL) in 1997. As a reason for the league's existence, Siegal had become tired of waiting for opportunities to develop for women in the sports industry. Therefore, she was motivated to ensure that young girls had a chance to compete as athletes in baseball games. "I want my four-year old daughter to have a place to play baseball," she said. "My daughter, Jasmine, symbolizes all of the other daughters from around the world who want a chance to participate. This is what the WBL is all about; creating opportunities for the daughters of the world."[41]

Because of Siegal's leadership, during the Summer of 1999 the four-team WBL began its inaugural season in Beachwood, which is a U.S. city in the state of Ohio. Since 1999, the WBL has been an active and progressive organization. To illustrate, the league and/or its teams have participated in or sponsored various baseball events. In 2002, for example, the WBL had conducted a Leadership and Women's Baseball Conference in Orlando, Florida, promoted and provided an All-Star Baseball Tour across North America, and finished behind one team each from Australia and Japan to win a bronze medal at the Women's World Series in Tampa, Florida. Then, in 2003 the WBL was represented at the University of Rhode Island in the U.S. Scholar Athlete Games, at the Dreams Park Tournament played in Cooperstown, New York, and at the Amateur Athletic Union (AAU) National Championships in Fort Meyers, Florida. Finally, in 2004 the WBL was directly or indirectly involved with the International Girls Baseball Championships in Toronto, Canada, the Dreams Park Tournament that was played again in Cooperstown, New York, and the 15U team tournament for girls and boys in the Dominican Republic. These events clearly indicated that this women's baseball league had met two of its primary objectives, that is, to build ties in baseball on the national and international levels and to promote baseball to girls through clinics, high profile adult games and encouragement.[42]

Besides the previous information about America's WBL, women's baseball has existed in Australia since the early 1900s. However, Australia's women-only baseball leagues first developed in the 1990s when the Victorian Women's League began to operate. Because of the Victorian Women's League's competitiveness and its international reputation and success, Australian women's baseball teams won World Championships in 2001 and 2002, and placed second to Japan in the 2003 Women's World Series at the Gold Coast in Queensland, Australia. Indeed, these results indicate why women's baseball in Australia is an established and popular sport that will grow even more prominent after 2004.[43]

As an aside, during early 2004 MLB formed a partnership with the eight-team National Pro Fastpitch women's softball league (NPF). This affiliation is part of Commissioner Bud Selig's Initiative on Women and Baseball, which is a program designed to build a stronger relationship with the female sports audience and strengthen the family fan base. Formerly known as the Women's Pro Softball League (WPSL), the NPF organized in 1997 to provide elite female athletes an opportunity to compete as professionals. After play was suspended during the 2002 season, the league restructured and explored expansion. Whether the NPF will flourish somewhat depends on the support from MLB. "With Major League Baseball's involvement with our league, it's sure to open new doors for women's athletics," said Sacramento Sunbirds third baseman Jaime Foutch. Anyway, in 2004 and thereafter the NPF plans to develop grassroots programs, launch marketing and media campaigns to generate local and national awareness of the sport, and encourage young female athletes to showcase their skills and abilities on the playing field and in the community.[44]

This concludes Chapter 1's analysis of MLB and its international business strategies and relationships, and also the discussion about other baseball leagues such as the CBL and WBL. To consolidate and highlight the chapter's contents, the following Summary is presented.

Summary

This chapter contained five distinct topics that were organized into sections. In total, these topics encapsulated the global business strategies of MLB and secondarily, other baseball leagues. First, the purpose and structure, and the responsibilities, business activities and ventures of MLBI, which is the international division of MLB, were identified and then discussed. Established in 1989, MLBI has evolved into the organizational unit that represents the league's member teams and as such, is accountable for all of the international business aspects of MLB. Second, to acknowledge the globalization of baseball as a sport, at least ten specific foreign sports markets were identified and listed as countries, and then analyzed with respect to baseball's presence and prestige in those countries. The most prominent markets, relative to their fan bases and relationships with MLB were Japan,

Mexico, Puerto Rico, the Dominican Republic and Venezuela. Then, there were Cuba, selected European nations and finally, China and Russia. These countries' sports environments and business alliances with MLB, if any, reflected how much the sport of baseball had grown in popularity both internationally and in various nations' communities.

Third, this portion of Chapter 1 focused on the economic and social factors and reasons that, in part, explained why foreign athletes have been scouted, recruited and signed as baseball players to contracts by MLB teams. Interestingly, if this trend continues throughout the early to middle 2000s, then the NL and AL will likely develop and implement a variety of global policies, procedures and rules that reflect the cultural backgrounds, interests and economic statuses of their foreign players. Fourth, several relevant international baseball concerns and issues were listed and examined. These matters included the league's Latin American baseball academies and drug test programs, the implications of a worldwide international draft system that incorporates all amateur and professional baseball players, three proposals for a World Cup of Baseball to be held in 2005 or thereafter, and the formation and demise of the CBL. Relative to the globalization efforts and successes of MLB, the significance of each issue was mentioned. Lastly, Chapter 1's content concluded with a table that listed five foreign cities as viable sites to place a MLB franchise after 2004, which was followed by some facts about women's baseball leagues and events in America and Australia.

In turn, Chapter 2 focuses on the NFL's global business strategies that are represented by the league's domestic and foreign activities, alliances, events and relationships. According to the research performed by and publications of many sports experts, the NFL is the U.S.'s most popular and successful professional sports league. Basically, the chapter's content examines why, when, where and how the league has developed its global presence and thereby evolved from a national into an international organization. In short, the reader realizes that the various economic and social forces, issues, problems and trends that influenced the NFL are, to some extent, different than those that have affected, and will likely impact MLB, and the NBA, NHL and MLS.

Notes

1. For the history of team relocation and league expansion in MLB, see Frank P. Jozsa, Jr. and John J. Guthrie, Jr., *Relocating Teams and Expanding Leagues in Professional Sports: How the Major Leagues Respond to Market Conditions* (Westport, CT: Praeger Publishers, 1999); James Quirk and Rodney D. Fort, *Pay Dirt: The Business of Professional Team Sports* (Princeton, N.J.: Princeton University Press, 1992); Charles C. Euchner, *Playing the Field: Why Sports Teams Move and Cities Fight to Keep Them* (Baltimore, MD: Johns Hopkins University Press, 1993); Mark S. Rosentraub, *Major League Losers: The Real Costs of Sports and Who's Paying For It* (New York, N.Y.: Basic Books, 1997); Kenneth L. Shropshire, *The Sports Franchise Game: Cities in Pursuit of Sports Franchises, Events, Stadiums, and Arenas* (Philadelphia, PA: University of Pennsylvania Press, 1995); Neil J. Sullivan, *The Dodgers Move West: The Transfer of the Brooklyn Baseball Franchise to Los*

Angeles (New York, N.Y.: Oxford University Press, 1987); Paul D. Staudohar and James A. Mangan, eds., *The Business of Professional Sports* (Champaign, IL: University of Illinois Press, 1991).

2. American professional baseball and the other big-league sports are being transformed by globalization, a term that refers to the growing flows of people, goods, images and inform- ation across national boundaries. Because of the attractions and pressures from global markets, sports franchises may loosen their connections to local communities. Rather than downgrade their hometown interests, perhaps teams will build cultural and economic bridges to foreign countries. This outlook is discussed in Michael Clough, "The (Multi) National Pastime: As Professional Sports Go Global, Will Local Communities be Shunted Aside?" *The Los Angeles Times* (31 March 1996), M1. According to Clough, to become global major league teams "need to expand their efforts to bring together kids from the all- to-separate worlds that exist in large U.S. cities. One way to do this is to sponsor teams and tournaments consciously organized to transcend the segregation of city and suburb." Furthermore, teams "should become more active partners in the growing efforts of cities, states and regions to develop their own international relationships." For analytical discussions about the theories and social aspects of globalization and sport, see Peter Donnelly, "The Local and the Global: Globalization in the Sociology of Sport," *Journal of Sport and Social* Issues, Vol. 20, No. 3 (1996), 239–257; Jean Harvey, Genevieve Rail, and Lucie Thibault, "Globalization and Sport: Sketching a Theoretical Model For Empirical Analysis," *Journal of Sport and Social* Issues, Vol. 20, No. 3 (1996), 258–277; Brian Stoddart, "Convergence," *Journal of Sport and Social* Issues, Vol. 21, No. 1 (1997), 93–102; Donald R. Richards, "A (Utopian?) Socialist Proposal For the Reform of Major League Baseball," *Journal of Sport and Social Issues*, Vol. 27, No. 3 (2003), 308–324. In Richards' view, the implementation of the luxury tax and revenue sharing are not adequate measures to reestablish fan loyalty in MLB. Rather, he prefers that municipalities own teams and that the reserve clause be used to assign players to particular teams for their careers. These reforms, according to Richards, would control salaries and allow tickets to be priced at levels for families with modest incomes to attend games. Also, a predetermined salary structure makes player competition a function of longevity and not the market. Besides globalization, there are other business matters with respect to the future of MLB. Those involve, respectively, questions about revenue sharing, multimillion-dollar player contracts, price inflation of tickets, small-market teams, new stadiums, television deals and players' drug tests for steroids. With respect to how globalization would be affected by the public's ownership of franchises, Richards remarked in an email that, "From a strictly administrative perspective, I don't see the globalization of sport issue as having much impact on the technical workability of public ownership of teams. The non-owner trustees of teams could still hire players, for example, from whatever country they choose. Leagues could expand into foreign markets as long as the foreign-based franchises play by the same rules that apply to all teams." Then, in the email Richards further elaborated about professional sports leagues as follows, "The internationalization of sport is part and parcel of its growing commodification with an eye to its marketability and profitability. These are substantial obstacles to the realization of any alternative structure for MLB, NFL, etc. that places emphasis on the values of local identification, stability and allegiance that makes 'fandom' meaningful." For a further discussion of related topics, see Rick Harrow, "Some MLB Business Issues to Examine," at <http://www.sportsbusinessnews.com> cited 9 March 2004.

3. There are several articles that discuss various aspects of the activities and the formation, development and strategy of MLBI. For example, MLB's international organizational unit is mentioned in Terry Lefton, "Global Grand Slam," *Brandweek* (18 October 1999), 20–22;

Dennis W. Organ, "Baseball and Global Capitalism," *Business Horizons* (September/October 2002), 1; Claire Smith, "The Game Looks to Foreign Fields," *The New York Times* (27 October 1992), B9, B12; Mike Hiserman, "The Growing Globalization of MLB," at <http://www.sportsbusinessnews.com> cited 25 November 2002; Larry Eichel, "MLB's 'Vision' of a Global Game," at <http://www.sportsbusinessnews.com> cited 23 October 2003; Larry Stone, "Selig Discusses Cancellation of Overseas Opener," at <http://www.sportsbusinessnews.com> cited 27 March 2003; "All-Star Game Ratings We're Talking Japan," at <http://www.sportsbusinessnews.com> cited 19 August 2003.

4.   MLB's efforts to secure apparel contracts, international broadcasts and video deals, and licensing agreements have generated more cash flows for its member clubs. For more about these topics, see Stefan Fatsis and Suzanne Vranica, "Major League Baseball Agrees to $275 Million Deal in Japan," *Wall Street Journal* (31 October 2003), B4; Kelly Grimes, "Global Access Sends Major League Baseball Overseas," *Business Wire* (30 April 1996), 43; "Intelsat Beams Baseball Worldwide Via Fiber, Uplinks," *Fiber Optics News* (4 August 2003), 1; Mike Hiserman, "World Series," *The Los Angeles Times* (23 October 2002), U1; Paul Dykewicz, "Spotlight: Baseball's All-Star Game Goes Global," *Satellite News* (21 July 2003), 1; "MLB Announces New Licensing Agreements," at <http://www.sportsbusinessnews.com> cited 5 August 2003; "MLB.com to Video Stream MLB Playoffs to Overseas Markets," at <http://www.sportsbusinessnews.com> cited 25 November 2002. Besides the league, various baseball teams have pursued or signed broadcast agreements. See Chris Zelkovich, "Blue Jays May be Headed to Global," at <http://www.sportsbusinessnews.com> cited 25 November 2002; "A's Return to Spanish Radio," at <http://www.sportsbusinessnews.com> cited 19 August 2003; Sean Wood, "Rangers Target Hispanic Fans . . . Again," at <http://www.sportsbusinessnews.com> cited 27 March 2003; Bill Griffith, "Red Sox Adding Spanish Broadcasts This Year," at <http://www.sportsbusinessnews.com> cited 27 March 2003; Adam McCalvy, "Select Brewers Games to be Broadcast in Spanish," at <http://www.sportsbusinessnews.com> cited 13 February 2003. With respect to the network arrangements to broadcast the New York Yankees and Tampa Bay Devil Rays series of games in April of 2004 at the Tokyo Dome, see Richard Sandomir, "YES Network Will Focus on Yankees in Japan," at <http://www.sportsbusinessnews.com> cited 30 March 2004.

5.   The team competitions and player traditions that influence Japan's high school baseball games and tournaments are vividly illuminated in Ken Belson, "High School Baseball . . . in Japan," at <http://www.sportsbusinessnews.com> cited 26 August 2003. Reflecting on Koshien, which is Japan's most prestigious baseball tournament for high school players, sports commentator Masayuki Tamaki said, "The tournament no longer matches the era. When Japan was growing fast, we needed [a] fighting spirit. But now, it's each man for himself. We have to think more creatively." For an interpretation of *wa* and how the sport of baseball has changed in Japan during recent decades as a reflection of society, see Carter Gaddis, "Baseball and Japan," at <http://www.sportsbusinessnews.com> cited 30 March 2004. American Michael Westbay, who lives and works in Japan and operates web site japanesebaseball.com, said that "Making sacrifices for the family or for the company were very strong values, especially in pre-war and post-war Japan. Starting from the Walkman generation of the 1980s, though, self sacrifice has slowly eroded away. It hasn't left baseball, . . . But I don't thing that it is reflected or appreciated by society any longer."

6.   In Japan, a company's stock may rally when its' sports team plays well. Some investors look for themes to focus their investments and frequently target the shares of companies whose teams excel. For examples and results, see Eric Bellman, "Trying to Leverage Success in Japanese Baseball," at <http://www.sportsbusinessnews.com> cited 19 August 2003. With respect to this phenomenon, AIG Global Investment chairman Robert Howe

said, "Investors are hoping fans will go in a celebratory mood to buy more at the Hanshin Department store and they will ride the Hanshin railways back and forth around the city waving their team flag. It's completely ludicrous, but that's what makes this an exciting and inefficient market."

7.   In fact, amateur and professional baseball are extremely popular sports in Japan. Indeed, the Japanese fans are obsessed with the sports. For selected business aspects of Japanese baseball, see Calvin Sims, "Japanese Leagues Worry About Being Overshadowed," *The New York Times* (30 March 2000), 3; "Japanese Players and Baseball Cards," at <http://www.sportsbusinessnews.com> cited 3 December 2002; Eric Fisher, "MLB Finally Taking Notice of Far East," at <http://www.sportsbusinessnews.com> cited 19 August 2003; Doug Struck, "Japanese Appreciative of Their Exports," at <http://www.sportsbusinessnews.com> cited 19 August 2003; Ken Belson, "Baseball in the Land of the Rising Sun," at <http://www.sportsbusinessnews.com> cited 3 April 2003; Chris Isidore, "By All Appearances, Japan is Living MLB TV," at <http://www.sportsbusinessnews.com> cited 13 November 2003; William C. Rhoden, "MLB and Japanese Baseball," at <http://www.sportsbusiness-news.com> cited 3 December 2002; Richard Sandomir, "Its Good For MLB to Open Their Season in Japan," at <http://www.sportsbusinessnews.com> cited 16 March 2003; Marc Topkin, "Making MLB Heading to Japan—Feel Comfortable," at <http://www.sportsbusin-essnews.com> cited 23 March 2003; Chris Isidore, "The International Pastime," at <http://cnnmoney.printthis.clickability.com> cited 13 April 2004. With respect to the preparations to schedule the Yankees-Devil Rays games in Tokyo, the Rays' general manager Chuck LaMar commented, "It's a daunting task. But the commissioner's office and the players association has done a fantastic job. Their attention to detail has been second to none. The comfort level they have given us, not only from a business standpoint but from a personal standpoint, has been fabulous." According to sportswriters such as Sandomir, Japan is baseball's most crucial market and the place where the New York Yankees' owner George Steinbrenner and the Yomiuri Giants' owner Tsuneo Watanabe might collaborate to promote each other's franchises. Relative to Japan's assets, in late 2003 American real estate investment firm Colony Capital of Los Angeles agreed to buy the 48,000-seat Fukuoka Dome and the Sea Hawk Hotel and Resort from Daiei Inc., which is Japan's third largest retailer. Interestingly, the Dome is the home stadium of the national baseball champion Fukuoka Daiei Hawks. According to the agreement, Daiei Inc. will control the team while Colony Capital permits the Hawks to use the Dome for 30 years. For more details about the deal, see Ken Belson, "Building a Ballpark in the Land of the Rising Sun," at <http://www.sportsbusinessnews.com> cited 4 December 2003.

8.   Some of the MLB teams, especially those located in the U.S. southwest and west, have effectively marketed their franchises in cities throughout northern Mexico. This strategy is examined in Rob Evans, "U.S. Baseball Expects Big Hit in Mexico," *Amusement Business* (8 July 1996), 19–20; Justin Martin, "Can Baseball Make it in Mexico?" *Fortune* (30 September 1996), 32–33; Joel Millman, "Diamondbacks Look to Mexico to Fill More Seats," *Wall Street Journal* (27 July 2002), B1; "Baseball Hot in Mexico," *The Charlotte Observer* (17 July 1998), 4B. Besides those articles, to read about the excitement at the MLB exhibition games that were held in Mexico City during early 2004, see Jose De Jesus Ortiz, "Mexicans Far From Believers in MLB Dream," at <http://www.sportsbusinessnews.com> cited 16 March 2004; Joe Capozzi, "MLB in Mexico, is Italy Next?" at <http://www.sports-businessnews.com> cited 16 March 2004; Kevin Baxter, "A Not so Glorious Ending For MLB's Weekend in Mexico," at <http://www.sportsbusinessnews.com> cited 16 March 2004. Despite the Mexican fans' disappointment and behavior at the Florida Marlins and Houston Astros game that finished in a tie after nine innings, MLB's vice president for in-

ternational relations Paul Archey said, "We've really targeted Mexico City. Soccer has a hold on Mexico City—no doubt about it. And that's a place where we felt we needed to go play to help create some further excitement, exposure."

9. For why Hermosilla, Mexico City and Monterrey are important cities to MLB, see Eric Fisher, "Hoping Les Becomes Los Expos For 2004," at <http://www.sportsbusinessnews. com> cited 22 August 2003, and Mark Asher, "Viva, Monterrey, Mexico and Los Expos," at <http://www.sportsbusinessnews.com> cited 19 August 2003. Other information about Mexico's baseball market is in Rob Evans, "U.S. Baseball Expects Big Hit in Mexico," 19–20; Dick Kaegel, "Baseball May Not be King in All Mexico, But it is in Hermosillo," at <http://www.kansascity.com> cited 8 April 2003; Michael Morrissey, "Will MLB be Holding Exhibition Games in Mexico City This Year?" at <http://www.sportsbusinessnews. com> cited 20 February 2003; David King, "How About Dueling Permanent Homes For Les/Los Expos," at <http://www.sportsbusinessnews.com> cited 17 December 2003; Mary Jordan, "Mexico and Les/Los Expos," at <http://www.sportsbusinessnews.com> cited 2 October 2003.

10. During the early 2000s, MLB radically diversified and added international coaches, managers and owners to authoritative positions in the sport. For more information about the minority groups and individuals who have taken leadership positions in U.S. professional baseball, see Barry M. Bloom, "Diversity Producing Key Leaders," at <http://www. mlb.com> cited 15 May 2003; Stefan Fatsis, "Disney Nears Sale of Baseball Team to Businessman," *Wall Street Journal* (14 April 2003), B5; Elisabeth Malkin, "The Mexican Billionaire in Search of the American Dream," at <http://www.sportsbusinessnews.com> cited 25 November 2002. When Mexican Arturo Moreno purchased the Anaheim Angels in 2003, his franchise had incurred a $6 million loss. Yet, Moreno committed $146 million to four free agent players. Because the team will be competitive in 2004, ticket sales and revenues from sponsorships and advertisements increased and Moreno said the team made $80 million in total revenue during 2001, which could double by 2005 when the club enhances its radio and television deals in English and Spanish. For Moreno's plans, see Bill Shaikin, "Arte Moreno's Angels Spending Spree May Not be Done," at <http://www.sports-businessnnews.com> cited 14 January 2004.

11. See the "Expos Complete Successful San Juan Homestand," at <http://www.mlb.com> cited 21 April 2003, and "Expos to Begin Play in San Juan Today," *The Charlotte Observer* (11 April 2003), 4C. The concerns of MLB officials, team owners and players to schedule games in San Juan in 2004 are discussed in Jeff Blair, "Are Los Expos Done in Puerto Rico For 2004?" at <http://www.sportsbusinessnews.com> cited 2 September 2003; Stephanie Myles, "Montreal Reaction to Likely Return to San Juan," at <http://www.sportsbusiness-news.com> cited 23 October 2003; Stefan Fatsis, "Montreal Expos: No Place to Call Home Plate," *Wall Street Journal* (7 August 2003), B1.

12. During the summer of 2003, the NL Montreal Expos played 22 regular season home games in San Juan, Puerto Rico. For why the San Juan area is an attractive professional baseball market for MLB, see Kevin Baxter, "Los Expos in Puerto Rico," at <http://www. sportsbusinessnews.com> cited 6 March 2003. This topic was also discussed in John-Thor Dahlburg, "Looking Beyond Ball and Bat to See What Baseball Really Stands For in Puerto Rico," at <http://www.sportsbusinessnews.com> cited 19 August 2003, and Murray Chass, "Deal All But Done, Expos Set to Play 20 Games in San Juan," at <http://www.sportsbusin-essnews.com> cited 25 November 2002. For why the Expos will play 22 home games during the 2004 regular season in San Juan, see "Its Official—Les/Los Expos Return For 2004," at <http://www.sportsbusinessnews.com> cited 11 December 2003, and Stephanie Myles, "Los Expos Set to Return to San Juan," at <http://www.sportsbusinessnews.com>

cited 4 December 2003. Indeed, to prepare for the Expos Puerto Rican businessman and sports promoter Antonio Munoz—who had paid MLB $10 million for the games—and local authorities on the island had contributed to the renovation of Hiram Bithorn Stadium. That is, the facility's capacity increased to accommodate 20,000 fans, more outfield seats were added along with new artificial turf and scoreboard, and the locker rooms were renovated. These improvements may convince baseball officials to move the Expos to San Juan after the 2004 season concludes. This update was discussed in "Improved Stadium Awaits Expos in Puerto Rico," at <http://si.printthis.clickability.com> cited 13 April 2004.

13.   See "Baseball Has Been Very, Very Good to the Dominican," at <http://www.sports-businessnews.com> cited 19 August 2003, and Joe Posnanski, "Few Baseball Dreams Realized But Many Dashed in Dominican Republic," at <http://www.kansascity.com> cited 8 April 2003. Because of the nation's plentiful supply of talented players, sports agents dominate the Dominican market. Locally known as *buscones* or finders, some agents operate outside the law when they charge exorbitant commissions, steal signing bonuses outright and threaten players to extract additional payments. The president of Hispanics Across America Fernando Mateo said, " ... regulation of the *buscones* is the next battle now that Major League Baseball has announced plans to implement drug testing." To read about this problem, see Steve Fainaru, "MLB May be Looking to Regulate Dominican Agents," at <http://www.sportsbusinessnews.com> cited 18 September 2003. Furthermore, because the nation is not subject to the amateur draft, MLB teams can sign players for less money than it would cost to sign an equally talented U.S. prospect. However, baseball clubs insist to see government issued birth certificates after some Dominican players had falsified their documents to appear more youthful. For how players regard the sport, 21 year old Texas Ranger prospect Juan Carlos Senreiso said, "There are many baseball players who play baseball for the love, but there are also many that come from poor homes, and they try to reach the major leagues to help their families. There is a lot of poverty here." See Kathleen O'Brien, "In the Dominican is Baseball a Ticket to Paradise?" at <http://www.sports businessnews.com> cited 24 February 2004. For other references about Latinos in professional baseball, there is G. Leticia Gonzalez, "The Stacking of Latinos in Major League Baseball," *Journal of Sport and Social Issues*, Vol. 20, No. 2 (1996), 134–160, and Alan M. Klein, *Sugarball: The American Game, the Dominican Dream* (New Haven, CT: Yale University Press, 1991).

14.   The U.S. embargo and economic conditions have not diminished Cuban fans' enthusiasm for baseball even though games are played with basic equipment in obsolete ballparks. This scenario was discussed in Steve Cummings, "Baseball and Cuba," at <http://www.sportsbusinessnews.com> cited 19 August 2003; Wright Thompson, "Cuban Ballplayers Have More Than Most, But Still Not Enough," at <http://www.kansascity.com> 8 April 2003; Stefan Fatsis, "Cuba, Si. Stardom, No," *Wall Street Journal* (17 August 2001), W4; Mark Hyman, "Where *Beisbol* is the Stuff of Revolution," *Business Week* (15 May 2000), 28, 30.

15.   See S.L. Price, *Pitching Around Fidel: A Journey Into the Heart of Cuban Sport* (Hopewell, N.J.: Ecco Press, 2000), and Milton H. Jamail and Larry Dierker, *Full Count: Inside Cuban Baseball* (Carbondale, IL: Southern Illinois University Press, 2000). Despite Castro's threats, baseball scouts and sports agents operate in Cuba. To avoid detection, some scouts and agents pretend to be journalists. This matter is discussed in Wright Thompson, "Some Baseball Scouts in Cuba, But the Risks Are High," at <http://www.kansascity.com> cited 8 April 2003. According to Cuban baseball commissioner Carlos Rodriguez, MLB scouts "come undercover. They come on false passports. They come with a list of 30

athletes, and they go throughout Cuba visiting them. They are violating our laws, and they end up in jail."

16.   For professional baseball in Venezuela, there were several web sites consulted such as "Venezuelan Baseball League," <http://www.geocities.com> cited 2 October 2003. Other online sites for professional baseball in Venezuela include <http://iml.jou.ufl.edu/projects-/Fall02/Landino/index.html>, <http://iml.jou.ufl.edu>, and <http://www.lvbp.com>.

17.   During 2002 and 2003, the economic conditions in Venezuela impacted the country's sports programs. For why the winter season games were suspended, see Peter Wilson and Nick Benequista, "Not a Great Season For the Venezuela's Professional Baseball League," at <http://www.sportsbusinessnews.com> cited 20 January 2003.

18.   MLB Commissioner Bud Selig and MLBI officials fully expected American-style professional baseball to gradually become a more popular sport in various European nations during the early 2000s. For this perspective, see John Vinocur, "Baseball in Europe, " at <http://www.sportsbusinessnews.com> cited 19 August 2003; Rafael Hermoso, "With Los Expos a Success, MLB Looking at Further Expanded Horizons," at <http://www.sportsbusinessnews.com> cited 22 August 2003; Gordon Edes, "Making it Sound so Easy For MLB to Play Games in Europe," at <http://www.sportsbusinessnews.com> cited 27 March 2003; "Baseball Hits Home Run in Europe, Latin America," *Video Age International* (October-November 1991), 44.

19.   Boston Red Sox executive Larry Lucchino wants the Sox to schedule games in England and/or Italy soon. Furthermore, he is a proponent of a baseball World Cup tournament that includes teams from Europe. For Lucchino's views, see Gordon Edes, "MLB in Europe in 2005?" at <http://www.sportsbusinessnews.com> cited 22 September 2003.

20.   China's interest in baseball was nearly eliminated during the 1966–1976 Cultural Revolution. Since then, however, the sport has modestly revived itself. For the status of baseball in China, see Michael A. Lev, "Baseball in the People's Republic," at <http://www.sportsbusinessnews.com> cited 21 August 2003. MLB's agreement with the China Baseball Association to promote baseball in advance of the 2008 Summer Olympics in Beijing is described in Barry M. Bloom, "MLB and China Sign a Working Agreement," at <http://www.sportsbusinessnews.com> cited 1 December 2003.

21.   The sport is discussed in Kim Palchikoff, "Youth Baseball in Russia," at <http://www.sportsbusinessnews.com> cited 19 August 2003. According to Palchikoff, "Until about 10 years ago, the Russians did not know the difference between a baseball and, as one coach put it, a bobsled. Youth baseball was nonexistent, since children traditionally play hockey in the winter, soccer in the summer and basketball in between. And the numbers [of baseball] players are growing around Russia and in the republics of the former Soviet Union, including Ukraine, the Baltics, Belarus, and Georgia, which all had teams but not the money to send youngsters to the championships [European Juvenile Baseball Championships]."

22.   By nation and based on 2001–2003, the percentages of foreign ballplayers in MLB is reported in "Foreign Legions," at <http://sportsillustrated.com> cited 4 April 2001; David King, "Baseball—The Global Game," at <http://www.sportsbusinessnews.com> cited 25 November 2002; "Growing Number of Major Leaguer's Born Outside the USA," at <http://www.sportsbusinessnews.com> cited 3 December 2002; John Donovan, "Globalization of the Grand Old Game Hits All-Time High," at <http://cnnsi.com> cited 17 July 2003. With respect to recent data about team rosters, the numbers and percentages of foreign-born players in MLB declined from 230 or 27.8 percent in 2003 to 227 or 27.3 percent in 2004, which is the first decrease in six seasons. The top five countries represented by the players included the Dominican Republic with 79 or 35 percent, Venezuela with 45 or 20 percent, Puerto Rico with 36 or 16 percent, Mexico with 16 or 7 percent and Canada with 11 or 5

percent. After Canada there was, respectively, Japan, Cuba, Panama, Australia and South Korea, Columbia and the Netherlands Antilles. In the minor leagues, however, the proportion of international players with contracts had increased from 46 percent in 2003 to 47.6 percent in 2004. The largest number of foreign-born minor league players emigrated from the Dominican Republic and then Venezuela, Puerto Rico, Canada and Mexico. Nevertheless, during early 2004 more than 200 of baseball's talented players from Latin American countries were unable to get visas to enter America. That occurred because minor leaguers need a H-2B, which is a quota-limited visa established at 66,000 per year. Consequently, it is the U.S. Congress' decision whether to remove the restrictions on the entry of minor league players into America. If the limits are not removed, perhaps such baseball teams as the Los Angeles Dodgers and New York Yankees will relocate one or more of their minor league clubs to the Dominican Republic, Mexico, Puerto Rico or Venezuela. Meanwhile, foreign MLB players qualify for a P-1 visa, which has no cap. These topics are discussed in "First Drop in Seven Years," at <http://si.printthis.click-ability.com> cited 13 April 2004, and "Spitballing the Minors," *Wall Street Journal* (22 April 2004), A18.

23. See Bob Dutton, "Royals Have Shifted Direction in Latin America But Still Trying to Catch Up," at <http://www.kansascity.com> cited 8 April 2003; Joe Posnanski, "Spanish Lessons," at <http://www.kansascity.com> cited 8 April 2003; Dick Kaegel, Baseball Has Become America's Game," at <http://www.kansascity.com> cited 8 April 2003. For the vote spread and other information about Tony Pena's AL Manager of the Year award, see "McKeon, Pena Easy Manager of the Year Winners," at <http://sportsillustrated.cnn.com> cited 13 November 2003.

24. Beside his fielding and hitting performances with the Mariners, during 2001 Ichiro Suzuki was a commercial success for professional baseball and the club in Seattle, Washington. See Susan G. Hauser, "Japanese Baseball Stars Turn Seattle Radio Bilingual," *Wall Street Journal* (10 July 2001), A16; Alexander Blenkinsopp, "Asian Invasion: Baseball's Ambassadors," *Harvard International Review* (Spring 2002), 12–13; John Shea, "The City by the Bay's Connection to Japanese Baseball," at <http://www.sportsbusinessnews.com> cited 3 December 2002. Interestingly, before he entered MLB Suzuki had dedicated himself and trained in the Japanese sports system to develop and become a superstar. Similar to other such great Japanese baseball athletes as the New York Mets' second baseman Kaz Matsui and Los Angeles Dodgers' pitcher Hideo Nomo, he relentlessly improved his skills as a batter and fielder. This devotion to excellence in sports by Japanese players is discussed in two books. Authored by Roger Whiting, those are *You Gotta Have Wa* (Lincolnshire, IL: Vintage Publishing, 1989), and *The Meaning of Ichiro* (Boston, MA: Warner Books, 2004). The former book examined the ethos of Japanese baseball and the hardships it placed on *gaijin* (foreign) participants, and the second book discussed the transformation of America's national pastime by the new wave of Japanese players and described the ways in which Japanese baseball is associated with social codes of harmony and sacrifice of self. Indeed, Whiting emphasized how Suzuki practiced baseball with his father for hours a day, from age three to high school. For a review of *The Meaning of Ichiro*, see Chaz Repak, "Ecstasy in the Ballpark," *The Wall Street Journal* (2 April 2004), W6. In Repak's view, it is Japanese baseball and fans that are being transformed because many of the nation's finest players have left to join MLB in America since the late 1990s. As he stated it, "Ichiro's success in 2001 led to Ichiromania, including a museum [in Japan] displaying everything from his first bat to the retainer he wore as a teenager." Furthermore, Repak notes that, "Such an approach [three-hour practices on game days and the 1,000-fungo drill] builds up a team's *wa* or harmony, which is foreign to the U.S. version of the game."

25.   For a sample of articles that discuss Hideki Matsui's entry and performance in the AL, and his affect on the Yankees and MLB, see Ken Belson, "More Japanese Baseball Stars Heading to America," at <http://www.sportsbusinessnews.com> cited 3 December 2002; Marc Topkin, "Yankees International MVP Readies For Media Circus," at <http://www. sportsbusinessnews.com> cited 6 February 2003; Skip Rozin, "Godzilla to the Rescue?" *Business Week* (3 March 2003), 95; Tyler Kepner, "Yankees Expanding Their International Horizons," at <http://www.sportsbusinessnews.com> cited 25 November 2002; Mark Cannizzaro, "Godzilla (Matsui) is Missed," at <http://www.sportsbusinessnews.com> cited 19 August 2003. Besides the emigration of Suzuki and Matsui, Japan's industrial leagues have downsized because of the stagnant economy and tight corporate budgets. The baseball experience of 28 year old relief pitcher Kazuhiro Takeoka is discussed in Martin Fackler, "Baseball Players Are the Latest Casualty of Japan's Slump," *Wall Street Journal* (7 January 2004), A1–A2. For another example of players leaving Japan, the AL's Chicago White Sox signed for one year the relief pitcher Shingo Takatsu who is considered one of the country's greatest professional baseball athletes. Japan's consul general Mitsuo Sakaba said, "For the area's 7,000 Japanese and 20,000 Japanese-American, Mr. Takatsu's signing by the Sox is epoch-making. It's a happy day. I shall support with much stronger enthusiasm White Sox games." See Maudlyne Ihejirika, "Japanese Fans and the Chicago White Sox," at <http://www.sportsbusinessnews. com> cited 30 January 2004. In April of 2004, baseball fans in Japan had the opportunity to watch Hideki Matsui perform when the New York Yankees and Tampa Bay Devil Rays competed in a series to open MLB's season. See "Baseball: 18 Teams to Start April 5; Season Opener in Japan," *The Charlotte Observer* (25 January 2004), 14F. Prior to that series, however, the Yankees defeated the Yomiuri Giants in an exhibition game at the Tokyo Dome, which was the first Yankees appearance in Japan since 1955. During that game, the former three-time Japanese Central League MVP Matsui hit a home run to right-center field and at the location where 'Godzilla' earned his legend in the ten years he performed for the Giants. According to a sportswriter, "After the final out, Matsui stepped on a small cage at home plate and was interviewed briefly. He took off his cap and waved toward every section of the Tokyo Dome, while fans eagerly snapped photos and cheered." Those results are reported in Pete Caldera, "Matsui Home Run Thrills Fans in Japan," *The Charlotte Observer* (29 March 2003), 9C. Based on the series of games in Japan, according to the Los Angeles Dodgers senior vice president Tommy Lasorda, "Baseball has become global now. It's getting much bigger, much bigger around the globe." Lasorda's statement was presented in Barry M. Bloom, "Playoff Atmosphere in Tokyo," at <http://mlb.mlb.com> cited 30 March 2004. For Kazuo Matsui's auspicious first game as a rookie player from Japan and whether he will earn his three-year $20 million contract, see "More Matsui Mania," *The Charlotte Observer* (7 April 2004), 6C, and John Donovan, "Game Face," at <http://sportsillustrated.cnn.com> cited 13 April 2004.

26.   Because African Americans do not have access to groomed baseball fields and expert instruction, and given the decline of the black two-parent household and the passionate neighborhood volunteer coach, young blacks in America have generally lost their incentive to play sandlot and organized baseball. Those circumstances are examined further in Tom Verducci, "The African-American Baseball Player is Vanishing. Does He Have a Future?" at <http://www.sportsillustrated.cnn.com> cited 17 July 2003. For evidence that the black presence in MLB is vanishing, consider that there were first, seven African Americans named to the 2002 All-Star team compared to 15 in 1972; second, 13 black pitchers in the majors including only five starters; third, only 19 blacks younger than 26 years old performing in the majors; fourth, the Boston Red Sox did not have a starting pitcher or every-day black player for the first time since 1961.

27. See Arturo J. Marcano and David P. Fidler, *Sealing Lives: The Globalization of Base-ball and the Tragic Story of Alexis Quiroz* (Bloomington, IN: Indiana University Press, 2003). For two Internet articles about this topic, see Jim Souhan, "Latin American Acad-emies Becoming the Norm," at <http://www.sportsbusinessnews.com> cited 14 January 2003, and Gary Marx, "An Expose on Baseball Training Facilities in Latin America," at <http://www.sportsbusinessnews.com> cited 19 August 2003.

28. Ibid. Besides the sports academies in Latin American nations, another labor issue is the manufacture of baseballs in Turrialba of Costa Rica. Factory workers in Costa Rica typically earn $2,750 per year while the average MLB player averages nearly $2.4 million. In one plant, temperatures might rise to 95 degrees and some workers have suffered repetitive stress injuries because they are paid $.30 to produce each baseball, which Rawlings Sporting Goods sells for $14.99. The MLBPA's Donald Fehr said working conditions at the plant had not been brought to his attention. For more information about the production of baseball's in Costa Rica, see Tim Weiner, "Costa Ricans Sweat Details For Major-League Baseballs," *The Charlotte Observer* (25 January 2004), 10A.

29. MLB Commissioner Bud Selig's Office circulated the Standards during the Fall of 2002. For some reason, the document did not apply the MLR's on minor league operations to the baseball academies in Latin America. Because the minor league facilities in North America were included in the Standards, was MLB negligent and discriminatory against Latin children and young men? For reforms of the Standards, see Arturo J. Marcano and David P. Fidler, "Memorandum," at <http://www.sportinsociety.org> cited 2 October 2003.

30. For how MLB's drug test program is structured and conducted, see "Baseball to Start Testing Latin American Players," at <http://cnnsi.com> cited 4 September 2003, and Steve Fainaru, "MLB to Consider Drug Testing For Foreign Players," at <http://www.sportsbusin-essnews.com> cited 19 August 2003. As to the penalties for steroid use in MLB, the first positive test results in treatment; the second positive is a 15-day suspension or $10,000 fine; the third positive is a 25-day suspension or $25,000 fine; the fourth positive is a 50-day suspension or $50,000 fine; and the fifth positive is a one-year suspension or $100,000 fine. Because those penalties have not effectively deterred drug use by MLB players, the U.S. Congress might pass legislation that would formally designate androstenedione, which is a steroid precursor, and more than two dozen other steroid-like supplements as controlled substances. Even so, apparently fans do not seem to care whether professional baseball athletes consume performance enhancing drugs as discussed in Steve Wilstein, "Shadow on the Game," *The Charlotte Observer* (1 April 2004), 1C, 3C. With respect to what baseball officials think about and how they reacted to drug use restrictions on players, Wilstein says, "Commissioner Bud Selig, chafed about the focus on steroids, issued a drug policy gag order on management, hoping it would make the problem go away. He told Congress he favored a tougher anti-doping program, similar to the one used in the minors [U.S. professional baseball leagues]. Union chief Donald Fehr stood up to Selig and politicians, insisting that stricter drug testing invades the privacy of players."

31. Ibid. As reported prior to the start of MLB's 2004 regular season, approximately 5–7 percent of the 1,438 drug tests, plus 240 retests that were completed with respect to all players during the 2003 season had turned up positive, which amounts to 86 tests based on a midpoint of 6 percent. Indeed, such megastars as the San Francisco Giants' Barry Bonds and the New York Yankees' Jason Giambi had to testify before a committee regarding the use of THG, which is a recently discovered steroid. Since MLB players were told in advance of the tests, there appears to be a greater usage of performance enhancing drugs by players than perceived. See John Donovan, "As Steroid Use Goes, Baseball's Numbers Just Don't Add Up," at <http://sportsillustrated.cnn.com> cited 20 November 2003.

32.   See Tom Singer, "MLB.com Looks at the Concept of a World-Wide Baseball Draft," at <http://www.sportsbusinessnews.com> cited 3 December 2002, and Thomas Harding, "MLB and MLBPA Still Working on World-Wide Draft Plan," at <http://www.sportsbusinessnews.com> cited 25 November 2002. According to Harding, "The concept of expanding the amateur draft worldwide was discussed during negotiations for the collective bargaining agreement, but the sides couldn't agree on a number of issues. The next step is for several figures representing Major League Baseball's management counsel to join with representatives of the Major League Baseball Players Association to try to hash out the issue."

33.   This topic is further explained in Gary Klein, "Global Draft," *Los Angeles Times* (3 June 2003), D6; Kevin Kelly, "Worldwide Draft Caps Wealthy Teams' Monopoly," at <http://www.sportsbusinessnews.com> cited 19 August 2003; Dave Sheinin, "A World-Wide Baseball Draft Could be a Logistical Nightmare," at <http://www.sportsbusinessnews.com> cited 19 August 2003.

34.   See George Gross, "Former MLB President Paul Beeston Wants a Baseball World Cup by 2005," at <http://www.sportsbusinessnews.com> cited 25 November 2002; Murray Chass, "A World Event Could Solve All-Star Blahs," *The New York Times* (9 July 2002), D3; Jerry Crasnick, "Baseball May [be] Headed to the Caribbean," at <http://www.sportsbusinessnews.com> cited 3 December 2002; "Baseball World Cup Could Get Green Light Soon," at <http://www.sportsillustrated.cnn.com> cited 13 November 2003; Barry M. Bloom, "Baseball World Cup Being Planned For 2005," at <http://www.sportsbusinessnews.com> cited 13 November 2003; "The World Cup of Baseball," at <http://www.sportsbusinessnews.com> cited 25 November 2002.

35.   MLB is committed to organize a World Cup baseball championship. This effort was discussed in Barry M. Bloom, "MLB Looking at World Cup in 2005," at <http://www.sportsbusinessnews.com> cited 1 August 2003; Amy Shipley, "Baseball Looking to Internationalize," at <http://www.sportsbusinessnews.com> cited 19 August 2003; Albert Chen, "Inside Baseball," *Sports Illustrated* (28 April 2003), 66. Before the tournament, however, MLB must obtain agreements from the International Baseball Federation (IBF) and the MLBPA. Although the players union is concerned about the drug test program, that organization supports the World Cup and MLB's interest in hosting the event in America during 2005. For such potential issues with the World Cup, see Murray Chass, "Problems With Proposed MLB 2005 World Cup," at <http://www.sportsbusinessnews. com> cited 10 February 2004, and Pete Caldera, "Players to Consider Testing For Cup," *The Charlotte Observer* (29 March 2003), 9C. As indicated in Caldera's article, the MLBPA's chief operating officer Gene Orza stated that the union might agree to the drug testing guidelines established for the Olympics as a requirement for a World Cup of Baseball tournament before the 2005 regular season. The IBF's president Aldo Notari has also stated that his organization will not endorse the tournament unless the Olympic guidelines are applied to the drug testing of players.

36.   Again, see Barry M. Bloom, "MLB Looking at World Cup in 2005." Besides those proposals, during late 2003 Commissioner Bud Selig expressed his interest in the tournament when he said, "I think in a certain sense it really motivates people, me and all of us in baseball, to see how the game will be, because the game is being played at such a high level in so many countries that the World Cup makes even more sense. And I want to repeat, as disappointing as that loss—U.S. national team defeated by Mexico for Olympics qualifier—was, it points out why a World Cup makes sense, because quality baseball is being played in a lot of places. This could be really good, really good." See Mike Bauman, "Bud Believing in a Baseball World Cup," at <http://www.sportsbusinessnews.com> cited 13 November 2003. With respect to the Olympics and drug tests, during March of 2004

Selig said his goal is zero tolerance at the major league level, which is the program for all 40-man roster players in the minor leagues. Those players are tested year-around for steroids, over-the-counter nutritional supplements and recreational drugs, and punished after a first positive test. Meanwhile, internationally players are banned two years after the first positive test and for life if a second test is positive. "What you need to produce a World Cup is to have the same stringent, well-written, well-documented policy for the U.S. and all other countries in the world," commented Selig. "We need to have a policy that conforms to the Olympics. I trust we can bridge that gap. We can't have a World Cup without it." For his and other MLB officials' views, see Barry M. Bloom, "Bud a Baseball World Cup and Drug Testing," at <http://www.sportsbusinessnews.com> cited 29 March 2004.

37. See Geoff Baker, "Backers Pitch Merits of New League," *Toronto Star* (21 November 2002), D5, and John Lott, "Baseball North," *National Post* (22 February 2003), B10.

38. For specific strategies of the CBL and expectations of league executives, see Shi Davidi, "Canadian Baseball League Counting on Communities," at <http://www.sportsbusinessnews.com> cited 18 May 2003, and "Canadian Baseball League Moving Forward," at <http://www.sportsbusinessnews.com> cited 25 November 2002.

39. After only two months of regular season play, the CBL's suspension was imminent. See Kevin Rothbauer, "Goodbye Canadian Baseball League," at <http://www.sportsbusinessnews.com> cited 19 August 2003; "Canadian Baseball League to Conclude Inaugural Season After All-Star Game," at <http://www.canadianbaseballleague.com> cited 6 September 2003; Graeme McElheran, "Goodbye Canadian Baseball League," at http://www.sportsbusinessnews.com> cited 19 August 2003. Besides the death of the CBL, minor league baseball teams struggle in Canada. For example, in Ottawa the Lynx have experienced poor attendance at games. "It's the same old story," said the Lynx's owner Ray Pecor, "It's been a disaster. My dad would tell me that (owning this team) has been a lot more heart than anything else. Some games, there have been maybe 25 people watching. That makes me cry. I'd love to have 4,000 (spectators) a game. We're not charging too much for tickets . . . we're not charging too much for parking . . . so what is it? What are we doing wrong? The facility is so good, the community is so good . . . and the team will be as good or better than last year. But it can't continue to go the way it's going." See Tim Baines, "City of Ottawa— Not a Baseball Town," at <http://www.sportsbusinessnews.com> cited 23 March 2004.

40. Since the middle of the 1990s, Monterrey officials have desperately yearned for a big-league franchise. As a center for industy, the city has excellent transportation links and the potential to draw fans from a vast area and border towns such as Nuevo Laredo. Furthermore, the City is home to 58 of Mexico's 160 Little League organizations and the Cuauhtémoc Brewery that produces Tecate and other Mexican beers. Jose Maiz Garcia, who is the owner of the local Sultans professional baseball team said, "Your bring the Expos to Mexico and you are globalizing. If we had the team here, 104 million Mexicans could follow the team, plus the 25 million Mexicans working in the States." To read about Monterrey and MLB, see Justin Martin, "Can Baseball Make it in Mexico?" 32–33; Hugh Dellios, "Monterrey Wants the Expos," at <http://www.sportsbusinessnews.com> cited 10 February 2004; "Yanqui Doodle Dandy," *Wall Street Journal* (20 February 2004), W11. As cited in the latter article, "Manifestly, Latin America has plenty of budding A-Rods [New York Yankees' $250 million player Alex Rodriguez] and millions more baseball fans. Isn't it time to give them a real chance to root for the home team?"

41. The WBL is determined that girls have the same visions of diamond [shape of baseball field] glory as boys. When girls become adolescents, they are discouraged to play baseball

alongside boys. For how the WBL has fulfilled childhood dreams, see "Women's Baseball League Inc.," at <http://baseballglory.com> cited 1 December 2003.

42.   Ibid. Besides the WBL, in 1992 there was an American women's baseball organization. This league is discussed in "American Women's Baseball," at <http://womensbaseball. com> cited 1 December 2003. For more insight about the sport during the early 1990s, see Gai Ingham Berlage, "Women's Professional Baseball Gets a New Look: On Film and in Print," *Journal of Sport and Social Issues*, Vol. 16, No. 2 (1992), 149–152.

43.   At the 2003 Women's World Series, Japan and Australia teams tied for first place in the regular pool play with won-loss records of four–two, while America finished third at one-five. In the Gold Medal Game, Japan outscored Australia four–one. See "2003 Women's World Series," at <http://www.wibba.com> cited 1 December 2003. With respect to the Series, the New England Women's Baseball League was denied entry because of a rule that allows one team per country. Regarding that decision, the organizer of the Series and pre- sident of American Women's Baseball, Jim Glennie stated, "If you dilute that, it takes away the special feeling of belonging to the national team. I gave that some thought and talked it over with Australia and Japan. But we came away with the decision that we'd stick to the rule." See Maureen Mullen, "Small World at Women's Series," at <http://www.sportsbusinessnews.com> cited 19 August 2003. Finally, for women's baseball programs in Australia, see "History of Australian Women's Baseball," at <http://womens baseball.com> cited 1 December 2003.

44.   Since the U.S. women's softball team won gold medals in the 1996 and 2000 Olympic Games, and more than 1,700 collegiate softball programs exist in America, MLB repre- sentatives contend that female softball players are an untapped natural resource market. As such, the league's support of the NPF seems to be a worthwhile investment. From another perspective, the NPF welcomes MLB's interest in professional women's softball. According to Sacramento Sunbirds general manager Glenn Wolff, "The ability to partner with MLB will not only add credibility to the Sunbirds organization and the NPF but will allow us to showcase the talents of many great players and reach a new level of sponsorship opportunities for the coming years." For more about this topic, see Mark McDermott, "MLB Set to Support New Women's Professional Softball League," at <http://www.sportsbusin-essnews.com> cited 23 March 2004, and "National Pro Fastpitch," at <http://profastpitch. com> cited 23 March 2004. To read more information about the history of the sport, there is Mary L. Littlewood, *Women's Fastpitch Softball—The Path to the Gold: An Historical Look at Women's Fastpitch in the United States* (Columbia, MO: National Fastpitch Coaches Association, 1998).

Chapter 2

National Football League

Between the late 1890s and 1910s, the sport of professional team football in America was chaotic, disorganized and in disarray. This scenario had primarily occurred because of three unique factors. Those were first, the inflation of teams' salaries; second, professional football players' unwillingness to make long-term commitments to, and remain with one club; and third, professional teams' employment of college and university football players who were still enrolled as students in their schools. As a result of this unstable situation, in 1920 an organizational meeting was held that included the representatives of four independent professional football teams, which were each located in the U.S. Midwest. At that Canton, Ohio meeting the group reached an agreement. That is, the representatives decided to establish the American Professional Football Conference, which was renamed later that year as the American Professional Football Association (APFA). After a reorganization of teams, in 1922 the APFA changed its name to the National Football League (NFL), which then consisted of 18 U.S.-based teams that included a Native American club titled the Oorang Indians and its great player Jim Thorpe, who was a double gold medal winner at the 1912 Summer Olympic Games in Stockholm, Sweden. Based on that background information about the formation of the league, the NFL is the focus of this chapter in *Sports Capitalism*.[1]

Besides the NFL, since the middle of the 1920s seven other American professional football leagues, besides the NFL, were organized and had briefly existed in the U.S. Eventually, five of the leagues had to dissolve their operations, one disbanded into the NFL and another one, which was the American Football League, was forced to merge with the NFL in 1969. Those seven leagues had to consolidate their organizations, merge or fail as businesses because of several reasons. To illustrate, some of the leagues had teams with inept or inexperienced franchise owners and executives who lacked sufficient business management talents and marketing skills to successfully operate their professional football clubs for profits. Meanwhile, other officials of the football leagues and teams did not cooperate and negotiate with America's broadcast networks to secure any local, regional and/or national television and radio contracts. Furthermore, there were leagues' teams that played in obsolete stadiums at inferior home sites and thus had earned below-average cash inflows from their ticket sales and concessions at games during their regular season home schedules. Finally, some of the leagues contained franchises that experienced a mixture of short- and long-term demographic, economic and financial hardships. The World Football League (WFL), for example, was formed in 1973. As the league's decision makers, some of the WFL's team owners were basically unqualified to be professional sports entrepreneurs. Therefore, they had likely misallocated the organization's resources and underfinanced the business aspects of their franchises. Besides those factors, several of the WFL's team coaches and general managers had lacked name recognition and reputations as football leaders, most of the league's teams had played their home and away games in dilapidated and/or undersized stadiums, and the majority of team rosters had predominately consisted of inexperienced rookies and mediocre, semiprofessional football players. When sports fans, potential investors and the media discovered that the league had grossly inflated and falsified its total game attendances and also miscalculated some teams' home attendances in published reports, the WFL lost its credibility, and then ceased operations and folded in 1975.[2]

Twenty-five years before the WFL failed, the NFL had periodically scheduled exhibition and/or preseason games at sites in Canada to attract football fans and increase its international exposure, that is, beyond the U.S. market. The City of Ottawa welcomed various NFL games in 1950–1951, Toronto in 1959–1961, Montreal in 1961 and 1969, and Hamilton in 1961. Since those games were well-attended by fans who resided in the metropolitan areas surrounding the respective cities, from the middle of the 1970s to the early 1980s other foreign cities had served as home sites for NFL exhibition and/or preseason games. That is, Toyko hosted an NFL game in 1976, Mexico City in 1978 and London in 1983. To attain even more worldwide exposure, in 1986 the NFL sponsored its first annual American Bowl series game, which was played before 82,000 spectators at Wembley Stadium near London. Subsequently, in response to the growing global interest in and demand for American professional football competitions, the NFL decided to extend this series of games, which have successfully continued into the early 2000s.[3]

To be consistent with the format, style and organization, and the type of analysis that was presented in Chapter 1 for MLB, Chapter 2 explores why, when and how the 82 year old NFL has gradually evolved to become a prominent and prosperous international sports league that represents the popularity and globalization of American-style professional team football. Given that premise, this chapter will incorporate and integrate the respective business and sports-specific alliances, events, innovations, opportunities, threats and trends, which are reflected as international business strategies, that the league has experienced and/or managed to accommodate in order to achieve its mission.

As such, the primary topics and other matters themes to be considered and highlighted hereinafter in Chapter 2 are arranged in four distinct parts and discussed as follows. First, this chapter provides some relevant facts, statistics and other historical information about the American Bowl series games, and then examines the formation, development, failure and finally, the reemergence of the World League of American Football (WLAF) in 1995, which was renamed the NFL Europe (NFLE) in 1998. As described in this chapter, it is because of huge dollar payments and subsidies from the NFL that have permitted the NFLE's teams to continue their operations as ongoing sports and business organizations. In the second section of Chapter 2, the purpose and fundamental business activities, programs and other strategies of the NFL International (NFLI) are identified and explored. Because of this discussion, the readers of *Sports Capitalism* will be informed and educated about why the league has assigned the NFLI with the multifaceted task of seeking worldwide commercial deals, investments and ventures.

After the WLAF, NFLE and NFLI are scrutinized, the third portion of Chapter 2 analyzes the sport of American football with respect to the NFL's presence, image and market power in a diverse group of non-U.S. nations. The six foreign countries selected were Japan, Canada and Mexico, which are places where the league has regional offices, and then England, Spain and China, which are NFL markets. Regarding the status of professional football organizations in Canada, the role and success of the Canadian Football League (CFL) and its business and sports-specific deals, if any, with the NFL are clarified. Interestingly, this relationship reveals how the two professional leagues independently co-exist as football groups, but to some extent cooperate to control the quality and supply of professional football for the benefit of sports fans who are located in North America and, in part, international markets. In the chapter's fourth section, a recent sample of the NFL's outreach and grassroots programs for the youth in European nations and other countries are identified and briefly described. In short, the discussion of these special activities and events indicates why the rewards and risks associated with competing in and winning football games and tournaments appeals to and interests millions of foreign-born children, teenagers and young adults.

Chapter 2 concludes with a Summary and Notes. The contents of the Summary reconfirm that the globalization of American football is a reality and highlight the NFL's primary international business strategies based on the league's activities, interests, relationships and successes. Meanwhile, the Notes contain the research sources that are listed in the Selected Bibliography of *Sports Capitalism*. As stated on a previous page, the first topic presented in this chapter is the history and operation of the NFL's European professional football league.

WLAF-NFLE

During the initial five years when the NFL had established the American Bowl series, the City of London in England hosted one football game in 1986 and another game in 1987. One year later, there were single American Bowl series games played in London and also in Goteborg, Sweden and Montreal, Canada. In 1989, there were two games with one each held in London and Tokyo, Japan, and then in 1990, single games were played in Berlin, Germany and again in London, Montreal and Tokyo. At the 1990 series, an estimated total of 200,000 football fans that lived on three continents had attended the four games. As a result of the series' extensive international media coverage and exposure, and because of the enthusiastic crowds at such venues as nearby London's Wembley Stadium and Tokyo's Korakuen Dome, the NFL's executives and team owners were thrilled and encouraged by the publicity from, and turnout at the four games. To display that success and summarize those events, Table 2.1 was prepared to represent a 16-year history of the NFL's American Bowl series. What do the tabled columns indicate? First, they denote, in part, that 70 percent of the series' games were held in Berlin, London, Mexico City and Tokyo. Thus, the sports fans in these cities enjoyed and supported professional football events. Second, only one game was played in Sydney, Vancouver, Dublin, Monterrey and Goteborg. Evidently, the fans in these cities preferred to watch other sports such as ice hockey and soccer. Third, for some reason the current NFLE cities that have not hosted an American Bowl series game through 2001 included Dusseldorf and Frankfurt in Germany, Amsterdam in the Netherlands and Glasgow in Scotland.[4]

Because of the growth in stadium attendances from football fans and the media coverage at the NFL's exhibition and preseason games that were played abroad during the middle to late 1980s, and due to the league's appeal, exposure and longevity in America, the ten-team WLAF was launched in 1991. Even though the games in the American Bowl series were not played in the U.S. as reflected in Table 2.1, the WLAF originally consisted of seven North American clubs and one team each that was located in the medium to large cities of Barcelona, Frankfurt and London. Early on, the league had experienced some relatively moderate but short-lived fan support during the 1991 and 1992 regular seasons. It was, however, the below average attendances, inferior player performances, and thus the poor quality of games that crippled most of the WLAF teams, and especially the seven clubs that were based in the U.S. where an economic recession had inflicted damage on the economy and thereby reduced consumer spending and business investment. In retrospect, a portion of America's sports fans had perceived and evaluated the league's players to be untalented castaways and not high-caliber professional football athletes. As result of the fans' attitudes, after the 1992 World Bowl was played between the Sacramento [California] Surge and Orlando [Florida] Thunder, the NFL franchise owners approved a proposal from the World League's Board of Directors to suspend the league's operations and then restructure the WLAF. The NFL owners made this decision, at least in the short-term, to preserve cash by the elimination of teams' subsidies. In the long-term, however, it meant that the NFL desired to allocate more resources and appropriate additional funds to upgrade and support the WLAF's international franchises, and enlarge those clubs' marketing budgets.[5]

After the development of a new business plan, in 1994 the NFL partnered with the Fox television network and announced the formation of a new joint venture. From that deal, a six-team World League was organized. It was based in Europe and scheduled to begin play in 1995. That year, the WLAF had reemerged as a professional football league without any clubs located in America. Rather, one each of the league's teams was placed in the cities of Amsterdam, Barcelona, Dusseldorf, Edinburgh, Frankfurt and London. To conclude the WLAF's first season, nearly 24,000 exuberant fans watched the Frankfurt Galaxy defeat the Amsterdam Admirals 26–22 and win the 1995 World Bowl championship game. Then, to attract more international exposure and recognition, in 1998 the WLAF changed its name to the National Football League Europe (NFLE).[6]

Table 2.1 American Bowl Series Games, by Country and City, 1986–2001

Country	City	Years	Games
Australia	Sydney	1999	1
Canada	Montreal	1988/1990	2
	Toronto	1993/1995/1997	3
	Vancouver	1998	1
England	London	1986–1993	8
Germany	Berlin	1990–1994	5
Ireland	Dublin	1997	1
Japan	Tokyo	1989–1996/1998/2000	10
Mexico	Mexico City	1994/1997–1998/2000–2001	5
	Monterrey	1996	1
Spain	Barcelona	1993–1994	2
Sweden	Goteborg	1988	1

Note: The countries are listed in alphabetical order. Between 1986 and 2001, the number of series games per Year ranged from one to four.

Source: "NFL International Historical Results," at <http://www.nfl.com> cited 25 November 2002.

For a distribution of Seasons, victories in World Bowls and the Attendances at games associated with the WLAF and NFLE European teams, Table 2.2 was created. It indicates, for those seasons, that the Amsterdam Admirals and London Monarchs were the least, and the Rhein Fire and Frankfurt Galaxy the most successful teams at winning championships in the World Bowls. For the ten World Bowl games played during the two periods between the seven European teams, the average attendance per team was approximately 41,000 spectators. In 1991, the London Monarchs defeated the Barcelona Dragons before 63,000 fans, which was the highest attendance at a World Bowl game. As an aside, during the team's last season in 1998 the London Monarchs were renamed the England Monarchs. Besides the Monarchs, since 1998 the Barcelona Dragons have discontinued its operations and in 2004, a team called the Centurions based in Cologne, Germany had joined the NFLE.

Relative to specific regular season game statistics, the WLAF-NFLE's average team attendance during the seasons reflected in Table 2.2 was about 12,000–17,000 per game. Alternatively, the NFL's teams had averaged nearly 60,000–65,000 per game. As such, the two leagues' large attendance gap denotes, in part, that the NFL is the superior sports organization and why it must subsidize the operations of the teams in the NFLE.

During the 1991–1992 and 1995–1997 seasons the WLAF, and in the 1998–2003 seasons the NFLE, had each struggled to improve their teams' brands, images and performances in the home city markets. That is, to become a legitimate and the

**Table 2.2 WLAF-NFLE European Teams, World Bowls and Attendances,
              1991, 1995–2003**

Team	Seasons	World Bowls	Attendance
Amsterdam Admirals	11	1	24
Barcelona Dragons	11	4	42
Berlin Thunder	5	2	43
Frankfurt Galaxy	11	5	36
London Monarchs	6	1	63
Rhein Fire	9	5	40
Scottish Claymores	9	2	38

Note: Seasons are the teams' number of regular seasons at the home site. World Bowls are the teams' number of appearances in a World Bowl. Attendance is the teams' average home attendance at the World Bowl games. The 1992 World Bowl, which is excluded from Table 2.2, was played in Montreal, Canada between the Sacramento Surge and Orlando Thunder. The Rhein Fire and Scottish Claymores joined the NFLE in 1995 and the Berlin Thunder in 1999. Because its attendance averaged 7,000 in Barcelona, the Dragons folded after the NFLE's 2003 regular season.

Source: "NFL Europe," at <http://www.nflef.com> cited 13 October 2003; *NFL International* (New York, N.Y.: National Football League, 2002), 287–289.

more popular sport, and thus compete with professional soccer for the support of Europe's sports fans, and for recognition from the European sports establishment. Nevertheless, since the late 1990s the NFLE has evolved to be the most prominent professional football organization that subsequently trains, and otherwise prepares and develops U.S. and international athletes for the NFL. Furthermore, the NFLE currently serves as the most reputable forum where players from all nations can compete to impress the owners, general managers and coaches of teams in the NFL and perhaps the professional scouts and team officials in the CFL and other nations' football leagues. Although the NFLE teams' operations result in deficits that amount to $15–25 million each year in Europe, the league generates fees, income from contracts and other business revenues from sports fans and companies across the globe to support the marketing and distribution of NFL television and radio broadcast rights, and the production and promotion of football clothing, equipment and merchandise. To illustrate how that has occurred, besides the international exposure and cash inflows from the American Bowl series' exhibition and preseason games in Tokyo and other cities, in early 2000s the NFLE conducted numerous non-contact flag football programs throughout Europe and the league's 2002 World Bowl championship game was broadcast in 150 countries to a global population that was estimated to be 200 million people.[7]

   Despite the NFLE's business environment and progress, and its teams' competitiveness and publicity, during the middle of 2003 the NFL club owners had met and evaluated whether to terminate their European league and replace it with teams that were a current member of the U.S.-based Arena Football League and/or Continental Football League. After a serious debate that resulted in an agreement, in September of 2003 the NFL owners decided to retain and continue to subsidize the NFLE's operations through the league's 2005 season. Apparently, there were some NFL franchise owners who convincingly argued that the incremental benefits from the NFLE's presence such as its European marketing coverage, which provides programming for the NFL Network, and its teams' experiences to attract and train qualified coaches, officials and players, had marginally outweighed its administrative, operating and player costs. Despite that outcome, during early 2004 the NFL decided to develop a long-term business plan that would consider the relocation and/or termination of a portion of the existing NFLE franchises, and perhaps would evaluate the expansion of the six-team league into various medium to large cities in Asian and Eastern European countries.[8]

Based on the analysis of, and reports from several of Europe's sports executives, journalists and broadcasters, NFL Commissioner Paul Tagliabue has realized that there are some deep-rooted concerns, misconceptions and prejudices by European traditionalists about the historical development and entertainment value of American-style professional football and how the NFLE operates as a business. For example, three specific issues that have surfaced during the early 2000s are listed as follows. First, some well-intentioned government and business leaders and sports officials who are from European countries have not completely accepted professional team football as a viable sport because of the game's complex rules and violence, and its overtly American image. Second, despite the supposedly long-term unification forces of the European Union (EU), local and regional government authorities and the sports federations and fans in nations throughout Europe are incompatible, distant and highly fragmented. Third, the NFLE and the sport of American football must compete with amateur and professional baseball, basketball, cricket, ice hockey, rugby and soccer leagues and clubs for its European fan base. Especially in contrast to the latter three sports, American football teams, players and coaches have a unique kind of contact or interaction that does not appeal to or interest millions of Europeans. In short, to overcome the market barriers and differences between institutions and households in foreign countries, the NFLE must adapt its brand, image and product to the European sports culture such as the NBA teams had accomplished during the 1990s and early 2000s.

Certainly, frequent exposure and wide television coverage are essential elements for the NFL and its teams to develop broad, loyal and passionate fan bases in global markets. To that end, during the 2003 regular football season approximately 70,000 hours of NFL programming, which ranged across 24 time zones in more than 30 languages, was transmitted to 60 broadcasters in 223 foreign countries and territories. Besides the broadcasts of games and football scores on weekends, the NFL's international media partners and sponsors, and television affiliates received such league shows as the NFL Blast, and the league's GameDay, Satellite News Service and Super Bowl Memories. Specifically, those four programs and other NFL events were distributed to inform, educate and entertain the world's football and other sports fans. In total, the programs featured special game highlights, 'popular plays of the week' segments, teams' press conferences, players' profiles including their contributions to community activities, music videos and sports stories recorded from fans in nations throughout the world. In particular, to capture the sport of football's passion and pageantry the Super Bowl Memories program provided a history of the most memorable moments of the NFL's more than 36 championship games that have been played as Super Bowls in such American cities as Los Angeles and San Diego in California, and Miami and Tampa Bay in Florida. Indeed, those types communications, exposures and programs are crucial business investments for the NFL to compete against the other U.S.-based professional sports leagues for global market share, and to further grow its sport and expand its organization worldwide during the 21st century.[9]

To penetrate international sports markets, the NFL was restructured during the middle of the 1990s. As such, a new organizational unit was formed. This development is discussed next and then followed by the activities, alliances, events and programs, or business strategies that the league has implemented in various countries.

NFL International

After the WLAF had resumed its regular season game schedule in 1995, one year later the NFL Properties (NFLP), which was a division of the NFL, had aggressively started to extend the NFL's brand from America to overseas markets. To become more efficient, the NFLP then consolidated its numerous offshore marketing campaigns and placed them in a new division titled the NFL International (NFLI). As such, this organizational unit was established to create a unified department for the league's foreign markets, to streamline the activities and plans of the NFLP and NFLE, and to provide the NFL with innovative marketing and promotion programs that would be sold for profit to existing and potential affiliates, licensees, partners, sponsors and/or vendors across the globe.

To further globalize the league's games and other products and services, since the late 1990s the NFLI has progressed as a unit and its strategies have been moderately successful. To illustrate, in 1998 Germany's SAT1 and Spain's TV3 television networks had agreed to broadcast key segments of the NFLE's games for the first time. That is, both networks had joined with five other European broadcasters to provide exciting football plays and other highlights from the NFL's teams' regular season games. In 1999, the league's NFLI signed a well-publicized business agreement with Keith Prowse International (KPI), which then was the world's leading entertainment travel company that besides sports, also provided services for theatre, concert and attraction sale projects. According to its agreement with the NFLI, KPI became an authorized ticket agent for foreign fans who wanted to purchase tickets and ticket-inclusive packages to exhibition, preseason and regular season NFL games. For other business strategies to market and promote American professional football and the NFL, by early 2000 the NFLI had succeeded to enroll more than 1,000,000 children from foreign nations in Flag

Football programs. Furthermore, the international unit had coordinated football promotions with 68 sponsors, arranged for 56,000 hours of NFL programming to be broadcast in 24 languages to households in 182 countries, and developed football-related internet web sites to be read in German, Japanese and Spanish. Finally, during January of 2003 the NFLI sponsored a $1.6 million Super Bowl advertising campaign to especially attract athletes and other adult sports fans and viewers in the United Kingdom, which is the world's second most valuable market with respect to television sports rights fees.[10]

According to a statement made in 2002 by the NFLI's senior vice president and managing director Douglas Quinn, "Our focus for the future is to continue to provide our existing and potential new fans with the highest quality entertainment experience while delivering our business partners the maximum value from their NFL association." To fulfill that vision, during 2002 the NFLI had proceeded to establish business partnerships with at least 30 corporate sponsors and 18 multinational companies, earn an estimated $100 million in consumer sales, and maintain strategic business relationships with such leading retailers as Foot Locker, Deportes Marti, Japan Sports Vision and Wal-Mart. In short, with creative marketing programs and corporate alliances the NFLI has successfully promoted the NFL's image worldwide and thereby generated an enormous amount of extra revenues for the league from the sale of NFL games, merchandise and programming to companies and sports fans in numerous foreign countries.[11]

Based on the aforementioned activities, facts and other information about various aspects and performances of the WLAF, NFLE and NFLI, the next portion of Chapter 2 emphasizes the types of international business events and programs, and otherwise global strategies that the NFL and/or NFLI have implemented and managed with respect to marketing football and the league in selected nations. Because of the differences that exist between countries' cultures, social environments and economic systems, the respective topics and contents that are highlighted and discussed about football, and especially regarding the worldwide business of the NFL, will vary by nation.

NFL Strategies by Country

After the WLAF had resumed its regular season schedule in 1995, the NFL decided to establish regional branch offices in three geographically dispersed countries. To identify where and when the NFL's offices originated, the respective countries were Japan in 1996, Canada in 1997 and Mexico in 1998. Because the three offices represent, in part, an example of the NFL's global long-term priorities and most-valued investments, if applicable the league's interests, sponsorships and partnerships, and the football events and business developments in those nations are presented first, which are then followed by the league's business alliances and ventures in other foreign countries.

Japan

In 1934, American football games and other events came to fruition in Japan when Paul Rusch, a U.S. schoolteacher, organized some local amateur teams. When the allied armies maintained a military presence in Asia during the middle to late 1940s, the sport grew more popular and expanded there especially during the 1950s and 1960s. To provide competitive football games across the nation in the 1970s, Japan's largest companies had formed an X-league. This group included approximately 71 football teams, which were each ranked and then placed into one of four tiers. Between the late 1970s and 1980s, the Japanese economy had boomed and the sport of football attracted the support of Japanese fans, and in 1989 the fourth annual American Bowl series game was played in Tokyo between the NFL's Los Angeles Rams and San Francisco 49ers. In that contest, the Rams defeated the 49ers 16–13 in an overtime period, which thrilled the Japanese spectators who had attended the game. Nonetheless, by the early to middle 1990s Japan's national economic recession, and the stock and real estate markets that crashed, had significantly reduced the incentives for consumer expenditures on entertainment activities. These conditions, in turn, diminished Japanese's attendances at football games for which ticket prices remained surprisingly high in the midst of a deteriorating economy. As a result, the nation's sports fans gradually shifted their interest and support from football leagues, teams and players to the emerging amateur soccer leagues and to professional baseball organizations.[12]

Despite a sluggish economy and consumer's pessimism about the country's future, from the middle to late 1990s to the early 2000s the NFL continued to provide its football programs in Japan. That is, the league marketed the sport by negotiating licensing agreements and signing sponsorship deals and television and radio contracts, and by implementing grassroots activities such as flag football programs for Japanese youth. From its new office in Tokyo, which had opened in June 2001, the league streamlined and structured its international strategies in Japan's market to profitably exploit business opportunities there. Accordingly, the league provided programming services to its broadcast partners such as NHK-BS, NTV terrestrial, Gaora and SkyPerfecTV, and also promoted fan and player development activities in various cities. Moreover, the NFL formed strategic alliances with Toyota and VISA, and partnerships with Japan Sports Vision, Marubeni and Reebok. Because of these sports events and business relationships, during the early 2000s approximately 9,000 Japanese athletes played in football games on teams in more than 200 colleges and nearly 160,000 elementary and junior high school students participated in flag football programs.[13]

Notwithstanding the NFL's outreach and grassroots efforts since 1996, and its investments in football programs marketed to teenagers and young adults, undoubtedly the most popular Japanese sports events continue to be baseball and soccer games, and sumo wrestling matches. In contrast to those three sports, to schedule football seasons for teams and thus operate a sports league requires excessive amounts of equipment and money, and a large playing area of land, which is a very scarce resource in and surrounding Japan's densely populated cities. Furthermore, a moderate to large percentage of Japanese consumers view American football games as violent and injury-prone events, which are played by huge men who wear bulky shoulder pads and butt opponents' heads with their helmets.

Since football's fan base in Japan is relatively small, a growing portion of Japanese corporations has provided their teams with minuscule budgets to operate. Moreover, because of company layoffs and cost savings during the 1990s and early 2000s, it is exceedingly difficult to organize a football team and field a squad of employees from one business organization. Japanese football players, therefore, are not given any special perquisites or privileges by their employers and generally are not respected for their athletic skills by Japan's sports fans. Those attitudes toward organized sports by companies and fans are why the formation of high-quality, full-fledged professional football leagues in Japan are basically only a remote possibility. Perhaps Japan's NFL Managing Director Hikaru Machida was overoptimistic in 2002 when he declared, "Japanese fans embrace the NFL with a unique blend of awareness and emotion. Participants play the game at an increasingly competitive level. This combination bodes well for the NFL and the sport of football."[14]

Canada

Since 1997, the NFL's business alliances and its television broadcasts and marketing campaigns have noticeably expanded to promote professional team football as a sport in Canada. The following examples illustrate a few of those activities and programs. To broadcast NFL games in various Canadian provinces and/or cities during the league's regular seasons and its playoffs and Super Bowl championships, the NFLI initiated and formed partnerships with such telecommunications companies and cable television networks as Global, The Score, RDS and Rogers Cable. Besides those broadcasters, there were international consumer goods companies like Frito-Lay, Gatorade, Pepsi and Pizza Hut who incorporated the NFL brand and logo, and the league's image as an entertainment provider in the advertisements and sales promotions of their beverage and/or food products.

Those and other marketing projects continued into 1999 when the NFL signed a four-year, seven-figure contract with Canadian beer company John Labatt Ltd., who then agreed to advertise Budweiser beer in four television spots during regular season games. Then, during 2003 the NFLI concluded a lucrative two-year deal with Craig Media Inc. This company provided the broadcasts of at least 17 NFL Monday Night Football games to four Canadian stations that were located in Alberta, Manitoba, and in Ontario on Toronto/one, which was the first over-the-air television station launched in Toronto since the early 1970s. Finally, despite some minor concern and opposition from a few Canadian network executives, it was the digital channel named NFL Network that had expectations to broadcast league games and other professional football programs in Canada during 2004 or 2005. To be presented on cable and satellite systems, the channel's content was scheduled to consist of NFL game analysis, reports and archival footage, and home shopping shows and replays. For sure, those advertising and television network programming alliances, and the fan and player development in-market programs designated as American Bowl series games, NFL Canada Days and Practice with the Pros, were each marketing campaigns that required significant financial investment, coordination, leadership and trust between various NFL officials and the respective affiliated broadcasters. In regard to the league's strategies with respect to its Canadian office, NFLI vice president Gordon Smearton recently said, "The integrated marketing programs from our top partners have taken the NFL to a new level in Canada. Our local office provides the creative and promotional support to drive the NFL's development across the country."[15]

In short, the increase in exposure from marketing campaigns to, and the broadcast of games played by American professional football teams for Canadian fans are commercially worthwhile but long-term ventures since, during 1997, the NFL had originally established a five-year alliance with the CFL to jointly cooperate and build the Canadian people's awareness of and interest in the sport of professional football. For more details about the two leagues' business agreements, relationships and shared responsibilities, the following section titled the *CFL* discusses why and how these top-notch professional football organizations amicably co-exist and interact, yet have competed for market share in each other's sports markets.

CFL

Because of a lopsided U.S.-Canadian dollar exchange rate during the early to middle 1990s, which had resulted in the accumulation of deficits by the CFL and frequent salary cap violations by its teams, in 1997 the NFL loaned $5 million to that Canadian professional football league. As a condition of the loan agreement, the CFL had permitted veteran players to reject their teams' best salary offers and to join NFL clubs in those players' option years. This condition became reality, for example, in 2002 when 12 above average athletes switched from the CFL to the NFL. The players who emigrated were primarily former CFL quarterbacks who had been stars but could earn much more in salaries as NFLE starters or even millions of dollars as second- or third-string NFL quarterbacks. Regardless, only a small percentage of the eligible players have changed leagues since the late 1990s. Consequently, the loan agreement was extended to the early Spring of 2004. Therefore, CFL players are allowed to sign with NFL clubs in their option years while the leagues work together to support the game of football in Canada with initiatives that include NFL/CFL High School Coach of the Year, Reebok NFL/CFL Flag Football and an elementary school physical education program.[16]

The partnership between the leagues, in part, reflects the CFL's dismal sports economic environment and reveals the league's flawed business model relative to the NFL. Before Michael Lysko became its Commissioner in 2000, the CFL was pressured, despite a debt balance that exceeded $1 million, to allocate more money from its bank accounts to several undercapitalized teams. When Lysko became Commissioner, however, he publicly criticized the distribution of money and the business decisions of two popular CFL franchise owners. As a result of that controversy, a serious dispute occurred between him and various CFL team owners who had feared that at least 30 of the league's sponsors would panic and terminate their agreements. These owners were evidently mistaken in their beliefs, however, when in fact a few new sponsors had decided to join with the CFL and promote professional football and the indebted league throughout Canada. Besides the burden from teams' deficits, other financial issues had emerged about the league's operations. It was discovered that, for several years, an underground economy existed in the CFL whereby some of the clubs' star players had been secretly compensated by corporate sponsors or with side payments from the franchise owners. Thus, many teams' designated salary caps, with respect to their roster of players, were routinely violated and thus not enforced by the owners. In turn, that action created salary escalation that inflated teams' costs and deflated their profits. As a solution, Commissioner Lysko had strongly suggested to the CFL owners that the NFL's collective bargaining agreement with the NFLPA was a superior business model because team officials and players must sign binding statements and swear that non-contractual player payments are illegal and unauthorized. Furthermore, to ensure compliance the NFL Commissioner and his or her office staff periodically measure teams' aggregate and players' individual salaries, and then financially penalize any owners who had violated the caps. Nonetheless, when the Canadian media obtained insider information and then published reports that criticized the dispute between the Commissioner and owners, the CFL's Board of Governors chose to fire Lysko.[17]

Because of a newly adopted democratic committee system, and with pledges from the Governors' to communicate and cooperate, it appeared that unity had seemingly returned to the CFL in 2002. Then, because of better governance within the CFL, the teams' regular season game attendances improved, the league received higher ratings on its teams' televised games, corporate partnerships and sponsorships rose, and a troubled franchise like the Montreal Alouettes avoided filing for bankruptcy. Nevertheless, due to the apathy of Canada's football fans and the persistent gap in the exchange rate between the U.S. and Canadian dollars, there were struggling CFL franchises, particularly in Hamilton and Toronto. After those teams' home attendances and cash inflows dwindled, during the middle of 2003 the CFL's Commissioner Tom Wright announced that the league had assumed managerial control of the Hamilton Tiger-Cats and Toronto Argonauts. That is, during one month, the owners of those two storied franchises, which were each located in Canada's Southern Ontario provinces, had yielded their teams' operations to the league. In retrospect, the two football club failures in the CFL resembled what occurred in the NFL during the 1920s and 1930s when some of the league teams, led by inept and/or inexperienced franchise owners, had played their home games at sites in inferior U.S. sports markets. Ultimately, several of those NFL franchises were urged to relocate or terminate operations because of low game attendances at their respective home stadiums and because of other factors such as a shortage of financial capital and wrong-headed management decisions. So, if the difference in exchange rates between the U.S. and Canadian dollars continues or grows wider, and Canada's professional football fan base shrinks especially in the large metropolitan areas, the CFL may be forced to merge with the NFL. Predictably, the wealthiest and most stable CFL franchises would survive despite the merger and possibly be permitted to enter the American or National Football Conference of the NFL. Interestingly, this movement of franchises occurred in 1970 when ten AFL teams were allowed to join divisions within the NFL's American Football Conference (AFC). Thus, since most NFL teams are relatively prosperous and financially secure, the entry of CFL clubs into the NFL is a more likely outcome from a merger than an existing NFL club in Seattle, Buffalo, Detroit or Minneapolis moving across the U.S. border to such cities as Calgary, Ottawa, Quebec or Winnipeg in Canada.[18]

Mexico

Although the sport does not imminently threaten the success of the country's baseball and soccer programs, amateur and semiprofessional football games and events are popular entertainment activities in Mexico, which arguably is the NFL's largest and most lucrative international market. Since the early 1900s, Mexicans athletes have organized teams and played football games. Besides a college group of clubs that calls itself the Major League, teenagers and young adults play on teams in football leagues, which are located in cities throughout Mexico. Established during the early 2000s, the 2 year old Tochito football league, for example, involves an estimated 100,000 enthusiastic participants who are 8-18 years old. This organization also includes a 48-team league for emerging athletes who are 12-14 years old. Because football games are enjoyed and primarily played by youngsters who participate at the grassroots level, and given the nation's close proximity to the U.S. border states of Arizona, California, New Mexico and Texas, these factors partially explain why football has become an increasingly popular sport in Mexico particularly during the 1990s and early 2000s.[19]

Since its regional office opened there in 1998, the NFL has aggressively advertised and promoted American professional football games and other league events to households and businesses in the Mexican economy. Indeed, these marketing efforts have been successful. To illustrate, during 2002 the DirecTV, ESPN, Fox Sports, Grupo Imagen, Televisa and/or TV Azteca networks had broadcasted all regular season and postseason NFL games in Mexico on various cable and satellite channels, and on radio networks. According to reports from the NFLI, at least ten business partners such as Campbell's Inc., Gatorade, Nestle and VISA had spent an estimated $10 million on NFL-themed advertisements and other promotions in various Mexican cities. Furthermore, the U.S.-based professional football league sponsored integrated marketing displays that were featured in Mexico at retailers like Deportes Marti, Suburbia and Wal-Mart. Lastly, other events and programs such as non-contact flag football, in-market player and cheerleader appearances, and American Bowl series games had exposed the NFL's products and thereby provided Mexicans with entertainment options to play and watch, and therefore learn and respect American-style football.[20]

Because of the growth in the country's professional football fan base, in 2002 the NFL sold $16 million of NFL-franchised goods and merchandise to twenty million Mexicans. As one of the NFL's business strategies, when the nation's economy improves and market opportunities emerge, the league grants its licenses to small to medium sized Mexican companies that can efficiently produce, promote, sell and distribute quality products. These retailers know the preferences of local customers and are aware of how to effectively merchandise and transport NFL products to individuals and families who live in Mexico's urban and rural areas.

When the Mexican peso was devalued during the middle of the 1990s, the country experienced an economic crisis. As a result of that condition, many local retailers went bankrupt and other companies had to move their businesses to China, India and to other low wage countries. In the majority, however, the Mexican firms that manufactured and/or marketed NFL goods, as a full-time business, were able to survive the economic crisis and during the late 1990s and early 2000s, those companies realized greater revenues and higher profits from their sales of football products.

According to league statistics, during 2003 there were two Mexican players in the NFL and 27 Latino players who were listed on NFL training camp rosters. Before their tryouts at NFL-sponsored camps, those athletes likely played on independent Mexican clubs or on U.S. Division II and III college football teams where their outstanding performances attracted the attention of professional football coaches, general managers and scouts, and obviously sports agents. When the NFL's mini-camps concluded, generally the most promising Mexican and other foreign-born players were assigned to play for teams in the NFLE for one or more regular seasons. This assignment was intended to expose those players to various game situations and also, to provide them with an opportunity to become competent professionals by improving their offensive and defensive skills for preparation to qualify for teams and perform in the NFL.[21]

In the Appendix, Tables A.3 and A.4 indicate the numbers and countries of the international players who appeared on NFLE and NFL team rosters during specific months. For the six NFLE teams listed in Table A.3, there were a total of 64 foreign players, which represented approximately 17 percent of the rosters in March of 2004. With respect to the distribution of those athletes, 18 or 28 percent were from Germany, nine or 14 percent from Japan, eight or 12 percent from France, seven or 11 percent from Mexico, and six or ten percent from England. Interestingly, the 18 Germans played for the Berlin Thunder, Cologne Centurions, Frankfurt Galaxy or Rhein Fire, and the three athletes from Scotland performed for the Scottish Claymores. Regarding the team positions of the international players, 15 or 23 percent were defensive linebackers, 12 or 18 percent played on offense as wide receivers and seven or 11 percent excelled as kickers. Generally, the majority of the remaining players were assigned to teams as running backs, cornerbacks, defensive tackles and tight ends.

For the 28 NFL teams listed in Table A.4, there were 66 international players, which means an average of less than four percent on each team. Accordingly, 14 or

21 percent were natives of Canada and 10 or 15 percent of Germany. About the distribution of the 66 athletes, 19 or 27 percent played on the Jacksonville Jaguars, Minnesota Vikings or San Diego Chargers, and one each on the nine clubs listed at the bottom of the table. Because of strong leg speed likely developed during soccer practices and games, several of the international players were kickers or punters for their teams. Those included, for example, the Tampa Bay Buccaneers' Martin Gramatica from Argentina, Arizona Cardinals' Bill Gramatica from Argentina, San Francisco 49ers' Jose Cortez from El Salvador, Oakland Raiders' Bill Janikowski from Poland, and from Canada there were the San Diego Chargers' Steve Christie, Indianapolis Colts' Mike Vanderjagt and New Orleans Saints' Mitch Berger. Meanwhile, the other NFL foreign athletes played various team positions on defense or offense. For some reason, however, very few of the 66 men had trained to be a quarterback, which is a position on offense that requires passing skills and experiences at calling plays to score first downs and touchdowns. Furthermore, it should be recognized that because of players' injuries, trades and retirements, the teams' rosters as reported in Tables A.3 and A.4 frequently change in numbers and distributions.

As a demonstration of the league's respect, in 2002 NFL officials attended the inauguration of the Mexican Football Hall of Fame, which is located in Mexico City. Besides honoring those players who were top performers, this ceremony celebrated American professional football for its long and storied history in Mexico. To that end, there have been a variety of NFL teams that have excelled to win championships and thus are adored by sports fans who reside in Mexico and other nations below the U.S.' southwest border. Because of their geographic locations and winning traditions, the most popular NFL teams in Mexico have been the Cowboys from Dallas, Texas, the Dolphins from Miami, Florida, and the Raiders from Oakland, California. If the football team plays competitively in its division and conference, and establishes a regional and foreign fan base, the expansion franchise in Houston, which is nicknamed the Texans, will likely become a popular NFL team in Mexico and perhaps throughout countries in Latin America.[22]

In short, the NFLI in New York City and since 1998, the NFL's office, which is headquartered in Mexico City, have collectively aroused a passionate and grassroots fan base in that foreign nation. This excitement occurred specifically in Mexico because of the competition between teams at the American Bowl series games, extensive television coverage and other media programming, and business alliances with local and regional retailers, partners and sponsors, and nationwide with corporate partners. To highlight that progress, in 2002 the NFL Mexico Managing Director Will Wilson summarized the efforts to promote professional football and the league's games and merchandise south of the U.S. border when he said, "With our continued investment in the market through integrated marketing programs, we expect to continue to build our fan base and deliver value for a growing list of partners."[23]

Britain

For various economic and sports-related reasons, during the middle to late 1980s American professional team football, as represented by the NFL, had become more accepted as a sport and entertainment event in Britain. When the British amateur and professional soccer league teams experienced a modest contraction of their fan bases because of hooliganism and rowdy behavior by spectators who attended their games and international tournaments, the NFL suddenly grew more popular and the league's games appeared throughout England on terrestrial television channels. Furthermore, the American Bowl series games played in London stadiums had attracted large and enthusiastic crowds in 1983 and again in 1986–1989.[24]

Nonetheless, during the early 1990s the novelty of the sport had waned and as a result, Britain's passion for and interest in American-style football games and the NFL began to fade. This occurred, in part, when England's professional soccer leagues revised their marketing strategies and retargeted their soccer programs to attract and entertain families. Likewise, British sports commentators who announced professional football games on the country's terrestrial channels had failed to inform and educate television viewers about team strategies, player performances, and the entertainment values of American-style football competition. Meanwhile, the U.S. Dream Team became an international success at the 1992 Summer Olympic Games in Barcelona. As such, after American-style basketball had become popular and penetrated England's marketplace, a significant portion of the country's sports fans shifted their allegiance and support from the NFL to the NBA.

In August of 1993, London hosted an American Bowl series game. When this event concluded, and after the league's revenue streams from the sales of football clothing, equipment and merchandise had gradually diminished, the NFL decided to shrink its presence and the sport's exposure in Britain. To reallocate its resources and abundant money reserves, as previously stated in this chapter, during the middle to late 1990s the league invested in and opened regional offices in Japan, Canada and Mexico.

Based on published newspaper articles and other research materials about the league, in 2003 the NFL had apparently reversed its strategy in England. According to NFL vice-president for planning and development Alistair Kirkwood, the new goals established then by Commissioner Paul Tagliabue and team owners was to "push the league into popular culture" and "make football stars to be household names within a few years." To achieve that objective, the league implemented a multimillion-dollar, five-year marketing plan in England to increase the consumers' demand for American football and make the NFL one of the leading sport brands in the nation. Interestingly, the plan had contained four unique marketing components. First, the NFL signed a contract with a British terrestrial television network named Five, which assumed responsibility to broadcast a prime time U.S. professional football show each week; second, various types of print, radio and outdoor advertising would be intensely used to promote the NFL to sports fans throughout the country; third, key agreements were concluded with consumer product partners such as Budweiser, EA Sports and Reebok to promote the NFL brand and league games and events in their advertising; and fourth, newly designed NFL merchandise and a line of women's clothing would be marketed in London and other major cities.[25]

Besides the strategy revision adopted in 2003, the NFL increased its sponsorship of many flag and other football programs that were organized at the grass roots level to appeal to kids and prospective athletes throughout England. As developed by the NFL, those programs are designed to teach children how to develop specific and useful football-related skills, and how to interpret the basic procedures and rules of American football games. During June of 2003, there were football teams composed of 12–14 year old English and Scottish gridiron players who competed against each other in scheduled games to become the group's champion. When the tournament had concluded, the winning club advanced to the eight-team European School Final, which was played in Glasgow, Scotland.[26]

Spain

After NFL officials had finalized their negotiations in March of 2002, they endorsed a three-year marketing agreement with the Spanish soccer club, F.C. Barcelona. Essentially, the contract requires that the American football league would promote F.C. Barcelona and its activities in the U.S., and that the professional soccer team would promote the games of the NFLE's Barcelona Dragons in Spain and also informs Spanish sports fans about the NFL's teams. Furthermore, there were other important business and sports-related matters included in the agreement. Those inclusions, for example, recommended that NFL teams and the F.C. Barcelona club exchange stadiums to play exhibition games, display shields on each other's uniforms, share advice about broadcasting, licensing and sponsorship deals, provide teams with the rights to use trademarks for promotions, and lastly, cooperate to schedule and advertise American football games in Spain and amateur soccer programs in U.S. elementary and secondary schools.[27]

To highlight the historic significance of the marketing agreement, NFL Commissioner Tagliabue commented to the media, "We're doing this as part of the growing globalization of sports, combining the best of American and European sports." Besides the remarks of the Commissioner, the NFL's Alistair Kirkwood graciously expressed his sentiments about the league's relationship with F.C. Barcelona as follows, "The NFL's historic alliance with F.C. Barcelona represents the first time the two leading sports in their respective countries have joined forces to promote each other's activities. This groundbreaking relationship, along with our close ties with local government, sports federations, and commercial partners throughout Europe, are examples of the kinds of partnerships that are keys to our continued success."[28]

As an aside, the Commissioner of MLS, Don Garber voiced his opinion when he proposed that his organization should be allowed to join and participate in the NFL-F.C. Barcelona alliance, although Paul Tagliabue is apparently more interested in the NFL's presence in Europe than any relationship or involvement with the

U.S.-based professional soccer league. "We're in the soccer business," Garber stated. "We want to be part of the growth of the sport [soccer] in this country [U.S.] and are ready to do what's necessary to accomplish this."[29]

China

During January of 1987, an estimated 300 million Chinese citizens watched an NFL regular season game that was broadcast on the China Central Television (CCTV) network. Lyric Hughes, the president of a Chicago-based company named TL International, viewed the game on television in Peking with some prominent Chinese sports journalists. "They were very, very enthusiastic," remarked Hughes. "They cheered all the good plays and touchdowns, although I'm not sure they understood what was happening. They asked a lot of questions about the crowd— what the people were wearing and eating." Hughes' observations, in part, relate to how words that are connected with a sport translate from English into Chinese. In China, for example, football is dubbed ganlanqiu, which means 'olive ball,' and a quarterback sack translates into 'capture and kill.' Anyway, encouraged by the huge Chinese television audience that watched the game, TL International prepared a ten week NFL postseason package of games that aired on the CCTV network from February to May of 1987.[30]

As a prelude to the 2008 Summer Olympic Games in Beijing, since the early 2000s the NFLI's managing director Doug Quinn has been negotiating with top Chinese government and sports officials and various promoters to schedule NFL exhibition and/or preseason games at stadiums in Shanghai in 2005 and Beijing in 2007. As a result of his communications about games, Quinn maintained that China has strong economic incentives to further develop and upgrade its sports programs and modernize the country's facilities to support the proposed football games and other international events in Shanghai, Beijing, and perhaps more Chinese cities. To successfully reach an agreement and arrange for the broadcasts of the respective games, during 2004–2005 Quinn must allocate sufficient time to complete the required paperwork and to secure commitments from the Chinese sports authorities in a binding contract. Interestingly, the football games to be played in Shanghai and Beijing would fulfill the NFL's strategy of scheduling games and other events in countries that have built world-class stadiums to host a popular global event such as a summer or winter Olympic Games. Moreover, NFLI executives are convinced that the exposure from televising professional football games in China would further broaden the NFL's fan base and boost its image with respect to Asia's corporate community and the continent's media companies.

The previous section completes the analysis of how the NFL, and professional football teams and games are represented in certain nations. As mentioned before in this chapter, it is important that each U.S.-based professional sports league effectively design, sponsor, manage and operate international grassroots and outreach programs, which may include camps, clinics, games, tours, workshops, tours, championship series and other tournaments. To be popular, those activities and events must provide entertainment for players, other participants and spectators. They also should inform, educate and teach foreign children, teenagers and young adults about the rules of a contact sport such as football. To that end, the next section describes some unique American-style football projects that the NFL and NFLE have jointly organized and invested in to entice young athletes in Asian and European countries to learn, play and enjoy.

Grassroots Football Programs

The NFLE's primary web site, nfleurope.com lists some grassroots activities and other events that the league and its parent, that is, the NFL have sponsored in Europe. Besides a Beginner's Guide to Football, which is an eight page summary of the sport, this online source lists the team rosters, game schedules and scores, and other related information about the NFL Global Junior Championship tournament (GJC), NFL Flag Football World Championships (FFWC), European Federation American Football's Wilson European Junior Championships (EJC), European Amateur Football competitions (EAF), and the NFL Experience (EX). For each activity and/or event posted at the NFLE's site, there are links displayed on the home pages that provide updated and interesting professional football news and other details with respect to teams' games and players, and tournaments. To illustrate, the following content highlights some specific competitions and results about the significant grassroots programs that are listed and discussed on <http://www.nfl europe.com>.

GJC

This grassroots event is an annual multination football tournament that had originated during 1997. That year it was played in New Orleans, Louisiana before Super Bowl XXXI, which featured the NFC's Green Bay Packers and AFC's New England Patriots. As it was organized, the tournament was originally a single game designed to showcase the skills of talented, junior American football players on teams from Europe and Mexico. At GJC I in New Orleans and II in Chula Vista, California, Mexico defeated Europe and at GJC III, which was held in Fort Lauderdale, Florida, Europe beat Mexico. Because of football's growing popularity and its development in North America and foreign countries, during 2000 the GJC expanded to four teams. One team was from Canada while the other three had performed in Europe, Panama and the U.S. In 2001, Japan joined the GJC and that increased it to a five-team tournament. At the GJC VII, which was held in San Diego, California during the week of Super Bowl XXXVII, an American team placed first and a Canadian team finished second. When the tournament concluded, at least ten players who had performed for the U.S. championship team, and one player each from the Canadian and European teams, were recruited and eventually signed national letters of intent to compete in a football program at an American college or university. At <http://www.nfleurope.com, there are specific links to the GJC competitions and archives. In turn, these links provide information about the

previous tournaments, and team rosters and outstanding players. In short, the GJC represents an opportunity for pre-college and college-age players to compete against their peers from other countries and furthermore, the tournament is a marketing event that promotes the sport of football and thus benefits the NFL and NFLE.[31]

FFWC

This type of program is a ten-team international flag football tournament that involves boys and girls who are 12–14 years old. At the tournament in 2003, there were well-prepared teams from Australia, Austria, Canada, Japan, Mexico, Netherlands, Spain, South Korea, Thailand and the U.S. that had competed. With respect to the tournament's purpose, the NFL's Senior Manager of Fan Development and Events Michael Stokes said, "This [FFWC] is further proof that flag football is a safe and fun way to learn the fundamentals of American football. Flag football favors speed and skill over size and strength and is a great game for boys and girls from around the world."[32]

Interestingly, during the 2003 FFWC that was played in Tokyo, Japan, nearly 60 percent of the teams that participated contained girls on their squads. Canada, which finished in ninth place, had placed two girls on its roster and three of the semifinal teams in the tournament also listed girls on their rosters. The winning team at the FFWC was Mexico's Los Diabilitos. That squad, which won the championship without losing a game, included an impressive athlete named Maricela Lopez. Spaniard running back Natalia Hurtado was another star player because she was selected as the Female Tournament Most Valuable Player. "Natalie is an outstanding player and she runs the ball very well," said a Spanish team spokesperson. Besides the FFWC in Tokyo, during May of 2003 there were ten teams that consisted of 11–14 year old boys and girls from England who competed in FFWC games played at Saffron Lane, Leicester. To praise that tournament, the NFL's Flag Football Officer for the United Kingdom Gerry Anderson commented, "We have a good mix of school and club teams taking part in the English finals and the standard of play should be very good." In sum, based on articles that reported the enthusiasm of the boys and girls who had participated in the various FFWCs, it is expected that the NFL will continue to support and perhaps expand the FFWC to the urban cities and rural areas of other nations. For example, in 2003 more than 400 players and coaches from 23 Shanghai schools participated in China's first NFL Flag Football clinic. That event, which was broadcast on channels CCTV-5 and G-Sports, covered such football movements as passing, receiving and running routes, and included a scrimmage game. During 2004, China's national final football tournament highlighted the best teams from Beijing, Guangzhou and Shanghai.[33]

EJC

The British American Football Association (BAFA), European Federaton of American Football (EFAF) and the NFLE jointly organized the EJC. This competition is a bi-annual tournament that represents the best American football programs, which exist in European countries. Besides the teams from Austria, Czech Republic, France, Germany, Great Britain, Italy, the Netherlands and Sweden, Russia generally has entered a football team in the competition. To qualify and play for teams in the EJC, the players must be 15–19 years old.[34]

At the 2002 EJC tournament, which was held between international teams in Scotland's Broadwood Stadium, Russia defeated Austria 20–0 to win the Group A classification and Germany beat Great Britain 34–6 to triumph in the Group B category. In the championship game, Russia outscored Germany 26–20 to become the EJC's titlist. This final score reflects, in part, Russia's steady progress to upgrade its American-style football programs, at least for the junior level of play.

To illustrate the nation's interest in the sport, the first Russian football league was established in 1995. Seven years later, there were two football teams in Moscow, named the Bears and Patriots, and six clubs in the Ukraine. According to team spokesman Alexander Simanchev, during 2003 more than 1,000 kids played football in Moscow. For professional football entertainment, Russians usually watch NFL games by satellite, especially when the Super Bowl is broadcast on national television each year to approximately 10,000,000 viewers. Despite the Russians who complain that American football games are too rough, complex and fast-paced, Moscow's teenage athletes seemingly enjoy the sport and an opportunity to compete in the EJC tournaments.

EAF

Several well-managed EAF programs have been scheduled and successfully operated in Europe during the early 2000s. First, in the late Spring of 2001 there were player tryouts held in England at the NFLE's residential flag football and summer tackle camps. Located in London, one camp opened for 11–15 year old players who had attended to improve their flag skills, while the other camp existed for 15–19 year old knitted junior players. Specifically, at the flag camp youngsters were taught such important football movements as how to play various defensive positions and how to run the offensive receiver routes at short and long distances. That camp, which was conducted by the NFLE's Gerry Anderson, featured coaches and teachers who had earned their badges through the government-approved Leaders' Award.[35]

Second, during the Summer of 2001 some youth, who aspired to be college and professional football players in America, had attended four-day camps in Scotland and Spain. Basically, these EAF programs emulated the structure and style of the NFL and NFLE training workouts that those leagues' professional players had experienced. At the camps, coaches taught kids about the fundamentals of

American football and how athletes must develop their blocking, passing, tackling and running skills to win games. The kids were also trained at daily workouts, received special coaching tips and allowed to gauge their progress in the sport by reviewing their previous offensive and defensive performances during video and theory sessions. In Scotland, former Scottish Claymores receiver Scott Couper introduced the sport of football at the camp's sessions. Couper emphasized to the group that, to be competitive, players should physically and mentally condition themselves to deal with the rigors of the workouts. He also encouraged them to leave the camp with enough confidence, experience and ability to apply their athleticism and skill during games.[36]

Finally, during 2003 the NFL and BAFA conducted a group of clinics for coaches at three regional European sites. In a single comprehensive course, the foreign coaches who attended the clinics learned the fundamental football positions on defense and offense, and the basic movements on how to block and tackle opponents. When the clinics ended, the instructors advised the coaches to apply their knowledge and illustrate to players how to effectively block other linemen and tackle backfield runners.

EX

During 2000–2002, an interactive theme park titled the NFL Experience had toured in countries such as Germany, Scotland and Spain. The theme park's activities permitted youngsters from the countries to discover how it feels, for example, to run through and around a group of opponents, catch a winning touchdown pass and kick a field goal at 50 yards from the goal posts. To some observers, these and other experiences appeared to be boring, risky or perhaps too dangerous for kids to perform. At the park, however, there were soft, inflatable equipment sets that recreated the feelings and emotions of playing an actual game of American football in a fun environment. For example, youngsters that are challenged may simulate the path of a fullback, who drags his/her tacklers to the end zone for a score by running on a giant inflatable set while attached to a bungee cord. Furthermore, children had the option to bounce through blocking dummies for a first down, catch passes while running along the field's sidelines at full speed, or play quarterback and throw short, medium and long yardage passes to shifty wide receivers and other teammates. To diversify the EX's events, while the theme park toured Germany the interactive area included an exhibition stage that featured cheerleaders from Berlin's amateur football teams. Therefore, as a fun and happy experience, although the EX primarily entertains youngsters, it motivates them to watch their favorite NFL heroes on television, and it also encourages them to join a local team and play supervised American football games with classmates from their schools and with friends in their neighborhoods.[37]

The previous paragraph completes an overview of the most popular NFL and NFLE grassroots programs that had existed in Europe during the early 2000s. Certainly, the effects of the international activities and events benefited those who participated and the two leagues. That is, the NFL and NFLE have provided the programs to challenge, educate and inform foreign children and teenagers about the sport's fundamentals. Moreover, the programs tried to teach aspiring athletes the skills that are necessary for them to be successful players in American-style football games and to win championships at tournaments played in Europe, America and elsewhere.

In this chapter, the final American professional football organization identified is the National Women's Football Association (NWFA), which was formed during 2000 by entrepreneur Catherine Masters. With headquarters in Nashville, Tennessee, the NWFA is the largest league in the world for women who play full contact football. To meet the nation's demand for women's football, between 2000 and 2004 the number of members had increased from two to 37 teams, which were located in 23 U.S. states. Indeed, eight teams independently existed in medium sized cities in Ohio and Tennessee, and three each in Pennsylvania and Texas. In the 2003 season, each team played eight games and competed for a division title in order to qualify for the playoffs and then the World Championship Game. With respect to the demographics of its market, the league's typical fan is a single/divorced female with a college education. On averge, she is an Internet user, fitness enthusiast and pet owner, who enjoy camping/fishing and possibly extreme sports events.[38]

Since 2000, the NWFA's media exposure has impressively expanded because of the sport's growing popularity and fans' enthusiasm for the league's product. There have been feature stories and interviews about the league on such programs as the NBC Today Show, CBS Evening News and CBS Morning Show. Moreover, information about the league has been presented on the Tonight Show with Jay Leno, the Connie Chung Show and on such cable networks as Nickelodeon, Spike TV, MSNBC and CNBC. The *Baltimore Sun, Boston Globe, Cleveland Plain Dealer, New York Times, New York Post* and *Washington Post* newspapers, and *Advertising Age, Arrive Magazine* and *Southern Living* have included articles regarding the women's sport and organization. Moreover, the NWFA' web site, womensfootballassociation.com has generally recorded between one and three million hits per month. During the teams' April-July regular season games, playoffs and championship game, some of the advertisers have included CNN, ESPN Radio, Essere Corporation, Fox Sports TV, Street & Smith Sports Business and USA Today. Based on the NWFA's success thus far, president and chief executive officer Catherine Masters states, "Enjoy the game and remember, you are part of creating some pretty cool history for women's sports. And, if you happen to see me running around, stop and say 'Hello.' It's your support of the teams and league that are making us so proud." In short, the NWFA has the leadership, structure and uniqueness to survive as a professional football organization in America. Consequently, if the league decides to expand beyond the U.S., then a site in a city of southern Canada and/or northern Mexico would be the most attractive locations.[39]

To consolidate and highlight the international growth, development and prosperity of the NFL and American professional football as previously discussed in the contents of Chapter 2, a Summary follows next. When the Summary concludes, there are Notes. Then, Chapter 3 is presented. For that chapter, the topics are concerned with the international business strategies of the NBA and the globalization of American-style professional basketball.

Summary

Between 1920 and 2004, the NFL had succeeded to organize and develop in the U.S. as a professional team sport, and also to prosper as an entertainment business. Meanwhile, during that period the sport of football had gradually established a presence in several foreign countries, especially since the early 1990s. To analyze those historical facts and developments, the league's establishment and growth in America were briefly described. Then, Chapter 2 explored why, when and how the NFL became a global organization whose teams and games are currently recognized and admired by millions of sports fans in numerous nations on various continents. Therefore, to identify and discuss the international sports-related and business activities, events, partnerships, programs and any additional relationships that compose the international strategies of the NFL, and to learn about the league's alliances and affiliations with hundreds of government officials, private and public companies, and other groups abroad, the chapter was arranged into four distinct sections.

First, Chapter 2 reviewed the formation, struggle and failure of the WLAF during 1991–1992 and then its reemergence and development in 1995–1997, and later as the NFLE from the late 1990s to the early 2000s. As the 11-year history of this professional football league is presented in the chapter, there was a table that denoted some facts and statistics about the American Bowl series, which are annual exhibition and/or preseason games that have been played by various NFL teams in foreign cities since 1986. After that topic is presented, another table displayed the game attendances and results of World Bowl championships won by the European-based WLAF and NFLE teams during the leagues' postseasons in 1991 and 1995–2003. Although some NFL franchise owners are doubtful about the NFLE's future and whether the league's annual multimillion-dollar subsidy payments should be continued, the readers of *Sports Capitalism* will appreciate and comprehend how the NFLE's exposure and presence in Europe has contributed to the spread and success of the NFL and its teams, and American-style football, throughout Europe and in other regions of the world.

After the revival of the WLAF and progress of the NFLE are discussed, the chapter's contents then described the purpose, structure, performance and other aspects of the NFLI. As the research disclosed, the NFL established this organizational unit in 1996. Its basic function was to target, manage and aggressively market and promote the league's strategic international short- and long-term business and sports-related activities, events, plans and programs. From its location within the NFL's headquarters in New York City, the NFLI has been directly responsible to expand the league's global fan bases and increase its revenues in markets relative to such competitive sports organizations as MLB and the other

U.S.-based professional team sports leagues. To successfully accomplish the NFL's business goals, the NFLI has been involved with matters related to and about such activities as worldwide cable and satellite systems and various television and radio broadcast networks, American Bowl series games, European non-contact flag football programs and multination amateur and professional football tournaments, relationships with global football fans and the league's affiliated business partners and sponsors, the development of the NFLE and its respective World Bowl championships, and the recruitment and employment of amateur, college and professional football players who may be citizens of foreign countries. Based on the unit's progress since the middle to late 1990s, it appears that during the early 2000s the NFLI will gradually extend its authority, responsibility and power within the NFL and thus continue to market and promote American professional football games, grassroots programs and other league-related events as entertainment options for sports fans in nations across the planet.

Following a discussion of the NFLI's worldwide endeavors and accomplishments, Chapter 2 then focused on the role of American football, and the extent of the NFL's presence, and its types of strategies in six foreign countries. That is, to further penetrate consumer markets and expand the sport of football, in the middle to late 1990s the league set up a regional office in Japan and then in Canada and Mexico. Since these nations represented the NFL's primary international markets, this portion of the chapter emphasized the prominent business agreements, partnerships, sponsorships and programs that have been negotiated and activated with respect to each location of the three offices. As the progress of Canada's office is described, there are facts presented about the relationships that exist between the U.S.-based NFL and its northern counterpart, the CFL. When the description of the business activities of the three offices concludes, there was information about the football environment, NFL fan base and the league's presence, if any, in Britain, Spain and China. Although the NFL's ability to penetrate small to medium and medium to large markets has varied by country, the league reputedly possesses a variety of economic resources and large amounts in bank deposits to greatly enhance its exposure abroad and further its ambition to become the world's most well-known international sports organization.

The final two topics included in Chapter 2 were some of the grassroots junior football programs, clinics and other entertainment events that the NFL has sponsored and implemented, especially in European countries since the late 1990s, and the NWFA. Generally, there are NFL officials and their European colleagues and promoters who have been assigned to organize, manage and operate these types of football-related activities. That is, some American and European football officials have jointly established international games and tournaments between nations' teams, scheduled coaching and player instruction workshops, and also provided football camps and clinics to educate children and to develop the athletic skills of foreign teenagers and young adults who want to learn the sport's fundamentals and compete in American-style football games and youth league championships. Besides those activities, other NFL programs have been established to introduce youngsters to the intensity and thrills of American football games as they participate in an interactive theme park that has toured European cities during festivals and holidays. Based on Chapter 2's content, the research of the NFL revealed that the league has become a more powerful international sports and business organization, which will further globalize its brand, exposure and market share during the 21st century.

Notes

1. The chronology of professional football, from 1869 to 2001, is documented on pages 278–289 in the *NFL 2001 Record & Fact Book* (New York, N.Y.: National Football League 2001). Besides the league's history, there is information about the American and National Football Conferences and records, rules, teams and player statistics, and the 2000 Season in Review. For other NFL history and tradition, see Roger G. Noll, ed., *Government and the Sports Business* (Washington, D.C.: The Brookings Institution, 1974); James Quirk and Rodney D. Fort, *Pay Dirt: The Business of Professional Team Sports* (Princeton, N.J.: Princeton University Press, 1992); Frank P. Jozsa, Jr., *American Sports Empire: How the Leagues Breed Success* (Westport, CT: Praeger Publishers, 2003); Frank G. Menke, *The Encyclopedia of Sports*, 5th ed. (Cranbury, N.J.: A.S. Barnes and Company, 1975); David S. Neft and Richard M. Cohen, *The Sports Encyclopedia: Pro Football*, 5th ed. (New York, N.Y.: St. Martin's Press, 1997); Robert W. Peterson, *Pigskin: The Early Years of Pro Football* (New York, N.Y. and London, England: Oxford University Press, 1996); *Sports Encyclopedia* (New York, N.Y.: Ottenheimer Publishers Inc., 1976). For other books that relate, in part, to the culture, power and globalization of professional sports, see Alan Bairner, *Sport, Nationalism, and Globalization: European and North American Perspectives* (Albany, N.Y.: State University of New York Press, 2001); Allen Guttman, *Games and Empire: Modern Sports and Cultural Imperialism* (Chapel Hill, N.C.: Columbia University Press, 1994); Toby Miller, Geoffrey Lawrence, Jim McKay, and David Rowe, *Globalization and Sport: Playing the World* (Thousand Oaks, CA: Sage Publications, 2001); Hans Westerbeek and Aaron Smith, *Sport Business in the Global Marketplace* (New York, N.Y.: Palgrave Macmillan, 2003. In the Selected Bibliography of this book, there are four dissertations that relate to various aspects of professional sports leagues, which include football. Those are Michael E. Dobbs, "The Organization of Professional Sports Leagues: Mortality and Founding Rates, 1871–1997," Ph.D. diss., University of Texas at Dallas, 1999; James J. Grice, "The Monopolistic Market Structure of Professional Sports Leagues," Senior Thesis diss., Colorado College, 1987; Frank P. Jozsa, Jr., "An Economic Analysis of Franchise Relocation and League Expansion in Professional Team Sports, 1950–1975," Ph.D. diss., Georgia State University, 1977; Daniel A. Rascher, "Organization and Outcomes: A Study of Professional Sports Leagues," Ph.D. diss., University of California at Berkeley, 1997. Other books that involve the business and/or economics of professional sports include Henry G. Demmert, *The Economics of Professional Team Sports* (Lexington, MA: D.C. Heath and Company, 1973); Paul Downward and Alistair Dawson, *The Economics of Professional Team Sports* (London, England and New York, N.Y.: Routledge, 2000); Mark S. Rosentraub, *The Real Costs of Sports and Who's Paying For It* (New York, N.Y.: Basic Books, 1997); Paul D. Staudohar and James A. Mangan, eds., *The Business of Professional Sports* (Champaign, IL: University of Illinois Press, 1991).

2. A list of the current and former U.S. professional football leagues is in Appendix A of Eric M. Leifer, *Making the Majors: The Transformation of Team Sports in America*

(Cambridge, MA: Harvard University Press, 1996). Given Leifer's list, it is interesting to read why and how the NFL had decided to form its European league, that is, the WLAF during the late 1980s and early 1990s. For example, see Gerald Eskenazi, "Pro Leagues in America Eye the Globe," *The New York Times* (9 April 1989), 19; "Rozelle Looks to Europe," *The New York Times* (21 March 1989), B13; Gerald Eskenazi, "Global N.F.L. Game Plan: Springtime Play Overseas," *The New York Times* (20 July 1989), A1; "1990 Opener is a Global Enterprise," *The New York Times* (2 August 1990), B11; Ferdinand Protzman, "N.F.L. a Big Hit in West Germany," *The New York Times* (12 August 1990), 29. For the WLAF's history, see "World Football League Quick History," at <http://wflfootball. tripod.com> cited 6 October 2003; "WFL Europe," at <http://www.wfl.com> cited 13 October 2003; "World League Renamed NFL Europe," at <http://www.nfl.com> cited 11 March 1998. In sum, the final three articles discuss such topics as why and how the WLAF formed, the financial contributions of the league's investors, specific owner's interests in professional football, cities which were granted franchises and those teams that failed, the recruitment of coaches and players, and reasons for the league's collapse. As described by one sportswriter, "After a brief period of success, chronically poor attendance financially crippled most teams. Dogged with the reputation of being filled with NFL has-beens, castaways, and problem-children, the WLAF failed to garner consistent fan support in the United States." See Ariel Simon, "Touchdown!" *Harvard International Review* (Winter 2001), 12–13.

3. Since 1950, the NFL has scheduled exhibition and preseason games outside the U.S. The dates, sites, opponents and scores are reported in "NFL International Historical Results," at <http://ww2.nfl.com> cited 25 November 2002. For selected games and season attendances between 1950 and 2001, see the *NFL 2001 Record & Fact Book*, 281–289. As an aside, on page 369 of the *Fact Book* are the dates, sites, teams and scores of 52 international games. Indeed, the majority of those listed are American Bowl games.

4. For a breakdown on how each team had performed in the American Bowl series, see "American Bowl Results (1986–2000)," at <http://www.tinfl.com> cited 9 October 2003; "American Bowl Series," at <http://www.nfl.com> cited 9 October 2003; "NFL International Historical Results."

5. See various pages of the "World Football League Quick History" and "WFL Europe," and pages 286–287 of the *NFL 2001 Record & Fact Book*.

6. For the NFLE teams and seasons, and the results of the World Bowls see "National Football League Europe," at <http://www.nfleurope.com> cited 13 October 2003. Some World Bowl results are also mentioned in the *NFL 2001 Record & Fact Book*, 287–289. For the teams' players, the NFLE relies on the NFL. To illustrate, during early 2004 the NFL listed 229 players, including 18 quarterbacks that would be transferred to NFLE teams. When quarterback Chad Hutchinson was assigned to the NFLE, the Dallas Cowboys' coach Bill Parcells commented about Hutchinson's assignment. "He is going to play over there. Now, quite frankly, it's been my experience if a guy goes over to Europe and he can't play over there, he is going to have a hard time playing over here." See "QB Hutchinson Among 229 NFL Europe Invitees," at <http://sportsillustrated.cnn.com> cited 10 February 2004.

7. See "N.F.L. Europe Loses $20 Million," at <http://www.sportsbusinessnews.com> cited 3 December 2002; Franz Lidz, "Achtung! Football Does a Flip-Flop," *Sports Illustrated* (24 June 2002), 56–57; Ariel Simon, "Touchdown!" With respect to the NFLE's presence overseas, Simon made the following statement. That is, "Whether American football will attain the type of global popularity enjoyed by baseball and soccer remains to seen. Nonetheless, its success in Europe should not be overlooked. The league's continued survival is a salient reminder that globalization is not only opening trade barriers, increasing

political interdependence, and encouraging democratization, it also involves the extension of local cultures into new international arenas."

8. Because of NFLE team attendance problems since the middle of the 1990s, rumors have circulated that some NFL owners want to terminate the league's six-team experiment in international relations. According to NFL International managing director Doug Quinn, "This is the first time, I think, that a lot of owners really took a hard look at the business. We have a commitment to move forward, which is very gratifying. Now we need to work on improving the structure and business model of NFL Europe. For more insights on how the owners and NFL Commissioner Paul Tagliabue have evaluated the NFLE's long-term prospects, see Eric Fisher, "NFL Owners Will Keep NFL Europe Alive," at <http://www.sportsbusinessnews.com> cited 18 September 2003; Ivan Carter, "Is the End Near For NFL Europe?" at <http://www.sportsbusinessnews.com> cited 19 September 2003; Scott Miller, "Paul Tagliabue on the Importance of the NFL in Europe," at <http://www.sportsbusinessnews.com> cited 25 November 2002; Leonard Shapiro, "The Commish (Paul Tagliabue) on NFL Europe," at <http://www.sportsbusinessnews.com> cited 3 December 2002.

9. Since the late 1990s, the NFL has successfully increased its efforts to establish media partnerships and broadcast its regular season and playoff games, and Super Bowls across the globe. Some results are reported in "NFL Expanding Their Broadcast Horizons," at <http://www.sportsbusinessnews.com> cited 4 September 2003; Steve Donohue, "Rebranding Key to NFL Europe," *Electronic Media* (23 March 1998), 36; "NFL Experience Gears Up For New Season of Fun," at <http://www.nfleurope.com> cited 12 October 2003; "NFL Experience Rolls on Through Europe," at <http://www.nfleurope.com> 12 October 2003; Erin White, "Is Europe Ready For Some Football?" *Wall Street Journal* (15 January 2003), B4; Stefan Fatsis, "Can New $220 Million NFL Deal Appease Restive Owners?" *Wall Street Journal* (16 December 2003), B1, B11. Besides those reports, there is a list of networks in each country or territory that broadcasted NFL programs. To identify the NFL's international programming during 2003, and the league's agreements with sports channels in China and Japan, see "NFL Coverage Spans the Globe—Agreements Bring Football to Japan, China," at <http://www.nfl.com> cited 4 December 2003. The article contains an alphabetical list of the broadcast networks in each country or territory or from Afghanistan to Zimbabwe.

10. See *NFL International* (New York, N.Y.: National Football League, 2002); "NFL International is a Success," at <http://ww2.nfl.com> cited 25 November 2002; "NFL International Signs Outside Licensing Deal," at <http://ww2.nfl.com> cited 25 November 2002; Don Garber, "NFL Sets Up Unit to Plot Overseas Pitch," *Brandweek* (14 October 1996), 14.

11. For the purposes, activities and programs of the NFL's international organizational unit, which is the NFLI, see various editions of the media guide, *NFL International*. Besides an Overview, this publication includes information about the NFLI's Vision, Media, Development and Partnerships, and about its offices in Canada, Mexico, Japan and Europe.

12. Paul Rusch, the American Bowl series and Japan's X-League are discussed in Ken Belson, "NFL Continues to Market Itself in Japan, " at <http://www.sportsbusinessnews.com> cited 19 August 2003. Specifically, Belson describes how the league promotes football through licensing agreements and television contracts, and with grassroots activities like teaching flag football. Accordingly, sports management is a new field in Japan and most teams are run by executives who are more interested in placing their logos on uniforms than finding good players to wear those uniforms. That is, players are treated as employees rather than football specialists. Besides, it was during 2003 that football was played on the high school, college and industrial levels in Japan. For how Japanese players qualify as professional football players, see Kit Stier, "Jets Hope to Break Into Japanese Market," at <http:

//www.sportsbusinessnews.com> cited 19 August 2003. Interestingly, Stier discusses the skills of two Japanese players in the NFL. Those athletes are the New York Jets' wide receiver Yoshinobu Imoto and San Francisco 49ers' linebacker Masafumi Kawaguchi.

13.   See "NFL Football Heads to Japanese TV," at <http://www.sportsbusinessnews.com> cited 25 November 2002. For an overview of the programs in Japan's NFL office, see "NFL Opens Office in Japan," at <http://ww2.nfl.com> cited 25 November 2002, and the *NFL International* booklet. In general, the league's office in Japan is designed to better service business partners such as broadcasters NHK, Gaora and SkyPerfecTV, take advantage of business opportunities and promote development activities for football fans.

14.   Besides Mr. Machida's statement, which is contained in the Japan section of the *NFL International*, the booklet provides the names, addresses and telephone numbers of such international contacts as NFL Europe, NFL Mexico, NFLI Canada and NFL Japan.

15.   Since it opened in 1997, the NFL Canada office has become the league's central organization for business operations in Canada. See Wayne Washington, "Craig Lands NFL Monday Night Football Rights," *The America's Intelligence Wire* (9 May 2003), 1; Terry Lefton and Matthew Grimm, "Labatt in Seven-Figure NFLI Deal For Budweiser North of the Border," *Brandweek* (4 January 1999), 10; William Houston, "NFL Network in the Frozen North," at <http://www.sportsbusinessnews.com> cited 19 August 2003. The contacts and specific activities of the Canada office are described in the *NFL International* booklet. Interestingly, during 2003 the AL's Toronto Blue Jay's president Paul Godfrey was involved in the organization of a digital cable television channel that would broadcast the home games of the Blue Jays, NHL Toronto Maple Leafs and NBA Toronto Raptors. According to a sports reporter, this deal might lead Godfrey to eventually bid for an NFL franchise to be located in Canada. For the benefits of this media convergence, see Dave Perkins, "Merger of Toronto Sports Properties Could Happen," at <http://www.sportsbusinessnews.com> cited 11 July 2003.

16.   In 2003, the maximum salary of CFL roster players was $150,000 while it exceeded $200,000 for entry-level NFL players. Because of the U.S.-Canadian exchange rate, during 2002 NFL players on practice rosters could earn as much as some players on CFL team rosters. As such, the Calgary Stampeders surrendered four players to the NFL. For more about this topic, see "CFL Happy With NFL Partnership," at <http://www.sportsbusinessnews.com> cited 3 December 2002. The extension of the NFL/CFL Alliance into the Spring of 2004 is discussed in "CFL Extends NFL Agreement," at <http://www.sportsbusinessnews.com> cited 4 December 2003.

17.   For some specific reasons why the CFL has experienced financial hardships and other news about the league, see David Naylor, "Canadian Football League and Debts Unpaid," at <http://www.sportsbusinessnews.com> cited 3 December 2002; Idem., "In the Canadian Football League, When a Salary Cap Isn't a Salary Cap," at <http://www.sportsbusinessnews.com> cited 3 December 2002; Sean Fitz-Gerald, "All is as Well as Can be Expected When it Comes to the Canadian Football League," at <http://www.sportsbusinessnews.com> cited 3 December 2002; "Canadian Football League Looks at Expansion," at <http://www.sportsbusinessnews.com> cited 3 December 2002. Other economic and financial aspects of the CFL are reported in "CFL Enjoying a Renaissance of Sorts," at <http://www.sportsbusinessnews.com> cited 20 November 2003, and Mark Harding, "These Are Heady Days For the Canadian Football League," at <http://www.sportsbusinessnews. com> cited 3 December 2002. Interestingly, sportswriter Harding reports on the revival of the Montreal Alouettes during the early 2000s. As stated by the president and chief executive officer of the Alouettes Ellis Prince, "Club presidents and governors now take off their team hats and put on league hats at meetings. They've realized that what they had before were nine campfires. Now, they're a proud partner in the CFL."

18. For the relocation and expansion of professional sports teams, see Frank P. Jozsa, Jr. and John J. Guthrie, Jr., *Relocating Teams and Expanding Leagues in Professional Sports: How the Major Leagues Respond to Market Conditions* (Westport, CT: Quorum Books, 1999), and Frank P. Jozsa, Jr., "An Economic Analysis of Franchise Relocation and League Expansion in Professional Team Sports, 1950–1975," Ph.D. diss., Georgia State University, 1977. The CFL's takeover of its failing teams is discussed in Sean Fitz-Gerald, "CFL Makes it Official: They Now Control Another Franchise," at <http://www.sportsbusinessnews. com> cited 19 August 2003; Jim Cressman, "London Argonauts Are a Possibility," at <http: //www.sportsbusinessnews.com> cited 19 August 2003; "Cost of Business in the CFL is Way Up!!" at <http://www.sportsbusinessnews.com> cited 26 August 2003. As such, the latter article reports on the cost structures and debts of such CFL clubs as the Hamilton Tiger-Cats, Toronto Argonauts, Calgary Stampeders, Winnipeg Blue Bombers and Saskatchewan Roughriders.

19. See Sarah Talalay, "NFL Looking to Grow Latin Fan Base," at <http://www.sportsbusinessnews.com> cited 13 November 2003; Jenalia Moreno, "NFL Boosts Mexican Economy," at <http://www.sportsbusinessnews.com> cited 19 August 2003, and Ross Atkin, "Mexico in the Super Bowl? Hmm ...," *The Christian Science Monitor* (22 January 1997), 1. For why Mexico is a primary NFL market, see Murray Chass, "Mexico is Now in Picture For Possible Expansion," *The New York Times* (10 June 1994), B17; Jenalia Moreno, "NFL Not Quite Ready For That Mexican—Cowboys/Texans Pre-Season Game," at <http://www. sportsbusinessnews.com> cited 25 November 2002; "Super Bowl to Focus on Hispanic Market," at <http://www.sportsbusinessnews.com> cited 30 October 2003. During the week of Super Bowl XXXVIII in Houston, Texas, the NFL sponsored Latino Day and Kids Workshop, which were programs aimed at the Hispanic population in the Houston area. For more information about the programs, see page 30 of the *Super Bowl XXXVIII Game Program* (Houston, TX: National Football League, 2004). The NFL's recent plans with respect to marketing football in America's southwestern and western States and in Mexico are reported in Sam Walker, "Adios, NFL!" *Wall Street Journal* (5 December 2003), W4; Idem., "The (Non) Internationalization of the NFL," at <http://www.sportsbusinessnews. com> cited 11 December 2003; "NFL and Hispanic Fans," at <http://www.sportsbusinessnews.com> cited 3 February 2004. As mentioned in the latter article, the NFL plans to boost sales to Hispanic consumers, in part, by offering 220 games each year on Hughes Electronics' DirecTV Latin American LLC and sponsoring conferences for young Hispanic entrepreneurs. Furthermore, during the 2003–2004 regular season the NFL sold tee shirts with Spanish language phrases and held a Hispanic summit in Houston, Texas. Regarding the league's marketing programs, the chief executive of Latin Force David Perez said, "If you're ignoring these [women and foreigners] populations, you're ignoring your current and future fan base." For the NFL's broadcasts and promotions, and the league's average number of viewers per game during 1995–2002, see Stefan Fatsis, "Salaries, Promos and Flying Solo," *Wall Street Journal* (9 February 2004), R4, R10.

20. The *NFL International* highlights the activities of the NFL Mexican office, which was established in 1998. This office is also discussed in "Scoring Drive," *Business Mexico* (October 1998), 12–15, and Brendan M. Case, "The NFL Heads to Mexico City," at <http: //www.sportsbusinessnews.com> cited 3 December 2002. For other partnerships and sponsorships, see "Visa International Becomes the Official and Preferred Payment Card," *PR Newswire* (22 October 1998), 1, and "Visa, NFL Join in Deal For Foreign Marketing," *American Banker* (16 November 1998), 1.

21. The NFL team rosters are listed at the nfl.com web site. Furthermore, see Jim Carley, "Hispanic Players in the NFL," at <http://www.sportsbusinessnews.com> cited 19 August

2003. In his article, Carley provides comments from such Hispanic football players as Tampa Bay Buccaneers' kicker Martin Gramatica, Carolina Panthers' wide receiver Marco Martos, and Houston Texans' linebacker Antonio Rodriguez, who played for the NFLE's Barcelona Dragons during 2003. After his seasons at Mexico's Monterrey Tech, Rodriguez denoted that, "It's definitely a different level of football here [in the U.S.]. It's much more intense. One of the most difficult things for me is the defenses are so complicated." See also "Foreign-Born Players in the NFL," at <http://ww2.nfl.com> cited 25 November 2002.

22.   The football environment in Mexico and ceremony are briefly described in "Mexican-American Football HOF Makes Presentation in Canton," at <http://www.profootballhof. com> cited 6 August 2003, and Brendan M. Case, "The NFL Heads to Mexico City."

23.   NFL Mexico general director Will Wilson's quote was extracted from the *NFL International* booklet, which has unnumbered pages. Furthermore, in Barry Janoff, "The NFL Heads to Mexico to Market the League," at <http://www.sportsbusinessnews.com> cited 25 November 2002, Wilson says, "Mexico is one of the NFL's most important areas outside of the United States. An average of 3 million fans watch NFL games on Mexican TV per week, a relationship that started more than 30 years ago."

24.   See "American Bowl Results (1986–2000)," *NFL 2001 Record & Fact Book*, 278–289 and "NFL International Historical Results."

25.   This marketing effort introduced the NFL's star players to fans in the United Kingdom. For more about the campaign, see Daniel Thomas, "American Football to Launch $5m UK Push," *Marketing Week* (15 May 2003), 10. As an aside, to evaluate the social aspects of women's football the promoters should read Jayne Caudwell, "Women's Football in the United Kingdom: Theorizing Gender and Unpacking the Butch Lesbian Image," *Journal of Sport and Social Issues*, Vol. 23, No. 4 (1999), 399–402.

26.   For flag football action during the Summer of 2003, see "British Youngsters Battle," at <http://www.nfleurope.com> cited 13 July 2003, and "Flag Qualifying Tournaments Begin," at <http://www.nfleurope.com> cited 12 October 2003. Flag football is the NFL's core international grassroots program. It helps kids and teenagers learn the basics of American football. During 2003, there were an estimated 1,000,000 boys and girls located in 20 countries around the world who had participated in flag football games and championship tournaments. Those nations included, for example, Australia, Austria, Denmark, Israel, Korea, New Zealand and Thailand.

27.   See "NFL Finalizes Deal With F.C. Barcelona," at <http://ww2.nfl.com> cited 3 December 2002, and George Solomon, "FC Barcelona (Football Club) and the NFL Team Up," at <http://www.sportsbusinessnews.com> cited 3 December 2002. Relative to the agreement, NFL commissioner Paul Tagliabue said, "We are excited about this new association with F.C. Barcelona, which we believe is a ground-breaking moment for sport in Europe and the United States. It is the first time that the two strongest, most popular sports in their respective continents have joined forces." As an aside, during 2000 FC Barcelona was ranked as the eighth wealthiest soccer club in the world with revenues of $113.8 million.

28.   Alistar Kirkwood's statement appeared in the *NFL International* booklet and Commissioner Tagliabue's in the article by George Solmon, "FC Barcelona (Football Club) and the NFL Team Up."

29.   Ibid. For some interesting facts about the fundamentals of American Football, see "Beginner's Guide to Football," at <http://www.nfleurope.com> cited 9 October 2003. This document includes such basic information as football's end zone, field dimensions, kickoff, first down, moving the ball, the pass and tackle, scoring, touchdown, extra point and two-point conversion, field goal, safety, turnovers, fumble, interception, two sides of the ball, offense, and the assignments of offensive and defensive players.

30.   To learn about China's interest in American football and NFL games, and the NFL's plans for China, see Frederick C. Klein, "On Sports: Gridiron Broadcasts Behind the Great Wall," *Wall Street Journal* (20 January 1987), 1; Curtis Eichelberger, "NFL Considering Heading to China For Pre-Season Games," at <http://www.sportsbusinessnews.com> cited 2 January 2003; "NFL Looks to China as Next Stop," *The Los Angeles Times* (1 January 2003), D4; Thomas Heath, "NFL Has Ambitions For China," *The Washington Post* (1 August 2002), D1. About the publicity from a preseason football game played in Osaka during August of 2002, NFL International managing director Doug Quinn commented, "The big payout is people buy into the NFL brand and watch NFL football. They want to watch their Japanese players. We want to get Japanese players on U.S. NFL teams." The University of California's Marshall School of Business professor David M. Carter agrees with Quinn. Carter said, "Player development is huge. The NFL is taking a page out of the NBA playbook. The number of imports form the NBA helps generated fan interest in foreign countries. Basketball has a head start." It appears, therefore, that the opportunities for football players from China and other countries to perform in the NFL improved during early 2004 when the league evaluated a rule such that each team would add one spot to its practice squad, which would be reserved for a foreign player. About that rule, the Atlanta Falcons' general manager Rich McKay stated, "The main question is whether it's implemented this year or next year. It's a matter of taking a look at it and seeing how many international players are really ready to play." See Mark Maske, "NFL Opening Their Doors to Foreign Players," at <http://www.sportsbusinessnews.com> cited 11 March 2004.

31.   The GJC games and tournaments were reported in "Stars of GJC VII Sign National Letters of Intent," at <http://www.nfleurope.com> cited 9 October 2003, and "History of the Global Junior Championships 1997–2002," at <http://www.nfleurope.com> cited 12 October 2003. During Super Bowl XXXVIII week in Houston, Texas, the NFL Global Junior Championship VIII was held between football teams from America and those from Canada, Japan, Mexico and Russia. See "NFL Global Junior Championship," *Super Bowl XXXVIII Game Program* (2004), 28.

32.   For more game results of the Flag Football World Championships, see "Girl Power," at <http://www.nfleurope.com> cited 9 October 2003; "Mexico Crowned Flag Football Champs," at <http://www.nfleurope.com> cited 12 October 2003; "Flag Qualifying Tournaments Begin," at <http://www.nfleurope.com> cited 12 October 2003; "USA World Champions," at <http://www.nfleurope.com> cited 12 October 2003; "NFL Flag Football," *Super Bowl XXXVIII Game Program* (2004), 157.

33.   Ibid. Furthermore, during 2003 there were flag football in-season games and a city final tournament played in Shanghai, China. For a brief description of the football clinics and television coverage of 'Warriors Crown,' which is China's national football tournament, see "China Holds First NFL Flag Football Clinic," at <http://www.nfl.com> cited 4 December 2003.

34.   The information about the EJC games, players and tournaments appeared in "European Junior Championship Lineups Unveiled," at <http://www.nfleurope.com> cited 12 October 2003; "EJC Qualification Begins," at <http://www.nfleurope.com> cited 12 October 2003; "Russia Are Champions," at <http://www.nfleurope.com> cited 9 October 2003; "Russians Keen to Prove Worth," at <http://www.nfleurope.com> cited 13 October 2003.

35.   For the EAF programs and other amateur football news, see "Coaches Clinic," at <http://www.nfleurope.com> cited 9 October 2003, and "Flag and Tackle Summer Camps Announced," at <http://www.nfleurope.com> cited 12 October 2003.

36.   See "Summer Lovin' For Youngsters," at <http://www.nfleurope.com> cited 12 October 2003. According to the former Scottish Claymores' wide receiver Scott Couper, who scored ten touchdowns and totaled 1,000 yards in a seven-year career, "If young aspiring

players want to know what it takes to get on the right track to play at the highest level, then this is an ideal introduction. They [players] will realize that physically and mentally you have to condition yourself to deal with the rigours of a demanding training camp, but the main thing is they will leave with more knowledge and ways to improve their game."

37.   Since 2000, the NFL Experience's activities in Europe have increased in popularity. To read about the interactive theme park, see "Berlin Welcomes YOU and the NFLX," at <http://www.nfleurope.com> cited 9 October 2003; "NFL Experience Rolls on Through Europe;" "NFL Experience Gears Up For New Season of Fun." Besides Europe, this program also was presented in Houston, Texas during Super Bowl XXXVIII week. At that event, the NFL Experience served to supplement and expand opportunities for fans to enjoy all the sights, sounds, and thrills of the Super Bowl. See "The NFL Experience," *Super Bowl XXXVIII Game Program*, 30.

38.   During early 2004, three media guides and a cover letter and promo video were received from the NWFA's vice president Debby Lening. Thus, the information about the league that was discussed in Chapter 2 was extracted from the *2002 SupHer Bowl* (Pittsburgh, PA: National Women's Football League, 2002); *2003 Championship* (Nashville, TN: National Women's Football Association, 2003); *2004 Media Guide* (Nashville, TN: National Women's Football Association, 2004). To read more about the NWFA, see Hillary Johnson, "Just Give Us the Damn Ball," *The New York Times* (22 October 2000), 80–88; Monique Walker, "A Powerful Draw," *Pensacola News Journal* (26 May 2001), 1D–5D; JoAnne Klimovich Harrop, "SupHer Bowl Puts on Good Show," *Pittsburgh Tribune-Review* (28 July 2002), C1; Carrie Ferguson, "Founder and CEO of a Dream," at <http://www.tennessean.com> cited 9 June 2003; James T. Black, "Nashville's Dream Team," *Southern Living Magazine* (August 2001), 64, 66–69.

39.   In March of 2004, the Cincinnati Sizzle, LLC was awarded a team license in order to join the NWFA for the 2005 season. The club is owned and operated by Ickey Woods, who was a running back for the NFL Cincinnati Bengals, and Ickey's wife Chandra. Regarding the team's preparation for the 2005 season, Ickey denotes that, "Our ladies are itching to play. We are going to get them suited up and use the exhibition games this season to get them prepared for next year." About the Sizzle's competitiveness, NWFA president Catherine Masters states, "When we held the tryouts in Cincinnati, every single woman that participated seemed to be a top notch athlete so we expect great things from this team." Those comments were reported in "Women's Football League Getting Ready to do the Ickey Shuffle," at <http://www.sportsbusinessnews.com> cited 23 March 2004. Besides the growing popularity of and interest in the NWFA, the 20-team Women's Professional Football League (WPFL) scheduled its sixth season in the summer of 2004. The teams in the U.S.-based WPFL each compete in ten games per season and players earn $1 per game plus a portion of the gate proceeds. Some athletes such as the WPFL's executive director Beth Markell are enthusiastic about the opportunity to play professional football. She said, "They would pat me on the head, thinking that I was a dreamer with no understanding of the real adult world. Playing football means that now, when a 10-year-old girl says to me, 'I want to play professional football when I grow up,' I am living proof that she can be whatever she wants to be." See Marshall Lubin, "Women's Professional Football Hits Long Island," at <http://www.sportsbusinessnews.com> cited 13 April 2004.

Chapter 3

National Basketball Association

Since the early 1920s, several independent, professional basketball leagues have existed for one or more years in America. If the Women's National Basketball Association (WNBA), various professional developmental leagues and the National Basketball Association are excluded, the destinies of the nation's other professional basketball leagues are briefly summarized next in chronological order. Formed in 1925, the American Basketball League had to restructure and became a regional organization after the completion of its regular season in 1931. Then, the National Basketball League (NBA) was organized in 1937. Eleven years later, however, the NBA absorbed it while the Basketball Association of America, after three seasons, evolved to become the NBA in 1949. Established for one season, the Continental League dissolved in 1961 and in 1975, the American Basketball Association (ABA) terminated its operations after nine seasons and four of the ABA's most successful teams—Denver Nuggets, Indiana Pacers, New Jersey Nets and San Antonio Spurs—were admitted to and joined the NBA. Finally, because of illegal business practices conducted by its co-founders, the World Basketball League lasted three years and then folded in 1992. In short, despite the occasional entry of competitive leagues, the NBA has survived to gradually become the dominant professional basketball organization in the U.S. and according to some sports experts, is the most prominent sports entertainment group in the world.[1]

Between the late 1940s and early 1980s, the various NBA Commissioners and the league's numerous team owners had primarily concentrated their marketing efforts and financial investments into the development and growth of professional basketball in the North American market. After that 35 year period, however, NBA Commissioner David Stern began an international campaign to energize and transform his organization and thus expand the league's brand, image, exposure and market power into nations across the globe. In part, because of Stern's leadership, perseverance and vision, and the convergence of cultural trends, economic factors and business opportunities within and between various countries and continents, basketball gradually became a popular international sport that has auspiciously propelled the NBA into the 21st century.

The theme, purpose and scope of Chapter 3 is to analyze why, when, where and how the NBA has achieved its phenomenal international presence and success, especially since the middle to late 1980s when Commissioner had initiated his marketing plan. To provide an analysis, the chapter is divided into five key parts or sections with each depicting the league as reputedly the world's most recognized and well-known professional sports organization. Indeed, the research performed for *Sport Capitalism* indicates that the NBA's global ambition and its worldwide activities, events, interests relationships and trends are collectively represented as business strategies in Chapter 3's content. Therefore, those topics and other matters are highlighted and reflected in this portion of the book and briefly summarized as follows.

In the first part, the league's international strategies are identified and discussed based on two relatively recent time periods. Because of how events occurred, those periods were from the middle to late 1980s to the middle 1990s, and then from the middle 1990s to the early 2000s. About midway between those two periods, Commissioner Stern and the NBA's franchise owners had evaluated their organization's status and progress, and as a result, decided to expand the number of teams in the league. Thus, when the two clubs joined the NBA one was placed in the City of Toronto, Canada and the other in Vancouver, Canada. Accordingly, those expansions are portrayed as business strategies and then examined early in Chapter 3. Furthermore, the league's global strategies have included various agreements with licensees, partners, sponsors and vendors that obligated numerous U.S. and foreign private sector companies to promote the NBA brand and products in their advertisements, promotions and sales campaigns. Consequently, this part of the chapter also provides some facts and reasons about how those companies were mutually involved with and supported the worldwide business strategies of the league.

For the chapter's second part, the NBA officials' decision to aggressively expand the league's international presence by establishing more fan bases and thereby further penetrating selected nations' sports markets is discussed in this section of Chapter 3. These results were realized, in part, when and after the NBA had increasingly scheduled teams' exhibition, preseason and regular season games abroad. The league, furthermore, signed contracts as it linked its operations with various U.S. and foreign cable and satellite systems and television channels and networks, which committed those organizations to broadcast the professional basketball teams' regular season games, and the playoffs and championship series in cities and remote regions of countries throughout the world. Undoubtedly, this strategy had created lucrative business opportunities for the NBA to successfully promote and sell its teams' apparel, equipment and merchandise, and for affiliated companies to market and distribute basketball shoes, jerseys and other products to sports fans everywhere.

As depicted in section three of this chapter, it has been the responsibility of the league's teams to discover, scout, recruit, draft and employ the most skilled amateur and professional basketball players in the world. Given those tasks, increasing portions of the athletes are natives of and live in various foreign countries. Accordingly, the import of international basketball players is a relevant issue that reflects the globalization of the sport and the NBA. Therefore, the content in this portion of Chapter 3 examines why many athletes from other countries, and especially from eastern and western European nations have been particularly proficient performers for various NBA teams at the guard, forward and center positions. Interestingly, this result occurred even though foreign players' basketball court savvy, skills, training practices and experiences were not necessarily compatible with or complementary to the traits, styles and personalities of many NBA athletes from America. Besides those issues, Chapter 3's third section also discusses the entry, exposure and marketing of Chinese player Yao Ming, and his economic impact on the Houston Rockets franchise, and on the league's U.S. and international commerce and the growth of that business.

After an analysis of the league's foreign players including Yao Ming, the fourth component of Chapter 3 appears. That is, this section describes the sport of basketball and, as appropriate, the NBA's presence and market strength in various European countries, and in China, Mexico and Africa. This information explicitly indicates why the sport of basketball and the U.S.-based league are increasingly admired and respected by millions of international fans that, for generations, have rooted for cricket, ice hockey, rugby and soccer clubs, and for teams in leagues of other sports. Because of the NBA's worldwide marketing, promotion and exposure, this portion of the chapter also displays a table that lists the populations of five medium to large foreign cities and areas of those cities that, during the early to middle 2000s, might be considered and possibly selected as home sites for existing NBA teams and/or expansion franchises. Relative to that decision, the reasons are given for why the league's owners would choose one or more of those sites as future locations.

The fifth and final part of Chapter 3 discusses, in part, the number and presence of international athletes who have performed for teams in the WNBA. Moreover, this part highlights the achievements and contribution of a few outstanding foreign-born players. To some extent, those facts and statistics denote the role and status with respect to how women's professional basketball and the WNBA have progressed in America. When the fifth section ends, there is a Summary of the contents and then the Notes, which will conclude Chapter 3.

International Strategies

By the late 1970s, the NBA had become a tattered, dispirited and risky sports organization and business. That circumstance happened because several of the league's franchises experienced below average attendances in their home arenas and thus operating deficits. Furthermore, numerous players on teams reputedly consumed such illegal drugs as marijuana, cocaine and heroin, the television ratings of regular season professional basketball games on sports networks ranged from disappointing to deplorable, and there was an acrimonious relationship between the league's commissioner and team owners, and the National Basketball Players Association (NBPA), which is the union that represents the league's players. Despite those troubles, during the early to middle 1980s a former University of North Carolina All-American basketball player named Michael Jordan had entered the league. Meanwhile, the NBA's Commissioner David Stern had begun to cleverly apply his enormous managerial talents and well-designed marketing policies to confront and partially resolve the most serious of the aforementioned issues and problems. Then, during 1988–1989 Stern and the league's team owners evaluated and approved the entry of four new franchises, which would be located in the U.S. In short, those actions by the league's officials and a robust American economy inspired the NBA to promptly move forward and further implement its international strategies. When this occurred, the league's global progress was immediate, profound and profitable, especially from a short-term business perspective.[2]

To illustrate those affects, by 1990 approximately 200 million households in foreign countries had tuned in and watched regular season NBA games on television. Furthermore, the league's merchandise appeared for sale to innumerable consumers in 40 nations, and at least 100 former NBA players had performed for foreign teams that competed in 12 or more European countries. Finally, the media's statistics denoted that professional basketball games had become an enjoyable entertainment attraction to millions of fans who lived in such diverse countries as Australia, Israel, the Soviet Union and Zimbabwe. As the sport became increasingly popular among athletes who played it in those and other nations, several competitive and well-known retail food, industrial and service firms negotiated, obtained licenses from and established marketing partnerships with the NBA. In turn, these alliances improved the firms' international exposure and likely their sales revenues, profits and market shares. Those companies, in part, consisted of such shoe manufacturers as Converse, Nike and Reebok, plus apparel and basketball producer Spalding, and also McDonald's, which is a fast food giant, and American Airlines, a transportation corporation and Lipton, a tea company. Besides the producers of those specific products and services, in Italy, Spain and Japan for example, there were various publishers that devoted their magazines' contents to the performances and news about local, national and international amateur and professional basketball leagues, teams, players, games and other events of the sport. In short, this worldwide brand exposure and contract activity meant that, before the early 1990s, the NBA had surpassed the global developments and business expansions as experienced by the other U.S.-based professional sports leagues.[3]

Because of the job losses from the U.S. economic recession and the limited seat capacities of various U.S. professional basketball arenas, during the early 1990s the league and some of its teams had incurred an alarming and unexpected drop-off in attendances. To offset that decline and corresponding cash flow deficiency, the NBA and several franchise owners tried to exploit other and perhaps new sources of revenue. That is, more money flowed in from the sale of basketball paraphernalia and children's merchandise at retail outlets, installation and lease of professional seat licenses, club seats, skyboxes and luxury suites in arenas, higher food, clothing, merchandise and ticket prices at games, and an increase in teams' product sales from the league's expenditures on newspaper, radio and television advertisements, and promotions. With the respective franchise owners' approval, many NBA clubs had decided to implement one or more of those business incentives and/or marketing tactics. For even more incremental revenues, during 1992–1994 the league established a new concept shop in Melbourne, Australia and also liberally issued licenses and permits to local vendors who had experiences in selling clothing, equipment and merchandise in selected Asian and Latin American countries and communities. Although those projects had successfully boosted the league's and most of the teams' cash flows in the short-term, Commissioner Stern and the NBA owners concluded that the global expansion of franchises, as a strategy, would be a promising long-term solution to any revenue shortfalls for the league. Alternatively, perhaps the league's decision makers had studied MLB's entry into Montreal, Canada in 1969 and Toronto, Canada in 1977, and/or felt pressure by the threat of NFL and National Hockey League club relocations and league expansions, to be sufficient reasons for placing NBA teams beyond the U.S. border. Anyway, in the middle of the 1990s the league boldly implemented its decision to increase membership via expansion.[4]

After the NBA had announced to the U.S. and foreign media that two new franchises would be awarded to compete in their respective divisions and conferences in time to start the 1995–1996 season, and that each franchise would be located outside America's boundaries, there were several corporations, single investors and syndicates that had each prepared and submitted business plans and offered more than $100 million to acquire the rights to the franchises. After a thorough evaluation of the plans and bids that were received from companies, individual investors and other prospective ownership groups, the league's existing team owners unanimously approved the respective pro forma financial statements and managerial strategies of two franchisees and then reached an agreement with them. One new owner was selected to place an NBA club in Toronto to be nick-named the Raptors and the other in Vancouver to be titled the Grizzlies. Thereupon, those clubs began their regular season game schedules in the Fall of 1995.

During the franchise's first four seasons in Vancouver, the Grizzles underperformed against NBA opponents on the basketball court. When the team won only 23 percent of its regular season games at the 20,000-seat General Motors Place arena, the hometown basketball fans became critical about the coaches' efforts and apathetic about the players' teamwork, which caused the Grizzlies' home attendance to rank well below the league average. As a result of indifference and the lack of support from local fans, the team's players gradually became demoralized and the club renegotiated only a few sponsorship deals with the local business community and other organizations in the Vancouver metropolitan area. After two ownership changes, it was apparent by the late 1990s that the Canadian-based franchise had incurred immense operating losses and likely deteriorated by millions of dollars in market value. Because of those circumstances, the club needed to extensively revise its player roster and search for a new home site in North America. Subsequently, during early 2001 the Grizzlies' owner Michael Heisley appealed to the NBA Board of Governors to unanimously support his proposal for the relocation of the franchise out of Vancouver. After the Board approved his request, in the Summer of 2001 Heisley moved the team from Vancouver to Memphis in the State of Tennessee.[5]

In the early 2000s, Memphis, which was named after an Egyptian city and recognized for Beale Street and the home of the 'blues' music, was ranked in population as a medium sized southern port city where Elvis Presley's 14-acre

Graceland Mansion is located. More significantly, Memphis is the site of a 32-story, 20,000-seat stadium named the Pyramid Arena. The Arena, which is a publicly financed entertainment facility, has been promoted to tourists as the world's third largest pyramid. As a financial gift to the Grizzlies, Memphis' taxpayers agreed to finance the Arena's renovation costs while the Federal Express Inc. spent millions of dollars to acquire and retain the Arena's naming rights. Essentially, the relocation from Vancouver to Memphis was completed to improve the team's long-term performance and reduce its operating deficits and debts. As an aside, during the 2002–2003 regular season the Grizzlies best player was Pau Gasol, a tall, rangy Spaniard who won the NBA Rookie of the Year award for his performances as a forward on offense and defense.[6]

During the late 1990s and early 2000s, the NBA continued its marketing campaign to actively promote and sell the sport of professional basketball to sports fans throughout the U.S. and in numerous foreign countries. One aspect of the league's campaign was to strategically expand its business relationships by signing short- and long-term agreements with more corporate sponsors and partners from the media and technology industries. In 2000, for example, the league and Internet search company Yahoo! Inc. signed a multiyear, integrated contract that included content distribution, commerce and communication initiatives. Indeed, this complex deal involved several communication and sport activities. First, it meant that each day Yahoo! Sports provided sportscasters with the video highlights of teams, player statistics in real time and various audio live game and on-demand broadcasts. Second, Yahoo! Broadcast committed to forward original NBA web-based shows, press conferences and events to the print media and television networks. Third, Yahoo! Auctions had to establish itself as a primary source for league-sanctioned, online auctions that would attract sports fans and retail companies on a global basis. Fourth, Yahoo! Shopping was assigned to develop an international front for the NBA Store on NBA.com, which is regarded as the Internet's most prominent and comprehensive online basketball store. Fifth, Yahoo! Geocities was obligated to supply users with the information to access the league's contents, logos and markets, which assisted professional basketball fans to develop their own personal web sites based on the NBA or their favorite teams.[7]

Besides the league's innovative agreement with Yahoo! Inc., in 2002 the NBA extended its four-year global marketing partnership with U.S. beer manufacturer and distributor Anheuser-Busch and its 18-year relationship with the Gatorade Company. With respect to the former alliance, it was the advertising staff at Anheuser-Busch's Budweiser, which is the world's top ranked beer, who agreed to promote the NBA's games that were broadcast on the Spanish television station Telemundo, and also to subsidize the costs of scheduling adult basketball programs in various cities within Mexico and Spain. Relative to the league's other partner, the Gatorade Company had to expand its commitment with the league overseas, that is, to create NBA-themed advertising and establish other marketing programs, promote NBA exhibition and preseason games, support basketball grassroots activities, and develop NBA-themed premium and merchandising retail events. Based on Gatorade's partnership with the NBA, PepsiCo Beverages' International vice-president David Knight commented, "With . . . the league [NBA] becoming increasingly popular among fans around the globe, it was a natural for us to do more with the NBA overseas."[8]

By late 2003, NBA Commissioner David Stern had committed to and/or encouraged the completion of several international projects that involved the league. The projects' overall purpose was to motivate consumers, especially those sports fans that lived in foreign countries, to spend their disposable incomes on the NBA's products and services. Some of the key projects included the construction of a modern NBA City theme restaurant in the Dominican Republic, freestanding retail stores in Asia and Europe, and boutiques in large department stores such as the El Corte Ingles in Spain. As a result of establishing those and other businesses abroad, the league certainly expected to inflate its nearly $500 million in cash inflows from international markets for the sales of food, merchandise, player posters, school supplies, and assorted basketball clothing such as hats, jackets, shoes, socks, team jerseys and pants.[9]

Based on the discussion of the topics thus far in Chapter 3, between the early to middle 1980s to the early 2000s the plan and thus essential elements of the league's strategy to become an international organization were based on creative advertisements, promotions and other types of marketing campaigns overseas, the placement of one each expansion team in the Canadian cities of Toronto and Vancouver, renegotiation and implementation of agreements with global partners, sponsors, vendors and distributors, and the construction of new retail stores and specialty shops abroad. Indeed, the NBA successfully applied one or more of those elements in several nations.

Nonetheless, the league had met the foreign demand for professional basketball, in part, with commitments from affiliates to ensure that the NBA's regular season games, annual playoffs and championship series were globally broadcast on cable and satellite communication systems and television and radio networks. Furthermore, the league had scheduled several NBA teams to play exhibition and preseason games at sites in foreign countries. Those topics are to be discussed next, followed by why, when and how foreign basketball players were scouted, recruited, trained, drafted and hired to perform for various teams in the U.S.-based professional league.

Global NBA Broadcasts

During the late 1980s to early 1990s, some historical forces and events had affected the global sports industry and America's professional leagues, which included the NBA. That is, communist totalitarianism collapsed in the Soviet Union, free market economies evolved in many nations, hundreds of American consumer companies expanded into international markets because of globalization, and new cable and satellite systems and television networks emerged and supplied their broadcast services throughout the world. After the U.S. men's Dream Team, which was a basketball group led by the NBA Chicago Bulls' shooting guard Michael

Jordan and other superstars, had won gold medals at the 1992 Summer Olympic Games in Barcelona, professional basketball suddenly became a more popular and admirable sport for consumers in markets across the globe. Thus, the previous economic, social and/or political facts, and the Olympic Games' experience and exposure of Jordan and the Dream Team, revealed to the world that American basketball games and tournaments and NBA events had an immense and unexploited international fan base. In short, it was the sport, and the league and many of its players that strongly appealed to millions of passionate and die-hard fans everywhere.

When the Toronto Raptors and Vancouver Grizzlies began their regular season of play in 1995, a package of televised NBA games that included the All-Star Game and Final Championship tournament appeared on the Total Sports Network (TSN), which then was the only Canadian cable channel to broadcast professional basketball games. The excitement generated from those games stimulated basketball fans' interest in other league programs such as the NBA Action and Inside Stuff. Therefore, by the late 1990s it was Jordan's fabulous skills and the Chicago Bulls' six championships that were factors, which significantly had expanded the NBA into markets on cable, satellite, and television sports networks, particularly in such nations as Argentina, France, Greece, Italy, Mongolia, Namibia and Spain. According to a global survey presented to sports fans during the early 2000s, basketball had ranked ahead of soccer as the most popular sport of teenagers. This success prompted McDonald's Corporation senior vice president for worldwide marketing to acknowledge that "[NBA Commissioner] David Stern is certainly the best brand manager in sports—and he's one of the best brand managers in any business today."[10]

In 2002, most of the NBA teams' 82 regular season games were broadcast in 42 languages to basketball addicts and other sports fans in 212 countries. To reach that vast audience of viewers and thereby generate abundant hours of international programming, the league had prudently signed a number of binding contracts with 148 different broadcast networks. Despite the wide differences in economic, political and religious ideologies and values between Americans and the majority of people in foreign countries, eventually NBA games even appeared on household television sets in such assorted nations as Afghanistan, Iran, Iraq, Libya and North Korea. Besides those television agreements and countries, the league had also renewed its contracts with telecasters in Hong Kong, Iceland and Portugal, and for the first time, there were games broadcast to households in Azerbaijan, Kazakhstan and Saudi Arabia. To measure how geographically widespread the coverage of games was then, in 2002 the league's most intense and widely viewed annual game series that determines a championship team, which is the NBA Finals, had reached 2.5 billion people who were represented in 36 languages including Arabic, Creole, Hindi, Maltese and Tagalog. In short, the NBA's worldwide midweek and weekend game distributions became the most powerful factor that increased the sales of the league's products relative to the broadcast business of any other U.S.- or foreign-based professional sports organization.[11]

For television viewers, the major national terrestrial channels in Germany broadcasted NBA game highlights each day during the 2002 and 2003 seasons. Because of the programming power and advertising revenue derived from the league's games, the channels created more local, regional and national contents for their respective news and sports broadcasts. The NBA's vice president of international television and marketing partnerships Scott Levy had the following observation about those sports programs. "With this varied and extensive television coverage, fans in Germany will have the opportunity to watch the world's greatest basketball players in action."[12]

To increase basketball's worldwide popularity and exploit the league's brand and image in various markets overseas, before the 2003–2004 season there were preseason games played, for example, in Barcelona, Mexico City and Paris, and in San Juan, Puerto Rico, while two regular season games occurred in Saitama, Japan. Even though the league's previous game in Spain was held in 1994, an enthusiastic crowd in Barcelona watched the western Conference's Memphis Grizzlies battle the 2003 European League Champion, which was F.C. Barcelona. Likewise, the other cities had also previously hosted preseason NBA games. Since 1992, the NBA had staged 15 basketball games in Mexico City at the Palacio de los Deportes, which was the site of the 1968 Summer Olympic Games. To highlight the significance of one event, the Dallas Mavericks' and Mexico's native son Eduardo Najera returned home to compete in an October 2003 game. Najera's presence aroused the crowd and his play received nationwide press coverage in Mexico and in the city newspapers of countries throughout Latin America. Meanwhile, in Paris the NBA champion San Antonio Spurs, led by Virgin Islands' center Tim Duncan and French point guard Tony Parker had challenged the Memphis Grizzlies at Bercy Arena. For the league's fourth appearance since 1993, some NBA teams had also played exhibition games in Puerto Rico. Finally, at Japan's Saitama Super Arena, which is the venue for the 2006 Federation of International Basketball Association (FIBA) World Basketball Championship for Men, the NBA's Los Angles Clippers and Seattle SuperSonics met to open their regular seasons as western Conference opponents. With respect to the strategic importance of playing exhibition, preseason and regular season games in foreign cities, NBA Commissioner David Stern said, "Although our games are available on television in over two hundred countries there is nothing quite like showcasing our stars during the live game experience to cement our relationship with the growing base of international NBA fans."[13]

To conclude this portion of Chapter 3, it is relevant to mention that the league's award-winning production and programming division, NBA Entertainment produces NBA TV, which is a 24-hour television network, and schedules weekly television shows and exclusive contents for each of the NBA teams' web sites and for the league's official web site, NBA.com. Remarkably, during 2003 approximately 40 percent of the Internet traffic on NBA.com originated from computers at international locations. This relatively large percentage of traffic reflects, in part, to what extent the league has penetrated global markets and thus, is thoroughly enjoyed by basketball and other sports fans outside of North America.

As the globalization of American-style basketball and the media broadcast's of NBA games gained momentum during the 1990s and early 2000s, for various economic and sports-specific reasons an increasing proportion of the league's teams had aggressively scouted, recruited and drafted foreign players to fill those clubs' active rosters. Because of the players' experiences as professionals, training habits and basketball skills, a swelling corps of the most talented athletes from European nations and elsewhere have won the hearts and minds of America's sports fans, and also proved that they can successfully compete in the NBA and become superstars for such teams as the Cleveland Cavaliers, Dallas Mavericks, Denver Nuggets, Houston Rockets, Sacramento Kings and San Antonio Spurs. To determine why, when and which basketball players have been hired to compete for these and other franchises in the league, the following section of this chapter is presented.

Foreign Players

During the early 1980s, fewer than ten international basketball players were listed on the active NBA rosters as of the regular season opening games. The small number occurred because of the league's internal problems and some players' consumption of illegal drugs, the affects of other factors such as the cultural differences and language barriers between countries, and America's basketball fans' perception that foreign sports players were inferior athletes who lacked the natural ability to be competitive. This meant that most NBA teams rarely scouted small, medium-sized or tall talented athletes from outside the U.S. In short, 20 years ago it was too risky and therefore not an economic incentive for the league's franchise owners to actively recruit, offer contracts to, and invest their financial capital in amateur and professional basketball players from abroad. After the early 1980s, however, those circumstances gradually changed and so did the attitudes of fans, league officials and team owners about foreign athletes.

That is, beginning in the middle to late 1980s some well-known international players earned respect by competing for teams in the NBA. For example, the Houston Rockets' Hakeem Olajuwon and the New York Knicks' Patrick Ewing and Washington Bullets' Manute Bol excelled as players by blocking opponents' shots at the hoop and/or leading their club in rebounds. Besides the outstanding performances of those three athletes, even more impressive was how some men's foreign national basketball teams had improved their competitiveness and won important international tournaments. To illustrate, either in 1987 or 1988 these four events were newsworthy. First, a Yugoslavian team led by Vlade Divac, Dino Radja and Toni Kukoc defeated a U.S. team to win the Junior World Championships in Bormio, Italy; second, a Brazilian club that featured such great players as Oscar Schmidt and Marcel Souza won a gold medal at the Pan American Games in Indianapolis, Indiana; third, a club from Italy nicknamed the Tracer Milan and that performed at a McDonald's Open tournament in Milwaukee, Wisconsin, nearly beat the hometown Bucks, which is an NBA club; and fourth, a U.S.S.R. team that had five Baltic nationals among its top six players defeated an American team in the medal round at the Summer Olympic Games in Seoul, South Korea. In contrast, U.S. women's basketball teams performed brilliantly and won gold medals during the 1980s and 1990s at the Summer Olympic Games in 1984, 1988, 1992 and 1996.[14]

Between 1990 and 1995, five other special international basketball teams excelled when they played U.S. teams. In 1990, a club from Yugoslavia won gold medals at the World Championships in Buenos Aires and at the Goodwill Games in Seattle, Washington. Meanwhile, at the fourth McDonald's Open, which was held in Barcelona, the NBA New York Knicks needed an overtime game to beat Scavolini Pesaro and win the title. With respect to another event, in 1994 U.S. coach Don Nelson surprisingly had to call a time out at the World Championships in Toronto to revise his team's strategy against a Russian club that surged and scored points. Lastly, in 1995 an American team that was favored to win finished a disappointing seventh at the World Championships in Athens, Greece. Indeed, except for the Dream Team in 1992, it was apparent that by the early to middle 1990s America's long-standing global basketball supremacy and U.S. men's teams' dominance had eroded at international tournaments. For the readers' interest, what factors may have contributed to the decline in the U.S. basketball teams' performances against foreign clubs?[15]

According to many sports analysts and other experts, several reasons explain why the quality gap between American and international basketball players had narrowed then and continued to shrink from the middle of the 1990s to early 2000s. In turn, those results justify why NBA teams increasingly recruit and draft foreign-born players who were from nations in Africa, Asia, Europe, South American and elsewhere. From an analytical perspective, five reasons are cited to explain the use of international players by teams in the NBA. One, since the early 1990s the pool of U.S. college and university basketball players that graduated with academic degrees completed in four or five years had relatively declined. That is, rather than play for four years on a college or university team to upgrade their skill level, develop strength, gain experience and acquire the mental discipline in order to become potentially better professional athletes, numerous first-rate U.S. college and university players had declared their eligibility and entered an NBA draft after their freshman, sophomore or junior years at school. Furthermore, after evaluating their abilities, some college and university athletes feared that a serious illness or injury would possibly deny them an opportunity to sign a lucrative NBA contract, earn income from endorsements, and thus cause them to forfeit future wealth and a glamorous career in professional basketball. So, even though they were mentally and physically unprepared and undisciplined, since the early 1990s many top-notch U.S. amateur basketball players decided to forego one to four years of college and a university degree to perform for teams in the NBA, National Basketball Development League (NBDL), which is the NBA's developmental league, or in a foreign basketball organization.

Two, there is a relatively large supply of experienced, mature and talented international athletes who have become available since basketball's popularity began to soar globally in the early 1990s. To illustrate, by 2003 the number of professional basketball clubs outside the U.S. exceeded 2,000. "I was making $100,000 at [the] age [of] 16 playing professionally in France," said San Antonio Spurs guard Tony Parker, who could play there throughout the year to build confidence, and to enhance his reputation and develop proficient basketball skills. Furthermore, after the European League and FIBA's Super League merged in 2002, a majority of the superior international players were then forced to compete against each other, which motivated those players to improve their game strategies and skills. Three, the NBA teams' owners, general managers and coaches realized that its refreshing to negotiate contracts with and employ outstanding foreign players who have not been coddled or spoiled by their elders since elementary school because of their athletic achievements on the basketball court. In contrast, besides their arrogance, immaturity and trashy language, generally America's superior high school basketball stars have become increasingly inferior and unmotivated students who attend college simply to play sports and not to study for and complete an academic degree. "Let's face it," said Sacramento Kings' personnel director Jerry Reynolds, "You're better off taking a guy who's been well-coached and playing pro in Europe or somewhere else as opposed to some 18–19 year old phenom from the States who can't play a lick." Because of those beliefs and other concerns, the majority of NBA teams will increasingly demand the talents of experienced international basketball players.[16]

Four, an increasing number of NBA franchise owners have budgeted larger amounts of their teams' future cash flows to build global person to person relationships and communication networks in order to locate, scout and recruit foreign players. In fact, to collect intelligence and personal information about athletes there are national and international formal and informal systems of agents, coaches, scouts and even fans that research publications and forward, by electronic mail, the various profiles, stories and reports about foreign players to many NBA teams. This data, in turn, compels coaches and managers to separate the mediocre athletes from future star players based on their recent basketball performances. Five, while the officials of foreign teams typically allocate an extraordinary amount of time to patiently develop their players' talents, in America the National Collegiate Athletic Association (NCAA) regulates the number of hours its member college and university teams can practice during the season and postseason. In short, if employment trends continue in the sport of basketball, the proportion of foreign-born athletes that play on NBA clubs will expand to possibly 50 percent or more by 2010.

To measure and account for the influx of NBA players who were not from the U.S., and to identify which countries these athletes had emigrated from, there have been raw values recorded and various statistics published in reports since the middle 1990s. Interestingly, a few key percentages reflect those values and statistics. The number of international basketball athletes drafted by NBA clubs, for example, had increased from three in 1994 to 17 in 2002, which represents a total of 31 players in eight years. Seven, or respectively 22 percent of those drafted were natives of Serbia-Montenegro and 12, or 39 percent were collectively from Brazil,

Croatia, France, Greece, Poland and Russia. The dozen players remaining had emigrated in equal proportions from 12 countries such as Argentina, Iceland, Macedonia and Senegal. For more facts about this topic, in 2003 the NBA teams' rosters for the opening day, regular season games contained 65 international players from 34 countries and territories. Specifically, Serbia-Montenegro supplied eight, or 12 percent of the players; Canada, Croatia and France provided four each or 18 percent of the total; and China, Nigeria and Slovenia furnished three each or 13 percent of the foreign-born players. To recognize the players and respective teams of five league All-Stars, there was Lithuania's Zydrunas Ligauskas of the Cavaliers in Cleveland, Ohio, Canada's Steve Nash and Germany's Dirk Nowitzki of the Mavericks in Dallas, Texas, Serbia-Montenegro's Peja Stojakovic of the Kings in Sacramento, California, and China's Yao Ming of the Rockets in Houston, Texas. Interestingly, the NBA included a player from every continent during games played during the 2002–2003 regular season.[17]

As the percentages indicated, a variety of European countries have been primary sites for the NBA teams to locate, scout and recruit athletes, and to draft and develop them to be competent as professional basketball players. The next portion of this chapter discusses why, how and which European nations and areas have generally provided the NBA with players who successfully mastered the sport's fundamentals and acquired the mental discipline and physical strength to become professional basketball's international superstars.

European Basketball Players and Sports Environment

As clarified in Chapters 1 and 2, respectively, MLB's international players have tended to emigrate from Latin American countries and the NFL's from Canada and Mexico. Alternatively, in the NBA a generous portion of the league's foreign-born players are from cities in small to medium sized Eastern and Western European nations. From a historical view, even though amateur and professional soccer are Europe's most popular and prevalent sports, American basketball has experienced an above average growth rate in market share among Europe's sports fans, especially since the early to middle 1990s. As such, the interest of and participation by fans and the involvement of youth organizations and sports officials has led to the competitiveness and professionalism of basketball players who frequently began to play games in their European elementary and secondary schools and then, if qualified, joined company's teams in the respective country's advanced professional leagues.

In the middle of the 1980s, there were some very competitive leagues and well-prepared teams in nations throughout Europe. As a result, between 1986 and 1989 a few NBA teams had focused on and succeeded to draft such outstanding international players as Croatia's Drazen Petrovic by the Trail Blazers in Portland, Oregon, Lithuania's Sarunas Marciulionis by the Golden State Warriors in San Francisco, California, Croatia's Dino Rajda by the Celtics in Boston, Massachusetts, and Serbia-Montenegro's Vlade Divac by the Lakers in Los Angeles, California. Besides those four athletes, for various franchise- and game-specific reasons other European basketball players were scouted, recruited, drafted and then signed to teams' contracts. That is because the players were well coached and trained to effectively perform such basic skills and motions as dribbling and passing a basketball and accurately shooting it, and agile enough to move their bodies with surprising athleticism that reflected years of experience from playing as amateurs and/or professionals on national basketball teams in their home country.[18]

Since the philosophy and methodology of European junior basketball coaches is to teach and train young athletes, and not necessarily insist that they must win games and tournaments, those coaches emphasized unselfish behavior and the team concept rather than focusing on individual players who could perform razzle-dazzle movements and attempt to complete one-dimensional plays. Consequently, there are very few playground basketball games or helter-skelter scrimmages conducted in junior European basketball programs because players there must spend most of their leisure time practicing the game with coaches. At those practices, the coaches provide guidance and instruct the players how to dribble, pass and shoot a basketball, which are skills to be learned and repeated in drills. While scouting at a recent biennial European Basketball Championship tournament, the NBA Indiana Pacers' president and former Boston Celtics legend Larry Bird highlighted and stated, "Our [U.S.] guys are more skilled, but they've gotten away from fundamentals, and often European players know the game better." Meanwhile, the Dallas Mavericks' president of basketball operations Donnie Nelson further contrasted the improving European basketball environment to the individual-oriented and selfish play in NBA games as follows, "Coming to Europe was like a liberation or revival. You would have five guys passing and moving without the ball. They played the way I think [basketball originator James] Naismith intended it to be played."[19]

In America, meanwhile, the teenagers who play basketball on youth league teams receive a relatively modest amount of basic instructions from, and participation in drill practices with, their coaches. Thus, the high school and summer league teams are needed with respect to upgrading U.S. players' skills for college and university sports programs. The European system of training and developing players while youths, however, is significantly different than in America. Essentially, young and talented European basketball players are expected to sign long-term contracts with local clubs or company-sponsored teams even in their early teens, and as those players age, they progress through the system by competing for that club or team. Indeed, in European countries an authorized basketball contract generally binds a player to one team for several years. Then, when the player's contract nears expiration, he may renegotiate it with his club, or wait until the contract expires and plan to enter his name in the NBA draft. To acquire the world's best athletes, some NBA teams such as the Utah Jazz draft have drafted young European players and then assigned them to play on a team in their home country to improve their skills and conditioning until a roster slot had opened for them to join the Jazz, who are located in Salt Lake City. To illustrate, during the early 2000s Europe's player development system enhanced the talents of several prominent athletes including Russia's Andrei Kirilenko, Spain's Raul Lopez, Slovenia's Bostjan Nachbar and Georgia's Nikoloz Tskitishvili. As such, by 2003 Kirilenko and Lopez had played in games for the Jazz, Nachbar for the Houston Rockets and Tskitishvili for the Denver Nuggets. Other than those players, during the 2004 regular season the Cleveland Cavaliers' Zydrunas Ilgauskas, who is 7 feet 3 inches and from Lithuania, had matched or outperformed the top centers in the league. After eight years, Ilgauskas had finally displayed the shooting touch and passing ability that defines European players. According to Cavaliers coach Paul Silas, "Right now [March 2004], I can't think of any one center in the East [Conference] that's any better, and of all centers, I can't think of that many that are much better."[20]

According to reports confirmed by knowledgeable NBA officials, included in many of the basketball contracts signed by professional players from Europe and elsewhere are specific sentences, clauses and phrases that are intentionally ambiguous and difficult to translate into English. Because of the confusion, teams frequently violate the terms of those players' contracts. Apparently, their respective teams frequently violate the contracts. Furthermore, to avoid payment of taxes levied by multiple government offices, some foreign team owners have secretly negotiated alternative contracts with their star players. In those documents, the players' salaries and/or fringe benefit amounts may be significantly less than what appeared in the original contract and the conditions of employment may be vastly different. To improve accountability, therefore, during the early 1990s the FIBA and NBA agreed that disputed contracts of foreign players must be adjudicated by an international arbitrator. If an arbitrator decides to void a contract's terms and/or conditions after reviewing the evidence, the player is eligible to file a statement with the proper authorities and become a free agent. For creditability and consistency of their standards, the two basketball organizations have periodically inspected international players' contracts to ensure that the compensation values, terms and conditions of employment as stipulated in the documents can be easily and clearly interpreted into English and are legally enforceable through arbitration.[21]

A controversial issue that involves the employment relations with European players, especially those drafted by an NBA franchise, are the specific rules that apply to the prices of buyouts. A delicate situation may occur, for example, when an American or foreign sports agent signs an international amateur or professional basketball player, and then later redirects that player to a team that is willing to include settlement fees as a buyout condition in a contract offer. During the early 1990s, the NBA's Collective Bargaining Agreement stipulated that the league's teams could spend up to $250,000 for an international players' contract. This relatively low amount was established to allow such small-market NBA clubs as the Denver Nuggets, Memphis Grizzlies and Orlando Magic to have an equal opportunity as the large-market teams to sign contracts with the best foreign players. Furthermore, the payment was set at $250,000 to avoid a bidding war that had occurred, for instance, in MLB when teams had to compete to sign elite baseball players from national and company-sponsored clubs in various Asian countries. Because of the bidding process, MLB teams' costs soared and the franchises incurred operating deficits. Anyway, by the early 2000s the minimum buyout of contracts for teams who pursued international basketball athletes had increased to $350,000 and generally players were willing to pay a portion of that expense. In short, given the transactions and experiences that have occurred about labor issues in the players' market, the legal enforcement of contracts and buyout clauses will gradually make it less complex for NBA teams to draft and sign international players, especially those athletes who had committed to play on various teams in European nations.[22]

Since the early 1990s, the majority of NBA teams have scouted and recruited outstanding players who had attended and participated in American and European basketball camps. At the camps, which are frequently sponsored by shoe corporations and other sports equipment companies, the coaches usually allocate time to teach the fundamentals of basketball to rookies and veteran international players. If the camp is held in America, besides the U.S. athletes who attended, there are experienced and talented foreign players who may also be invited to participate and workout for professional teams' coaches and scouts. After the players compete, occasionally the personnel directors of company-sponsored teams and the sports agents that represent national teams overseas, may sign U.S. athletes to contracts although European teams have generally limited the number of Americans on their rosters. Similarly, at the camps the coaches and scouts of NBA teams evaluate foreign players. If those athletes' performances are exceptional, they are signed by an NBA club and then reassigned to a developmental league such as the Continental Basketball League or NBDL.

As a special event for young foreign basketball players and other athletes, the NBA established an annual summer camp series, which was titled Basketball Without Borders, in 2001. That year, in the City of Treviso, Italy, 50 12–14 year old kids from Bosnia, Croatia, Macedonia, Slovenia and Yugoslavia attended the summer camp whose programs promoted and encouraged youth to accept the principles of friendship, goodwill and understanding through sport. Two NBA players from the former Yugoslavia and five other professional players conspicuously interacted with the kids who had participated at the camp. During 2002 and 2003, similar summer camps were held for youth, respectively, in Istanbul, Turkey and again in Treviso. Besides playing basketball games at the camps, the young athletes were taught by the professional players and program officials how to develop their leadership skills, and how to resolve personal conflicts and strive to live a healthy, drug-free life. The camps held in 2002 and 2003 were sponsored, in part, by well-known international corporations such as American Airlines, Gatorade, Nike, Spalding and Sprite, and in Turkey by the Garanti Bank and in Treviso by United Colors of Benetton, which is the firm that owns Treviso's basketball team in the Italian league. Lastly, several FIBA officials assisted and contributed their experiences and expertise to organize and/or host the Basketball Without Borders programs.[23]

Regarding the NBA's strategies and future plans with respect to leagues and teams located in Europe and to the employment of European players, the NBA's

International vice president Andrew Messick has explored three strategic options. These options were first, to create a new foreign-based professional basketball league that would compete for fans against the existing national and company-sponsored European teams; second, to apply the NBA's most successful marketing and management practices after becoming involved with and supporting European leagues and their clubs' games and tournaments; and third, to place an existing NBA team and/or an expansion franchise in a major medium to large European city such as Barcelona, Berlin, Brussels, Madrid, Munich, Paris or Rome. Whether the NBA eventually implements one or more of those options will be based, in part, on the amount of television and radio revenues derived from the respective local and national overseas markets, and on other factors such as currency exchange rates and the ticket prices at games, arena capacities, fan bases and teams' travel costs with respect to sites in each city.[24]

In the sport, certainly the most marketable and publicized athlete to enter and play in the NBA since the Los Angles Lakers' Shaquille O'Neal, and before the Cleveland Cavaliers' LeBron James has been Yao Ming, a native of Shanghai, China. His journey into and impact on the league, and how the international professional basketball business has changed because of his entry, are interesting events to ponder. That said, an overview of Ming's presence in the league and his affects on professional basketball across the globe are discussed in the next portion of this chapter.

Yao Ming

As the son of parents who played basketball on various Chinese teams, and recognized as a cultural icon since he became a teenager, in 1996 Yao Ming was 16 years old, seven feet and three inches tall, and wore a size 18 in Adidas sneakers when he attended a Nike Inc. party in Shanghai to honor the Sharks, which was an excellent local basketball team that Nike had sponsored. Six years after that party was held, the discussions and strategic business meetings between Chinese basketball authorities, the Sharks' negotiators, American sports agents and marketing executives, and NBA officials had concluded. As a result, Ming signed a professional basketball contract to play for the Houston Rockets after he was selected first in the NBA draft by the franchise. As a Rocket, his four-year employment contract, excluding incentives, had been valued at $18 million. According to the terms established in the agreement, it was reported that Ming and the Sharks would equally share approximately $9 million or 50 percent of the contract's amount, and the remaining money would be redistributed among China's governmental sports agencies. With respect to fans' expectations about Yao in Houston and the $18 million he received to perform for the Rockets, in his rookie season Ming averaged 13.5 points and 8.2 rebounds per game, hit 52.2 percent of his shots and became a league All-Star player.[25]

Because of Yao's decision to play for the Rockets in the NBA and not for a European national team, there were six provincial Chinese television networks, which included 12 regional channels that had broadcasted 30 of the Rockets' 82 games during the 2002–2003 regular season to an average audience estimated at 250–350 million people. Besides the sponsors' advertisements, promotions and other marketing campaigns during the broadcasts of those games, the NBA decided to open a branch office in Beijing and expand its administrative staff in Hong Kong, create a Chinese web site, plan to launch a Chinese basketball magazine, and for several years, will likely schedule and play exhibition, preseason and perhaps regular season games in Beijing, Shanghai, and in other large Asian cities. To illustrate, the first-ever NBA preseason games in China were scheduled during October of 2004 at the 17,500-seat Capital Stadium in Beijing and at the 11,500-seat Shanghai Stadium. "We are happy to work with the NBA to bring these highly anticipated games to China. We know that these games will not only bring enjoyment to the basketball fans, but most importantly, to spur the development of our elite players," said the president of the Beijing Municipal Bureau of Sport, Sun Kanglin. Eventually, NBA-themed retail stores, specialty shops and restaurants might be built in China for the country's consumers and especially its sports fans. Meanwhile, because of Ming's exposure and status in Houston, during the 2002–2003 season the Rockets' television ratings skyrocketed and the team's home attendances measurably increased at its new arena, which is named the Toyota Center, and the club improved its standing in the Western Conference. Moreover, the franchise's arena, catalogue and Internet sales of apparel, merchandise and team equipment also beat estimates because of Houston fans' interest and willingness to attend home games and/or watch local television stations to cheer for the Rockets' Chinese player at the center position and his club.[26]

Based on his charisma, maturity, sense of humor and potential as an international professional basketball role model, Ming had expected to earn an estimated $4–6 million per year in endorsements by promoting the products of Apple Computer, Gatorade, PepsiCo Inc. and Visa International. After Yao's deal with Nike had expired, during 2003 he signed a long-term contract to promote Reebok's products. Ming then endorsed a multi-year deal in early 2004 to be part of McDonald's global marketing campaign. With respect to that deal, the marketing director of the group that represents the Rockets' center said, "Yao is extremely selective in picking blue chip companies to align himself with. McDonald's has a great history of working with athletes. They have produced fantastic ads and this alliance will help them further penetrate the Chinese market, which is one of their important goals." Furthermore, his business connections in China included deals with wireless service and mobile telephone companies. Besides those promotions by Ming, in 2002 the Rockets earned more revenues when the U.S. distributor for the Chinese Yanjing Beer Group Corporation leased billboard space inside the Toyota Center, which is a five-year deal valued at $6 million.[27]

According to one of Yao's closest marketing advisers, Erik Zhang, Ming had received numerous proposals from Chinese business firms to make television commercials for products sold in China. Given China's focus on expanding business activity and economic development, Zhang said, "For Chinese companies with multinational aspirations, sports are something that will help them get there [international recognition]." As an aside, Erik Zhang is one of Yao's Chinese-born cousins. During 2002, Zang had attended the University of Chicago, which is in the State of Illinois, as a business student. While at the school, he joined with several other students and a professor to form a team and prepare a product brand strategy for Ming in China. After studying the Chinese's consumer markets, and conducting research in that country to measure Yao's popularity and what he could become as a businessperson, the marketing team developed an interactive database to determine the correlation and a fit between the core values associated with Ming and the core values evoked by specific products and brands. As result, in a professional but confidential and unpublished report, the team had analyzed how a change in the world's political climate or a debilitating injury from playing basketball with the Rockets would affect, if at all, Yao's endorsement potential. As an advisor to the team and its project, the University of Chicago clinical professor of marketing Jonathan Frenzen said, "He [Yao] is a perfect bridge from communist China to the New China, and from the New China to the rest of Asia and the United States."[28]

Encouraged by Yao Ming's presence with the Rockets in Houston, Texas, and his influence on professional basketball worldwide, the NBA had scheduled single 2003 preseason games in Barcelona, Mexico City, Paris and San Juan, an opening regular season game in Saitama, Japan, and one each 2004 exhibition games in Beijing and Shanghai. Therefore, based on the growing trend of the league's teams to play overseas, what are some relevant facts and information about how amateur and/or professional basketball and the NBA are respected in various countries and/or areas besides North America? For this chapter, the nations identified and studied about basketball and the league were China and Mexico and the area of interest was the African continent. Consequently, the topic of global basketball markets is discussed next followed by a table that lists five foreign cities that may qualify as potential sites for NBA franchises. After the tabled data is reviewed, an update on the international aspects of the WNBA is presented.

Global Basketball Markets

China

Based on the research for *Sports Capitalism*, the Chinese started playing basketball games during 1893. As the sport had evolved in China during the middle to late 1890s and throughout the twentieth century, it eventually developed into an instiution that became deeply rooted in the country's culture and society, and a national pastime since the middle of the 1930s. To illustrate the sport's appeal, growth and popularity, when coaches identify Chinese kids as promising athletes and potential professional players, a portion of them may attend a state-run basketball academy to be trained and taught how to develop their skills when they play various positions during games on defense and offense. Later, as teenagers, the most talented of the players from academies are then selected to attend tryouts and perhaps qualify to join a team in the professional China Basketball Association (CBA). This sports organization has established itself as a solid middle tier league ranked below similar basketball leagues in Italy and Spain but above those in Turkey and Russia. The majority of the CBA's players, therefore, were handpicked at a young age to be identified and segregated as athletes who would acquire the necessary skills to become professional basketball players in the country's primary league. Because of the types of sport development systems in the nation, to a large extent the CBA's players must realize and accept that China's authoritative government will intervene in and control their professional sports careers. Except for special circumstances, those players will never be free as American and European athletes are, to enter a market and pursue the highest money amount that was bid for their basketball talents.[29]

During 1987, Sung Tao was the first highly touted Chinese basketball player to be drafted by an NBA team. For undisclosed reasons, however, Tao never relocated from China to play the sport for a club in America Then, in the early 2000s it was the athletes Wang Zhi-Zhi at seven feet tall and Mengke Bateer at six feet and eleven inches, who were followed by Yao Ming at seven feet and five inches that became the first Chinese players to perform for teams in the NBA. Despite the heights, abilities and experiences of these athletes, and the country's previous basketball victories in various Summer Olympic Games and in the Asian Championships and other global tournaments, sport pundits do not regard China as a major power or an international role model in the sport of basketball. For how the NBA evaluates the quality of Asian basketball, according to Commissioner David Stern China is "one of many frontiers" that also include France, India and countries in Africa. That is, to become a global basketball superpower China must dedicate and efficiently allocate its sports resources to achieve specific objectives with respect to the development of players and global success in games and tournaments. To illustrate what the nation needs to implement, the International Basketball Federation's (IBF) Patrick Baumann has recommended that China expose its players to better competition and other styles of play as performed by amateur and professional teams from America, Europe and elsewhere. Baumann also suggests that, in order to improve, China needs to "upgrade facilities [school gymnasiums and basketball arenas], identify young players sooner [in elementary and junior high schools], further educate coaches [about basketball fundamentals and game strategies], and be willing to accept outside help [assistance from sports athletes and instructors in other countries]."[30]

Although the Chinese basketball system is intrinsically problematic because of customs, traditions and politics, China's government bureaucrats expect the country's best men's and women's teams to provide superior performances at the 2008 Summer Olympic Games in Beijing. According to the beliefs and interests of Chinese national authorities, besides the nation's hospitality to sports fans, the media and tourists, and the country's investments in infrastructure, an excellent basketball performance at the Olympic Games will ultimately improve the economic growth of companies, especially those in Beijing and Shanghai, and likewise benefit China's international businesses in Africa, America, Asia and Europe.

Mexico

At the 1936 Summer Olympic Games held in Berlin, Germany, before America defeated Canada in the men's championship game, Mexico had won a bronze medal in basketball and in 1999, the nation placed fourth at the World University games. Since then, Mexico has not been successful in winning its games at international basketball tournaments even though an estimated six million Mexicans play the sport.

Relative to the nation's professional sports structure, a national Basketball Federation has existed in Mexico for more than a decade. With respect to that organization, the country's top basketball players either perform for teams in the CIMEBA, CIBACOPA or LNBP league. Organized as a group more than 30 years ago, the CIMEBA operates its schedule of games and tournaments independent of the Federation. Nevertheless, because of low attendances at games and cash flow problems that have adversely affected the league, the number of its teams had to decrease from 18 in 1993 to eight in 2003. Alternatively, during 2003 the CIBACOPA contained ten teams while the LNBP is a new professional basketball league that is affiliated with the Federation. To be more specific, The LNBP consists of approximately 11 teams and has an operating relationship with the CNI, which is the LNBP's minor basketball league. As to their teams' exposure to sports fans in markets, these professional basketball organization's home and away games are not broadcast on Mexico's local or national television networks, and the country's newspapers provide little content and few statistics about each league's teams, players, seasons and tournaments. In short, the Mexican Basketball Federation (MBF) and the various professional leagues and teams are unstable and generally not a widely popular sports group.[31]

Because of Mexico's struggling national economy, political turmoil and immense social capital needs, there are insufficient amounts of economic resources allocated by the Mexican government to construct or maintain the nation's public basketball facilities for amateur youth organizations and for athletes who play on elementary and secondary school teams. As a result, kids that play basketball on courts in their neighborhoods must attempt to score points with shots at crooked rims without nets, while the rims are attached to trees or flimsy backboards. Since local governments neglect Mexico's public school playgrounds, grass and weeds generally grow unattended through a basketball court's cracked asphalt. Despite those conditions, however, in popularity basketball ranks moderately behind soccer but nearly equal to baseball as a national sport. If so, what is the support for and status of a well-known professional basketball player who was born and had played the sport in Mexico?

Latin American sports fans have idolized the Dallas Mavericks' Eduardo Najera, a native of Meoqui, Chihuahua and a graduate of, and former basketball star at the University of Oklahoma since he became the second Mexican-born player to perform in the NBA. His fame was highlighted when television sports anchor Enrique Garay said, "Eduardo is as popular as any soccer player in Mexico right now [in 2003] because of his courage, his heart, [and] the way he plays. He shows the way the Mexicans are because we have to work hard, harder than most of the people." For more about Najera, during the Mavericks' 2002–2003 regular season the burly Mexican, who had played at the center position but was periodically injured, still managed to score 6.7 points and 4.6 rebounds per game. Because of his work ethic and willingness to interact with fans and autograph seekers before and after games, Najera obviously is the favorite player of Dallas' 152,000 Hispanic residents. As a result of that behavior, the support from fans has benefited this Mexican basketball player. To illustrate, besides the U.S.-based Accident & Injury Pain Centers Group, Bimbo Bakeries and Nike Inc., the other companies that Najera had or has relationships with and endorses their products and services include Telcel, which is Mexico's largest mobile-telephone service, and Anheuser-Busch, which is North America's biggest brewer. Although Najera's performance with the Mavericks has not been exceptional, he contributes to the league's and team's successes.[32]

Since the middle of the 1990s, Mexico's TV Azteca has broadcasted the NBA's regular season games, All-Star Weekend and the Final Championship series on its network. Besides that exposure, during 2002 the Hispanic network Telemundo signed an agreement with the NBA to televise the league's 2002–2003 regular season games and its All-Star weekend in Spanish to sports fans who live in Mexico and other Latin American countries. In short, because of the television coverage and American and Hispanic fans' interest in and respect for Eduardo Najera, the NBA will continue to expand its brand, product line and marketing campaign in Mexico.[33]

Africa

Although soccer is this continent's primary sport for various populations, such organizations as the FIBA, Basketball South Africa (BSA), and especially the NBA and WNBA sponsor and operate basketball events and programs, and market amateur and professional basketball to Africa's sports fans. Since the early 1990s, there have been one or more NBA and/or WNBA representatives who had specifically visited Africa on three occasions. To highlight those visits, during 1993 Commissioner David Stern and a contingent of professional coaches and players, and other league officials traveled to Kenya, Zaire and South Africa to conduct basketball clinics for African youth. Besides providing the sports clinics, the group met and spoke about their experiences and efforts in the nations with the former African National Congress' president Nelson Mandela. Then, in 1997 two WNBA players had volunteered to tour South Africa and present basketball programs and encourage those kids and women that were interested to play the sport. The third visit occurred in 2003 when the best 100 players, who were aged 16–20 years old from 19 African countries had assembled at the American International School of Johannesburg to receive basketball instructions from NBA players and to participate in worthwhile education and social programs. As expressed by BSA president Vusi Mgobhozi, the "Africa 100 Camp is designed to promote, expose and strengthen the culture of basketball among the continent's youth."[34]

To highlight the benefits of the latter basketball program, at the Africa 100 Camp there were four enthusiastic African-born NBA players who had served as coaches. Those players were the Congo's Dikembe Mutombo, Cameroon's Ruben Boumtje Boumtje, and Senegal's DeSagana Diop and Mamadou N'diaye. Besides the four coaches who had given basketball instructions and led organized drills and practices, the Camp's participants had an opportunity to attend educational seminars and learn about the lifelong and real benefits of personal leadership, healthy living, ways to prevent HIV/AIDS, and programs that deal with drug abuse and addiction problems. Furthermore, a Reading and Learning Center was established at the Ithuteng Trust, which is a Johannesburg school for troubled youth. The Center was formed, in part, to supply thousands of books, resource guides and materials to African children who attend the Trust, and to install and operate desktop computers, printers, servers and educational software the Dell Computer Company had donated. According to an NBA legend and the league's community ambassador Bob Lanier, "With the things that go around the game—the referees, better facilities, more organized structure—[African] guys that are good athletes will blossom, and 10 years from now, you'll [fans will] be reaping the benefit."[35]

Thus far, the topics and other contents in Chapter 3 suggest that the NBA will eventually place one or more of its teams outside of North America. Based on the literature read for *Sports Capitalism* and on the league's strategies for the early to middle 2000s, Table 3.1 lists five international cities that Commissioner David Stern has alluded to or mentioned in interviews, newspaper articles or reports to be potential NBA sites for an existing team and/or expansion franchise. Why did Stern identify sites in these five cities?

As future NBA markets, each foreign city in Table 3.1 has some sports- and business-related strengths and weaknesses. That is, if the league decides to consider relocation or expansion to one or more of the cities, there are economic and soc-

Table 3.1 Foreign NBA Cities, Post 2004

City	Nation	Population	Area
Barcelona	Spain	1.5	3.9
Beijing	China	6.6	9.3
Berlin	Germany	3.2	3.9
Mexico City	Mexico	8.6	21.3
San Juan	Puerto Rico	.4	2.0

Note: City and Nation are self-explanatory. Population is the 2003 city population in millions. Area is the city's 2003 metropolitan area population in millions.

Source: "The World Gazetteer," at <http://www.world-gazetteer.com> cited 1 November 2003.

ial benefits and costs for the specific franchise and also for the local communities, fans and visiting NBA teams. With respect to site selection, it is the capacity and configuration of a basketball arena, the exposure provided by and the number of regional and national television and radio networks, print media coverage, and the quality and wealth of the team's local ownership that are important factors for the NBA to evaluate and measure about each city. Since demographics matter, then Barcelona and Berlin are each considered to being moderate-sized European cities. While Berlin currently hosts an NFLE team, the NFLE's Barcelona Dragons had to suspend its operations after the 2003 season because of low home attendances. Furthermore, those two cities are located at long distances from the U.S. eastern and western coasts.

Mexico City, which is the most populated city and has the largest metropolitan area in Table 3.1, is situated hundreds of miles south of the U.S. border. Also, Mexico's capital city is polluted and its population has a relatively low per capita income and high poverty rate. Likewise, Beijing has an abundant population but unlike Mexico City, must soon construct a high-quality basketball arena for the 2008 Summer Olympic Games. In turn, this facility would probably be of sufficient size and modern architecture to support an NBA team after 2004. However, the legal and political environments in China are risky and uncertain regarding the enactment and enforcement of contracts, property rights and individual freedoms. San Juan, meanwhile, is a tourist attraction and entertainment city that has hosted several of the games and series played by MLB and NBA teams. As such, Commissioner David Stern considers it to be a potential site for a team. In short, based on those and other factors the optimal locations to eventually place an NBA club are Mexico City and then Berlin, Barcelona and finally, Beijing and San Juan. Other international cities with medium to large populations that are future sites but not listed in Table 3.1 include, in no specific order, Frankfurt in Germany, London in the United Kingdom, Madrid in Spain, Monterrey in Mexico, Paris in France and Rome in Italy.

Besides the previous content, the final topic examined in this chapter is information about the presence, exposure and status of prominent international players in the WNBA, which is the premier women's professional basketball league in America, and perhaps in the world. When this discussion is completed, a Summary section and the Notes conclude Chapter 3.

WNBA

Between 1978 and 1992, three national professional women's basketball leagues were organized in America. For one or more economic and/or sports-specific reasons, eventually each league had to terminate its operations. The majority of those leagues' teams failed, in part, because of cash flow problems, which resulted from poor attendances at home games, and from inflated player salaries, excess operating costs and overhead relative to the respective leagues' and teams' budgeted amounts, inability or lack of foresight to negotiate and endorse local and national television and radio contracts, and/or inferior managerial decision-making by the teams' owners and league officials. After the three leagues had folded, it was the NBA's Board of Governors who realized that local sport markets and fan bases existed to support professional women's basketball, especially in some of the medium to large cities of the U.S. After research studies confirmed their beliefs, in 1996 the Governors unanimously approved the formation of the WNBA. When it was organized, the WNBA included two primary groups, that is, the Eastern and Western Conferences. Each Conference contained four teams that were located in such medium sized or large American cities as Charlotte in North Carolina, Houston in Texas, Los Angeles in California, New York City in New York and Sacramento in California. In exchange for a proportion of the revenues from the WNBA's national television contracts and its sponsorships and licensing agreements, the NBA's club owners agreed to pay the new league's expenses. Because the typical WNBA team on average has operated at a loss, to maintain operations the league's teams require a sizable amount of dollars in subsidies from the NBA. Given those circumstances, it means that the women's league has not moved any previous or current teams nor expanded its franchises to sites in cities beyond the U.S. borders.[36]

Since the late 1990s, the WNBA has matured as a sports organization and the numbers of international players on the league's team rosters have increased at the beginning of each regular season. That is, the teams' rosters listed less than ten foreign players in 1997 and at least 30 in 2003. That year, there were six players from Australia, three from Brazil and Russia, two from Canada and the Czech Republic, and one from 14 other nations such as Bulgaria, Cameroon, Germany, Hungary, Mali, Poland and Turkey. During the 2003 season, which was played from May to September, the WNBA Seattle Storm's roster included two international players who were special athletes. One player, who was Korea's Sun Min Jung, had been the top international selection from the 2003 WNBA draft and the other player was Australia's Lauren Jackson who had played on the 2003 All-Star team. Furthermore, the Congo's Mwadi Mabika excelled for the 2003 western Conference champion Los Angles Sparks and Poland's Margo Dydek played well enough to be an All-Star selection from the San Antonio Silver Spurs. Because of their skills and performances, these athletes were the outstanding international players in the WNBA.[37]

The global exposure of American women's professional basketball and the league has expanded during the early 2000s. In 2003, for example, the WNBA's regular season games were televised in 183 countries and territories around the globe as 62 telecasters reported those events in 26 languages. Morcover, the league had signed inaugural short- and long-term agreements with ten broadcasting companies in seven geographically dispersed countries. Those nations included Angola, China, Indonesia, Macedonia, Mozambique, the Philippines and Turkey. Based on the sport's global market penetration, the NBAE's vice president of International Television and Media Scott Levy stated, "Women's basketball is [currently] one of the fastest growing sports around the world."[38]

Although the women's network named Oxygen was uncertain whether to renew its two-year programming agreement with the WNBA after the completion of the 2003 season, and despite a 23 percent decline in its average attendances between 1998 and 2003, as a long-term project the league requires financial support based on various statements made by Commissioner David Stern and decision-makers on the NBA's Board of Governors. Even so, the WNBA will not likely expand in size and place any teams at sites in cities or rural areas outside the U.S. before the 2006 or 2007 regular seasons.[39]

As an aside, the new three year old American Basketball Association (ABA) was not discussed earlier in Chapter 3 because of its brief history. Organized during 2002, the ABA completed its 2003–2004 regular season with five clubs based in America and two located in Mexico, that is, in Juarez and Tijuana. According to the league's web site, the organization's mission "is to offer exciting, fast-paced, fan-friendly, professional basketball to families at a reasonable price, while providing a platform for top level players and coaches to showcase their talents in a competitive market." In the long term, the ABA seeks to be a nationally recognized and respected professional basketball league with franchises in major U.S. and international markets. With headquarters in the state of Kansas, this men's league is ambitious. To illustrate, during 2004 the ABA intended to expand by at least 17 teams with one club in Vancouver, Canada and another in Mexico. The team in Vancouver is expected to consist entirely of Chinese players and perhaps an expansion team in Los Angeles, California will be composed of Hispanic basketball athletes. Furthermore, the league has encouraged each of its member franchises to complete their rosters with one or two international players. Due to exhorbitant travel costs and other barriers, however, the ABA is not anticipating any expansions beyond America, Canada and Mexico. For more information about the ABA's leadership, structure and plans, visit its web site at <http://www.abalive.com>.[40]

Summary

Chapter 3, in sum, focused on the managerial strategies that included international alliances, broadcasts, markets, players, sponsorships and other business relationships, which have portrayed, according to some experts, the NBA to be the world's leading and most popular global sports organization. Since there are several unique themes, events and problems that relate to the globalization of the league, Chapter 3 was divided into several components.

First, the league's international strategies were identified and discussed relative to two distinct time frames. That is, those periods extended from the early to middle 1980s to the middle of the 1990s, and then from the middle 1990s to the early 2000s. During the initial period, Michael Jordan joined the NBA and Commissioner David Stern implemented a global business plan. Besides the actions of Jordan and Stern, there were other major activities. One, the league's teams aggressively scouted, recruited, drafted and gradually employed more foreign players for their active rosters. Two, the league formed business partnerships and teamed with corporate sponsors who advertised, promoted and otherwise marketed the NBA brand in North America and in nations overseas. Three, the league organized the NBA Dream Team, which was led by the Chicago Bulls' Michael Jordan and other superstars who won a gold medal in basketball at the 1992 Summer Olympic Games in Barcelona, Spain. Four, after studying the sport markets and fan bases in various Canadian cities, the league approved the expansion of one franchise each to Toronto and Vancouver in time for the Raptors in Toronto and Grizzlies in Vancouver to open the 1995–1996 regular season.

During the second period, the league's teams increasingly added outstanding international players, particularly the superstars on clubs in European countries, to their full-time active rosters. Furthermore, the NBA continued to market its brand and extend its exposure in countries of Africa, Asia, Europe and Latin America. How did the league accomplish that feat? In part, the NBA signed licensing agreements and contracts with sponsors and vendors, and formed partnerships with various U.S.- and foreign-based companies; initiated marketing, promotional and sales campaigns to advertise and sell its apparel, merchandise and other products abroad; and, created new and entertaining basketball programs that were broadcasted on the Internet and cable and satellite systems, and on television and radio networks across the globe.

Second, this section of Chapter 3 examined the specific U.S. and international cable and satellite systems, and the television channels and networks that the league used to communicate and contract with to broadcast an increasing portion of its regular season games, and its playoffs and final championship series to basketball addicts and other sports fans in various foreign markets. Besides those business deals and relationships that were established, the content in the chapter's second section elaborates on how the league scheduled numerous exhibition and preseason games overseas to showcase its players and teams. In short, those events promoted American-style basketball as a growth sport and as an alternative form of entertainment, especially for the international fans who had been dedicated to teams in amateur, semiprofessional and professional baseball, cricket, ice hockey, rugby and soccer.

Third, this portion of Chapter 3 explains the influx of foreign players into the NBA that occurred during the 1980s, 1990s and early 2000s. As a result of this information, the readers of *Sports Capitalism* acknowledge and understand why the NBA's team owners have been motivated to discover, recruit, draft and employ highly skilled amateur and professional players from various countries, and how the experiences and playing styles of international players have influenced U.S. athletes and the sports fans and markets in America, Canada and other nations. Because the import and success of European players in the NBA, and especially of China's Yao Ming have attracted attention across the globe, and been an important factor in the development and growth of professional basketball and the league from a business perspective, those topics are examined in further detail in this section of Chapter 3.

Fourth, the research accomplished for *Sports Capitalism* and the specific topics that emerged in the chapter revealed some interesting and pertinent facts and other information about how basketball has become embedded in various nations' cultures and societies. The research also exposed, in part, to what extent the NBA is recognized and revered by sports fans in such foreign countries as China and Mexico, and in African nations. In these countries and other parts of the world, American-style basketball is extremely popular among kids and a large proportion of the NBA's regular season games, playoffs and championship series are televised on local, regional and national television networks to millions of households. As such, this section essentially described how the sport of basketball and the league are represented in the two aforementioned countries and Africa. Finally, a table lists data for five international cities that Commissioner Stern contends are potential and viable relocation and/or expansion sites for one or more NBA franchises. Then, after some remarks about each city, they were ranked from first to fifth as preferred NBA sites. In short, the contents present a few key facts about the cities' qualities, that is, their attributes and deficiencies based on geographic location and population, and on the income and wealth of the cities' residents. If the NBA's Board of Governors vote and decide to approve the placement of a team outside the borders of the U.S. and Canada after 2004, those cities are reasonable places to consider as the location of one or more professional basketball franchises.

Fifth, the core contents of Chapter 3 conclude with an overview of the WNBA's operations and aspects of the league's business relations. This section also highlights the performances of foreign players who excelled during the WNBA's 2003 regular season and in the championship series. Lastly, there is a brief discussion about the global exposure and worldwide television broadcasts of the women league's games.

After an analysis of the international business and sport-specific ventures and strategies of MLB in Chapter 1, the NFL in Chapter 2 and NBA in Chapter 3, *Sports Capitalism* presents the NHL in Chapter 4 and MLS in Chapter 5, which are each profiled and explored from a global perspective. In short, Chapters 4 and 5 analyze the foreign activities, alliances, events, operations and relationships, and thus the business strategies of the most prominent U.S.-based professional leagues in ice hockey and soccer. As discussed, the chapters emphasize the crucial factors that have determined the worldwide growth and prosperity of the NHL and MLS, and how those leagues have struggled to become established global sports business organizations during the 20th century and early 2000s.

Notes

1. For the history and economics of the various professional sports leagues in America, see Roger G. Noll, ed., *Government and the Sports Business* (Washington, D.C.: The Brookings Institution, 1974); James Quirk and Rodney D. Fort, *Pay Dirt: The Business of Professional Team Sports* (Princeton, N.J.: Princeton University Press, 1992); Frank P. Jozsa, Jr. and John J. Guthrie, Jr., *Relocating Teams and Expanding Leagues in Professional Sports: How*

the Major Leagues Respond to Market Conditions (Westport, CT: Quorum Books, 1999); Frank P. Jozsa, Jr., *American Sports Empire: How the Leagues Breed Success* (Westport, CT: Praeger Publishers, 2003). Besides those books, professional basketball and/or the NBA are discussed in Andrew D. Bernstein, *NBA Hoop Shots: Classic Moments From a Super Era* (San Francisco, CA: Woodford Press, 1996); Walter LaFeber, *Michael Jordan and the New Global Capitalism* (New York, N.Y. and London, England: W.W. Norton & Company, 1999); Alexander Wolff, *Big Game, Small World: A Basketball Adventure* (New York, N.Y.: Warner Books, 2002); Terry Pluto, *Loose Balls: The Short, Wild Life of the American Basketball Association—As Told by the Players, Coaches, and Movers and Shakers Who Made It* (New York, N.Y.: Simon & Schuster, 1990); Martin Tarango, *Basketball Biographies* (Jefferson, N.C. and London, England: McFarland & Company, 1991); Ron Smith, Ira Winderman, and Mary Schmitt Boyer, *The Complete Encyclopedia of Basketball* (London, England: Carlton, 2001). To read articles about the operation and failure of American professional basketball leagues such as the World Basketball League and International Basketball League, see "Hard Pills to Swallow," *Time* (17 August 1992), 16; Mark Robichaux, "International Basketball League Shoots for a Following—WBL, in Its Third Year, Hope to Cash in on Growing Popularity of Sport," *Wall Street Journal* (25 January 1990), B2; "IBL's Slam Appears on Verge of Closing Its Doors," at <http://www.sportsbusinessnews.com> cited 3 December 2002.

2. Between the late 1970s and 1980s, the NBA transformed itself from a national into a global business organization. This change is discussed in Jack McCallum, "Tomorrow the World," *Sports Illustrated* (7 November 1988), 58–63, and Jeffrey A. Trachtenberg, "Playing the Global Game," *Forbes* (23 January 1989), 90–91. During the 1990s and 2000s, the developments of NBA.com and nine other Internet sites have attracted visits from millions of American and foreign web users, who learn about the league's events, teams and players. Regarding the league's approximately 29 million online visits per month that originate from outside the U.S., the NBA Entertainment's senior vice president of interactive services Brenda Spoonemore stated, "We have these incredible ambassadors. Clearly basketball is one of the most participated-in sports worldwide. It's a great feeling for us. It clearly tracks with the rest of our business." See Sarah Talalay, "The Internationalization of the NBA Continues," at <http://www.sportsbusinessnews.com> cited 2 January 2004.

3. See Linda Deckard, "Global Expansion Next Step For NBA?" *Amusement Business* (22 April 1991), 35–36; Marc Weingarten, "Site by Site, N.B.A. Takes on the World," *The New York Times* (14 November 2002), G2; Gordon Simpson, "*Inter*National Basketball Association," at <http://www.insidehoops.com> cited 30 June 2003; Carl Desens, "The NBA's Fast Break Overseas," *Business Week* (5 December 1994), 94; Greg Pesky, "Spanning the Globe," *Sporting Goods Business* (November 1993), 36; Kevin B. Blackistone, "David Stern on Basketball's Global Game," at <http://www.sportsbusinessnews,com> cited 25 November 2002. During a conference call in early 2004 between NBA teams, the owners discussed taking the league overseas. With respect to expansion abroad, Sacramento Kings co-owner Gavin Maloof said, "I think it's a way away. Not within five years, maybe 10 years. But I think it can become a reality." For where the league may expand, see Jaime Aron, "2 Owners Like Vegas For Expansion Team," *The Charlotte Observer* (23 January 2004), 4C. Besides those views, Deputy NBA Commissioner Russ Granik said the league has requested that former Madison Square Garden and New York Knicks president Dave Checketts examine the viability of placing a franchise in Europe. For why NBA Commissioner David Stern sees a possible team move by 2010, see Ross Siler, "Is the NBA Really Looking at Global Expansion?" at <http://www.sportsbusinessnews.com> cited 10 February 2004. Regarding the league's globalization plans, Stern said, "I was sitting with a

fan in Tokyo who was from Mexico. She was visiting from Guadalajara and was taping, using an inch-thick mini-camcorder. I was scratching my head. On the other side of me were folks from Shanghai and Beijing because they're going to host the Rockets and Sacramento Kings next October [2004]. There really is a coming together of the world." See George Diaz, "NBA Going Global," at <http://www.sportsbusinessnews.com> cited 20 February 2004.

4.   To read about various aspects of the NBA's progress and plans, see Daniel Eisenberg, "The NBA's Global Game Plan," *Time* (17 March 2003), 59–60; Larry Stewart, "It's Not Futbol, But NBA's Global Appeal is Growing," *The Los Angeles Times* (8 June 2002), W6; Alexander Wolff, "Expanding to Europe Could be in the Cards For the NBA," at <http://sportsillustrated.cnn.com> cited 26 June 2003; Percy Allen, "NBA Tips Off in Japan," at <http://www.sportsbusinessnews.com> cited 30 October 2003; Ken Belson, "The NBA is Talking Japanese," at <http://www.sportsbusinessnews.com> cited 30 October 2003; Frank Hughes, "NBA Not Strongly Embraced in Japan," at <http://www.sportsbusinessnews.com> cited 30 October 2003; "Stern and Granik Get Ready For a New NBA Season," at <http://www.sportsbusinessnews.com> cited 23 October 2003. In response to a question about overseas expansion, Stern said, "I was asked at a press conference, are we planning to come to Europe with franchises, and I said that it ultimately depends on new buildings, fan interest getting higher as well, a pricing model that would work so that the fans who did want us would be willing to pay the kinds of prices to support a team, and ultimately ownership as well. There are lots of hurdles there [Europe] to overcome." Furthermore, during an interview in March of 2004 Stern reaffirmed his commitment to global expansion when he stated, "If you can schedule the Portland Trail Blazers in Orlando, you can schedule the (Los Angeles) Lakers, who would not be flying from L.A. but from Boston, to do their European trip. Yes, I think we will see an NBA franchise in Europe someday and NBA-sanctioned leagues on other continents. I think we're talking about some place among Spain, France, Italy, Germany and England (for potential expansion)." Interestingly, the league has hired a firm to analyze foreign facilities, marketing options and potential fan interest. See Sekou Smith, "David Stern Expects to See the NBA in Europe," at <http://www.sportsbusiness-news.com> cited 30 March 2004.

5.   For the Grizzlies' relocation from Vancouver, Canada to Memphis, Tennessee and the other movements of teams in the NBA, and MLB and the NFL, see Frank P. Jozsa, Jr. and John J. Guthrie, Jr., *Relocating Teams and Expanding Leagues in Professional Sports*, 17–42, 67–100. For team relocations in the NHL between 1967 and 2001, see Frank P. Jozsa, Jr., *America Sports Empire*, 26–28. With respect to expansion, during 2004 the Carolina Bobcats began its first season as an NBA team. Earlier, the franchise had proceeded to search across the globe for a new general manager. One candidate interviewed was Maurizio Gherardini, who at that time was the general manager of the Italian club Benetton Treviso. According to the Bobcats' executive vice president Ed Tapscott, "He [Gherardini] has a unique eye for talent. He believes in working within a budget—not just buying talent, but developing talent. This guy is absolutely the best general manager in the international game." For this strategy, see Rich Bonnell, "Tapscott Hits Europe in Bobcats GM Search," *The Charlotte Observer* (9 October 2003), 1C, and Idem., "Tapscott Says Italian is Serious GM Candidate," *The Charlotte Observer* (10 October 2003), 2C. Indeed, Tapscott and other NBA executives have turned to international players trained in foreign leagues for the refined skills U.S. prospects generally lack. For why the Bobcats pursued international basketball players, see Rich Bonnell, "Gone Global," *The Charlotte Observer* (20 April 2003), 1F, 4F.

6. The information about the facilities, players and histories of each NBA team is available at the league's web site, <http://www.nba.com>.

7. For more details about the multi-faceted global contract between the NBA and Yahoo! Inc., see "The NBA, WNBA and Yahoo! Announce Groundbreaking Global Agreement," *Business Wire* (11 September 2002), 9–19. According to Commissioner David Stern, "By establishing this agreement with Yahoo!, we believe we can considerably enhance NBA. com and WNBA.com as full-service destinations for everyone interested in basketball. Yahoo! provides us with a wide range of services, all geared towards driving traffic and meeting the needs of NBA and WNBA fans."

8. See "Gatorade and NBA Enter Global Partnership," *AsiaPulse News* (8 November 2002), 49, and "Anheuser-Busch & NBA Extend Global Partnership," *PR Newswire* (10 December 2002), 4. With respect to the former deal, Gatorade's vice president for PepsiCo Beverages International David Knight remarked, "With players from all over the world making a greater impact in the NBA and the league becoming increasingly popular among fans around the globe, it was a natural for us to do more with the NBA overseas." Regarding the latter contract, "We are proud to play a role in the continuing international growth of Budweiser and believe our global brand truly benefits from the extraordinary marketing and strategic direction that accompanies everything Anheuser-Busch does," said Commissioner Stern.

9. Those and other capital projects are discussed in Daniel Eisenberg, "The NBA's Global Game Plan," 59–60. Other proposed investments and strategies for the league are reported in "The NBA Needs to do Some Globetrotting," *Business Week* (19 July 1999), 19, and Percy Allen, "David Stern Still Looking to Globalize the Game," at <http:///www.sports-businessnews.com> cited 6 November 2003.

10. For why and how the NBA had expanded its worldwide television presence by the late 1990s, see Mike Reynolds, "Full Global Press," *Inside Media* (1 February 1995), 22; Marc Gunther, "They All Want to be Like Mike," *Fortune* (21 July 1997), 51–53; Frank Lawlor, "NBA Czar Reaches Out to World," *International Herald Tribune* (4 February 1999), 17; Christopher Clarey, "France's Newest Passion: The N.B.A.," *The New York Times* (16 June 1993), B9.

11. See "NBA Renews International Television Agreements," at <http://www.sportsbusin-essnews.com> cited 25 November 2002, and Eric Fisher, "The NBA Continues to Use TV to Drive Its Product Internationally," at <http://www.sportsbusinessnews.com> cited 25 November 2002. Interestingly, during the middle of the 1990s NBA Canada was established to negotiate and maintain national broadcasting deals for the Raptors in Toronto and Grizzles in Vancouver, and to arrange business relationships with Canadian companies. However, in early 2004 Maple Leaf Sports and Entertainment had attempted to take control of NBA Canada by persuading the NBA to drop its 75-mile regional territorial boundary that applies to the teams' marketing and regional television broadcasts. This deal is very im-portant according to one Raptors official who remarked, "I think the way the league per-ceives this whole move, it is pretty interested in expanding into Europe and this develop-ment in Canada could act as a pilot program for those European countries." For more about the negotiations, see Robert MacLeod, "Toronto Raptors Looking to Take Control of NBA Canada," at <http://www.sportsbusinessnews.com> cited 24 February 2004.

12. During 2003, NBA games, highlights and features were televised in Germany through Premiere World, DSF, ProSieben, Sat. 1, ARD, ZDF and RTL channels. For this announce-ment, see "NBA Blankets Germany With TV Agreements," at <http://www.nba.com> cited 21 May 2003.

13.   See "NBA Renews International TV Deals," at <http://www.nba.com> cited 21 May 2003; "NBA Announces International Preseason Schedule," at <http://www.nba.com> cited 4 August 2003; "Coca-Cola NBA Jam Session Debuts in China," at <http://www.nba.com> cited 25 September 2003.

14.   For how the world has gradually closed the gap with the U.S. in basketball player abilities as represented on a timeline that extends from 1972 to 2002, see Alexander Wolff, "The Decline of U.S. Dominance," at <http://sportsillustrated.cnn.com> cited 25 June 2003, and Idem., "The Rest of the World Nearly Has Caught Up to the U.S.," at <http://sportsillustrated.cnn.com> cited 26 June 2003. In Wolff's view, "For years, foreign coaches humbly studied the American way, soaking up every last detail and applying it systematically. Now, as smugness sets in Stateside and more and more kids the world over play the game, parity has snuck up on the U.S."

15.   Ibid.

16.   Those and other viewpoints about the expansion of foreign players in the NBA are expressed in four articles. See Mike Wise, "The Globalization of the NBA," at <http://www.sportsbusinessnews.com> cited 25 November 2002; Barbara Barker, "The Internationalization of the NBA," at <http://www.sportsbusinessnews.com> cited 25 November 2002; David Shields and Phil Poynter, "Foreign Guys Can Shoot: That's Why the N.B.A. is in the Import Business," *The New York Times Magazine* (3 March 2002), 56; Peter Gwin, "Transatlantic: How Europe is Shaping US Basketball Hoops," *Europe* (June 1997), 33. Even more revealing about the use of foreign athletes in the NBA, of the 60 total players represented in a 2004 mock draft as reported on a web site, there were 12 or 20 percent listed from outside of America. Those players included four from Russia, two from Brazil and one each from Denmark, Latvia, Serbia-Montenegro, Slovenia, South Korea and the Ukraine. The draft order, teams, players' names and countries appear in "2004 Mock Draft," at <http://www.nbadraft.net> cited 13 April 2004.

17.   See Adrienne Lewis, "Foreign Imports," *USA TODAY* (4 June 2003), 3C, and "International Players in the NBA," at <http://www.nba.com> cited 21 May 2003. For a distribution of foreign players in the NBA, see Table A.5 in the Appendix. The table indicates that a total of 61 players existed on the rosters of 27 professional teams during early March of 2004. Also, eight or 13 percent of the basketball athletes were natives of Serbia-Montenegro, four or six percent each from Canada, France, Republic of Georgia and Slovenia, and three or five percent each from Brazil. The Spurs in San Antonio, Texas and Jazz in Salt Lake City, Utah had the most international players at six while the Bulls in Chicago, Illinois and Wizards in Washington, D.C. played their games without foreign athletes. For sure, in recent seasons the western conference's Spurs and Jazz have generally outperformed the eastern conference's Bulls and Wizards on the court. Indeed, the Spurs' Tim Duncan from the Virgin Islands and Tony Parker from France, and the Jazz' Andrei Kirilenko from Russia and Carlos Arroyo from Puerto Rico have excelled, respectively, as players for their clubs. Kirilenko, for example, made the 2004 all-star team. About representing his country at the game, in an interview Kirilenko stated, "I was born in Russia, it's my country. I like the NBA, that's my dream, but Russia is my country. It's all about business, profession in America—like money, job—but my heart is in Russia." For the interview, see "Global Mailbox: Andrei Kirilenko," at <http://www.nba.com> cited 20 April 2004. For the interviews of two Canadian players in the league, there is Johannes Berendt, "Kickin' Style," at <http://www.nba.com> cited 20 April 2004, and "Global Mailbox: Jamaal Magloire," at <http://www.nba.com> cited 20 April 2004. Besides Table A.5 and those articles, Table A.6 shows the distribution of those 61 international players by position. That table denotes that 26 or 43 percent of the foreign players were assigned to their clubs as a center, 23 or 37 percent as a forward and 12 or 20 percent as a guard. The centers are

generally the tallest players on the team. They must rebound missed shots at the basket and block the attempts by opponents to score points near the basket. The forwards score points on offense, rebound and play strong defense. Meanwhile, the guards set up plays and initiate fast breaks on offense, and play defense further away from the basket than the center and forwards. Based on the distributions in Table A.6, the NBA teams have seriously recruited international basketball athletes who are at least 81 inches or taller to play the center and forward positions.

18. The contrast in attitudes and skills between European and American professional basketball players are based on several factors. The reasons are partially examined in Michael Wilborn, "Basketball's New World Order," *The Washington Post* (6 September 2002), D1; Chad Ford, "European NBA Talent—Pay Later, Develop Now," at <http://www.sports-businessnews.com> cited 3 December 2002; Jerry Brewer, "NBA Embraces International Flavor," *Knight Ridder/Tribune Star News Service* (22 June 2002), 19; Alexander Wolff, "Foreign Intrigue," at <http://cnnsi.printthis.clickability.com> cited 28 June 2003.

19. Some NBA coaches and basketball analysts perceive that European basketball players may have improved significantly because of cultural factors. However, foreign basketball officials take a different view. "I hate it—the NBA ruined NCAA play, and now it's going to ruin the rest of the world. Too many of our young players are not learning the game as they should. European teams used to win with tactics, with teamwork. Our young guys aren't learning to be complete players anymore," said Slobodan Sarenac, the color commentator on basketball broadcasts for Serbia's national television network. For more about this viewpoint, see Tim Warren, "After the Pillage, European Basketball is Not Happy With the NBA Style of B-Ball," at <http://www.sportsbusinessnews.com> cited 16 September 2003, and Phil Taylor, "Will Foreign-Born Players Bring the U.S. Fans Back to the NBA?" at <http://sportsillustrated.com> cited 2 July 2003.

20. See Chad Ford, "NBA Scouting Becomes a World-Wide Experience," at <http://www. sportsbusinessnews.com> cited 3 December 2002; Stefan Fatsis, "The Continued Globalization of the NBA," at <http://www.sportsbusinessnews.com> cited 19 August 2003; Idem., "A Global Network of Scouts and Spies Hunts For NBA Gold," *Wall Street Journal* (26 June 2003), A1, A6. During the NBA's 2003–2004 regular season, some of the league's rookie international players had failed to meet expectations because their performances lagged. During late November of 2003, for example, 80 percent of the top scorers and 90 percent of the leaders in rebounds, assists and minutes played were Americans. One player who had disappointed his coach was the Detroit Piston's Darko Milicic who is from Serbia-Montenegro. According to the Phoenix Suns' president Bryan Colangelo, "Some of the young international players are being selected based on hype rather than reality." For other observations about the professional players, see Chris Broussard, "Americans Top Rookie Class," *The Charlotte Observer* (30 November 2003), 4F. Meanwhile, the Cleveland Cavaliers' Lithuanian center Zydrunas Ilgauskas averaged nearly 20 points, ten rebounds and four block shots per game against the Los Angles Lakers' Shaquille O'Neal and Houston Rockets' Yao Ming. Ilgauskas' performance is described in Chris Broussard, "Ilgauskas Living Up to Potential," *The Charlotte Observer* (21 March 2004), 4F. Besides Ilgauskas, six international players who were rookies in 2004 had made an impact in the league with their performances. Those players included the Phoenix Suns' Leandro Barbosa from Brazil, Utah Jazz's Raul Lopez from Spain, Golden State Warriors' Mickael Pietrus from France, Atlanta Hawks' Boris Diaw from France, Denver Nuggets' Francisco Elson from the Netherlands, and the Sacramento Kings' Darius Songaila from Lithuania. The game statistics of these players is discussed in Rob Peterson, "Fabulous Foreign Freshmen," at <http://www.nba.com> cited 13 April 2004. Even more impressive than the

rookies, three international players were identified as candidates to receive one or more major regular season awards in the NBA. The players were the Utah Jazz's Andrei Kirilenko from Russia, Dallas Mavericks' Dirk Nowitzki from Germany, and the Sacramento Kings' Peja Stojakovic from Serbia-Montenegro.

21.   Because of the increasing prominence of international players, the FIBA and NBA are expected to revamp and coordinate their respective contract and buyout systems. For some comments from club officials and scouts, see Chris Broussard, "The NBA and the Never Ending Search For Talent," at <http://www.sportsbusinessnews.com> cited 16 September 2003.

22.   For reforms with respect to the buyout system, see Darren Rovell, "Drafting European Players, Its Buyer Beware," at <http://www.sportsbusinessnews.com> cited 3 December 2002. According to Rovell, "Today, knowing the terms and the price of the buyout before drafting a prominent international player is essential. If an American agent signs a player at the onset of his professional career, he will be able to steer the player to a favorable foreign team, one that is willing to include buyouts in certain years of a long-term deal."

23.   At basketball camps, there are a number of agents, scouts and teams' personnel development officials who evaluate U.S. and international players. See Mike Fish, "European Invasion Has Prep Stars Focusing on Fundamentals," at <http://sportsillustrated.cnn.com> cited 17 July 2003; Kent Baker, "Professional Playing Opportunities For Non-Playing NBA Basketball Players," at <http://www.sportsbusinessnews.com> cited 19 August 2003; "Basketball Without Borders: Fact Sheet," at <http://www.nba.com> cited 13 August 2003; "Basketball Without Borders 2003 Fact Sheet," at <http://www.nba.com> cited 13 August 2003.

24.   To read about the NBA's options, see Tim Warren, "After the Pillage, European Basketball is Not Happy With the NBA Style of B-Ball."

25.   For Yao Ming's development as a basketball player in China, and his success in the NBA from a marketing perspective, see Stefan Fatsis, Peter Wonacott, and Maureen Tkacik, "A Basketball Star From Shanghai is Big Business," *Wall Street Journal* (22 November 2002), A1, A10; Jill Painter, "This Just In . . . Yao Ming is Big Business," at <http://www.sportsbusinessnews.com> cited 20 February 2003; Geoffrey York, "Live From China—The Legend of Yao Ming," at <http://www.sportsbusinessnews.com> cited 8 January 2003; Scott Soshnick, "Yao Ming and One Billion Chinese Basketball Fans," at <http://www.sportsbusinessnews.com> cited 3 December 2002; Brian Windhorst, "Yao is a Big Star," at <http://www.sportsbusinessnews.com> cited 20 February 2004; Rich Bonnell, "Yao's Arrival a Smooth One," *The Charlotte Observer* (20 April 2003), 4F; Danny O'Neil, "The Marketing of Yao Ming, a Work in Progress," at <http://www.sportsbusinessnews.com> cited 3 December 2002. Indeed, by early 2004 the NBA Rockets had leveraged Ming's popularity to attract and appeal to Asian sports fans who lived in the Houston area and elsewhere in Texas. That is, the club launched a campaign to market the amiable star to the city's Chinese community; advertised games in Chinese-language newspapers, radio and television; broadcasted a weekly Mandarin radio show that featured an interview with Yao; hired Mandarin speakers in its marketing department; initiated a Chinese-language web site and sold group tickets to Chinese community groups. To inform Asians about its games, the Rockets advertised heavily in such Chinese language newspapers as the *World Journal* and *Singtao Daily*, and sold three-game ticket packages that included one Rockets' game. Other NBA teams like the Golden State Warriors in the San Francisco area have also promoted Ming to their local fans in various ways. Those are reported in "NBA Wants to Turn Yao Admirers Into Team Fans," at <http://sportsillustrated.cnn.com> cited 6 April 2004. As an aside, during late 2003 the Toyota Motor Corporation almost finalized its purchase of the naming rights to Houston's new $202 million downtown arena. As a result, the arena was

expected to be renamed the Toyota Center. The deal prompted NBA Houston Rockets' president George Postolos to say, "Somebody is going to put their name on the arena. They are going to have an immediate association with our team, and a player that is a huge star in Asia." Toyota has recently expanded its presence in China and is the type of company that the Rockets had hoped to build a relationship with when the team selected Yao Ming as the first pick in the 2002 draft. For the arena's impact, see Megan Manfull and Jonathon Feigen, "Rockets New Arena May Have International Appeal," at <http://www.sportsbusinessnews. com> cited 19 August 2003.

26.   Ibid. Moreover, the reader should see T.C. Peng, "From Unknown to Stardom," *Chinese American Forum* (April 2003), 2–3, and <http://www.nba.rockets.com>, which is the Houston Rockets' web site. Meanwhile, the reasons for the NBA's preseason basketball games in Beijing and Shanghai were thoroughly described in "NBA Heading to China For Pre-Season Games," at <http://www.sportsbusinessnews.com> cited 17 February 2004. "The NBA China Games are the logical next step in the NBA's long-term relationship with Chinese basketball and Chinese fans. We have worked closely with the China Basketball Association, as well as the sports authorities of Shanghai and Beijing," remarked Commissioner Stern.

27.   For Yao Ming's various endorsement deals, see Gabriel Kahn, "Yo, Yao: What's Up With Chinese Ads in Texas?" *Wall Street Journal* (7 February 2003), B1, B4; Sam Walker, "Catch Yao Later," *Wall Street Journal* (7 February 2003), W4; "Slam Dunk," *Wall Street Journal* (9 January 2003), B5; "Basketball's Yao Ming Sues Coke For a Yuan," *Wall Street Journal* (27 May 2003), B4; Darren Rovell, "Is Reebok About to Sign Yao Ming?" at <http://www.sportsbusinessnews.com> cited 25 September 2003; Frederick Balfour, "It's Time For a New Playbook," *Business Week* (15 September 2003), 56; Peter Wonacott and Betsy McKay, "Yao is a Pitchman Torn Between Two Colas," *Wall Street Journal* (16 May 2003), B1, B4; Darren Rovell, "Yao Ming is Loving McDonald's," at <http://www.sports-businessnews.com> cited 20 February 2004. As reflected in Rovell's article, McDonald's has 560 restaurants in 70 Chinese cities and according to published reports, the company plans to open about 100 franchises during 2004. Even so, the franchises in China make up less than 2 percent of the total number of McDonald's restaurants in the world. "McDonalds has a great history of working with athletes. They have produced fantastic ads and this alliance will help them further penetrate the Chinese market, which is one of their important goals," claims the marketing director of Team Yao, Bill Sanders.

28.   For more about this topic, see "The Global Marketing of Yao Ming," at <http://www. sportsbusinessnews.com> cited 22 January 2003. "It doesn't take long, when you spend time with him [Ming] and learn what type of type of person he is, to realize that he has almost unlimited potential to do endorsements," said John Huizinga, who is the deputy dean of the faculty at the University of Chicago and Yao's officially registered agent.

29.   Jackie MacMullan, "Yao Ming and the History of Basketball in China," at <http://www.sportsbusinessnews.com> cited 27 February 2003; Idem., "The Sport and a Quarter of the World's Population," at <http://www.sportsbusinessnews.com> cited 27 February 2003; Mike Wise and Craig S. Smith, "How China Intends to Benefit From the NBA or China's Version of Democracy," at <http://www.sportsbusinessnews.com> cited 3 December 2002; "NBA Mulls Regular-Season Games in China," at <http://si.printthis. clickability.com> cited 2 October 2003; Gene Wang, "Is Yao Ming Bridging the Gap Between China and the United States," at <http://www.sportsbusinessnews.com> cited 6 March 2003. For other aspects about the history of professional basketball in China since the early 1900s, see Jeff Coplon, "Basketball in the World's Most Populated Country," at <http://www.sportsbusinessnews.com> cited 1 December 2003. To prepare the Chinese basketball team for the 2004 Olympic Games in Athens, Greece, the NBA Dallas

Mavericks' assistant coach Del Harris was named the coach of the Chinese National Team. Harris' experiences have included international basketball. He, for example, had coached six years in Puerto Rico, advised the Canadian National Team with respect to the 1994 World Championships, and served as an assistant to Team USA in the 1998 World Championships. About his effort and opportunity to coach a Chinese team, Harris said, "[My biggest challenge is] guard play. We have a lot of big guys. We don't have many [basketball players] in the 6-foot to 6-3 ranges by comparison. The long-range goal for the Chinese team is to be a serious competitor for a medal in 2008. It just has to be one step at a time." For more comments made by Harris during an interview, see Rob Peterson, "Q&A With Mavs Assistant Del Harris," at <http://www.nba.com> cited 6 April 2004. Besides Harris' evaluation, Yao Ming also believes that China's national basketball team has a chance to finish in the top eight at the Olympic Games in Greece. The guards, in Ming's opinion, are the weakest link of the team. As he states, "I don't think that the guards in China have enough experience in big international games. The big guys have played in many important games and know what it's like. Our guards need to be exposed to more of that high level of competition." See "Yao Has the Answers," at <http://www.nba.com> cited 20 April 2004.

30.   Ibid. Regarding Ming's presence in the league during 2004, NBA vice president Scott Levy said, "I don't think the Yao craze has died down at all, certainly not in China. The viewership there is as strong as ever, and that's only helped to broaden the interest in the entire league. Fans in China now also want to see LeBron James. They want to see Carmelo Anthony. They don't want a spoon-fed or watered-down version of the NBA. They're interested in all the same players and teams as we are in America." Meanwhile, former American dentist and sports promoter Dr. Leonard Bloom has struggled for five years to launch a basketball league in China. To that end, his eight-team university Friendship Basketball League was organized despite the lack of sponsorships and television contracts to promote the league. Indeed, Bloom has attempted to overcome China's ossified college sports system and the country's socialist sports programs by distributing Chinese training manuals that feature daily exercises, and by handing out a rule book that blends European and U.S. basketball rules translated into Chinese. Also, he developed new names, logos and uniforms for universities that had joined the league. To recoup the $1 million in costs spent by his Marquee Corporation, Bloom has become the exclusive agent for 80 of the league's college players for five years after they graduate. As a result, he will receive 10 percent of the contract amount of any player who becomes a professional athlete. Furthermore, the schools have allowed Bloom to sell league merchandise on their campuses including Friendship basketballs. For why sports are a growth industry in Asia and particularly China, and how the Friendship Basketball League was formed, respectively, see Eric Fisher, "Selling U.S. Professional Sports in China," at <http://www.sportsbusinessnews.com> cited 20 January 2004, and Karen Richardson, "Full-Court Press: Promoter Envisions NCAA in China," *Wall Street Journal* (22 April 2004), A1, A16.

31.   Mexicans adore basketball and the NBA. For information about the basketball leagues in Mexico, see "Introduction to Mexican Basketball," at <http://www.latinbasket.com> cited 27 October 2003, and Art Garcia, "Basketball's Popularity Growing in Mexico," at <http://www.sportsbusinessnews.com> cited 9 October 2003. Indeed, during 1994 a Continental Basketball Association team nicknamed the Aztecs played 28 home games at the 21,000-seat Sports Palace in Mexico City. According to the Aztecs' president Doug Logan, "We've talked with prospective (NBA) ownership groups in Mexico and the U.S. Commissioner (David) Stern has said the next expansion will be in Mexico City, but the next wave probably won't be until the year 2000. In the meantime, we're trying to build audiences." See Don Muret, "With CBA in Mexico City, Can NBA be Far Behind?" *Amusement Business* (6 June 1994), 13.

32. For how, when, where and why the Dallas Mavericks' Eduardo Najera became a basketball hero in Mexico, see Eddie Sefko, "Mavericks—Jazz Play Preseason Game in Mexico," at <http://www.sportsbusinessnews.com> cited 9 October 2003. Furthermore, see Scott Soshnick, "NBA's Mexican Born Player and Endorsement Opportunities," at <http://www.sportsbusinessnews.com> cited 3 December 2002; Joel Millman, "Young Maverick Sits on Sidelines But Stars in Ads," *Wall Street Journal* (27 February 2002), B1, B3. Interestingly, Najera and other foreign players in the NBA might play for their national teams in the Olympic Games. Mavericks' owner Mark Cuban has reservations about allowing his players to perform in the Games and other international tournaments. That is, he responded to criticisms from U.S. Olympic basketball team coach Larry Brown as follows, "Brown . . . isn't responsible to fans, and he gets paid regardless of what happens. If things don't work out, a player gets injured or he doesn't like the way things are going, he can do what he has done everywhere else, just leave. As the owner of the team, I can't do that." Cuban's views are reported in David Moore, "Pistons Coach Blasts Dallas Owner Cuban," *The Charlotte Observer* (9 February 2004), 4C.

33. See Sarah Talalay, "Miami Heat Continue Their Hispanic Marketing Efforts," at <http://www.sportsbusinessnews.com> cited 3 December 2002; Magaly Morales, "Telemundo Set to Begin Their NBA Coverage," at <http://www.sportsbusinessnews.com> cited 25 November 2002; "TV Azteca and the NBA Extend Broadcast Partnership," at <http://www.nba.com> cited 29 August 1998.

34. Because of urbanization and satellite television, Africa is a large potential market for the NBA. This observation was expressed in Ashley McGeachy Fox, "NBA Continues to Expand Their Horizons," at <http://www.sportsbusinessnews.com> cited 9 October 2003, and Alexander Wolff, "International Hoops," *The New York Times* (31 May 2002), A23. As sportswriter Fox denotes, "Soccer might be the top sport in Africa, but the NBA, along with the International Basketball Federation and Basketball South Africa, is working to make basketball a strong No. 2."

35. At the basketball camp, participants from across Africa were selected for their basketball skills, leadership abilities and dedication to the sport of basketball by the FIBA, in conjunction with participating basketball federations. See "NBA Players Unite For Africa 100 Camp," at <http://www.nba.com> cited 15 August 2003. With respect to the Camp, Commissioner David Stern said, "Basketball has the ability to bring people together and address important social issues at the same time. The Africa 100 Camp is an example of basketball's reach and the good that can come from gathering participants for learning on and off the court." Furthermore, as announced to the media the NBA had collaborated with FIBA to schedule Basketball Without Borders during 2004 in Rio de Janeiro, Brazil, and in Treviso, Italy and Johannesburg, South Africa. The camps, in part, included extensive community outreach activities, support for a Reading and Learning Center, educational seminars that addressed important social issues such as HIV/AIDS prevention, and instructions about how to be fit and healthy to play competitive basketball. About the African camp, New York Knicks' Congo-born center Dikembe Mutombo remarked, "Last year's Africa 100 Camp was a great event and I am very happy to return with the complete Basketball Without Borders program. All NBA players know how important it is to contribute to your community and to your homeland and I am honored to represent the NBA at Basketball Without Borders." With respect to each of the 2004 camps, the participants included 50 young players aged 16–17 from Latin America and the Caribbean, 50 from various European nations and about the same number from such African countries as Angola, Cameroon, Mozambique, Senegal and Nigeria. Generally, the players were chosen because of their basketball skills and their leadership and dedication to the sport. As a token

of appreciation, the NBA and FIBA planned to donate basketball, nets and rims to federations in the countries of the participants. Those and other details about the activities are reported in "Program to Encompass Three Continents in 2004," at <http://www.nba.com> cited 6 April 2004; "NBA Back in Africa For Basketball Without Borders," at <http://www. nba.com> cited 6 April 2004; "NBA Stars Return to Europe to Educate Youth," at <http: //www.nba.com> cited 6 April 2004. Interestingly, especially noticed as an instructor at Basketball Without Borders will be former NBA player Gheorghe Muresan, who played as a 7 foot 7 inch center from Romania. Although Muresan currently lives in the state of New Jersey, for almost a year he lived in Romania and managed the Romanian basketball team and the national team. For his contribution at the Borders' camp, Muresan will train the big men. "Yes, I will give them everything I know. I can't say I know enough basketball; you never know enough basketball. I know enough to show them a lot of moves from the post and the five. I will learn from them too at the same time, and I've got to teach them. It's a great chance to give back a lot of things I know. It makes me feel better too to give back to the kids." Other comments from Muresan are reported in Randy Kim, "Tall Tales: Catching Up With Gheorghe Muresan," at <http://www.nba.com> cited 20 April 2004.

36.   For the history of the WNBA to the late 1990s, see Frank P. Jozsa, Jr. and John J. Guthrie, Jr., *Relocating Teams and Expanding Leagues in Professional Sports*, 158–162. The NBA's web site, <http://www.nba.com> is an online source for information about the WNBA. Besides the WNBA, in America there is the National Women's Basketball League (NWBL), which began as a start-up organization with four teams during 2001. Basically, the NWBL has consisted of players who were former collegians with limited or no professional experience, and are mostly from schools located near each franchise. The league's teams, therefore, welcome WNBA players that cut their ties to European clubs. So, the six-team NWBL does not hesitate to compete with European teams to acquire WNBA players who are important to the organization's marketing and public relations campaigns. About the recruitment of foreign players, Springfield Spirit owner Steve Fox said, "If a player doesn't want to play in a country where they might not know the language, have to live in an unfamiliar place, and eat lousy food, then we offer them a chance to play here." Fox also stated, "The difference between our league and the WNBA is that we can offer players the opportunity who didn't play for a high-profile school. They have to play at a certain high level here." For more on this women's professional league, see Judy Van Handle, "NWBL Alive and Growing," at <http://www.sportsbusinessnews.com> cited 3 February 2004.

37.   The WNBA team rosters include international players who were active, injured and suspended. For a complete list, see "WNBA Players From Around the World: 2003 Season," at <http://www.wnba.com> cited 21 October 2003.

38.   For Scott Levy's comment about the WNBA, see "2003 WNBA Season to be Broadcast in 183 Countries," at <http://www.wnba.com> cited 21 October 2003.

39.   Specifically, the league's problems are discussed in Mike Peticca, "WNBA Not Concerned About Drop in Attendance," at <http://www.sportsbusinessnews.com> cited 16 October 2003, and R. Thomas Umstead, "Women's Network Unsure of Their Commitment to WNBA," at <http://www.sportsbusinessnews.com> cited 26 August 2003. To read about the WNBA's money problems and future, see Chris Isidore, "WNBA: Lovable Money Loser," at <http://www.si.com> cited 17 August 2001; "NBA Board of Governors Report," at <http://www.sportsbusinessnews.com> cited 16 October 2003; Lorraine A. Woellert, "For the WNBA, It's No Easy Layup," *Business Week* (1 May 2000), 102, 106.

40.   The ABA's web site at <http://www.abalive.com> includes links to the league office, franchise information, former players and where they are now, the 2004–2005 expansion teams, recent team standings, and other details such as announcements with respect to the

expansion dates and sites. Interestingly, an ABA expansion team will be placed in Charlotte, North Carolina in 2004, which is when the Charlotte Bobcats, a new NBA expansion team will begin its first season during the Fall. Regarding that decision, the ABA's co-founder Joe Newman said, "We know that the NBA's Charlotte Bobcats are starting next season, but the ABA and new owners felt strongly that the market was large enough and basketball fan support great enough to handle two teams. We believe that fans will love the fast-paced, high scoring, entertainment filled ABA style of play—at ABA affordable prices."

Chapter 4

National Hockey League

The National Hockey League (NHL) was formed in Montreal, Canada and initiated its first season in 1917. Besides the NHL, which is the focus of this chapter, there has been four other independent ice hockey associations organized as leagues in North America. After several seasons of play, however, those associations had to termin- ate their organizations and then dissolved, sold out or evolved into the NHL. That is, the seven year old National Hockey Association disbanded into the NHL after its final season in 1916, while the 14 year old Pacific Coast Hockey Association and the five year old Western Hockey Association had each failed and sold out to the NHL in 1925. Forty-seven years later, the professional World Hockey Association organized but then broke up in 1979. Even so, since the late 1890s other North American ice hockey groups currently exist or had operated for one or more seasons as either an amateur, junior, minor, semiprofessional or professional developmental association or league. Those organizations included, for example, the Amateur Hockey Association of Canada, Amateur Hockey League, American West Hockey League, Atlantic Coast Hockey League, Central Hockey League, Central Professional Hockey League, East Coast Hockey League, Eastern Canada Hockey Association, Federal League, International Hockey League, New Ontario Hockey League, North American Hockey League, West Coast Hockey League and Western Hockey League. In retrospect, it was because of below-average game attendances, limited budgets and insufficient cash flows, undercapitalized owners, unfavorable stadium leases and/or other economic, financial, marketing and management hardships that several of those leagues had to dissolve, merge or changed titles. Consequently, during the early 2000s the dominant professional ice hockey league in North America, and perhaps the world, was the U.S.-based NHL.[1]

Between 1942 and 1966, the NHL had consisted of Canadian teams in Montreal and Toronto and American teams in Boston, Chicago, Detroit and New York. Then, for various reasons from 1967 to 2004 eight teams received approval from the league to relocate and 24 new franchises joined the league. As a result of those relocations and expansions, during the 2003–2004 regular season the NHL's Eastern and Western Conferences each included three Canadian and 12 U.S. clubs, which totaled to 30 franchises. To be discussed later in this chapter from an inter- national sport and business perspective, the six Canadian teams were located in and played their home games at sites in the medium sized to large cities of Calgary, Edmonton, Montreal, Ottawa, Toronto and Vancouver.[2]

Before the format and organization, and an overview of the contents in Chapter 4 are presented, one issue that will likely influence the NHL's short- and long-term business activities, programs and prospects in North America and abroad is the expiration of the league's current collective bargaining agreement with the players' union in the Fall of 2004. Why are the types of clauses and provisions, and the terms and conditions in a new labor agreement of critical importance for the NHL team owners and the teams' players, and for the National Hockey League Players Association (NHLPA), Canadian Hockey League (CHL), and ice hockey and other sports fans?

Since the early 1990s, the NHL's enormous growth in revenue amounts has been exceeded by even larger increases in total player compensation, that is, in salaries and such fringe benefits as liability insurance and pension coverage. To be specific, during the early 2000s the league spent approximately 76 percent of its $1.9 billion in revenues on players' salaries and benefits, which is higher than the percentages that were spent in MLB, and in the NFL and NBA. Consequently, the NHL teams' operating losses per season had totaled $40 million in 1993–1994, and then increased to $218 million in 2001–2002 and one season later, $300 million. Because two of the NHL's franchises experienced bankruptcy in 2002, since then the market values of some of the league's existing teams have remained constant or perhaps declined. Accordingly, because of the depression in the franchise's market values, current club owners have been unable and/or unwilling to borrow more money and fund their operating losses, and also must raise their coupon interest rates to sell new debt securities. Given this dilemma, in its negotiations with the players' union in 2004 the league will likely seek a salary cap for its teams and/or restrictions on free agency. Meanwhile, the NHLPA would prefer to maintain the status quo, that is, to allow player salaries to be determined by the forces of demand and supply in the labor market. With a reported $300 million of deposits in its bank accounts, the league has prepared itself for a lengthy work stoppage. Likewise, the players' union has advised its membership to expect at least an 18–24 month shutdown of the league's operations. The NHL and/or NHLPA will make what compromises during the negotiations remains uncertain. It is assumed in this chapter, however, that the issues in the new collective bargaining agreement are resolved without a disruption from a union strike and/or owners' lockout, which means that the league's 2004–2005 regular season begins on schedule.[3]

Based on that premise, to analyze the international business and global strategies of the NHL, Chapter 4 is organized into five distinct parts or sections. In the first section, the purposes, events and commercial activities of the National Hockey League International (NHLI) will be exposed and examined. Similar to the international divisions that were established in MLB and the NFL, the NHLI, as an organizational subunit has been assigned the various marketing functions, responsibilities and tasks to expand the brand, image and fan base, and thus the market penetration and globalization of the NHL. After the NHLI is discussed, the second section highlights and describes the league's broadcast commitments with cable and satellite systems, media companies and American and foreign television and radio networks. This information will denote how the NHL compares to the other

U.S.-based professional leagues in *Sports Capitalism* with respect to international programming, exposure and market share.

Chapter 4's third section explores the eminent interests, topics and experiences that involve the league's ice hockey players and those professional athletes who play in various foreign hockey leagues abroad. This section, in part, includes some interesting facts and observations about the players on national teams, which are members of such larger worldwide organizations as the International Ice Hockey Federation (IIHF). Following the discussion of players, the chapter's fourth section also contains an analysis of the mission, organization, operations and business prospects of Canada's Federal Hockey League (FHL). The international aspects and global relationships, if any, of this new league will be identified and evaluated. Then, the fifth section describes what activities a World Cup of Hockey event entails and whether the international exposure from that type of tournament will increase the fan bases and short- and long-term business prospects of the NHL and of certain other professional hockey leagues that are based in foreign countries. Finally, some forward-looking but controversial options are presented and examined with respect to what the NHL's international strategies will be after 2004. Those options include, but are not limited to, the contraction and expansion of one, few or several of the league's teams, and the potential merger of the league with one or more professional foreign hockey leagues.

To consolidate and summarize the significant international business strategies which appeared as concepts and topics, and that were emphasized in Chapter 4, a Summary is presented after the fifth section is completed. Besides the important contents in each section, the Summary will also indicate if the NHL has progressed enough to become recognized as an international sports organization. When the Summary concludes, the Notes are listed. In short, the Notes contain the articles, books, Internet readings and any other documents and publications that were researched to learn more about professional ice hockey and verify the international business environment that matters to the NHL.

NHLI

The NHL Enterprises is the division that manages and controls the NHL's worldwide marketing and licensing commitments. As the division's organizational subunit, the NHLI is directly responsible for the development and implementation of the league's policies with respect to international ice hockey competitions, and for the league's global broadcast alliances, corporate partnerships and sponsorships, marketing campaigns, new and renegotiated media and licensing contracts, and the other NHL business activities and events that are typically conducted in nations besides the U.S. and Canada. This subunit, for example, controls the operations of The NHL Challenge Series, which was a program established by the league in 1993. Essentially, the Challenge Series allows the NHL teams to conduct training camps and participate in any exhibition, preseason and regular season games outside of North America. To illustrate, during 2001 the NHL's Stanley

Cup Champion Colorado Avalanche held their training camp in Stockholm, Sweden and the Vancouver Canucks played exhibition games against some teams from the Swedish national league. Furthermore, during the late 1990s and early 2000s a few regular season games between NHL teams were also played outside of North America. Since the middle to late 1990s, a few activities that involved the NHLI were several of the Winter Olympic Games and World Cup of Hockey tournaments, and the scheduling and implementation of various grassroots initiatives. The latter events, which included the EA Sports/NHL Global Championships, NHL Mall Tour, NHL Million Dollar Challenge and an All-Access Pass promotion, are each briefly described as follows.[4]

During 2003, EA Sports and the NHL combined their resources and offered ice hockey fans an opportunity to win a free trip to the league's All-Star Weekend in South Florida. At that event, local amateur teams composed of ice hockey players from North America and such European countries as Finland, Germany, Hungary and Switzerland had competed to become national and then world champions. Meanwhile, in the Spring and Summer of 2003 the NHL Mall Tour had traveled throughout Europe to showcase the league by featuring interactive ice hockey exhibits, fan activities and marketing displays of the sport. To present the activities of one tour, seven large Swedish malls were visited from April through June. At each mall, the hockey-themed attractions included NHL Slapshot, which enabled hockey fans to measure the velocity of their shots on goal and NHL Rapid Fire, which permitted athletes and other spectators to test and evaluate their goaltending skills. According to the NHLI's group vice president and managing director Ken Jaffe, "NHL on [Mall] Tour allows the League to promote and expose the NHL brand to Sweden's passionate hockey fans at a grassroots level, while at the same time leveraging the popularity of hockey during the NHL's most exciting time of the year, the Stanley Cup Playoffs."[5]

The NHLI's third grassroots initiative, which was titled the NHL Million Dollar Challenge, had rewarded the contest winners from various foreign countries with a free trip to All-Star Weekend and also a chance to shoot on goal for $1 million. Lastly, the All-Access Pass promotion entitled international winners of locally sponsored events the special right to attend scheduled All-Star Weekend activities and enter exclusive areas to meet and commingle with players, and furthermore, to engage in a VIP Behind the Scenes Tour, which was filmed and broadcasted during the World Feed of the NHL's All-Star Game. Besides the Czech Republic, Japan and Russia, there were at least six other countries that participated in the 2003 All-Access Pass promotion program. In short, during 2003 the NHLI organized and managed these and other global grassroots initiatives for exposure and to encourage more fan participation and interest in the sport of ice hockey and the NHL.

Based on the three previous paragraphs, the readers of *Sports Capitalism* now realize how the NHLI had developed unique initiatives and applied business strategies to expose and promote ice hockey and the NHL within and outside of North America. Given the information about what the subunit does for the league, the next section of this chapter focuses on some of the business activities and important relationships of the NHL with respect to the broadcast media and to affiliated firms that are NHL licensees, partners, sponsors and vendors, and especially those types of companies that operate in foreign countries.

Global NHL-Media Business

Since the late 1990s, the NHL had noticeably increased its global presence and thereby experienced reasonably good growth as an international sports organization. To illustrate, a few key facts reflect the league's operations that focused on worldwide marketing campaigns and exposure. First, in 1997 the NHL allowed a regular season series of games to be played by its teams beyond the borders of North America, that is, in Japan. The league's teams replayed the series there again in 1998 and 2000. Besides those specific competitions, in 2003 the NHL's fans and other ice hockey enthusiasts in 160 nations had the opportunity to observe numerous regular season games and other activities of the sport on their television sets. Those events had included the NHL All-Star Game, Stanley Cup finals and Power Week. Second, with the cooperation, expertise and resources of at least 50 international licensees and corporate marketing partners, during 2003 the league generated more than $1 billion in sales of its licensed products. Third, approximately 273 or 33 percent of the NHL's players had emigrated from 14 nations outside of North America. In 2003, for example, there were 71 players or 26 percent from the Czech Republic, 64 or 24 percent from Russia, 50 or 18 percent from Sweden, 38 or 14 percent from Finland, 25 or nine percent from Slovakia, and 25 or nine percent from other countries such as Germany, Latvia, Poland, Ukraine, the United Kingdom and Poland. For sure, those NHL players had excited the hockey fans in their respective countries and provided an incentive for foreign consumers to spend more money and purchase NHL programs and the league's products. In short, the former illustrations were three examples that represent the league's growing international presence and popularity relative to the various years cited.[6]

During the early 2000s, the NHL became a more aggressive business organization and attempted to further penetrate markets across. That is, the league had established commercial relationships with several American corporations. Some of those relationships resembled the types of activities and interactions that were performed by the international marketing staffs who represent MLB, and the NFL and NBA. In 2001, for example, the NHL teamed with Chicago-based Ignite Media to market and promote the league's primary web site, whose address is <http://www.NHL.com>. Because of this partnership, a portion of online traffic about events in professional ice hockey was diverted directly to the site. In turn, this traffic had likely increased the league's international e-commerce sales of ice hockey apparel, equipment, merchandise and supplies. Furthermore, the Ignite Media company developed new sponsorships for the NHL and Stanley Cup logos, and for the league's All-Star Game. According to the company's executives, the NHL was the first major sports league in North America to outsource its online advertising. "One of the things we really like about the NHL is that they're one of the first league's to look at all their assets and say interactive assets are important," said Ignite Media's president Hank Adams.[7]

Besides that business deal, in 2002 the NHL formed special strategic relationships with two other firms. Those corporations were Sun Microsystems and Globe-Cast North America. With respect to the former alliance, California-based Sun Microsystems became an official technology partner of the NHL and the NHLPA, which is the players' union. Basically, the agreement enabled the league to further extend its brand overseas, grow its international fan bases, and increase the NHL teams' revenues by streamlining communications and business processes. That is, Sun Microsystems' technology provided sports fans with instantaneous access to the real-time statistical coverage of more than 1,200 professional hockey games, and access to some historical data, merchandising programs and video highlights of the sport. This communication link was especially important to the league since, according to consumer surveys and research studies, the NHL's fan base and customers had ranked first among all professional sports leagues in the use of online software, broadband access, personal computer ownership and buying power on the Internet. Indeed the company's technology allowed the NHL Commissioner's office to easily communicate and conveniently conduct business transactions and negotiations more securely online with the league's 30 teams and, if necessary, with the players' union about contract disputes, transactions, schedules, waiver activity, scouting reports and other matters. Relative to the NHL's other business relationship, the Miami-based GlobeCast North American corporation, which was the world's largest provider of satellite transmission services for professional broadcast, enterprise multimedia and Internet content delivery in 2003, had agreed to manage the satellite distribution of the NHL's 2002–2003 regular season games, playoffs and Stanley Cup championship series to European rights holders for NHLI. Furthermore, GlobeCast agreed to deliver selected ice hockey games to various Asia-Pacific broadcasters in such nations as Korea, Indonesia and New Zealand. In short, those two partnership agreements reflect why the NHL is one of the leaders among the U.S.-based professional sport leagues with respect to using online communications to offer the league's games, products and other programs to hockey fans in countries across the planet.[8]

Interestingly, during 2003 the only Russian television channel that broadcasted NHL games via satellite was NTV-Plus. Therefore, since approximately 46 or 17 percent of the league's players were Russian-born athletes, broadcaster Alexandre Tkachev decided to call one Panthers' regular season game from Miami in Florida, Red Wings' game from Detroit in Michigan and Devils' game from Chicago in Illinois. According to Tkachev, "When I was young, there was only one sport in Russia and that's [ice] hockey. It's not soccer or tennis. It's [ice] hockey. It's kind of the national sport in Russia. I know hockey is a Canadian game, but it's a Russian game, too." Besides those three competitions, other native-speaking announcers called regular season games, which were recorded on television and then broadcasted later to hockey fans that had residences in the Czech Republic, Hungary, Japan and Spain. The examples, therefore, indicate how the NHL's teams and players have become more familiar to foreigners because of the league's games that appeared on television in Russia and other countries abroad.[9]

Based on the contents in the previous section of this chapter, it was primarily during the early 2000s when the NHL took decisive action to globalize its brand through various media outlets. Certainly, those partnerships and sponsorships boosted the league's worldwide exposure and fan support. Even so, from a business perspective the NHL's global progress occurred, in part, because of the quantity and quality of the foreign amateur and professional ice hockey players who had played the sport. As such, the next section of Chapter 4 focuses on how international athletes participate in ice hockey games and tournaments, and those players' relationships with the NHL and with foreign ice hockey federations and other sports organizations.

NHL International Players

When the NHL increased in membership from six to 12 teams in 1967, less than two percent of its players were born outside of North America. Nevertheless, during other league expansions in the 1970s and 1990s, the portion of international ice hockey players who were listed on teams' rosters continued to grow. For example, in 1975 the percentage of foreign-born players in the league was approximately two percent, in 1979 6.3 percent, in 1992 17.2 percent, and in 1999 23.9 percent. The largest ten-year percentage growth occurred, however, between 1989 and 1999 when the proportion of international players had nearly doubled, that is, increased from 12 percent to about 24 percent. Thus, as this influx of players into the NHL happened, the league's best foreign-born hockey players, who tended to be from Canada, had to increasingly compete for their teams to win division titles, conference championships and the Stanley Cups against superior athletes from Russia such as Sergei Fedrov, Pavel Bure and Alexander Mogilny, and against other European ice hockey superstars who had migrated to America from the Czech Republic, Sweden and Finland.[10]

From a cultural perspective, the NHL players from Canada, Europe and elsewhere generally have displayed a different attitude than American athletes who, for instance, play for teams in the NBA. That is, on average foreign-born NHL players seem to be less self-centered and egocentric than NBA players, and are generally perceived by ice hockey fans in North America as unselfish, disciplined and team-oriented. Because professional ice hockey athletes rarely brag or make outlandish and off-the-cuff statements to the media as, for example some MLB, NFL, NBA and MLS players do, it is the NHL hockey teams, rather than specific players that are evaluated and scrutinized by sports commentators and journalists. Indeed, the performances of ice hockey teams and not coaches or players, who receive the majority of analysis and coverage by the media. This observation implies that each professional sports league likely develops and implements different managerial and promotional strategies to penetrate markets and attract fans if based on the players' attitudes, behaviors, skills and performances. It is of special interest, therefore, to illustrate how European countries' and other foreign nations' athletes have affected the competitiveness and popularity of the NHL and influenced the hockey league's relationships with its international fans and global affiliates.[11]

Between 1950 and 2000, the NHL had gradually evolved to become the U.S.-based professional sports league with the greatest melting pot of athletic talent. For more than seven decades, it was predominately Canadians and not Americans or Europeans that excelled as the world's best professional ice hockey players. Because of their power and grace to skate with precision on ice rinks, the NHL's dominant stars were such Canadian legends as Gordie Howe and Henri Richard in the 1950s, Jean Beliveau and Bobby Hull in the 1960s, Guy Lafleur and Bobby Orr in the 1970s, and Wayne Gretzky and Mario Lemieux in the 1980s. Then, during the 1990s the mobility, strength and speed of Russians like Sergei Fedorov, Pavel Bure and Viacheslav Fetisov, and the skating maneuvers of numerous Europeans such as Finland's Jari Kurri, Czechoslovakia's Dominic Hasek and Sweden's Nicklas Lidstrom became skills more demanded by professional coaches and appreciated by fans since those game characteristics reflected the players' abilities to become competitive athletes in the NHL. Thus, other than the Canadians and Russians, there were many other outstanding players who were native-born European standouts. Those athletes, for example, included the Czech Republic's Jaromir Jagr, Sweden's Peter Forsberg and Finland's Teemu Selanne.[12]

To determine the number and percentage distribution of professional ice hockey players, that is, American, Canadian, European, Russian and Other players, who had performed on 12 NHL teams, six of which were based in the U.S.—with one team from each of the league's divisions—and six located in Canada, Table 4.1 was prepared. Given that objective, what do the numbers in the table indicate about the nationalities of players who were distributed among the 12 teams?

During the early portion of the 2003–2004 regular season, the data denotes that, on average, the 12 teams' rosters had included approximately three Americans, 14 Canadians, five Europeans, one Russian and between zero and one player from other nations such as Brazil and South Korea. Furthermore, the table shows that the collection of U.S.-based teams had employed proportionately more American players while the set of Canadian-based teams, on average, listed more Canadian and European players. Finally, the combined rosters of the two groups had included less than two Russian players per team. In short, Table 4.1 indicates that the NHL teams' owners, general managers and coaches tended to prefer ice hockey players from Canada and then players from Europe, America, Russia and lastly, from other nations. That is, Canadian players represented nearly 60 percent of the teams' rosters, Europeans accounted for 22 percent, Americans 13 percent, and the Russians and Other countries combined for 5 percent.

Besides the information presented in Table 4.1, there are other distributions of NHL players in Tables A.6 and A.7 of the Appendix. Table A.6, for example, indicates the composition of the league's 30 teams in March of 2004. Indeed, this chart shows that the teams' players totaled 124 or 16 percent from America, 404 or 53 percent from Canada, 178 or 24 percent from European countries, 46 or six per-

Table 4.1 Distribution of Twelve NHL Team Rosters, December 2003

Team	American	Canadian	European	Russian	Other
U.S.					
Boston Bruins	4	12	3	2	0
Dallas Stars	4	14	2	1	0
Detroit Red Wings	4	15	6	1	0
Minnesota Wild	2	16	6	1	1
Philadelphia Flyers	7	10	6	0	0
Tampa Bay Devils	3	13	5	3	0
Canada					
Calgary Flames	2	19	4	1	1
Edmonton Oilers	4	15	3	1	0
Montreal Canadiens	2	19	2	1	0
Ottawa Senators	3	12	6	2	0
Toronto Maple Leafs	2	13	9	1	1
Vancouver Canucks	1	11	11	1	0

Notes: The NHL's conferences, divisions and teams are, respectively, represented as follows. Eastern Conference: Atlantic Division, Flyers; Northeast Division, Bruins, Canadiens, Maple Leafs and Senators; Southeast Division, Devils; Western Conference: Central Division, Red Wings; Northwest Division, Canucks, Wild, Flames and Oilers; Pacific Division, Stars. The Other column includes the players, who were listed on team rosters but natives of other foreign nations such as Brazil, Kazakhstan and South Korea.

Source: The rosters of each NHL hockey team are listed at the web site <http://www.nhl. com>.

cent from Russia, and five or one percent from other nations. With respect to each of the team's rosters, in absolute amounts the New Jersey Devils had the most American players at nine. Meanwhile, the largest number of Canadians played for the Calgary Flames, of the Europeans for the Atlanta Thrashers and Vancouver Canucks, and of the Russians for the New Jersey Devils, New York Rangers and Philadelphia Flyers. Meanwhile, there were no Americans employed by the Vancouver Canucks, nine Canadians by the Colorado Avalanche and New York Islanders, one European by the Chicago Blackhawks and zero Russians by the Carolina Hurricanes and Florida Panthers. Finally, five or approximately 17 percent of the teams had zero players from other countries.

Alternatively, Table A.7 reflects the distribution of non-North American play-ers—Europeans, Russians and Others—by the position they played on the teams. During March of 2004, 43 or 18 percent performed as a center, 77 or 34 percent as a defenseman, 22 or 10 percent as a goalie, and 87 or 38 percent as a left or right wing. Based on the positions with the largest and smallest numbers of players, the most centers at five were with the New Jersey Devils, defenseman at six with the New York Islanders and Philadelphia Flyers, goaltenders at three with the Atlanta

Thrashers, and wings at five with the Buffalo Sabres. For the fewest number of players per position, six teams had zero centers, one team zero defensemen, 14 teams zero goaltenders, and one team zero wings. In short, those distributions indicated how the 30 teams had assigned 229 non-North American players to various positions during late March of the 2003–2004 regular NHL season.

During the 1980s and early 1990s, the attitudes, behaviors and skills of the foreign-born hockey players who performed during the games had been stereo-typed a priori by coaches and fans based on the athletes' home country or conti-nent. European players, for example, reputedly did not shoot the puck enough and therefore would score few goals. That is, those players tended to wait for the perfect or pretty play to develop before they attempted to vigorously move the puck and skate toward the goal and score points. Moreover, many international players had to overcome real and/or imagined psychological barriers when they tried to learn and speak English, interpret U.S. customs, laws and traditions, and adjust to how important it was to play for an elite team in the NHL and compete for a division title, conference championship and the Stanley Cup. Because of that mentality and the cultural ambiguities and different lifestyles in America, a portion of those foreign players did not perform up to team owners' expectations and standards on defense or offense during games. In order to avoid those and other issues, the NHL clubs' coaches and general managers decided to devote more energy and resources to scout, recruit and draft international ice hockey players, to stress how necessary chemistry and personality are as team concepts, and to implement social programs so that foreign-born players could gradually adjust to their new environment.[13]

Consequently, to incorporate international athletes and ensure that they be-came productive members of a U.S.- or Canadian-based professional sports organi-zation, some NHL teams hired tutors who had helped the players reduce and perhaps eliminate their language barriers. Other clubs, meanwhile, had established social events and personal activities to provide an opportunity and environment for those players from various nations to meet, communicate and interact between regular season games. A sample of the activities and events that were scheduled for a full team, or arranged for a group of international players to jointly participate in with their teammates included attending movies at local theaters, watching television shows, eating meals at restaurants, sharing families' and friends' birth-day parties, weddings and anniversaries, and establishing informal meetings whereby U.S. and foreign players might discuss and share information about current country-specific events, and about global cultural, economic and political news and social problems.

To further motivate their foreign-born ice hockey players from Eastern and Western European countries and other nations to perform as a unit rather than as individual athletes with conflicting playing styles, some NHL teams had to reform their game plans and then develop strategies and plays such that each hockey player had an assigned, yet flexible role on the team's defense and offense. That is, the types of skills that European players had developed from game experiences were blended with the passion and pride of North American players. When the league's coaches emphasized the team concept and took advantage of the abilities of all players on the roster, the clubs' competitiveness and players' performances tended to improve, especially in games where a goal made the difference between a win or loss.[14]

During the early to middle 1990s, the majority of NHL coaches realized that the players who had emigrated from Russia needed more time to adjust to the smaller ice surfaces that existed on North American rinks, and to the more physical styles of play as performed by Canadians and Americans. Eventually, however, the Russian players gained the respect of their teammates and opponents and thus, became formidable players in the league. Ultimately, some of those players will qualify for and join their countrymen in the Hockey Hall of Fame (HHF). One former Russian player inducted in the HHF was the New Jersey Devils' and Detroit Red Wings' Viacheslav Fetisov. After Fetisov played on ten world championship clubs, three Winter Olympic Games' medalist teams, two Stanley Cup champions during 1989 to 1998, and served as a professional assistant coach in 2000, he was inducted into the HHF in 2001. Another great Russian player was the New York Americans' and Toronto Maple Leafs' David (Sweeney) Schriner. Because he performed on teams that won two Stanley Cups in the 1940s, Schriner entered the HHF in 1962. The third Russian player, Vladislav Alexsandrovich Tretiak, was voted into the HHF in 1989 after his contributions for Soviet national teams that had earned ten world championships, nine European titles and Olympic gold medals in 1972, 1976 and 1984. According to M.R. Carroll, the author of *The Concise Encyclopedia of Hockey*, Tretiak" ... stands alone as the finest goalie international hockey has ever seen."[15]

To recognize the talents and achievements of more recent Russian players, in 1994 Sergei Fedorov won the Hart Memorial Trophy for his 56 goals, 64 assists and 120 points for the Detroit Red Wings. After he excelled at the center position during 1995–1997, Fedorov received a $12 million bonus as a reward for his accomplishments and helping his team score victories. Then, in 1999 Russian players Pavel Bure and Alexander Mogilny scored 90 and 45 points, respectively, for the Vancouver Canucks. When Sergei Priakin was allowed to leave his Soviet team because he had aged, and joined the Calgary Flames in 1989, NHL teams began drafting Russia's ice hockey stars so that, after perestroika, the floodgates opened and by 1999, that country was represented in the league by 42 of its best hockey athletes.

Although the import and assimilation of foreign-born hockey players into North America's culture and the league's teams has continued to progress, during the early 2000s there were some disputes that existed between the NHL office and various officials who worked for European leagues and/or international federations. Indeed, the following are relevant examples that illustrate and reveal how the globalization of the professional sports leagues, as depicted for the sport of ice hockey, have tended to create short-term conflicts. In turn, those and other problems may result in unique, but perhaps controversial long-term policy decisions implemented by each nation's governing sports authorities.

First, when 72 competitive players abandoned their European hockey clubs in 2001, one year later the NHL and IIHF negotiated and signed a three-year agreement. That document required the NHL to provide various European teams with $28 million in total compensation for those hockey players who had decided to seek careers in the U.S.-based league. According to one clause as stipulated in the contract, the amount of money paid to the European clubs had to gradually increase from $9 million in 2002 to $10.2 million in 2004. Nevertheless, since more than 330 of their players perform in the NHL, Europe's national teams undoubtedly realize that they are at a competitive disadvantage to recruit and employ local and talented athletes from European nations and thus win future international competitions such as the Olympic Winter Games, World Cups, and the IIHF and World Championship tournaments. Alternatively, the NHL's brand and logo, which have traditionally represented North American athletes, are jeopardized because so many of the league's players are not native-born Canadians or Americans. Furthermore, because Europe's best hockey players are recruited by and join teams in the NHL, U.S. sports officials are concerned that such clubs as the Canucks in Vancouver, Oilers in Edmonton, Islanders in New York, and Stars in Dallas will assign their premier players from North America to inferior or secondary positions on defense and to non-playmaking and pugnacious roles such as checkers and enforcers, who are sometimes called goons. To prove how the league's composition has changed, in 2002 the American high school and college athletes that were drafted by NHL teams equaled 35 ice hockey players, which was the lowest number of U.S. players drafted since 1998. Given the results of the 2002 draft, during the early to middle 2000s will the sports fans in such NHL cities as Atlanta, Montreal, Ottawa and Raleigh become more or less passionate about, respectively, the Thrashers, Canadiens, Senators and Hurricanes, if those fans know that 25 percent or more of those clubs' rosters contain native-born Europeans? In short, if employment trends continue it may be necessary for the NHL to eventually be renamed the North American-European Hockey League.[16]

Second, according to the IIHF's rules a nation's compulsory military service has priority over and supersedes the policies that are contained in an NHL players contract. Furthermore, as previously stated U.S. teams contribute money to a fund, which is used to pay the transfer fees of European athletes who sign contracts to play for teams in the NHL. With respect to those two policies, in 2002 there were two NHL first-round draft selections from Russia who were removed from their hotels in Los Angeles, California and then ordered by the Russian government to report for military duty in that nation's army. However, rather than report to CSKA Moscow, which is the former Red Army ice hockey team, both players returned to the club they had performed for in the Russian Super League, which then was named the Avangard Omsk. Based on the policies and government orders, Omsk' president Anatoly Bardin boasted about saving two talented players for Russia while CSKA Moscow's legendary Red Army coach Viktor Tikhonov denied any involvement of the players' affiliation with Omsk in the Super League. Interestingly, in response to the Russian's decision to seize the players, the NHL Anaheim Mighty Ducks' general manger said, "It's all about money and about transfer fees.

It's all about other favors too. The system is funny over there [in Russia]. There are things this country [U.S.] would consider illegal going on." For another reaction to what occurred with the relocation of the Russian players, the NHL Tampa Bay Lightning's assistant general manager Jay Feaster expressed his disappointment and declared, "This continues to be a web of intrigue. It's like a spy novel." Regardless, it was unclear whether or not the two players, Stanislov Chistov and Alexander Svitov, would ever be permitted to perform in the NHL.[17]

Third, because of the potential injuries to female athletes and perhaps for other gender-specific reasons, the IIHF prohibits women from competing in men's international sports tournaments whenever a separate women's category exists in the sport. This policy was challenged during early 2003 when Canadian Hayley Wickenheiser decided to play for Team Salamat, a second-division professional ice hockey team that was located in Kirkkonummen, Finland. Therefore, based on the IIHF's rule Wickenheiser became ineligible to play for the Canadian men's team at the 2003 World Championships since there was a separate women's hockey tournament that had been scheduled in China during the Spring of 2003. In an interview, the IIHF's president Rene Fasel expressed his concern about the safety aspects of women hockey, and the decisions of such female athletes as Wickenheiser when he commented, "As much as I admire the determination and the barrier-breaking commitment of the multiple world champion and the MVP [Most Valuable Player] from Salt Lake City, I am pretty sure there is no future in mixed hockey and there are several reasons why the IIHF does not want to promote women playing in men's leagues." Despite president Fasel's remarks, however, the IIHF has no jurisdictional control over the internal operations of the national governing sports organizations. Moreover, before 2003 Finland had amended its bylaws to permit women to play in men's leagues. Given those circumstances, then why did Wickenheiser opt to play professionally in Europe rather than on an affiliated-NHL minor league team in North America? According to reports from hockey insiders, she felt that it was in her best interest, safety and protection from injury to play on rinks in Europe's large, international-sized ice surfaces. Furthermore, for athletes that play on ice hockey teams in North America's minor leagues, aggressive body contact between players has generally been a common action during the games. However, it is inevitable that the globalization of the professional leagues in ice hockey will gradually force the reduction of gender barriers and other player restrictions. In short, this means that the IIHF and other international organizations will be obligated to reform their rules and allow women, if qualified as athletes, to tryout for men's professional ice hockey teams and perhaps for teams in the other men's U.S.-based professional sports leagues.[18]

Fourth, during 2003 a few of Europe's most experienced ice hockey officials met in Sweden to discuss whether or not to terminate the agreement that provided compensation for European teams whose players were chosen in the NHL draft. Indeed, since 1995 the NHL had paid about $10 million per year to European teams who had lost players that were drafted by the various NHL's clubs. With respect to that agreement, however, some ice hockey officials from Russia and the

Czech Republic, for example, complained that the dollar amounts of the compensation, which was approximately $200,000 for each player drafted, was woefully inadequate as a financial return to European team owners. Rather, those two country's representatives preferred the prior system of compensation whereby each European team directly negotiated for the release of its players with the NHL team that had drafted them. The president of the Russian Ice Hockey Federation Alexander Steblin emphatically contended that Russia deserved more compensation for its players than, for example, the amounts received by hockey teams in the Scandinavian countries. According to Steblin, "In Russia, it is the teams or the state that pay for everything. The clubs build and maintain rinks and each of them employ a minimum of 15 professional coaches at their hockey schools. That represents a huge investment and they deserve to be properly compensated for it." However, because of the extraordinarily high administrative and legal costs, there are ambiguous interpretations and confused terminologies associated with the sports contracts that are signed by and issued to hockey players in various European nations. As such, the NHL's Commissioner Gary Bettman demanded that officials in the European federations adopt a common approach to the development of regulations, which govern sports contracts, and mandate that those rules apply to athletes in each country. For self-interest reasons, Bettman's preference is to avoid the negotiation of player compensation amounts with individual countries. Because player contracts and compensation levels are multinational sports matters, those issues will probably be resolved collectively by the nation's ice hockey federations in the European Union with the participation and approval of Russia's top sports organization.[19]

With respect to the previous contents in this section of the chapter, the above average growth in the presence and use of international players by the NHL teams has created a variety of opportunities, threats and challenges that need to be addressed. That is, those issues such as player contracts should be evaluated and discussed by NHL executives and franchise owners with officials from international federations and the national federations in various nations. In short, there are several disputes and problems between ice hockey groups that must be equitably resolved before the NHL can effectively commit and implement its global business strategies, and therefore compete with the other U.S.- and foreign-based professional ice hockey leagues for sports fans and markets in Asia, Europe and elsewhere.

The next portion of Chapter 4 first examines the expected formation of two new professional ice hockey leagues in 2004, and then the failure of a North American minor hockey league in 2001. Those three organizations are, respectively, the new FHL in Canada and WHA in the U.S., and the former second-tier International Hockey League (IHL), which consisted of minor league teams in America and Canada. When the examination of those sport groups concludes, the chapter focuses on the international activities, competitiveness and implications of a World Cup of Hockey tournament in 2004 or during some year thereafter.

Alternative Ice Hockey Leagues

Federal Hockey League

Because of the weak Canadian dollar that existed during the 1990s and early 2000s, Canadian taxpayers' unwillingness to finance the construction of new hockey arenas, CHL teams' inflated player salaries and below-average revenue streams, and the economic burdens from excessive government bureaucracies, regulations and taxes, for several years a majority of the NHL teams based in Canada have experienced economic and financial difficulties. Since the middle of the 1990s, when the Nordiques moved from Quebec, Canada to Denver, Colorado and renamed the Avalanche, and the Jets from Winnipeg, Canada to Phoenix, Arizona and became the Coyotes, more than one of the remaining six NHL franchises in Canada have undergone hardships in the sports business. To illustrate, the Calgary Flames and Vancouver Canucks have estimated that their losses, as operating enterprises, are in the tens of millions of dollars. Meanwhile, the Molson Brewery Corporation of Canada sold its controlling interest in the Montreal Canadiens to a businessperson from the State of Colorado in America. Those and the other three hockey franchises' fundamental and persistent long-term problem has been that the team owners pay their players' salaries and benefits in U.S. dollars even though the teams' inflows of cash are received in Canadian dollars. To partially subsidize the operations of the country's professional ice hockey franchises, the NHL's Canadian Assistance Program was established to award monies to teams that have met predetermined quotas with respect to the sale of season tickets, rental of arena suites and the generation and collection of advertising revenues. Except for the league's Toronto Maple Leafs, the other five Canadian professional ice hockey clubs have obtained subsidies from the NHL's Assistance Program. Besides benefits from the Canadian Assistance Program, the Canadian government has put forth proposals to provide supplemental funds for the NHL teams' operations. In brief, the following are two of the proposals. One, a local, provincial and/or federal government agency would offer tax breaks and/or credits to ice hockey franchises based on the salary expenses of their team's players and two, one or more governments would allocate money from the national hockey lottery to the franchises in Canada to offset the clubs' losses. For various economic and political reasons, the legislators in Canada have not approved these and the other proposals to subsidize the Canadian-based NHL teams that have incurred operating losses and accumulated millions of dollars in debts.[20]

Despite the troubles of those franchises, during the early to middle months of 2003 it was reported that the ten-team FHL would be established as a sports organization based in Canada. As such, its founders made the decision to begin the league's inaugural season in September 2003. According to an official Press Release, the league's goal "is to bring our Pros home in order to provide top-notch professional hockey entertainment for kids, families and the average individual, at a price they can afford." However, because of unexpected delays that developed in order to finalize arena leases and secure some investors and owners, during the Fall of 2003 Commissioner John Larsen postponed the league's opening day games from September to January of 2004, and then to December of 2004. For how the league will function and operate as a business and sports entertainment entity that exists primarily to attract the loyalty and support of Canadian hockey fans, the following information is provided about its mission, organization and target market.[21]

According to the league's original structure, the FHL had planned to consist of five teams each in the East and West Divisions. The teams, which are to be located in Edmonton, Hamilton, Montreal, North Bay, Quebec City, Regina, Saint John, Saskatoon, Thunder Bay and Vancouver, were scheduled to play a 40 game short season. Since Edmonton, Montreal and Vancouver are current sites of NHL teams, the new league's sites predominately exist in small to medium sized cities that lack a major professional hockey club. Nevertheless, because of such issues as fluctuations in market conditions, unavailability of professional ice rinks and contractual disputes about leases, the teams' location are subject to change before, and perhaps during and after a regular season commences. Based on a breakeven attendance that was estimated to be 3,000 spectators per game, Larsen has projected that each team will charge approximately $17 per seat and average 5,000 fans at its home games.[22]

During the early to middle of July and September in 2003, the FHL held free agent evaluation camps in Vancouver and Toronto, Canada for ice hockey coaches and athletes to jointly conduct practices and workouts so that the athletes could compete for team positions. From his perspective, Larsen said the new league would seek to recruit and sign contracts with Canadian professional ice hockey players, who want to live and play games in Canada, but currently perform for minor league teams in North America and Europe. To be specific, Larsen told sportswriters that "In a nutshell what I want is to bring the boys back home here to play hockey before the people in this country and do it at a price that the kids, families and the average individual can afford." For the FHL teams to maintain ticket prices that are affordable and hopefully attract enough fans to regular season games, the players' average salary amount was estimated to be $1,500 per week.[23]

With respect to the league and teams' investors, the FHL prefers wealthy individuals and/or groups who agree to become franchise partners to support the organization's operations. Since he or she is referred to as a Senator, each partner will be involved in all major decisions that affect the business of the league. In turn, for each team a company must be organized, and one investor or an investor group will own the company. According to the league's bylaws, it must be a private company that includes no more than 100 individual investors as participants. Whether an individual or group owns a team, it is ultimately each owner's responsibility for the general management and overall direction of the club.[24]

How likely is it that the FHL will succeed in Canada and perhaps continue to provide ice hockey games after its first regular season? Without regional and national television contracts and/or major partnerships and sponsorships as revenue sources for the league's operations and the teams' cash flows, and given the presence of NHL clubs in three of its teams' cities, it is imperative that the FHL exist as a conservative, low-risk sports organization, which earns moderate profits. From a business perspective, and to remain economically competitive as a league, the FHL's teams must play games and provide events in their arenas that entertain ice hockey fans in the local community, and that appeals to those households, which enjoy watching fast-paced and contact sports games on television. Indeed, it is likely that the league's fan base will not include the avid supporters of current Canadian teams in the NHL or CFL, but will include those hockey fans that do not attend the home and away games of those teams. Although it wants to be recognized as an above average professional hockey organization, the FHL is equivalent to an upper-level North American minor hockey operation except that the league's teams are primarily located in the Canadian provinces of Ontario, Quebec and Saskatoon.

As an aside, if a long-term NHL work stoppage occurs in the Fall of 2004, an unknown proportion of the league's approximately 450 Canadian players will prefer to remain in North America and sign a contract to perform for an FHL team in Canada until the NHL can begin its 2004–2005 regular season. Certainly, the employment and presence of NHL players would provide the FHL with regional exposure, increase the league's fan base, and perhaps boost attendance at games, especially in the three Canadian cities that host an NHL club and perhaps in the provinces that lack a minor league hockey team. In short, if an NHL strike or lockout continues for months because the players' union representatives and league's team owners bicker about the language of, and the conditions and terms that belong in a new collective bargaining agreement, some of the FHL teams will draw reasonably large home game crowds and more cash inflows from concessions and parking fees at arenas, and from the sales of apparel and merchandise. In turn, the economic returns to the league's owners, partners and investors will appreciate because the NHL and NHLPA were unable and/or unwilling to jointly prevent a work stoppage.

World Hockey Association

After a 25-year absence, the WHA was reestablished to be a new ice hockey league as of late 2004, when its first regular season would begin operations. The league was originally conceived during the late 1990s when the former CFL Ottawa Rough Riders' president Allan Howell assumed the right to name his proposed league as the WHA. To attract disgruntled hockey fans in various North American and European cities, Howell and his partner, Nick Vaccaro decided to launch their league because of an impending NHL player's strike and/or team owner's lockout that would likely occur in the early Fall of 2004. To provide the maximum credibility and exposure for their start-up ice hockey league, during 2003 Howell and Vaccaro appointed the NHL Hall of Fame legend Bobby Hull to be the WHA's first Commissioner. When he agreed to be the league's Commissioner, Hull stated that "Our [WHA's] main objective is to bring professional hockey back to the families so that we can provide a guy and his wife and two or three kids with a night's entertainment that they can afford. We want to bring that back to the game, because I feel we're losing a lot of kids." Based on Hull's statement, it appears that the WHA and FHL officials have derived nearly the same mission and purpose for their organizations, and identified a similar market niche with respect to their customers.[25]

Although the league's goals, plans and policies were subject to change during the early to middle months of 2004, the WHA had initially proposed to place 12 teams in North American cities and four in European cities. Interestingly, to satisfy that proposal the league had proceeded to evaluate sites in 13 U.S. and three Canadian cities as viable locations for the WHA's teams. In the U.S., seven of the prospective cities that were screened did not contain an NHL franchise. Those Cities and their respective States included Birmingham in Alabama, Cincinnati in Ohio, Indianapolis in Indiana, Houston in Texas, Kansas City in Kansas, and Jacksonville and Orlando in Florida. Later, the WHA considered six other American cities to place teams. Those were Chicago in Illinois, Cleveland in Ohio, Detroit in Michigan, Minneapolis in Minnesota, Portland in Oregon and St. Louis in Missouri. Meanwhile, in Canada the cities of Hamilton and Winnipeg in Ontario and Quebec City in Quebec had each lacked an NHL team. Yet, for some reason there were no European cities identified and approved as potential team locations according to press releases from the WHA headquarters.[26]

For the league's specific policies and programs, the WHA's executives had recommended a $10 million salary cap per team, with an exemption allowed for each team to employ one star player. To attract enough qualified and talented ice hockey athletes who were also enthusiastic about playing in the WHA, and to make each teams' games a very entertaining sports event for spectators, Commissioner Hull said that "Smaller kids haven't been able to play [in professional hockey] because of the trappings (a widely used checking scheme). We're going to allow them to play. We're going to take out the center ice line and cut back on the size of these huge goalie pads that block most of the net. We'll have no-touch icing to speed up the game."[27]

In short, although Howell, Vaccaro and Hull expect their league's teams will play at a higher level than the clubs that currently exist in North America's minor hockey leagues, the WHA's officials are realistic and thus will not organize the league's schedule of games to match the competitiveness and unique styles of the NHL's teams and players. However, without the cash inflows from a lucrative television contract, the WHA's teams will struggle to earn sufficient operating revenues and attract enough national exposure to lure any American and Canadian ice hockey fans who are disillusioned and angry because an NHL shut down had occurred.

To reflect upon and predict the short- and long-term business successes and operational prospects of the FHL and WHA, what is presented next in this section is the history of the defunct IHL. Although the IHL existed in a different era and thus had a unique mission, composition and scope relative to the FHL and WHA, an examination of why the IHL failed, after a long presence as a minor league ice hockey organization, is an interesting and provocative topic for the readers of *Sports Capitalism* to consider.

International Hockey League

After 56 years in existence, the IHL officially folded its teams' operations during October of 2001. When it was founded, the league had started its initial regular season with four clubs. That is, the IHL consisted of two teams each in Detroit, Michigan and Windsor, Ontario. By 1995, however, the league had expanded to 19 teams but then eventually reduced its membership to 11 teams in 2001. After the league dissolved, five of the U.S.-based teams had to terminate their operations. But, one team located in Canada and five others in the U.S. joined the American Hockey League (AHL) to compete in the 2001–2002 regular season. To highlight the IHL's history in more detail, the following two paragraphs describe the rationale, composition and failure of the league.

In 1945, the IHL had formed to give American ice hockey players who had returned from World War II an organized schedule to compete and play games in the sport. As it was structured during the 1940s, the minor league organization filled a need in the marketplace because its teams generally played competitive hockey games in such U.S. small-market cities as Grand Rapids, Muskegon and Port Huron in Michigan, and Milwaukee in Wisconsin. As a subsidiary organization of the NHL, the IHL represented the type of hockey entertainment that appealed to fans who had resided in below-average populated cities. However, during the middle of the 1990s the IHL lost its local and regional roots when it added several teams that stretched the league's market boundaries from Orlando, Florida to Houston, Texas, and from Long Beach, California to Winnipeg, Canada. In short, because of the league's expansion, the teams' owners had to significantly increase their travel budgets and players' salaries.[28]

Because of the widespread dispersion of the league's teams, there were clubs located in such large-market cities as Chicago, Illinois and Detroit, Michigan, and in a medium-sized market like the city of Cleveland, Ohio, that had joined the IHL. Consequently, when the league switched from a regional to a national focus, which had ratcheted up the teams' operating costs, the owners of the small-city franchises were forced to fold their operations rather than spend excessive amounts of money for expenses, and to avoid short-term deficits and long-term debts. In a nutshell, the teams' financial dilemma was clarified by an AHL team general manager when he said, "They [IHL team owners] took big expansion fees and lived off them. They overspent on travel and players. They had illusions of grandeur. For a time, they thought they could even challenge the NHL or at least merge some teams." To provide a final observation about the organization's collapse, during June of 2001 the IHL's president and chief executive officer Doug Moss admitted, "With the landscape of minor league hockey continuing to evolve, the league's board of governors determined that this was a necessary decision."[29]

Based on the information in the last few paragraphs, it is imperative that the FHL and WHA officials avoid the marketing and managerial mistakes, and the cost miscalculations that were made by the IHL's executives and the league's team owners. To be successful in the long-term, therefore, decision makers within the new sports leagues, as business entrepreneurs, must provide entertaining and excit-

ing ice hockey games during the regular seasons, playoffs and championship series. Furthermore, before considering an expansion or relocation to any sites in
foreign nations, those officials must also control their teams' travel costs and
players' salaries yet penetrate the sport's local and regional markets.

In the next section, the global strategy and sports aspects of a World Cup of
Hockey tournament are explored. Then, the chapter's content explains whether the
NHL should eventually contract its operations and eliminate and/or merge one or
more of the weakest teams in various divisions, and/or place an expansion team in
a European city or at some other location outside of North America.

World Cup of Hockey

As an aftermath to a group of international hockey competitions, which included
the Summit Series in 1972 and 1976, Challenge Cup in 1979, Rendez Vous in
1987 and a series of Canada Cup tournaments held between 1976 and 1991, a
World Cup of Hockey tournament was first played in 1996. That year, the preliminary round of games took place in cities of Europe and North America and
then after the playoffs, the best-of-three final series was split with Game One in
Philadelphia, Pennsylvania and Games Two and Three in Montreal, Canada. During the tournament, which thrilled the ice hockey fans who had attended the games
and those who watched them on television, an underrated U.S. team defeated an
experienced Canadian team two to one. After the American victory and broadcast
exposure, athletes and other sports fans became more interested in ice hockey and
the sport modestly expanded in the U.S., especially among the nation's teenagers
and young adults. Interestingly, the international tournaments played during the
1970s, 1980s and 1990s, and the annual World Hockey Championships had paved
the way for the NHL's players to perform in the 1998 and 2002 Winter Olympic
Games.[30]

Between 30 August 2004, which was the first day of the 2004 Summer
Olympic Games in Athens, Greece, and 14 September 2004, which was the final
day before the NHL-NHLPA collective bargaining agreement had expired, the
second World Cup of Hockey was scheduled as a tournament. To arouse ice
hockey fans from across the globe, and also get the support of various nations and
the businesses and consumers in those countries, the 2004 tournament was expanded from six to eight teams. The European entries, which consisted of teams from
the Czech Republic, Finland, Germany and Sweden were scheduled to play in a
four-team round robin pool at venues in various European cities, as well as in
quarterfinal games that featured a format with Team One versus Four, and Team
Two versus Three. The four venues in Europe that hosted games were the Hartwall
Arena in Helsinki, Finland, Globe Arena in Stockholm, Sweden, Cologne Arena in
Cologne, Germany and the Saska Arena in Prague, Czech Republic. In the other
group, there was a pool of competitors that included teams from Canada, Russia,
Slovakia and the U.S. This group played games at the Bell Centre in Montreal,
Canada, Xcel Energy Center in St. Paul, Minnesota and the Air Canada Centre in

Toronto, Canada, which hosted the championship game on 14 September 2004. Given the news, rumors and predictions that will likely occur because of the imminent NHL work stoppage on 15 September 2004, the competitions at these seven arenas are expected to be sellouts.[31]

At the 2004 World Cup tournament, each teams' roster had listed 20 skaters and three goaltenders. To establish their rosters, the national hockey federations had to identify at least 18 team members by 1 February 2004 and the remaining five players had to be appointed by 20 June 2004 in order to complete the teams' rosters. To practice for the tournament, each team had conducted a ten-day training camp during early August 2004 and played two exhibition games prior to the start of the World Cup competition on 30 August. Because of the elite NHL players who would represent respective countries, and the expectation of and support from hockey fans in the eight nations, the tournament was guaranteed to be an international success. As expressed by the NHL's executive vice president Bill Daley, "For more than 30 years the NHL has participated in international hockey competition and the World Cup of Hockey provides a unique opportunity to showcase the game on two continents and adds to the list of historic international tournaments." Because of that exposure, the NHL and national hockey federations will use the event to advertise and promote the 2006 Winter Olympic Games that are scheduled for play in Italy.[32]

Since the early to middle 1990s, many NHL teams have experienced a decline in ticket sales, lower television ratings and higher operating losses relative to their regular season games and the league's postseason playoffs and Stanley Cup championship series. As a result, the popularity and prosperity of the national hockey leagues that exist in Germany, Finland, Sweden and Switzerland have undoubtedly humiliated the NHL's Commissioner Gary Bettman and the teams' franchise owners. Consequently, if the NHL's economic condition and business environment continue to deteriorate during 2004 and thereafter, there are three options that the commissioner and team owners may jointly consider to improve the league's short- and long-term growth and its commercial opportunities and prospects.

Although it is a risky option for the NHL, one strategy for the league's officials is to geographically expand and thus place an existing team(s) and/or a new franchise(s) at a site(s) in a medium sized or large European city. When the current NHL-IIHF agreement, which prohibits the NHL from locating its teams in Europe, expires in 2004, the former Swedish Ice Hockey Federation's president Rickard Fagerlund thinks that a relocation and/or expansion of one or more of the league's teams into Europe is a prudent decision for the NHL. To support his proposition, Fagerlund points out that the NHL Los Angeles Kings' owner Philip Anschutz has financial investments in several teams and arenas throughout Europe. Furthermore, Anschutz has been involved with the construction of sports stadiums in Berlin and London. Besides those activities, other multipurpose sports arenas have been completed and others are forecasted for completion in Cologne and Hamburg, Germany and in Prague, Czech Republic. Even so, some NHL and European leagues' executives, and decision makers in the NHLPA have disagreed with Fagerlund. These officials, for example, have stated that only a few existing European arenas have been erected to meet the NHL's standards for stadiums, and that time zone differences, increases in teams' travel costs and the dilution of the ice hockey player pools are other obstacles which may discourage the expansion of American teams into Europe. Meanwhile, the NHL's chief legal officer Bill Daley proposed that the IIHF should be involved in any team relocations to Europe. According to Daley, "To be successful over here [Europe], you [NHL] have to work co-operatively with the local federations and the IIHF. We would have no intention of going outside that construct." Nevertheless, the owner of a successful ice hockey team in Helsinki and the chairman of a consulting company that designs and operates arenas in several European cities, which is Harry Harkimo, prefers that the most important issue in the next agreement between the IIHF and NHL should be support for an increase in transfer payments to European teams who lose their outstanding players to the NHL teams.[33]

To repeat what MLB Commissioner Bud Selig announced during 2003, that is, he threatened to eliminate two of the league's small-market baseball teams through contraction, as another option the NHL could plan to reduce the number of teams in each of its conferences. To implement that option, the league would purchase one or more of the weakest hockey franchises, which have little opportunity to succeed, and then redistribute those players and other assets among the other franchises. During late 2003, Commissioner Bettman denied in press reports that his office or any of the league's franchise owners had considered the contraction of any existing teams. Rather than upset the NHLPA and scare the league's hockey fans and sponsors, Bettman's statement of denial was anticipated. However, during recent seasons about 50 percent of the NHL teams either did not change or had decreased their ticket prices for fans to attend regular season games, while in the teams' home arenas the average fees and payments had declined for individuals and organizations who had leased high-priced luxury suites and premium club seats. Moreover, the NHL expects to renegotiate a new television contract with ESPN and/or other broadcast networks. When concluded, those agreements will likely result in rights fees that amount to less than the current $120 million per year received by the league. According to an investment banker who is involved in discussions about the potential sale of several NHL teams, "There's just not enough revenue [for league teams] to share. There are only a couple of teams that make money and that's not very much."[34]

To organize a global super league, the NHL would need to combine its operations with those of one or more European hockey leagues. This is a third, but extreme and unlikely option. For various economic and league-specific reasons, this type of proposal has been opposed by the IIHF. That is, a merger of that magnitude would require sensitive, complex and controversial negotiations between representatives of the NHL, IIHF and various national ice hockey federations about arena standards, team locations, distribution of game and television revenues, regular season schedules and playoffs, unions and other matters. Furthermore, a merger would involve extensive economic compromises and concessions from those organization's officials, and perhaps trigger franchise movements and thus team and player dislocations. In short, during the early to middle 2000s the formation of an international super league, which would include all or a portion of the NHL teams and the successful clubs from prominent European leagues, is not a high-priority strategy that will be implemented by professional ice hockey's prominent leaders in North America and Europe.[35]

Summary

In retrospect, Chapter 4 analyzed the sport of professional ice hockey and discussed a variety of international activities, alliances, grassroots events and other business matters and relationships that comprise the global business strategies of the NHL. Also, the chapter reviewed the histories and operations of other hockey organizations that were, currently are, and will be located within the borders of North America. To entertain yet educate the readers of *Sports Capitalism*, Chapter 4 was composed of several interesting, meaningful and eminent ice hockey topics that were presented as opportunities, threats and issues that have or will involve the business environment of the NHL.

Because of the league's mission and its current and future operations as a worldwide business, the chapter's first section identified and revealed the NHLI as the organizational subunit of NHL Enterprises. Then, an examination of the subunit's affiliations, and its duties, responsibilities and tasks denoted how the NHLI has developed and operated to establish marketing campaigns in and provide revenues from sports consumers in numerous foreign nations. Because of its commitments and relationships with U.S.-based companies, and with non-American multinational corporations and national ice hockey federations and other groups, the NHLI has broadened the worldwide exposure and popularity of professional hockey, expanded the publicity of the NHL brand across the globe and increased the profits, if any, of the league's 30 member teams. During the early to middle 2000s, it is predicted that the NHLI will continue to extend its authority, resourcefulness and power within the NHL and thereby generate even more income for the league's teams from fans, businesses and other consumers and organizations that are located in Asia, Europe and elsewhere.

After an analysis of how the NHLI was organized and has matured as a subunit, the chapter's second section focused on specific agreements, and communication systems, broadcast networks and other commercial relationships that had been established between the NHL and American and foreign media companies. After the league issued more licenses to local vendors in various nations, and linked its business operations with national and international partners and sponsors to implement marketing campaigns and promotions abroad, those deals have marginally improved the teams' worldwide sales of apparel, merchandise and other ice hockey products and services. Moreover, since the middle of the 1990s the NHL's marketing and public relations divisions have negotiated and/or signed binding contracts with emerging cable and satellite systems and sports television networks to broadcast the teams' regular season games, and the league's playoffs and Stanley Cup championship series throughout the world. There are, for example, numerous NHL games that have been televised to millions of households in China and Russia, and in the majority of the Eastern and Western European countries. Finally, since the early 2000s the league has also expanded its presence on the Internet with the web site address of NHL.com, and thus increased professional hockey's worldwide exposure, fan base and market share.

The third section and largest portion of Chapter 4 was devoted to the league's increasing use of international athletes whose names appear on teams' active rosters. According to the coaches, those players are assigned key defensive and offensive positions during regular season and postseason games. This topic, of course, directly related to and involved the nationalities of the foreign players and their commitments to team owners and teammates, even though they maintain membership in the NHLPA. In the section, a table was presented that displays the number and distribution of NHL players from America, Canada, Europe, Russia and Other nations, who were listed on the active rosters of six U.S.-based and six Canadian-based teams and played during the 2003–2004 regular season. Then, the existence and importance of the IIHF and national federations such as the Russian Ice Hockey Federation were discussed because the policies of those sports organizations undoubtedly influence the decisions of the NHL's commissioner and franchise owners with respect to American and foreign players' salaries, buyouts and other contract benefits and employment conditions. As an issue, whether the present number and proportion of international players on the NHL's teams will change during the early to middle 2000s depends, in part, on economic, financial, political and social forces, and on events that occur in North America and in the ice hockcy athletes' respective countries.

To determine the current status, and anticipate the future operations of other professional ice hockey leagues that are likely to exist besides the NHL, the chapter's fourth section examined the organizations and prospects of two new leagues, that is, the formation of the FHL and WHA in 2004, and then explained the failure of the IHL in 2001. If an NHL work stoppage should occur in the Fall of 2004, perhaps a portion of the league's hockey players will decide that to maintain their fitness and skill levels, they should sign a short-term contract with an FHL team located in Canada or a WHA team placed in the U.S. or Canada. Since newly-organized professional sports leagues usually struggle for national exposure and their teams play to entice local fans to attend games during the first few seasons, a players' strike or owners' lockout in 2004 would each provide an opportunity for coaches and general managers of the FHL and WHA teams to recruit and hire NHL players. In turn, those players expect to improve their respective teams' quality, which generally results in even larger attendances and more ticket sales for teams at home and away games, and in more television exposure and thus revenues to be shared within the league.

To reveal what occurred when a longstanding American Hockey League had decided to expand from a regional to a national organization during the middle of the 1990s, there was a brief history and other information and facts about the IHL's demise. In short, that minor hockey league's small-market team owners lacked the resources, cash reserves and revenue streams to successfully compete with the league's medium to large market clubs that were located in cities across the U.S. and Canada. Thus, when the former franchises proceeded to fold their operations, the IHL was forced to disband in 2001.

Chapter 4's fifth section, in part, highlighted a few of the most prestigious international ice hockey tournaments that were held during the 1970s, 1980s and 1990s. Given the success of those events, however, the primary tournament described in this section was the World Cup of Hockey, which is an international competition between eight teams scheduled during August and September of 2004. The tournament includes teams with outstanding players from the CHL, NHL and the national leagues in Western European nations, Slovakia and Russia. A majority of ice hockey officials and promoters expect that the tournament's games will be exciting to watch, especially for hockey enthusiasts and other sports fans. If so, the competition will create a global surge and interest in the sport after the tournament ends in September.

When the description of the World Cup of Hockey concluded, three options were proposed for the NHL to consider as league strategies that may improve the hockey business. That is, for ice hockey to grow and succeed as an international sport, and for the NHL to expand as a business during the early to middle 2000s, the league should evaluate the short- and long-term economic benefits and costs of expansion and/or a franchise relocation overseas, the elimination of some existing teams, and/or a merger with one or more foreign leagues in order to establish an international super league.

Since those options are not mutually exclusive, alternatively the NHL may decide to equitably realign the composition and size of its conferences and divisions, and then move some teams to large cities in Asia, Europe or elsewhere. Furthermore, the NHL might also terminate a few of its weakest clubs located in the U.S. and Canada, or merge its operations with one or more of the European leagues to form the preeminent professional sports league in the world. In sum, since most of the NHL's franchises have experienced operating losses in recent years, and because the Canadian teams are especially disadvantaged because that nation's currency is generally undervalued with respect to the American dollar, the NHL team owners will likely consider and implement one or more of those options after a new collective bargaining agreement is signed with the NHLPA. In other words, the league will reposition and restructure its organization and then aggressively search for new international sports markets to penetrate.

Notes

1. There are books that, in part, discuss the history of ice hockey and the former and current professional leagues in that sport. For example, see Frank P. Jozsa, Jr., *American Sports Empire: How the Leagues Breed Success* (Westport, CT: Praeger Publishers, 2003); Spiros Bougheas and Paul Downward, *The Economics of Professional Sports Leagues: A Bargaining Approach* (Nottingham, England: University of Nottingham, 2000); Jeff Z.

Klein and Karl-Eric Reif, *The Death of Hockey* (Toronto, Canada: Macmillan Canada, 1998); Eric M. Leifer, *Making the Majors: The Transformation of Team Sports in America* (Cambridge, MA: Harvard University Press, 1996); Toby Miller, Geoffrey Lawrence, Jim McKay, and David Rowe, *Globalization and Sport: Playing the World* (Thousand Oaks, CA: Sage Publications, 2001); Roger G. Noll, ed., *Government and the Sports Business* (Washington, D.C.: The Brookings Institution, 1974); Hans Westerbeek and Aaron Smith, *Sport Business in the Global Marketplace* (New York, N.Y.: Palgrave Macmillan, 2003); Andrew Podnieks and Sheila Wawanash, *Kings of the Ice: A History of World Hockey* (Richmond Hill, On- tario, Canada: NDE Publishers, 2002); M.R. Carroll, Andrew Podnieks, and Michael Har- ling, *The Concise Encyclopedia of Hockey* (Vancouver, Canada: Greystone Books, 2001). Other interesting books about aspects of ice hockey include Dave Bidini, *Tropic of Hockey: My Search For the Game in Unlikely Places* (Toronto, Canada: McClelland & Stewart, 2002); David Cruise and Alison Griffiths, *Net Worth: Exploding the Myths of Hockey* (New York, N.Y.: Viking Press, 1991); Ken Dryden, *The Game* (New York, N.Y.: John Wiley & Sons, Inc., 2003); Debbie Elicksen, *Inside the NHL Dream* (Calgary, Canada: Freelance Communications, 2002); Morey Holzman and Joseph Nieforth, *Deceptions and Double- cross: How the NHL Conquered Hockey* (Toronto, Canada: Dundurn Press, Ltd., 2002); Michael A. Ribidoux, *Men at Play: A Working Understanding of Professional Hockey* (Montreal, Canada: McGill-Queens University Press, 2001); Doug Smith and Adam Frattasio, *Goon: The True Story of an Unlikely Journey Into Minor League Hockey* (Fredrick, MD: PublishAmerica, Inc., 2002). Besides those references, the history of the NHL is also documented on the league's web site at <http://www.nhl.com>. For two online sources that discuss the origin and development of ice hockey, see "IIHF: History of Ice Hockey," at <http://iihf.com> cited 12 November 2003, and "About the American Hockey League," at <http://www.monarchshockey.com> cited 29 November 2001.

2.   For specific information about the league expansions and team relocations that have occurred in MLB, and in the NFL and NBA, see Frank P. Jozsa, Jr. and John J. Guthrie, Jr., *Relocating Teams and Expanding Leagues in Professional Sports: How the Major Leagues Respond to Market Conditions* (Westport, CT: Quorum Books, 1999), and Frank P. Jozsa, Jr., "An Economic Analysis of Franchise Relocation and League Expansion in Professional Team Sports, 1950–1975," Ph.D. diss., Georgia State University, 1977. Because the sports of ice hockey and soccer have been less important elements of American culture, the NHL and MLS were excluded from that book. Yet, a brief history of the NHL is available in Frank P. Jozsa, Jr., *American Sports Empire: How the Leagues Breed Success*, 26–30. For season performances, various editions of *The World Almanac and Book of Facts* (Mahwah, N.J.: World Almanac Books, 1950–2002) contain facts about professional sports leagues, teams and players. Besides those references, there is information about ice hockey's Stanley Cup, player awards, career records, single season and game records, season leaders, All-Star games and the Hall of Fame. For example, see *Sports Illustrated 1999 Sports Almanac* (New York, N.Y.: Little Brown and Company, 1999).

3.   The NHL and its players are headed toward contentious labor negotiations because, in part, the league's 30 teams had collectively posted a $300 million operating loss during the 2002–2003 season. Indeed, the strategies of the league and players union are reported in Stefan Fatsis, "NHL Says Players' Salaries Put League in Financial Peril," *Wall Street Journal* (19 September 2003), B1, B3. As illustrated in this article, there is a bar chart that shows the growth in the NHL players' average salaries between 1993–1994 and 2002–2003. In another reading, the author discusses that the league might use the contraction of teams as a bargaining tool in the negotiations with the players' union. This approach, which was

applied by MLB owners during 2001, is described in Chris Isidore, "Skating on Thin Ice," at <http://cnnmoney.com> cited 16 October 2003. For the likelihood of a work stoppage, in an email Canada's Total Sports Network on-line producer Scott Cullen estimated the probability to be approximately 95 percent. On other issues besides a player strike or management lockout in the NHL, Cullen stated that no professional Canadian ice hockey teams were likely to relocate to America and that the WHA was finalizing its plans to establish a six-team league as of late April in 2004. According to Cullen, conceivably the WHA may permit 17 year old players to participate, especially super athletes such as junior hockey league player Sidney Crosby. Interestingly, this resembles Wayne Gretzky's presence on a WHA team in Indianapolis, Indiana during the 1970s.

4.   The international business activities of the NHLI division and quick facts about the NHLI's profile are listed in "NHL International," at <http://www.nhl.com> cited 8 March 2003. To read how NFL Enterprises changed operating officers during the late 1990s, see "A New Face at the NHL: Litner Seeks to Heighten Hockey's Global Profile," *Brandweek* (29 November 1999), 18. According to why he agreed to be the NHL's executive vice president and chief operating officer during 2002, Litner said, "I grew up near Boston [Massachusetts] very much a hockey fan with the [Boston] Bruins and Bobby Orr, so there was an emotional tie. On the business side, I've enjoyed my time in TV, but the NHL's positioned for growth and I wanted to be part of the group that capitalizes on that."

5.   See "NHL on Tour Visits Sweden," at <http://www.nhl.com> cited 26 September 2003. That online news article listed the dates, malls and locations of the league's 2003 tour, which was scheduled in Sweden. For other relationships between Sweden and the NHL teams and players, see Paul Hunter, "Maple Leaf Hype Fails to Score," *Toronto Star* (11 September 2003), 1, and Shawn P. Roarke, "Stars' Prospects Jump at European Assignment," at <http://www.nhl.com> cited 13 August 2003. With respect to international ice hockey fans, about 23 percent of the traffic on nhl.com originates from beyond North America and the NHL games in Sweden are reported there on television and in newspapers. Indeed, Swedish fans are likely to watch games played late at night. However, the global market represents about 5 percent of the league's total sales.

6.   The article, "NHL International" provides some interesting facts and statistics about the NHL's players, television programming, licensed products and partners, and the number and dates of games performed by the league's teams outside of North America.

7.   For more insights on how the NHL marketed its web site to increase online sales, see Rich Thomaselli, "NHL Markets Web Site," *Advertising Age* (20 August 2001), 14. With respect to this strategy, the NHL Enterprises president Ed Horn said, "The over-riding point is that we have never viewed our online business and offline business as separate entities. As far as growing the game and providing content to consumers, the online and offline are one. We have approached our business and run our business that way."

8.   The NHL's various broadcast agreements denote that professional ice hockey games are televised across the world. See "NHL Selects GlobeCast to Offer Hockey in Europe," *Communications Today* (25 October 2002), 1; "Sun Microsystems, NHL Form Strategic Relationship," *Presswire* (24 January 2002), 1; Hilary Cassidy, "Power Play: NHL Nets Broadcast Partners For Overseas Promos," *Brandweek* (11 December 2000), 9. In contrast to the broadcast of NHL games across North America, Canadian sports shows are starting to appear more frequently in America. For example, during late 2003 the Empire Sports Network beamed 'The Business of Sports' program to more than ten million U.S. homes and Fox Sports World broadcasted Winnipeg-based Fox Sports World Roundup nightly to 20 million American subscribers. For those programs and Canada's American Hockey League on U.S. television, see Chris Zelkovich, "Selling Canadian Sports Programming on American Sports Television," at <http://www.sportsbusinessnews.com> cited 15 December 2003.

Joe Del Baso, who had purchased the Canadian sports properties for Empire Sports Network, responded that the " ... production levels are high and they're quality shows." Meanwhile, Fox Sports World production and programming chief Dermot McQuarrie said, "It was a good, ready-made program that would stand up against any similar show. It doesn't hide the fact that it's Canadian and there's nothing wrong with that."

9.   Since the middle of the 1990s, Russia has lost approximately 65 percent of the country's good players to the NHL, East Coast Hockey League, American Hockey League or the Canadian Junior League. This loss explains, in part, why television station NTV has provided Russian hockey fans with coverage of the NHL games. See Michael Russo, "NHL Offers International Flair, Broadcasts Game in Russia," at <http://www.sportsbusinessnews. com> cited 6 November 2003. In Russo's article, Russian broadcaster Alexandre Tkachev stated, "It's hard for fans in Russia to keep connected with their favorite Russian players. By coming here [to America], we can announce it live and I can also interview the Russian players." As an aside, the New Jersey Devils' center Igor Larionov, who played 12 seasons in the Soviet Elite League and won Olympic gold medals with the Soviet team in the Winter games of 1984 and 1988, announced his retirement during the 2004 Stanley Cup playoffs. Since his debut in 1980 in the NHL, the 43 year old Larionov played on three Cup teams and finished his career with 169 goals and 644 points in 921 regular season games. His farewell to ice hockey will be in an exhibition game during December of 2004 in Moscow. To read about Larionov, see "Devils Center Igor Larionov Announces Retirement," at <http://nhl.com> cited 20 April 2004.

10.   For a listing with respect to the number of NHL players by birthplace and to the number of American, Canadian and other nations' players by season, as reported in 1999, see Elliott Teaford and Jim Hodges, "Sports Extra/NHL Preview," *The Los Angeles Times* (30 September 1999), 1. Interestingly, this article provides examples of how specific foreign players have adjusted to the NHL game style and to living in America. Those players mentioned in the article included Maxim Balmochnykh and Vitaly Vishnevski from Russia, Ruslan Salei from Belarus and Oleg Tverdovsky from the Ukraine.

11.   The contrasts in attitudes and cultures between professional basketball and hockey players are apparent in the way that the sports are promoted by the respective leagues and as covered in the media. This topic is described in Terry Frei, "NHL and NBA Choosing Different Marketing Strategies," at <http://www.sportsbusinessnews.com> cited 13 November 2003; Jim Hodges, "League of Nations: As the Number of European Players Continues to Grow, The NHL Reaches New Levels of Talent," *The Los Angeles Times* (30 September 1999), 1; "Alien Invaders Altering Look of the NBA," *Toronto Star* (17 October 2000), 6. As stated in the latter article, "Where the NBA differs substantially from the NHL is that aspiring basketball pros can assimilate more easily into the American 'style' through NCAA recruitment and the March Madness intensity at the university level. For NHL hopefuls, there is a quota for non-North Americans—only two foreigners per team—and therefore it's harder to be exposed to hockey on this side of the ocean."

12.   Which country produces the best hockey players? According to some observers, it is the nations in Europe. However, according to former U.S. coach Ron Wilson, who had guided the American team to the gold medal in the 1996 World Cup, "It's clear to me if you're looking for skills, you're looking for a European player. If you're looking for a guy who can score or grind, you look for a Canadian or American. It's sort of like the way we buy cars. If you're looking for something sports and flashy, you buy a German car. If you want a truck, you buy a Chevrolet Suburban." For these views, see Larry Wigge, "Global Ice Rink," *The Sporting News* (14 February 2000), 42, and Idem., "A World of Difference," *The Sporting News* (21 February 1994), 48–49. Regarding the differences in international

players who perform in the NHL, during his program called Hockey Night in Canada Don Cherry blamed French Canadians for booing the American anthem at the Bell Centre in Montreal, said that he wasn't surprised drug use in junior hockey was limited to Quebec, and then criticized European and French Canadian players for wearing visors during games. Cherry's comments are reported in William Houston, "Don Cherry and HNIC," at <http://www.sportsbusinessnews.com> cited 30 January 2004.

13.   See previous articles in the Notes such as "Sports Extra/NHL Preview," "Global Ice Rink" and "A World of Difference" for how the NHL team owners, general managers and coaches shifted their efforts and adopted social programs to provide comfort, hospitality and language tutors for their international players. This strategy seemed to positively affect the attitudes of many international players because several of them became superstars in the league.

14.   Ibid.

15.   The performance statistics of specific professional hockey players is reported online in the archives and history sections of the NHL teams' web sites at <http://www.nhl.com>. Also, there is players' all-time and season data in the hockey portion of *Sports Illustrated 1999 Sports Almanac*, 319–359. For how various European players had performed midway during the 2002–2003 regular season, see Darren Eliot, "The Euro Conversion Rate," at <http://www.cnnsi.com> cited 8 January 2003. As Eliot concludes his article, "In the end, that is what all of these European names prominently displayed across an array of pertinent scoring categories would seem to underscore. When it comes to scoring, the assimilation process of the last decade appears complete. There are no longer Europeans and North Americans, only NHLers. As cited before, a compendium of hockey leagues, teams and players, and the sport's special moments, jargon and lingo are presented in M.R. Carroll, Andrew Podnieks, and Michael Harling, *The Concise Encyclopedia of Hockey*. In that book, for example, the career of Soviet superstar Vladislav Tretiak is summarized on page 200. Interestingly, during early 2004 two articles highlighted the performances of hockey players. That is, at UEFA's 28th Congress French midfielder Zinedine Zidane was named Europe's top soccer player of the past 50 years. In a poll, Zidane collected more votes than Germany's Franz Beckenbauer and the Netherland's Johan Cruyff. Among the all-time best 20 European players, there were four from Germany and Italy, three from the Netherlands, two from England and France, and one each from other nations. Then, the candidates for various 2004 NHL awards were announced. Several international players had received nominations including Calgary's Jarome Iginla from Canada, Ottawa's Zdeno Chara from Slovakia and Daniel Alfredsson from Sweden, Atlanta's Ilya Kovalchuk from Russia and Calgary's Miikka Kiprusoff from Finland. Respectively, see "He's No. 1: Zidane Edges Beckenbauer as Europe's Top Player of the Past 50 Years," at <http://si.printthis.click-ability.com> cited 23 April 2004; "Anniversary Party: Best European Player to be Revealed at UEFA Congress," at <http://si.printthis.clickability.com> cited 23 April 2004; Shawn P. Roarke, "Trophies: NHL Announces Awards Finalists," at <http://www.nhl.com> cited 23 April 2004.

16.   During 2002, the IIHF-NHL agreement effectively failed to influence the number of Europeans who preferred to sign contracts with NHL teams. If that trend continues beyond 2002, the IIHF might reopen negotiations with the NHL to amend the agreement and increase the players' compensation levels. According to IIHF president Rene Fasel, "There is no player with NHL-potential who today will sign a long-term contract in Europe without an escape clause. So, if we didn't have an agreement, the NHL could have had virtually all players for free." See Barry M. Bloom, "The NHL and the World Hockey Federation Make Friends," at <http://www.sportsbusinessnews.com> cited 3 December 2002, and "Interna-

tional Hockey Leader Upset With the NHL," at <http://www.sportsbusinessnews.com> cited 3 December 2002.

17.   In Russia, the best hockey players who are in the military service tend to play for an army team. Otherwise, those players are not in the army. To determine whether there was a conspiracy within Russia to prevent hockey players from entering the NHL during the early 2000s, see Chris Foster, "Is the Russian Ice Hockey Federation Withholding Players From the NHL?" at <http://www.sportsbusinessnews.com> cited 3 December 2002. With respect to the emigration of Russian players, during late 2003 the 19 year old Nikolai Zherdev secretly left his club, CSKA, to join the NHL's Columbus Blue Jackets. If the Russian Hockey Federation had proved that Zherdev abandoned his military obligations, he would be ineligible to play in the NHL until those obligations are met. After the NHL-IIHF agreement expires in 2004, the Russian Hockey Association will likely renegotiate the transfer fees for players who had decided to join the American professional ice hockey league. According to author John Sanful, who wrote *Russian Revolution: Exodus to the NHL* (Worcestershire, England: Malvern Publishing Company, 1999), "The fascinating thing is that it's 2003, and 12 or 13 years ago we were talking about Sergei Fedorov coming over and talking abut the same team (CSKA) and the same people. It just shows that the more things have changed, the more they stay the same." For more details about players and transfer fees in this case, see Karo Yorio, "Russia, Defections, the NHL and Money," at <http://www.sportsbusiness-news.com> cited 15 December 2003. Meanwhile, the popularity and value of the NHL and its international players in European countries, and especially in Russia, is discussed in Rick Westhead, "NHL Expanding European Revenue Generation Potential," at <http://www.sportbusinessnews.com> cited 25 November 2002. In that article, the London-based sports marketing company Redmandarin's vice president Ethan Green said, "Eastern European countries aren't as attractive to American companies from a sponsorship standpoint because per capita income is comparatively lower there. A hockey crazy market is nice, but a hockey crazy market with a large population base and disposable income provides a better recipe for return on investment." Apart from the professional leagues, young amateur Russian hockey players continue to excel in the sport. For example, during early 2004 Russia defeated America in the Under-18 World Ice Hockey Championship to win its third title. For details about that victory, see "Russia Beats United States 3–2 For Under-18 Title," at <http://si.printthis.clickability.com> cited 20 April 2004.

18.   The role of women ice hockey players in professional leagues is depicted in Eric Duhatschek, "International Ice Hockey President Not a Fan of Girls Playing With Boys," at <http://www.sportsbusinessnews.com> cited 20 February 2003. About that topic, IIHF president Rene Fasel wrote in an editorial that, "Hockey is a tougher game than soccer, handball or basketball. You don't see girls playing in men's leagues in those sports. I don't think it would be healthy for Hayley [Wickenheiser], or any other female player, to go into a corner with a player who is determined to deliver a hard check." Even though the resistance to mix professional men and women hockey players involves safety and personal injury, there are active women's hockey leagues and their respective teams in Canada, China, Europe and Russia. For some interesting facts about the national women's hockey team in China, see Wayne Scanlan, "Chinese Women Hockey Team Overcoming Odds," at <http://www.sportsbusinessnews.com> cited 1 December 2003. Interestingly, although the Chinese team finished fourth in the 1994 and 1997 World Championships, and in the 1998 Nagano Olympics, the nation's sports bureaucrats have lost interest in subsidizing women's ice hockey because of the extreme competition from women's teams that exist in Canada, Finland, Japan, Russia and the U.S. As a result, less than 50 women players are active on teams to revive the sport in China. Because of the SARS outbreak during 2003, the Chinese team has struggled to schedule games. Alternatively, the schedule, standings, news, statistics

and teams of a Canadian-based women's league is reported in "National Women's Hockey League," at <http://www.dgp.utoronto.ca> cited 14 January 2004, and John Cook, "Professional Women's Hockey League Looking to Turn the Corner," at <http://www.sportsbusinessnews.com> cited 30 March 2004. With respect to the women's league, games have averaged about 100 spectators, which is less than ten percent of the group's total revenues. As such, teams will market their products to attract more men. "Right now the fan base that you get are young girls, you don't have the hard core hockey guy coming out to watch," said Oakville Ice's owner Bill Metcalf. "You don't do this to make money. I guarantee you that. Your best-case scenario is to break even. You have to have a passion for this and you do it to get involved with your community." Consequently, during 2004 and thereafter the NWHL will focus on improving its product to increase attendance and therefore gate receipts. Furthermore, NWHL president Susan Fennell has goals to encourage Hockey Canada to ease import restrictions, seek approval to increase the current limit of two non-Canadian players to six, establish a separate quota for American players, and close the competitive gap between the top trio of clubs in Brampton, Toronto and Calgary and the remaining teams. In Fennell's view, if the talent pool improves, there will be better competition during games, which means greater fan support. Even though the NWHL struggles for attention, Canada won its eighth Women's World Championship during early 2004 by defeating Sweden 7–1 and then an American team 2–0. Since the tournament began in 1990, Canada has lost only one game. For the tournament results, see "One-Sided Rivalry," at <http://sportsillustrated.cnn.com> cited 13 April 2004. Lastly, there is information about women's hockey and women's world ice hockey championships on pages 210–213 in *The Concise Encyclopedia of Hockey*.

19.   For the attitudes and beliefs of international club officials and federations with respect to the compensation amounts for European NHL draft choices, see Matthew Fisher, "European Hockey Official Look to Squeeze NHL For More Money," at <http://www.sportsbusinessnews.com> cited 13 February 2003. Foreign-born players who migrate to the NHL should somehow repay their federations. This recommendation was stated by the IIHF's president Rene Fasel in "IIHF Pres Says Players Should Compete in World Champs as Payback," at <http://www.sportsbusinessnews.com> cited 20 November 2003. According to Fasel, "If a player is earning $10-million a year, he should not forget about his federation that made it possible for him to be there."

20.   See "Just How Much of an Effect Will a Higher Canadian Dollar Have on the Maple Leafs," at <http://www.sportsbusinessnews.com> cited 6 November 2003; Dave Luecking, "The Future of Hockey in Canada," at <http://www.sportsbusinessnews.com> cited 3 December 2002; Bill Pennington, "Canadian Minor Hockey Fiasco(s) Makes it to the New York Times," at <http://www.sportsbusinessnews.com> cited 3 December 2002. Despite the struggles of NHL teams in Canada, during early 2004 some politicians from Winnipeg requested that the Pittsburgh Penguins' owner Mario Lemieux move his team to Manitoba's medium sized capital city. The new 15,000-seat MTS Centre and a solid ice hockey fan base are two reasons to consider Winnipeg as an NHL city. About the request, Winnipeg's deputy mayor Dan Vandal stated, "The reality is half the NHL teams are losing millions of dollars every year, and NHL hockey is being played in front of 3,000 or 4,000 people in the southern United States almost on a weekly basis. That's not sustainable. That's not major-league. Winnipeg is a major-league NHL town." See Ross Romaniuk, "What About an NHL Facility in Winnipeg," at <http://www.sportsbusinessnews.com> cited 5 January 2004, and Idem., "Winnipeg Interested in Getting the Pittsburgh Penguins," at <http://www.sportsbusinessnews.com> cited 5 January 2004. With respect to the league's finances, a study revealed that the 30 NHL teams had total operating losses of $272.6 million in the 2002–2003

season. Furthermore, the data showed that while the league's operating revenues increased from $732 million in 1993–1994 to nearly $2 billion in 2002–2003, the teams' player costs had risen from $414 million to about $1.5 billion during those years. The study's author, who was the former U.S. Securities and Exchange Commission (SEC) chairman Arthur Levitt Jr. commented that, "The results are catastrophic as I've seen in any enterprise of this size. They [the NHL] are on a treadmill to obscurity." This financial information about the NHL was listed in "Report Pegs Losses at $272 Million For League," *The Charlotte Observer* (13 February 2004), 4C. In addition to the bankrupt Ottawa Senators and Buffalo Sabres, a former chief accountant of the SEC discovered that three NHL teams had going-concern opinions and two other clubs did not have their finances audited. According to accountant Lynn Turner, "The one thing I know is they [NHL] can't continue down the road they are currently on or it would ultimately lead to a number of the other teams heading down the same path as the couple that have been in bankruptcy [protection]. Could this league even survive as 20 teams? I don't know. At some point in time you hit that number in the public's mind where they say, 'You know, I don't know if this is worth $50 a game.'" For why some NHL owners had to guarantee bank loans in order to keep their clubs solvent, see Paul Waldie, "NHL Armageddon 2004—The Bank(s) Are Calling," at <http://www. sportsbusinessnews.com> cited 20 February 2004. Despite those troubles, during March of 2004 it appeared that the six NHL teams in Canada would qualify for the playoffs, an event which had not happened since 1986 when the Montreal Canadiens defeated the Calgary Flames for the Stanley Cup. Because of the multi-year rise in the Canadian dollar, the small-market clubs in Canada have been able to better compete for free agent players with the U.S.-based franchises. "Any time you have the six teams in, it is good for the game and good for Canada," said the Ottawa Senators general manager John Muckler. "It is nice to see the Canadian teams compete for the Stanley Cup." Those comments were stated in Alan Adams, "Canada Thirsts For Six-Pack," at <http://www.nhl.com> cited 30 March 2004. However, despite the financial problems of Canadian-based teams, the Canadian Broadcasting Corporation (CBC) recorded that 3.9 million viewers watched the 2004 Stanley Cup playoff game between the Toronto Maple Leafs and Ottawa Senators. Those viewers represented the largest audience for a playoff game since 2002 and the highest rating of a first-round game since 1989. The numbers were reported in William Houston, "Stanley Cup Ratings Continue to Deliver in Canada," at <http://www.sportsbusinessnews.com> cited 20 April 2004.

21.   The FHL's headquarters is at 1006 Ogden Street Coquitlam, British Columbia, Canada, which was listed in the league's official press release in "New Canadian Pro Hockey League," at <http://www.federalhockeyleague.ca> cited 12 November 2003.

22.   The FHL's president John O. Larsen intended to own and control the Vancouver Seals Hockey Club. For Larsen's goals with respect to the league's operations and the expected locations of teams as of middle to late 2003, see "A New Hockey League in Canada," at <http://www.sportsbusinessnews.com> cited 19 August 2003; "FHL Finalizes Cities in Canada," at <http://www.federalhockeyleague.ca> cited 12 November 2003; "FHL: Teams," at <http://www.federalhockeyleague.ca> cited 12 November 2003; "FHL: League Updates," at <http://www.federalhockeyleague.ca> cited 12 November 2003; "FHL: General Information," at <http://www.federalhockeyleague.ca> cited 12 November 2003.

23.   The players that attended the evaluation camps received packages of items to use. Those items included hotel accommodations based on double occupancy, bus transportation to and from the arenas, all ice time, an FHL jersey and a professional evaluation from FHL directors of coaching and the scouting operations staff. See "FHL: Free Agent Evaluation Camp," at <http://www.federalhockeyleague.ca> cited 12 November 2003.

24. President Larsen claims that partners will receive 100 percent of the return on investment under the franchise agreement. According to Larsen "This is a tremendous opportunity for the right individual or group. We are convinced that the Federal Hockey League in participation with the Franchise Partners, will make our organization second to none." This statement was made in "FHL: Investment Opportunities," at <http://www.federalhockey-league.ca> cited 12 November 2003.

25. The history and operation of the original WHA during the 1970s is presented in "World Hockey Association," at <http://www.worldhockeyassociation.net> cited 25 November 2003. For how the new WHA will be organized, see Rod Beaton, "The New WHA Could Capitalize on NHL Labor Woes," at <http://www.worldhockeyassociation.net> cited 25 November 2003; "The World Hockey Association Concludes Two Days of Meetings in Toronto," at <http://www.worldhockeyassociation.net> cited 22 January 2004; Stephen Harris, "Clouded Future Remains For WHA," at <http://www.sportsbusinessnews.com> cited 11 December 2003. In the latter article, the NHL Philadelphia Flyers' center Jeremy Roenick told a reporter from the Philadelphia Inquirer newspaper, "I have had some friendly talks with Brett Hull and other people about the WHA starting up. They want to start up in 8–10 cities. If they can manage to pull that off, I would definitely be looking to go into one of those cities to help them start up the league." As the commissioner of the WHL, Brett's father Bobby Hull has stated that, "We see ourselves as an alternative, not a competitor. There are too many families that just can't afford to see an NHL game and, as a result, we are losing a whole generation of hockey fans. We need to get those kids and families back into the arenas." For Hull's vision with respect to the WHL, see Scott Pitoniak, "The Golden Jet on His New Hockey Dream," at <http://www.sportsbusinessnews.com> cited 23 April 2004.

26. The WHA was expected to form WHA2, which is a new minor ice hockey league with teams in Lakeland, Miami and Orlando, Florida, and in Jacksonville, Alabama and Macon, Georgia. For the home cities of WHA2 and WHA teams, see Paul Doyle, "At Least One Group Hoping NHL Armageddon 2004 Becomes Reality," at <http://www.sportsbusiness-news.com> cited 10 October 2003.

27. Ibid.

28. The early history and collapse of the IHL was discussed in Jeff Jacobs, "A Look Back at the International Hockey League," at <http://www.sportsbusinessnews.com> cited 3 December 2002. According to Jacobs, "The IHL continued to prosper, then the IHL got full of itself. The IHL stopped being the IHL. It signed former NHLers to fat contracts and played to the egos of new markets. The illusion was a delusion and ultimately, a fine old hockey league folded."

29. For more information on this topic, see "International Hockey League to Cease Operations," at <http://www.allsports.com> cited 25 November 2003; Ken Warren, "The Death of the IHL," at <http://www.sportsbusinessnews.com> cited 3 December 2002; Don Muret, "Demise of International Hockey League Leaves Several Scrambling For Dates," *Amusement Business* (11 June 2001), 8. In Muret's article, the Detroit Palace Sports & Entertainment's president Tom Wilson aptly described the league's problems. He said, "At the end of the day, we were losing seven figures on hockey and we don't have the luxury of propping up a second-tier sport. What was a regional league turned national in focus almost overnight, and the big city guys had the win-at-all-costs mentality in spending more money on the same players. The small market teams couldn't do that."

30. The international ice hockey tournaments that were held between the early 1970s and late 1990s are described in "World Cup of Hockey to Return," at <http://www.upi.com> cited 26 November 2003; Ken Campbell, "Toronto to be Major World Cup of Hockey Site,"

Toronto Star (20 September 2002), F2; "So What if NHL Shuts Down, World Cup is Coming to T.O.," *Toronto Star* (2 April 2003), E1.

31.   For more information about the 2004 World Cup of Hockey, see "Details Revealed For 2004 World Cup of Hockey," *Europe Intelligence Wire* (3 April 2003), 1; Terry Jones, "World Cup of Hockey to Return in 2004," at <http://www.sportsbusinessnews.com> cited 25 November 2002; "2004 World Cup of Hockey Schedule," at <http://www.si.com> cited 17 April 2003; "2004 World Cup of Hockey Information," at <http://sportsillustrated.cnn.com> cited 30 January 2004. The final article provides the World Cup's history and with respect to the 2004 tournament, it lists the venues, ticket information, broadcast partners, player selection and tournament format. Finally, see page 213 of *The Concise Encyclopedia of Hockey* for a brief overview of the World Cup tournament played in 1996.

32.   See Terri Frei, "World Cup a Tease of Global Proportions," at <http://sports.espn.go.com> cited 26 November 2003. Furthermore, a detailed history of the tournament was published in Patrick Houda and Joe Pelletier, *The World Cup of Hockey* (Toronto, Canada: Warwick Publishing Inc., 2002).

33.   Because of the NHL's economic problems and risky operations in North America, there is speculation that the league will relocate one or more teams to cities in Europe. This strategy was discussed in David Shoalts, "NHL in Europe—Not Anytime Soon," at <http://www.sportsbusinessnews.com> cited 24 September 2003.

34.   MLB Commissioner Bud Selig's threat to close two baseball teams in 2001 proved to be exaggerated. As to whether that strategy would be applied before or during the NHL negotiations by the NHL Commissioner Gary Bettman, see Chris Isidore, "Skating on Thin Ice."

35.   The potential of a global super hockey league that contains one or more of the NHL teams and various clubs from the European national federations was mentioned in the article "NHL in Europe—Not Anytime Soon." Interestingly, unlike the NHL, at least one European ice hockey league has a scoring system that awards a team three points for a regulation win, two points for a shootout victory and one point for a shootout loss. Furthermore, there are no ties or overtime. If teams are deadlocked at the end of regulation, they advance directly into a shootout. Those and other differences were identified in Eric Duhatschek, "What Makes European Professional Hockey Work?" at <http://www.sportsbusinessnews.com> cited 14 January 2004. In that article, Hamburg coach Dave King claimed that the NFL represents a good model for the NHL to liven up its games. According to King, "NFL football is a high, high-scoring game and that's really amazing because, if you look at the NFL, the players are bigger, stronger, faster—the same things we say about hockey players nowadays—but playing on the same-size field, they've found ways to improve the offence with some terrific passing schemes. Their rules favor offence versus defense and I think that's what we want in hockey." As an aside, when the NHL opened its regular season in Japan during 2000, one sportswriter called the league's drive for global expansion as 'mission proliferation.' In other words, the league seemed to be at cross-purposes with itself when the Pittsburgh Penguins and Nashville Predators played at the Saitama Super Arena in Omiya, Japan. That is, at that time the Predators were not a quality team in the NHL. The group and managing director of NHL International Ken Jaffe responded by saying that "While the NHL has a desire to promote the game internationally, it also has a responsibility to promote the game in North America and return value to the 30 member clubs in the league. So bringing Nashville to Japan has more to do with business, and promoting the team in North America, than it does with bringing the best product." For this perspective, see Shimbun Yomiuri, "NHL Short Sighted in Drive For Global Expansion," *The Daily Yomiuri* (5 September 2000), 1.

Chapter 5

Major League Soccer

Since the late 1960s, at least three prominent professional men's outdoor soccer leagues and one women's association were established in the U.S. For one or more reasons, however, each had failed. To identify those sports businesses, in 1967 the 12-team North American Soccer League, which decided that year to change its name to the United Soccer Association (USA), and the ten-team National Professional Soccer League (NPSL) had each began their first regular season. Because the USA was sanctioned by soccer's national and international governing organizations, which included the U.S. Soccer Federation and the Federation Internationale de Football Association (FIFA), it consisted of teams with players from Brazil, Canada, England, Italy, Paraguay, Ireland, Scotland and the Netherlands. The NPSL, meanwhile, was not sanctioned by those two govern- ing organizations. As such, that league struggled to recruit players who had feared of being suspended by professional soccer's eminent officials. Therefore, because of the leagues' bitter rivalries and small attendances at their teams' regular season games, in 1968 the USA and NPSL merged to form the 17-team North American Soccer League (NASL). Nonetheless, after one season of play only five U.S.-based teams had remained in the NASL. Besides those men's leagues, the eight-team Women's United Soccer Association (WUSA) played its first season in 2001. Two years later, however, the league had to suspend its operations.[1]

In retrospect, to promote soccer as a participation sport for young athletes and thus build a loyal fan base in America, the NASL became a semiprofessional league in 1969. Two years later, a team from Montreal, Canada and another one from Toronto, Canada were admitted to the NASL. When the Montreal team folded its organization in 1974, it was replaced by a franchise located in Vancouver, Canada. Then, to attract more sports fans, in 1975 the league's New York Cosmos team signed the great Brazilian athlete Pele to a three-year, $4.5 million contract. After other such international soccer stars as George Best, Bobby Moore, Frank Beckenbauer and Giorgio Chinaglia joined clubs in the NASL, its attendance doubled in two years. In 1977, Pele had retired from professional soccer although the league continued to exploit the sports markets and thus expand to 24 teams. During the late 1970s, however, the number of spectators at regular season games had gradually declined and so between 1981 and 1984, the quantity of teams fell from 21 to six. Because of fewer teams, lack of a national television contract and weak attendances at games, the NASL was forced to terminate its operations in March 1985. For ten years, therefore, there were no major profess- ional soccer leagues located in the U.S.[2]

After a successful men's World Cup tournament had concluded in 1994, the U.S. Soccer Federation and some World Cup officials from America cooperated to organize a men's outdoor soccer league. Consequently, this effort resulted in the formation of Major League Soccer (MLS), which proceeded to begin its first season in 1996. Initially, MLS consisted of two conferences with five U.S.-based teams in each conference. To further penetrate markets in America, the league added the Chicago Fire and Miami Fusion as expansion clubs in 1998 and then two years later reorganized itself into one conference with three four-team divisions. When the Miami Fusion and Tampa Bay Mutiny teams had to cease their operations before the 2002 season, the league returned to a two-conference format. Meanwhile, to globalize its brand and image during the early 2000s, MLS acquired the English language television rights to the 2002 and 2006 men's World Cup tournaments and the 2003 women's World Cup tournament. As a result of those acquisitions, the American Broadcasting Corporation (ABC), and the ESPN and ESPN2 networks each agreed to broadcast the three tournaments and the league's regular season games through 2006. In short, it was during the early 2000s that MLS had emerged as one of the premier professional soccer organizations in North America.[3]

To portray the history and the alliances, events, grassroots programs, relationships and other sports and business matters that involve the eight year old MLS from a strategic international perspective, and to discuss the sport of European football—hereinafter referred to as European soccer—and the suspension in 2003 of the WUSA, Chapter 5 is presented as a separate unit in *Sports Capitalism*. Indeed, the chapter is organized into four parts or sections that highlight the key international business strategies of MLS, and then devotes one section each for topics that relate to European soccer organizations and to the emergence and suspension of the WUSA. Because of the data, facts and other information presented in Chapter 5, this book's readers will learn, comprehend and respect why the sport of soccer and professional soccer leagues are essential components of the worldwide sports industry. In short, this chapter provides enough analytical contents to compare the business success and globalization of MLS with that of such leagues as MLB, and the NFL, NBA and NHL.

In the first section of this chapter, MLS' former, current and future international business strategies are exposed as topics and then discussed. Besides the insights and views of MLS' Commissioner Don Garber, the contents include various proposals whether to expand, contract and/or maintain the number and location of franchises in the league. Those proposals, therefore, are reviewed with respect to the teams' current and future sites in America and to prospective locations abroad.

After the league's various strategies are depicted, Chapter 5's second section focuses on how MLS had negotiated and succeeded to sign important broadcast agreements with a variety of cable and satellite operators and television networks to extend the coverage of its games into markets overseas and to encourage its participation in international soccer tournaments and other global events. The league, for example, had decided to increasingly advertise, promote and target its teams' soccer games and grassroots activities to Latinos in the U.S. and Hispanic audiences in Mexico and South American nations, and to households in such Asian countries as China and Japan.

This chapter's third portion is dedicated to exposing how and why the World Cup of Soccer has become such an important event for MLS and the teams that represent countries in Asia, Europe, Central America and other regions of the world. After World Cup championships were held in Uruguay, Italy and France, respectively, in 1930, 1934 and 1938, the tournament has been played every four years since 1950. Nevertheless, because the competitions had occurred since 1996 and therefore concerned MLS, this chapter's emphasis is on the World Cups that were completed in 1998 and 2002, and on various aspects of the tournament that is scheduled in 2006. Besides the World Cups, other soccer events alluded to in this section of the chapter were the European championships, Under-17 and Under-20 world championships, and international club tournaments like the European, Libertadores and Union of European Football Associations (UEFA) Cups.

In the fourth part of Chapter 5, some foreign soccer players who had decided to perform for MLS clubs are identified, which is followed by a discussion of why American athletes willingly agree to join the rosters of amateur and/or professional soccer teams that are based in nations abroad. Furthermore, this part highlights the intense competition and unique counteractions that existed among and between MLS teams and various European clubs to recruit, draft and sign America's 14 year old talent, Freddy Adu. Whether and how Adu's decision to play for the New York Cosmos will affect the short- and/or long-term business environments of MLS and the professional soccer leagues in other nations, is an interesting topic to evaluate for the readers of *Sports Capitalism*.

An overview of a few European soccer leagues and their clubs and players, and the reasons for the demise of the WUSA are presented in the final two sections of Chapter 5. Thus, to relate the operations of MLS with the status of soccer leagues overseas, with various teams in England, Italy and Spain, and with the viability of professional women's soccer as a sport and business, are topics that appear, respectively, in the fifth and sixth sections of this chapter. When the analysis of MLS and the contents of those sections are completed, Chapter 5 concludes with a Summary, which is followed by the Notes.

MLS International Strategies

Since the league's first competitive games in 1996, a MLS Cup championship series has been played between those teams that excelled during the regular season. This championship series has, in part, contributed to the development and growth of elementary, high school and college soccer programs in America. In turn, those programs have resulted in the improved performances by the U.S. men's national teams in soccer games at international tournaments. That is, since 1998 the nation's best men's teams have qualified for each of the World Cup tournaments and in 2002, the U.S. team performed well enough to play in the World Cup's quarterfinals. Thus, because of soccer's growing popularity in America's schools and the success of the country's national teams, after six seasons MLS had finally emerged as a potentially competitive professional sports organization from an international perspective. Given that progress, the league has become more globally respected by foreign soccer teams and officials. Moreover, America's national men's soccer clubs are expected to eventually challenge, and perhaps win one or more major international tournaments, against the best teams in the world from such organizations as Europe's Champions League, England's Premier League, Italy's Serie A and Spain's La Liga.[4]

After the former National Football Leagues' International senior vice president and managing director Don Garber became the MLS Commissioner in 1999, he initiated a variety of reforms and programs that have likely contributed to the league's long-term growth and its survival. In 2000, for example, Garber and team owners revised some of MLS' rules so that the league's policies would conform to international standards. To illustrate, the shootout was eliminated but overtime and a tie each became legal aspects of the teams' soccer games. Furthermore, during games the stadiums' clocks returned to counting up and official playing times were monitored only on the referee's wristwatch. Unfortunately, before these changes had occurred in 2000, the MLS franchises had collectively experienced $250 million in operating losses during the latter seasons of the 1990s, in part, because only a small percentage of the league's teams averaged at least 10,000 spectators in attendance per game. Nevertheless, by 2002 some teams' losses had significantly declined when their attendances at regular season home games increased to an average of almost 15,000. Based on those improvements in the league's popularity, in 2003 what were Commissioner Garber's aspirations for the future of American soccer and second, what were his business goals for MLS with respect to populations in North America and various foreign countries? The answer to that question primarily involves such subtopics as team sites, soccer stadiums and soccer markets. Because they are each discussed in the next several paragraphs, those subtopics are relevant to the future success of the league.[5]

Team Sites

Although the league's franchises in Miami and Tampa Bay were dissolved in 2002 because of poor attendances at games and the inferior performances of their teams, Garber has reported that MLS cannot establish and sustain a measurable and passionate base of fans in America until the league consists of at least 20 teams. Therefore, to accomplish that goal before 2008, the league has planned to expand its membership and encourage the entry of new teams that will be located at sites in North American cities and perhaps later in large urban areas abroad.

One U.S. city that seems to be an attractive place for a professional soccer team is Houston in the State of Texas. Located near the northwestern shore of the Gulf of Mexico with a population that exceeds four million, Houston is a large and diverse market where three annual soccer events have been held. Generally, those games had involved a combination of national soccer teams from the U.S. and

Mexico, or of MLS teams and soccer clubs from Mexico and European countries. During May of 2003, for example, an American and Mexican national team had competed at Houston's 69,500-seat Reliant Stadium. This is the two year old home facility of the NFL's Houston Texans and the site of Super Bowl XXXVIII, which was played between the Carolina Panthers and New England Patriots on 1 February 2004. Anyway, with respect to the competition of the two national soccer teams, they last met in a 2002 World Cup tournament game that the U.S. narrowly won by a score of two to zero. As an aside, the game played in May 2003 was broadcast live to hundreds of thousands of households in Mexico on Telemundo, which is a Spanish-language television network. Besides that exciting event, the U.S. team had also scheduled a series of games against three other foreign opponents who were, respectively, from Mexico, Japan and Argentina, in order to prepare for the FIFA Confederation Cup in June 2003 and one month later, for the Confederation of North and Central American and Caribbean Football (CONCA-CAF) Gold Cup. Founded in 1961, CONCACAF organizes international competitions that include the Champions' Cup, women's veterans and youth championships, qualifying tournaments for all FIFA competitions, and the biannual Gold Cup.[6]

Besides Houston as a location, the Canadian Soccer Association (CSA) has fervently campaigned to lure to metropolitan Toronto a MLS team that would primarily consist of native-born Canadian players. With a subsidy payment of $625,000 from the FIFA, the CSA has recommended that Canadian taxpayers and/or a syndicate of investors build a 30,000-seat natural grass stadium in Toronto to promote the city's bid to host the Women's World Cup tournament, which is scheduled in 2007. With respect to the proposal for a soccer stadium in Toronto's bid to be a MLS city, in early 2003 the CSA's president Andy Sharpe stated that, "A MLS franchise in Toronto would allow for the top 25 to 30 Canadian players to have an option of playing at the highest professional level in North America in front of a home crowd." Based on Commissioner Garber's plans to expand his league during the early 2000s, and the expected construction of a soccer stadium somewhere in Canada, Toronto appears to be an appealing site to locate a MLS expansion franchise before or in 2007 or 2008.[7]

To increase the league's presence in new medium sized sports markets, MLS has approved the bids submitted by two wealthy investors. As such, this decision allows each of the investors to acquire and own a new expansion team that will join the league in 2005. The first entrepreneur accepted by MLS was real estate developer and philanthropist Bert Wolstein. He selected Cleveland in the State of Ohio, which is an industrial, Midwest American city and the current location of MLB's Indians, NFL's Browns and NBA's Cavaliers as the home for his new professional soccer team. The other businessman that MLS welcomed as a team owner was Mexico's Jorge Vergara. He becomes a new franchise investor while serving as the current proprietor of his Mexican club, Chivas USA, which will likely be reestablished in San Diego, a medium sized city in southern California. If Vergara' team is competitive and ultimately a financial success after its relocation from Mexico, then perhaps another Mexican or Latin American capitalist will seek approval from the league to place a MLS club in Mexico City or Monterrey since those cities are excellent locations for a professional soccer team. In short, the cities of Houston, Toronto, Cleveland, San Diego and perhaps Mexico City and Monterrey appear to be attractive places for teams, as sports businesses, in MLS.[8]

During his interviews with the media and in press releases, Commissioner Garber has proposed that other medium sized and large market U.S. cities are considered as potential sites to place an MLS team. Listed alphabetically, these cities include Atlanta in Georgia, Louisville in Kentucky, Milwaukee in Wisconsin, Minneapolis in Minnesota, New York City in New York, Oklahoma City in Oklahoma, Philadelphia in Pennsylvania, Rochester in New York and St. Louis in Missouri. Nonetheless, because the typical MLS team has experienced operating losses during its existence, and due to weak attendances, lack of television broadcast agreements and inferior playing performances of the professional soccer franchises that failed in Miami and Tampa Bay, Florida, it is highly unlikely that MLS has the economic resources or fan bases to expand in size and then locate clubs in cities outside of America before 2008. This prediction would be challenged, of course, if an international and/or national soccer federation, and/or sports business entrepreneurs from America or one or more foreign countries had decided to invest in and construct a soccer-only facility to attract a current MLS team that seeks a new location, or to host a new expansion franchise. That is, the decisions of investors and/or taxpayers to build a single-purpose soccer stadium for a team are a critical factor for MLS officials to evaluate and incorporate in league operations as reflected in the following paragraphs.

Soccer Stadiums

According to his statements that appeared in various publications, Commissioner Garber has asserted that a soccer facility is a more valuable economic asset for the long-term survival and prosperity of a MLS franchise and the league than for a team to recruit one or more high-priced American and/or international soccer athletes. The Commissioner's hypothesis was revealed during 2002 when he declared, "We need our own stadiums so we can celebrate the game. Our teams need their own homes. I would much rather invest in bricks and mortar that will be around in 50 years than on the quick fix of buying some player who is gone in a couple of years." To further support Garber's thesis, the president of the Anschutz Entertainment Group (AEG) Tim Leiweke said, "Unless you have your own venues, it's difficult for it to make sense of 25,000 in a 100,000-seat stadium." Based on the viewpoints of Garber and Leiweke, what is the availability of soccer stadiums with respect to the teams in MLS?[9]

Between 1996 and 1998, there were no MLS teams that had played their home games in a made-for-soccer-only stadium. Then, during 2000 the 22,500-seat Columbus Crew Stadium was built by owner Lamar Hunt for the Crew, which is Hunt's MLS team that competed to win its home games in Columbus, Ohio. Although Columbus was the league's smallest market at that time, in 1999 the Crew's attendance exceeded 17,600 fans per game, a number that topped the average home attendance of each club in MLS. Then, in the middle of 2003 MLS' Los Angeles Galaxy opened its regular season in the 27,000-seat Home Depot Center, which is located in Carson, California. This $75 million soccer-specific facility is centered within an 85-acre sports complex that provides accommodations for those fans that attend the Galaxy's home games.[10]

For economic reasons, therefore, during 2003 a number of renovated or new soccer stadiums had either been designed and/or planned for construction to benefit MLS teams such as the Fire in Chicago, Illinois, and the Burn in Dallas, Texas, MetroStars in Secaucus, New Jersey and D.C. United in Washington, D.C. Besides the capital investment and economic revitalization that would occur surrounding the stadiums in those four cities, other business groups and/or investors had discussed the placement of soccer-only facilities in New York City and Rochester, New York. That is, AEG had intended to build the stadiums in Chicago, New York City and Washington, and the Dallas Burns' owner, which is The Hunt Sports Group, assumed responsibility to erect and partially fund a 17-field, 20,000-seat $65 million Frisco Soccer and Entertainment Center in Texas. Frisco, which is a booming suburb north of Dallas, combined with Collin County to provide $55 million of the cost and the Hunt's will cover the difference plus any cost overruns. Indeed, the stadium's construction began in early 2004. According to the Group's president John Wagner, "It doesn't matter what sport you're in, if you don't have the right kind of venue to play in, and don't have access to the right ancillary revenue, it's going to be a tough business." Meanwhile, during the early 2000s the City of Rochester secured $15 million in public sector funds to partially pay for its proposed soccer venue.[11]

In short, if those and other stadiums are completed at sites in U.S. cities for MLS clubs before or during 2007, then Commissioner Garber and the league's existing franchise owners are likely to discuss and then evaluate whether to place an expansion team in one or more foreign cities in 2008 or thereafter. As previously mentioned in this chapter, there are attractive international sites for MLS teams in a few Canadian and Mexican cities. Undoubtedly, the seasonal weather conditions and temperatures, local ownership, size of the metropolitan population, presence of other sports, extent of national television broadcast coverage, and the quality of soccer stadiums at sites in those cities are each relevant factors for MLS to include in the league's decision to select one or more foreign places as locations for current and/or new soccer franchises. If so, how important are consumer sports markets to the success of MLS teams and the league?

Soccer Markets

Because of MLS' eight plus years of existence, and the league's potential for national and international expansion and growth, a relatively small but dedicated fan base has gradually emerged in various U.S. cities and regions to attend professional soccer games and tournaments. Furthermore, during the early 2000s the sport of soccer had received more coverage from the media and thus moderately solidified its roots among professional sports fans. The overriding challenge for MLS officials after the early 2000s, therefore, is to educate, provide entertainment for and permanently convert the massive number of American children, youth and adults who have been or are active soccer participants and/or spectators, into passionate and committed fans of one or more of the league's teams. When they become die hard fans, for example, soccer enthusiasts are those people who will purchase a large number of regular season tickets and attend numerous home games, who will listen to sports announcers report the games' results on the radio or watch them on television, and/or who read about their favorite team on the Internet and in the sports section of a local, regional or national newspaper. In other words, these are the types of behaviors and loyalties that have been exhibited by the foreign fans who historically have supported such outstanding international teams as the Boca Juniors in Mexico, Milan in Italy, Real Madrid in Spain and Manchester United (Man U) in England.

To reach parity and remain competitive with the world's greatest soccer teams beyond 2004, the MLS clubs need to recruit, draft, sign and generously compensate the best amateur players from America's high schools and college sports programs, and from semiprofessional teams. This effort requires that the league's franchise owners each provide economic incentives to native-born U.S. players such as above-average salaries, performance bonuses and other benefits. To be sure, there is ample evidence that by 2007 the number of experienced and talented soccer players will significantly expand in America. There are at least three good reasons to justify and support that prediction. First, in 2003 the nonprofit American Youth Soccer Organization had included 50,000 teams that in total represented 650,000 boys and girls who were in the age group of 4–18 years old. Second, the U.S. Sporting Goods Manufacturers Association reported that 7.25 million Americans, who were 6–17 years old, had played soccer 25 or more times a year as compared to 4.75 million youth who had participated in baseball games. Third, the United States Soccer Federation's president Dr. Robert Contigugli recently made this comment about the sport, "To me, it's an incredible sociological and cultural phenomenon that's happened with youth soccer. It is the number one weekend family pastime in the United States. And now we're beginning to perform on the highest levels professionally." In short, thousands of elementary school, high school and college soccer players in America are second-generation athletes whose parents had encouraged them to participate in the sport when they were young children. If so, eventually the best performers of those youth will possess the ambition, skill and experience to join junior and semiprofessional soccer programs and then MLS teams to successfully compete, and therefore win World Cup championships and other major international soccer tournaments.[12]

The previous paragraphs conclude the discussion of soccer stadiums and markets. That said, to learn more about the international business of MLS, the next section describes how selected television deals and affiliations with partners and sponsors have exposed the league to sports fans in nations throughout the world.

Global Television and Media Agreements

During various years of the 1970s and 1980s, sportscaster Toby Charles hosted Soccer Made in Germany, which was broadcasted as a show on television. This program, which appeared for one hour on Saturdays, basically introduced the American audiences to soccer by describing games played by teams in the NASL. Since the 1980s, however, professional soccer games and international tournaments have been presented at an increasing rate on global television channels and networks. In 2003, for example, the Fox Sports World (FSW) network was authorized to broadcast the same-day delays of six foreign soccer games that were then played by teams from Argentina, Brazil, Germany, England, France and Holland. Meanwhile, other international soccer matches played by competitive clubs in Columbia, Ecuador, El Salvador, Guatemala and Spain were televised on Fox Sports Espanol or Gol TV, which then was a new Uruguay-based all-soccer satellite channel owned by Tenfield, S.A. In America, during particular seasons more than 100 games of MLS and the U.S. national soccer teams had received airtime on ESPN2 and Fox Sports. Furthermore, the Telemundo and Univision networks provided the coverage of competitive games involving some teams that were members of the Mexican Football Soccer Federation. Because of this international exposure from television, professional soccer games and tournaments have become considerably more affordable, entertaining, popular and fan-friendly, and thus a worthwhile business and an enjoyable sport for people and communities in numerous developed and underdeveloped nations across the globe.[13]

During the early 2000s, MLS and its broadcast affiliates collaborated to initiate a television campaign that would market professional soccer and the league primarily to Hispanic audiences in North, Central and South America, and then to other populations worldwide. To illustrate, in 2003 the Gol TV network had initially planned to program in Spanish and English about 800 soccer matches per year of various leagues, teams and tournament competitions that were scheduled in Mexico, and in nations of Central and South America. Rather than televise complete games, however, the Gol TV's broadcasts included the important news events and highlight shows that involved MLS teams. Since the league's ratings for games on ESPN generally measured a miniscule 0.1 or 0.2 in 2003, the sales and marketing staff at Gol TV had decided to limit the coverage of entire MLS events until the league had attracted more sponsors and a larger television audience in America.[14]

In early 2003, MLS was delighted to sign a four-year contract with Fox Sports International (FSI). The deal specified that FSI would nationally televise 25 of the league's regular season games and at least eight playoff games on FSW and Fox Sports en Espanol, and then to extend those broadcasts to Fox's affiliated networks in countries of Latin America and the Middle East. Besides the telecasts of teams' games, Fox also produced MLS Wrap as a program on FSW. MLS Wrap was created to be a weekly, one-hour studio-hosted show that included highlights of teams and games, league statistics, coach and player interviews, and an interactive email element with viewers. Besides the broadcasts on Fox Sports en Espanol, the league's weekly Saturday night games appeared in Spanish with the title, La MLS en Fox Sports en Espanol. With respect to the impact of those television agreements with Fox, MLS's chief operating officer Mark Abbott enthusiastically stated, "Major League Soccer is ecstatic about the opportunity to showcase our regular season and playoff contests, the competitive nature of our teams and the personality of our players on a cable network that has become a destination for soccer fans in the Western Hemisphere. Our fans have been clamoring for a weekly highlight show and Spanish-language broadcasts, and Fox Sports World has helped us deliver."[15]

To provide even more exposure of professional soccer games, teams and players, and tournaments to the Hispanic communities in America and elsewhere, midway during 2003 MLS announced the settlement of an integrated marketing and content agreement with Yahoo! en espanol, which then was one of the leading Spanish-language Internet portals. According to reports of what the agreement had included, the portal became the official online sponsor of MLS and the supplier of comprehensive online coverage of all the league's games and any other premier soccer events. During the 2003 soccer season, for example, Yahoo! en espanol had to place field board displays at various locations before all MLS regular season, playoff, international exhibition, All-Star and any of the Cup games. Furthermore, the all-inclusive sports section of Yahoo! en espanol, which was named Yahoo! Deportes and a subsidiary of Yahoo Inc., featured a special online area dedicated to the coverage of MLS. Indeed, that area included photographs, news, league statistics and special broadcasts of the Pepsi MLS All-Star Game and the Cup championship series. With respect to the league's relationship with Yahoo's portal, MLS's executive vice president of Marketing and Fan Development had declared, " We are excited to continue our partnership with Yahoo! en espanol and we are eager to leverage the power and reach of the Internet and their dominant position in [the] U.S. Hispanic online arena. This partnership will strengthen the popularity of our League, especially among U.S. Hispanics, who remain our core constituents."[16]

Based on the television and media agreements, and the other business transactions that have been cited, during the early 2000s it appears that MLS had partially shifted its marketing campaigns, resources and budgets from entertaining soccer fans in Asian and European nations to Hispanic audiences in the Americas. This transformation seemed to be a prudent decision since in 2002, Hispanics represented 30 percent of the spectators at MLS's regular season games. Also, there are many popular and skilled Latino athletes who have performed as players for the league's teams. Three of these soccer stars included the MetroStars' Amado Guevara from Honduras, D.C. United's Marco Etcheverry from Bolivia, and the Galaxy's Carlos Ruiz from Guatemala. In short, it seems evident that MLS officials will continue their efforts to reallocate a larger proportion of the league's capital investments and cash inflows to market teams' games and promote other events to Hispanic sports fans that live in North America and in several Spanish-speaking countries located south of the U.S. border.[17]

Similar to spectators of the other professional team sports, MLS fans are enthusiastic at games when the final outcome is in doubt and if the teams' players hustle and make a unified effort to perform at the highest level to defeat their opponents. To indicate when that occurs, in the next portion of this chapter MLS's presence in global soccer events is highlighted and described.

International Soccer Competitions

Because American sports fans have historically supported one or more of the professional teams in MLB, and those in the NFL, NBA and NHL during the 20th century, the soccer teams that represented the U.S. in various international soccer tournaments had received well-earned publicity, but achieved limited success. To be specific about the tournaments before 1999, two of America's best performances occurred in 1959 when a U.S. team won a bronze medal in the Pan American Games and again in 1991 when an American men's team won a gold medal at the Pan American Games. Then, in 1999 the national U.S. women's soccer team placed first at the World Cup championships, which were held in Pasadena, California. In other World Cup competitions, the four best performances by U.S. men's teams were those that had become a semifinalist for the Cup by winning two games in 1930, reached the second rounds of the Cup by one victory each in 1950 and 1994, and then qualified for the Cup's quarterfinals by defeating Mexico in 2002. The U.S. national team's achievement in 2002 was inspired, in part, by a last-place finish among 32 competitors at the 1998 World Cup, and also by the improvements in the attitudes and skills, and the experiences of the soccer players who had performed for franchises in MLS since the late 1990s. Therefore, based on the U.S. team's performance at the World Cup in 2002, there are several business and/or sport-specific implications that relate to MLS and to the presence and anticipated competitiveness of America's soccer teams and players at the 2006 World Cup tournament.[18]

Notwithstanding the U.S. national team's remarkable progress to play better and earn the respect of opponents in international soccer games and tournaments during the early 2000s, America remains relatively inferior and subordinate to many countries in establishing effective player development programs and systems for the nation's youth. Likewise, MLS is below average in quality and prestige when compared to the superior professional soccer leagues that exist in most eastern European nations and in such countries as Argentina, Brazil, Chile, Columbia, Mexico, Paraguay, Russia and Uruguay. For proof, simply consider an international tournament. That is, to identify the countries' teams that have won World Cup championships to 2002 there is Brazil with five trophies, Italy and West Germany each three, Argentina and Uruguay each two, and England and France each one. Those nations' teams that placed runner up in the tournament include West Germany with four second place spots, and Argentina, Brazil, Czechoslovakia, Hungary, Italy and the Netherlands each two, and Sweden one.

Nevertheless, before and after the World Cup tournament in 2002 some U.S. and foreign soccer athletes, coaches and officials expressed their concerns and opinions about the current and future status of amateur and professional soccer in

America as contrasted to various nations and areas in the world. The U.S. men's soccer team coach Bruce Arena, for example, has estimated that it would be at least five years, or until 2007 or 2008 before the necessary capital investments are made by local, state and federal governments, private investors and perhaps by MLS into junior programs and new facilities to organize, establish and sustain a first-rate soccer developmental system in America. Although some of the top U.S. professional soccer players are equally competitive with respect to their counterparts in leagues overseas, there are comparatively few outstanding players in America's high schools, college programs and minor league organizations. Furthermore, only the very best U.S. soccer players are recognized for their talents in the media, and there are no highly publicized international superstars, heroes or role models playing on American men's teams. Coach Arena, therefore, prefers that native-born American soccer players should be trained and earn their experiences within a U.S. developmental system. Also, he wants to place a quota on the import of amateur and professional soccer players from countries in Asia, Europe, and Central and South America. As MLS matures during the early to middle 2000s, and if American sports fans commit to attend games and otherwise support the league from a long-term perspective, eventually more U.S. national teams will compete for World Cup titles and qualify to play in the final rounds of other international tournament championships such as the Pan American Games, FIFA-sponsored competitions and the CONCACAF Gold Cup. With respect to the future advancement of U.S. soccer programs and the role of MLS players in global tournaments, Arena said "it will take time for the league [MLS] to produce a bigger supply of talent or follow top European clubs by spending millions on youth programs and facilities. MLS is taking baby steps ... but once the league clearly can see there is some light at the end of the tunnel, they'll make those investments. Right now it wouldn't be good business."[19]

When an American team qualified for the World Cup tournament during the early 1990s, that group primarily consisted of U.S. college players. To indicate, in part, how the investments in soccer players and programs differed at that time between various national teams, the entire U.S. Soccer Federation was valued at $1.5 million while Italy's roster of 22 players had collectively earned salaries of approximately $120 million. In 2002, 11 members of the U.S. national soccer team played for teams in MLS and the remaining 12 had performed for professional clubs in Europe. While the incomes of players in MLS were restricted by the league's multi-tiered compensation structure that rarely exceeded an amount of $270,000 per year, many of Europe's best players had signed lucrative multi-million-dollar contracts with their teams because of the soccer fan's passion for and interest in the sport, and due to the generous sponsorships of and money from European corporations. As a result, during the early 2000s a large gap had existed between the earnings of players on MLS teams and the incomes of professional athletes who performed on European soccer clubs. This meant that MLS and the league's team owners are at a huge salary disadvantage *vis-à-vis* the payments spent by clubs in the international leagues when there is a need to draft, sign to contracts and then retain the best American and foreign soccer players. Indeed, based on the dollars paid for players who make the teams' rosters, it appears that MLS owners rank on the same level as the senior soccer leagues in Europe and Latin America, or equivalent to the lower minor leagues in MLB and the NHL, or in parity with the developmental leagues in the NFL and NBA. Relative to the large differences between the salaries and total compensation of U.S. and foreign professional soccer players, and the power to recruit the best athletes available, the D.C. United's coach Ray Hudson commented, "There's no question talented players will always look for greener pastures. Their ambition drives them to higher, more established power leagues in the world. [Foreign] teams are always going to be out there looking to rob your nest." In short, to be competitive against top notch foreign teams like Man U, Juventus, Real Madrid and AS Roma, and win international tournaments, MLS and the league's team owners must be willing and able to sustain the personnel costs and thus bid millions of dollars to hire the world's superstar soccer players such as England's former David Beckham, Argentina's Gabriel Batistuta, Brazil's Ronaldo and Portugal's Luis Figo.[20]

For another observation about international competitions, the U.S. national men team's impressive performance at the World Cup tournament in 2002 denoted that the sports environment and market for soccer had unquestionably improved in America since the late 1990s. Whether MLS and the league's teams received any long-term economic and marketing benefits from that event, however, is indeterminate. Yet, a larger proportion of U.S. sports fans became more interested in the game and the number of soccer programs and youth leagues in America likely increased, especially among the households and school districts that were located in the suburbs of medium sized and large urban cities. Some historians have suggested that the sport of soccer appeals to suburbanites because it is free of certain aspects of modern America. That is, unlike games in the NFL and NBA, professional soccer is not a roughhouse or violent sport drenched in money, or an activity that is always dominated by muscular men and African Americans. According to many sports observers, the game of soccer in the U.S. is analogous to the happy families and suburban households who represent middle to upper class values.

In short, if the U.S. men's team makes a strong performance and achieves success at the World Cup tournament in 2006, American soccer players and coaches, and MLS as a professional sports organization, will each earn some well-deserved prestige and respect from the leagues, teams and federations of various foreign countries. Indeed, as sports writer Jerry Trecker said before the World Cup tournament in 2002, "It has long been recognized that soccer in the United States is a 'big event' prospect. League games—like those regular season NBA or NHL contests that sometimes seem rather ordinary—do not have the cachet of a World Cup. That's why success in this most important of all soccer championships is so vital for the growth of the American game."[21]

MLS and International Players

As it was organized and operated during 2003, MLS negotiated a salary amount with each athlete and then owned the contracts of all players who had signed to perform on teams in the league. Even though the league had established a salary cap, it was the responsibility of the teams' officials to decide which U.S. and foreign players to scout, evaluate and then commit to an agreement. Since 2000, MLS has increasingly attracted some international soccer superstars who had planned to relocate to America during the twilight years of their careers. Those athletes included, for example, such senior players as Yugoslavian midfielder Predrag Radosavljevic, Bulgarian forward Hristo Stoitchkov and Danish striker Miklos Molnar. Meanwhile, other well-known foreign players had decided to migrate to America, in part, when MLS created two new personnel designations. Those classifications were titled junior, for soccer athletes less than 23 years old, and transitional, for players who were 23–24 years old. Because of the organization's reforms, those rules allowed the league's franchises more freedom and fewer penalties for mistakes with respect to the assignment and allocation of foreign players. In turn, that flexibility encouraged several MLS teams to recruit and sign young athletes with long careers ahead of them such as Carlo Ruiz, who was MLS' 2002 Player of the Year. However, despite the positive affects that have occurred from the new classification scheme, some of the league's teams continue to flounder even with their more generous quota of international players who have usually provided team leadership and thus scored goals to win soccer matches during the regular season and U.S. Open Cup tournament.[22]

It was evident by the late 1990s when some of the coaches and general managers of inferior MLS franchises had realized that more highly skilled foreign players were needed for their teams to compete against the league's elite clubs and win conference titles. To illustrate, during 1996–1999 the New York-New Jersey MetroStars' coach Bora Milutinovic and general manager Charlie Stillitano had apparently used poor judgment when they chose the foreign players who would compete for their team. Because of the guidelines that the league had established for the distribution of players, the MetroStars' fans proceeded to criticize coach Milutinovic and MLS for the league's failure to supply the team with talented international athletes. However, general manager Stillitano admitted that the club did not retain enough cash or open a sufficient number of roster spots to negotiate with and sign to contracts the best foreign players who were available as free agents or those involved in trades with other teams. Consequently, to excel in MLS each coach must plan and learn to adjust the team's roster, and to exploit the talents of his domestic and international players in order to win regular season matches and qualify to become the league champion.[23]

To measure the number and position of foreign players in MLS, Tables A.8 and A.9 were constructed and located in the Appendix. As such, Table A.8 indicates that in March of 2004 a total of 70 international players appeared on the rosters of MLS teams. The largest number of players or seven had migrated from Jamaica, and an equal number or four each from Argentina, Canada, Columbia and

Mexico. Furthermore, such cities as Los Angeles in California and Dallas in Texas have above average Hispanic populations and more international players than cities with below average Latino citizens such as Chicago in Illinois and Kansas City in Missouri. Based on the distribution of players for the teams that are listed in Table A.8, the positions of those athletes are reflected in Table A.9. In that table, 30 or 43 percent of the players were midfielders, 19 or 27 percent forwards, 18 or 26 percent defenders and 3 or 4 percent goalkeepers. Proportionally, that means American professional soccer players have tended to be goalkeepers rather than midfielders. Because of their agility, mobility and speed, some foreign players are adept at defense and offense, and have the ability to act as links between defenders and strikers. Indeed, as midfielders they direct the pace and direction of the attack. Meanwhile, defenders prevent offensive penetration, win the ball and initiate attacks, and forwards or strikers assist and score goals, and win balls from defenders in the offensive one-third of the field. Therefore, Tables A.8 and A.9 indirectly depict the strategic roles of domestic and foreign players on MLS teams.

Besides the use of foreign players on MLS teams, there have been several international teams that preferred to sign contracts with American soccer athletes. Indeed, during 2003 there were approximately 100 talented U.S. soccer players who had performed for teams abroad, and especially for some of the competitive clubs in Europe. Indeed, this statistic indicates that because of America's steady investments in youth and national development programs, and given the incentive and opportunity to play for a franchise in MLS or overseas, the U.S. sport system had increased the production of topnotch soccer players during the early 2000s. Interestingly, this supply response also benefited European clubs who, for years, had viewed soccer players from the U.S. as a vast untapped pool of comparatively inexpensive, raw talent. Meanwhile, in European countries there had been a significant collapse of television deals with respect to sports and, for political reasons, players' passport applications and work permits were increasingly denied by nations' governments. Certainly, this forced foreign team owners to be conservative and not assume risks when the pursued Americans and other nations' athletes. Even though those imperfections still exist in the marketplace to prevent the free flow of talented athletes, on average the goal of MLS players is to play with or compete against the best soccer performers in the world. Besides, the players on most clubs in European leagues earn significant bonus monies because there are incentives in their contracts with teams. Those incentives may be based on points earned by the team, victories at away games and progress made by the team in such continental tournaments as the UEFA Cup, European Champion Clubs' Cup, Libertadores Cup, European Cup-Winners' Cup and the Champions League. In MLS's constant struggle to select and retain quality players from America and elsewhere, the league's deputy commissioner Ivan Gazidis responded to that problem in 2003 as follows, "MLS' goal is always to have U.S. stars and stars of the future playing in the United States. We [MLS] believe this is an important part of building the game here. That does not mean we have to have every U.S. star in MLS. [Thus] the generation of transfer fees as a source of revenue is not a priority for MLS."[24]

An increasingly popular and efficient personnel strategy, which is implemented by teams in foreign leagues but not authorized for those in MLS, is for one or more professional soccer clubs to loan their players for short-term periods to rival teams in the same or another division or conference of that league. There are three situations that may justify this type of activity. First, a loan could occur when a club wants to retain a young and productive player who is used only part-time by that club during regular season games. To get more playing time and experience in game conditions, and thus avoid sitting on the bench, the player is loaned to another team for a predetermined time. Second, a player who had signed a hefty long-term contact with a club, but is generally unwanted by that club because of an injury or inferior performance, may be temporarily loaned to another team. If the player regains his confidence and skill level, he will return and play for his original team, or he may be sold to another club for a reasonable amount of money. Third, rather than sell a current player for a reduced amount and incur a financial loss from that sale, a team owner may decide to loan the player out for a few games or even a season and then hope the player's performances improve. Later, if necessary the player would be allowed to return and help his original team win games. Besides being a good deal for the players, in each of the three cases cited both of the teams will benefit from a loan. For the 'lending' team, the player is given an opportunity to regain and/or further develop his skills and talents during regular season games and thus will return to his original team as a better performer. For the 'borrowing' team, there is rarely a large fee required to compensate the player nor is there a commitment made to keep the player on its roster after the loan period has expired. In short, since loaning players provide benefits to small, medium sized and large market clubs in foreign leagues, MLS should study the economic benefits and costs of how leagues' loan policies currently allocate players and if warranted, reform its rules and permit teams to exchange players during all or a portion of one season, or for one or more years.[25]

In order for MLS to grow and prosper as a sports organization from a global perspective, and based on the previous topics and subtopics discussed, it seems apparent that the league's teams need to recruit, sign and retain a portion of the world's best American and international athletes. When that happens, MLS can promote and market its superstars across the globe as MLB does for sluggers Barry Bonds and Sammy Sosa, and as the NFL does for quarterbacks Brett Favre and Peyton Manning, the NBA for scorers Allen Iverson and Shaquille O'Neal, and the NHL for skaters Mario Lemieux and Brett Hull. For MLS, the opportunity to publicize and exploit the talents of a potential superstar soccer player, who seems to have international appeal, may have been established during 2003. Who is the player and how did that opportunity occur for the league?

During August of 2003, the tenth biannual FIFA Under-17 World Championship of soccer was held in Finland. At the tournament, there were 16 teams equally distributed among four groups. In turn, each team had to compete to win a group title in a Finnish city. That is, in Lahti, Helsinki, Tampere or Turku. Then, the four group winners played against each other for medals at the 10,500-seat Finnair Stadium in Helsinki. For the U.S. team, there was one player who attracted the most interest and scrutiny from the hundreds of soccer club representatives, scouts and agents at the Championship. That player was 14 year old Freddy Adu, who had moved from the West African country of Ghana to America after his family won an immigration lottery in 1997.[26]

Because he excelled as a young athlete in Ghana, and then was an outstanding soccer player at youth events in Finland, Guatemala and South Korea, Adu had received an offer from an Italian club named Inter Milan before he was 12 years old. As such, that fame, recognition and performance compelled the U.S.-based shoe manufacturer Nike to sign Adu to a $1 million marketing contract during early 2003. After he decided to become a professional player and join a soccer league, Adu decided to negotiate with team representatives from Germany, Great Britain, Italy, Spain, the Netherlands and the U.S. There are international rules, however, that prohibit non-European-based athletes, including Americans, from performing for foreign teams without a European passport. Thus, rather than experience any bureaucratic delays or obstacles if he had tried to become eligible and compete for distinguished European teams such as Chelsea, Man U or Real Madrid, Adu instead chose to play for a team that operated near his residence in Potomac, Maryland. Indeed, he signed a prearranged six-year deal with MLS to perform for the D.C. United in Washington, D.C., which is the nation's capital city. Although Adu's multiyear contract had been estimated to be several hundred thousand dollars per season, this amount was reputedly much less than the salary offers he had discussed with officials of the European teams. After the deal with Adu had concluded, MLS' Commissioner Don Garber said, "This is a great day not just for MLS, but for soccer in America. We have arguably one of the top players in the world making a statement that is making a commitment to help grow the sport in this country." Besides his positive contributions to the exposure and popularity of MLS and the success of D.C. United, Adu should be well prepared to make the roster of the team that represents the U.S. in the 2006 World Cup Championship, if an American club does qualify for the tournament. Furthermore, to earn some international experience, hopefully he could compete for a position on the American team that participates at the 2004 Summer Olympic Games in Athens, Greece.[27]

Besides eligibility standards and geographic location, perhaps there were other factors and good reasons why Freddy Adu was motivated to accept a lower base salary and play for a soccer team in MLS and not for a world-renowned club in Europe. For some insightful facts and interesting revelations about professional European soccer leagues, teams and players, the next section of this chapter is presented.

European Soccer

During the early 2000s, several European soccer leagues, and a portion of those league's teams had experienced extreme financial hardships. Accordingly, some types of problems that Europe's teams encountered then included owner bankruptcies, unpaid wages, loan defaults, exorbitant overhead costs, player strikes and salary cap violations. For three reasons, such European clubs as Leeds United in England, Borussia Dortmund in Germany, Monaco in France and Valencia in Spain each incurred financial difficulties. Those reasons are highlighted as follows. First, the Bosman rule allowed foreign players on European teams to move freely between leagues, and thus to negotiate for higher salaries when their current contracts had expired. Because of that mobility and leverage, many foreign players demanded and received more money from their teams, which inflated their organization's expenses. Second, when the growth in television revenues declined across Europe, several national and international media networks renegotiated their contracts and provided less money to European federations, leagues and teams for the rights to broadcast games and tournaments. Third, some foreign franchise owners had decided to operate their teams like entertainment companies rather than, as non-profit public trusts. As a result, those teams' strategies and priorities switched toward maximizing net profits and financial returns and away from competitiveness and winning games regardless of costs. When the teams' owners, however, failed to restructure their organizations to be primarily a business rather than a sports firm, millions of soccer fans became disillusioned because of the high prices that were being charged by the teams for apparel and restaurant meals, and to subsidize risky for-profit business ventures. Consequently, the cash inflows and revenues of many teams declined while losses and debts increased. This, of course, adversely affected the teams' financial statements and ability to hire the best soccer players to win games.[28]

Based on those and other reasons like national recessions and government decisions, the following examples illustrate the financial predicaments of the soccer teams that had existed in four European countries during the early 2000s. In Germany, the Kaiserslautern soccer club needed about $20 million to settle a government tax obligations that had been incurred because of the financial irregularities conducted by the German club's officials. In Spain, there were eight first-division and 22 second-tier soccer teams that had voted in the middle of 2003 to delay the 2003–2004 season because of a disagreement about the allocation of television revenues. That dispute occurred when Gestsport, a subsidiary of Spanish pay-for-view television broadcaster Sogecable, offered $9.8 million less than the Spanish League had requested to air its games. Although Sogecable had broadcast agreements with such other top-flight Spanish teams as Barcelona and Real Madrid, the lower-level clubs needed the additional revenues to reduce their debts, which totaled about $2 million in 2003. In Italy, the budgeted salaries of soccer teams exceeded $100 million in 2002 for AC Milan, Inter Milan and Juventus. Those salary amounts had imposed an excessive financial burden on the three teams according to the Italian soccer federation president, Adriano Galliani. "Many clubs risk not surviving the next three years," said Galliani. "Club directors are partly to blame, but the moment has come for the players to understand and come to new agreements, otherwise many of them risk seeing their contracts only on paper." In England, apparently an oversupply of professional soccer teams had prevailed during the early 2000s. To rectify that market condition, Man U's chief executive Peter Kenyon stated, "Quite clearly, I don't think we can have four divisions of professional football any longer. There are too many clubs. That's not to say they can't all exist, but they can't all be professional and that has to be reviewed." Based on the financial dilemmas cited for each of the clubs in the four nations, some European soccer leagues' organizational structures and team operations need to be disassembled and then reconfigured to reflect the new free market economic environment and model that has evolved for organizations in professional team sports. In no specific sequence, the following actions and/or policies have been considered or implemented by public sector and/or private authorities, in part, to deal with the economic and financial problems, and uncertainties that impact the European professional soccer industry.[29]

Rather than approve a controversial recommendation to institute and enforce a leaguewide salary cap, which would misallocate resources, the Italian government has authorized the nation's professional soccer clubs to amortize their debts over ten, and not the normal three years. This public policy, according to some observers, had violated accepted accounting principles and also penalized the teams that suppressed current operating costs and successfully settled their long-term debts in three or less years. Next, in 2004 the UEFA had planned to introduce a licensing system. The system required that soccer club members must meet certain financial guarantees for them to compete in European competitions. Based on one estimate with respect to those guarantees, approximately 50 percent of the UEFA-affiliated clubs had fulfilled that criterion during the 2003 season.

To increase the teams' revenue streams and/or decrease their operating costs, other actions have been discussed, developed or proposed by various European league officials, club owners and other amateur and professional soccer groups and organizations. Such prestigious soccer teams as AC Milan, Arsenal, Man U and Real Madrid, for example, prefer not to pay their players' salaries and insurance premiums when those athletes participate in other events like the World Cup and European Championship. The G-14, which is a well-connected lobbyist that represents 18 well-off European clubs, had demanded that the FIFA redist- ribute its $1.5 billion collected from the World Cup, and that the UEFA share its $750 million from the European Championship to reimburse the teams who had provided players for those and other international tournaments. Furthermore, some European clubs like Italy's AS Roma and Spain's Real Madrid have sought to establish alliances and other business relationships with MLS, and with American companies who would be sponsors and partners. Indeed, the clubs' purpose is for those affiliated companies to promote professional soccer and the franchises' brand names and logos outside of Europe by selling such products as merchandise, tee shirts and video programs in the relatively untapped but prosperous U.S. sports market. In 2002, MLS's executive vice president of marketing and fan development Mark Noonan declared that league officials had spoke with some topnotch European clubs who wanted to expose their unique brands and uniform styles in America with tours, television programs and licensed sales. For MLS to collaborate with, and not try to out-compete the world's great soccer powers is a practical strategy that indicates good business sense. Since European broadcasters had reduced their expenditures on professional soccer programming during the early 2000s, there are plenty of operating and long-term benefits for MLS to commerially unite with foreign soccer leagues and various European teams, and thus contribute to the globalization of the sport.[30]

Besides those interactions, since 2000 a number of Europe's well-regarded soccer teams have increased their promotional activities in Asia to attract that continent's soccer fans. England's Newcastle United and the Chelsea Football Club, for example, have played a preseason match in Kuala Lumpur, which is a large city in Malaysia. Because soccer has gradually become the most popular team sport for people in Asian countries, Europe's premier soccer leagues and their respective teams have also used a variety of business relationships to penetrate consumer markets in nations such as China, Japan, Taiwan and South Korea. That is, some European teams decided to hire skilled soccer players who were popular athletes in Asia, while other teams affiliated with Asian clubs and linked with sponsors so that their merchandise would flow more freely around the globe. To illustrate, the London-based Arsenal soccer franchise purchased the rights to Junichi Inamoto, a midfielder from Japan. Meanwhile, Newcastle United signed a business contract with Dalian Shide, which was China's soccer league champion. That agreement included cross promotions, television arrangements and player exchanges between the two clubs. Finally, the Man U club switched its kit provider from a small English company to Nike, which is a powerful global sports corporation. In short, it is reasonable to assume that Europe's top soccer clubs will continue to focus on operations and increase the value of their organizations by establishing business alliances with American companies, initiating marketing campaigns and promotions on global television networks, expanding their brand names and fan bases into nations beyond Europe, and otherwise allocating their resources to satisfy the demands of soccer fans and sports consumers who reside in non-European nations. Indeed, that strategy will likely improve those soccer teams' current and future revenue streams from, and market shares in, other countries.[31]

For several years, one sports competitor based in Europe has been extremely successful and especially aggressive to promote and market itself around the globe. That soccer team is England's world renowned Man U. In the next portion of this chapter, the key business activities, relationships and marketing strategies of Man U are exposed. After that discussion concludes, there is an analysis of women's professional team sports and the suspension of the WUSA in 2003.

Manchester United

Because of its estimated worldwide base of 53 million fans, Man U is considered to be the most popular and valuable professional sports franchise on earth. How did that soccer team become so admired and wealthy as a business? To answer that question, the organization was founded as a railway workers' club team called Newton Heath LYR in 1878. Twenty-four years later, the team adopted its current name after experiencing financial problems during the late 1890s and early 1900s.

That is, when brewery owner John Henry Davies had invested his wealth in the club, he decided to rename it Manchester United rather than Manchester Central or Manchester Celtic. Then, in 1958 nearly 50 percent of Man U's players were killed in Germany as a result of a plane crash. Rather than fold its operations after the accident, in 1968 the team, including professional soccer's Player of the Year George Best, played outstanding and thus became the first English club to win the prestigious European Cup. As Man U's reputation gradually spread across the globe during the 1970s and 1980s, and after a victory in the 1991 Winner's Cup tournament, the team's executives decided to search for places in the world where the native professional sports were not popular. To appeal to international customers and penetrate markets, therefore, head executive and chairman Sir Roland Smith and his replacement Roy Gardner, and Scottish manager Sir Alex Ferguson each had provided the leadership and know-how for Man U to build its web site <http://www.manutd.com>, and to encourage fan clubs worldwide, expand merchandising outlets abroad, establish intercontinental television broadcast and distribution networks, and convince English Premier League officials to implement the same or similar marketing tactics and campaigns. In retrospect, it was the foresight of Man U's executives, the implementation of those strategies, and the club's dominance on the soccer field that explain how the franchise has created its wealth to become the world's greatest sports team. To further illustrate, there are some business aspects and other historical facts about Man U's organization that are interesting to reveal and evaluate.[32]

Between 1908 and 1993, Man U had won nine FA Premier League and ten FA Challenge Cup titles, two European Champions Club Cups and one World Cup Championship. Then, from 1994 to 2002 the team placed first to win seven more championships. Those included three consecutive titles in the Premier League and in 1999, other first-place victories in the Football Association Cup and Champions League tournaments. Those soccer triumphs, in part, are why Man U has become such a successful international business.[33]

As a private company whose securities are traded on the London Stock Exchange, Man U is a multi-diversified and profitable enterprise that markets and sells numerous types of products, from coffee mugs to bed sheets and scarves. The company, for example, owns and operates a subscription television service, which beams game highlights and player interviews to 75,000 subscribers on four channels that broadcasts this sports information at least 42 hours per week. Furthermore, the company sells credit cards, home mortgages, consumer loans and insurance policies, operates an online auction business that is similar to eBay, Inc., and owns a number of Red Café restaurants that are located from Manchester in England to cities in Singapore. Based on those and other commercial ventures, during fiscal 2002 this debt-free enterprise received $230 million in revenues and earned profits that exceeded $50 million. If the club's sources of revenue are expressed in percentages and dollars, approximately 39 percent or $90 million of the inflows consisted of ticket sales from soccer fans who had attended matches at the 67,700-seat Old Trafford stadium, which is the club's facility in Manchester and the largest stadium in England; about 36 percent or $83 million was derived from the sale of television rights for Premier League games and European and English Cup matches; nearly 18 percent or $41 million was provided from sponsorships and the company's financial services businesses; and, an estimated 7 percent or $16 million was generated in royalties from merchandise sales. For fiscal 2003, financial analysts had projected the club's revenues would grow by 13 percent to a larger total of $260 million.[34]

To further promote its brand name and thus increase the organization's future cash inflows and revenue streams, Man U successfully negotiated and extended its previous contracts, or had signed new agreements during 2003 with various media businesses, which included partners, sponsors and vendors. There were five deals that highlight the teams' business successes. First, because of a four-year $36 million extension of the club's agreement with an international mobile phone company, Man U's players agreed to continue wearing a Vodafone logo on their team uniforms during games. Meanwhile, Vodafone had committed to broadcast a variety of the club's content. That content encompassed season schedules and other news, still and video images, and the relays of soccer games to wireless devices throughout the world.[35]

Second, in a business alliance with the Australian Football League's Essendon Football Club, which then had a popular brand name and access to 1.1 million sports fans and 160,000 support and member organizations in Australia, a computer database was used to promote Man U in that country, and provide a market to sell replica strip and memorabilia to Australians, and also to advertise the sale of tickets of the team's games and events to consumers. In response to why that specific relationship was formed, Man U's director of business development Ben Hatton had concluded, "Of all the football clubs we've spoken to around the world, Essendon [Football Club] is the closest parallel to our business."

Third, after it attracted an audience of about 271,000 total spectators at stadiums in America during 2003 to watch three exhibition games against European soccer teams and one against a Mexican club, Man U agreed to play another four matches during the Summer of 2004 against opponents in the U.S. at Seahawks Stadium in Seattle, Washington, Soldier Field in Chicago, Illinois, Lincoln Financial Field in Philadelphia, Pennsylvania, and Giants Stadium in the New Jersey Meadowlands. According to plans, that series might also feature other European clubs such as Glasglow Celtic, Chelsea, Bayern Munich, Porto, A.C. Milan, A.S. Roma, Juventus and Liverpool. For its American tour, which included the four games played in 2003, the club had collected more than $7 million in revenues.

Fourth, in the media Man U announced that it would open a soccer school for boys and girls in the middle of 2004 at the Disneyland theme park in Paris, France. The school, which was to be operated by Nike, had invited parents to enroll their children in its sports programs because of Man U's world-wide reputation and exposure, and due to the expert instruction and training that the children would receive from highly qualified soccer coaches and instructors.

Fifth, during the early 2000s Man U and MLB's New York Yankees entered into a marketing alliance that committed the clubs to promote each other's brand name and specific sport. According to one part of the agreement, the YES cable and satellite channel, which at that time was owned by the YankeeNets Corporation, had the television rights to broadcast delayed coverage of Premier League matches to the New York-area market where there were at least 25 million people. Because of the television exposure of Man U's contests, a large number of American sports fans became more interested in the game of professional soccer and in the English club's visit to the U.S. in 2003 and then in 2004.

As an aside, during 2003 the NFL Tampa Bay Buccaneer's owner Malcolm Glazer had initially purchased enough of the stock shares of the Man U franchise to equal an ownership interest of 9 percent. Then, for some reason he increased his stake in the club to 10 percent and again to 15 percent. As of early 2004, Glazer had accumulated 16.3 percent, which is equivalent to approximately $215 million. With respect to that percentage, an editorial in the *Manchester Evening News* said that, "Glazer had no grasp of the passion Manchester United inspires in fans almost everywhere but the United States and, as owner, might even raise ticket prices to boost profits." A few stock market experts speculated that Glazer, who operated a property empire named First Allied and controlled a fish-oil business called Zapata, had acquired a portion of the shares of Man U to develop a global sports brand company. According to sportswriter Alan Cowell, "Mr. Glazer has said that he built up his stake in Manchester United for a variety of reasons including investment purposes. But, Mr. Glazer is unlikely to make a bid to take over the English team while Sir Alex [Ferguson] is locked in dispute over Rock of Gibraltar." Besides Glazer's minority investment in Man U, Irish horseracing tycoons J.P. McManus and John Magnier had proceeded to amass a 29.2 percent share of the club. Those two investors were speculators who had decided to accumulate a majority interest in the soccer company. Interestingly, in late 2003 Man U's stock price had soared more than 100 percent, in part, because of rumors that a takeover by Glazer or McManus and Magnier was imminent. Even after the stock price had increased, financial analyst Andrew Lee warned that several of the soccer club's players and many of its fans would be alarmed if Glazer attempted to own a sufficient number shares to become the boss of the franchise. "I would be very surprised if they [players and fans] would react well to someone non-British owning the club," said Lee. He also stated that " ... the last thing you need is discord among the fans and in the dressing room."[36]

When the British sports franchise had willingly sold its celebrated all-star player David Beckham to Spain's Real Madrid for approximately $41 million during 2003, it appeared that Man U had surrendered one of its most popular international attractions and a consummate specialist on the soccer field. That is, during his 13 years as a midfielder for Man U, Beckham had scored 86 goals in 387 matches and led the teams that won ten trophies. "In right-footed crosses and free kicks, he is brilliant, if not peerless," said the Los Angles Times' reporter Mike Penner. "Given enough space down the flank, or enough time while mulling his options over a dead ball, Beckham can break open a match with one flick of his foot. It's a spectacular skill, easy to splice into international highlight reels, and with it, he has built a formidable mythology." In retrospect, since Beckham's $7 million contract was scheduled to expire in 2005, which meant he could leave the

Sports Capitalism

club in that year, the multimillion-dollar transfer fee received from the sale of Beckham to Real Madrid may have been reinvested by Man U into marketing projects, used to further compensate the club's current coaches and players, and/or provided as dividends or bonuses to shareholders. Interestingly, since the late 1990s Real Madrid has spent at least $200 million in transfer fees to acquire several superstar players, besides Beckham, from other teams. Listed in chronological order, in 1999 Real Madrid signed Arsenal's French striker Nicholas Anelka for approximately $36 million; in 2000, F.C. Barcelona's Portuguese midfielder Luis Figo for $56 million; in 2001, Juventus' French midfielder Zinedine Zidane for $64 million; and in 2002, Inter Milan's striker Ronaldo for $44 million. Those and 11 other transactions are ranked by Year in Table 5.1, which indicates the leading transfer fees paid by and to European soccer franchises for players from 1997 to 2003. Interestingly, the table lists 15 trades that were valued in total at $658 million and Real Madrid's proportion of $197 million represented 36 percent of that amount.[37]

With those new players and perhaps the Premier Leagues' most famous defender, Roberto Carlos, along with Spanish superstar Raul Gonzalez, Real Madrid had successfully competed to win the European championships in 2002 be-

Table 5.1 European Player Transfer Fees, 1997–2003

Year	Player	Trade	Amount
1997	Denilson	San Paulo to Real Betis	35
1999	Nicholas Anelka	Arsenal to Real Madrid	36
1999	Christian Vieri	Lazio to Inter Milan	50
2000	Marc Overmars	Arsenal to Barcelona	35
2000	Hernan Crespo	Parma to Lazio	54
2000	Luis Figo	Barcelona to Real Madrid	56
2001	Lilian Thuram	Parma to Juventus	35
2001	Pavel Nedved	Lazio to Juventus	36
2001	Juan Sebastian Veron	Lazio to Manchester United	39
2001	Gaizka Mendieta	Valencia to Lazio	41
2001	Gianluigi Buffon	Parma to Juventus	45
2001	Zinedine Zidane	Juventus to Real Madrid	64
2002	Ronaldo	Inter Milan to Real Madrid	44
2002	Rio Ferdinand	Leeds United to Manchester United	47
2003	David Beckham	Manchester United to Real Madrid	41

Note: Year is when those teams had agreed to trade each of the players in exchange for a fee. Player is self-expanatory. Trade is each player's pre- and post-trade teams. Amount is the transfer fee in millions of dollars based on the exchange rates at the time of the transaction.

Source: Mike Penner, "Real Deal: It's the Marketing," *The Los Angeles Times* (18 June 2003), D1.

side 2003, and also had eliminated Man U in the quarterfinals of the European Champions League tournament. Although Beckham may struggle to qualify and start each match for Real Madrid, for sure his presence, personality and charisma will promote the club and its commercial interests, especially to soccer fans in European nations.

This concludes the portion of Chapter 5 that focused on European soccer. Indeed, this section included some information about the world's most valuable and marketable sports enterprise that is Man U, a brief profile of Real Madrid's David Beckham, and a table that reported the trades and amounts of transfer fees spent on European soccer players for six years. Before the Summary and Notes are presented, however, this chapter's final topic is an overview of the emergence and rapid decline, and then the final collapse of an American women's professional soccer league that occurred between 2001 and 2003.

WUSA

After America's spectacular soccer team victory at the 1999 Women's World Cup tournament played in Pasadena, California, during 1999–2000 a Discovery cable television executive, John Hendricks organized the WUSA, which had originally consisted of eight U.S.-based franchises. Initially, Hendricks and other investors contributed $40 million to pay the start-up costs and fund the league's operations for five years. The most prominent of those investors included the chief executive officers of such media companies as Continental Cablevision, Cox Enterprises and Communications, Comcast and Time Warner Cable. To promote and expose the new league, the Turner Network Television (TNT) and CNN/Sports Illustrated agreed to televise and broadcast the WUSA's regular and postseason games, and the Gillette Company and Proctor and Gamble's Era Max signed contracts to be the league's official sponsors.[38]

According to the league's business charter, the WUSA would officially own each franchise, provide payments for the players' salaries, which ranged from $24,000 to $85,000 per season, and ensure that each team paid no more than $800,000 in compensation. Furthermore, the league assumed the responsibility to assign all soccer players to specific franchises, that is, the athletes from colleges, the U.S. national team, and also the international players who were drafted by the franchises. Each team had to play 21 games per season, which extended from the middle of April to late August. After each of the regular seasons, the best clubs qualified for the playoffs and then the winners competed in the semifinals and championship series for the Founders Cup.[39]

Despite a unique but apparently ill-conceived and unrealistic business plan, the league's problems gradually worsened from its first season in 2001 to the final season in 2003. During those years, the WUSA teams' average attendance, for example, had declined from 8,100 to 6,700 and generally about 100,000 households had watched the teams' regular season games on television. Besides the low attendances at games and pathetic television ratings, the league's overoptimistic assumptions about the number of corporate sponsorships, and the level of merchandise sales and amount of debt balances led to an accumulation of the teams' operating losses. Consequently, the league's investors had to contribute nearly $60 million more for the payment of expenses and start-up costs, and additional amounts of $46 million in 2001, $24 million in 2002 and $17–19 million in 2003. Given the huge dollar bailouts and such sports statistics as team attendances and the demographic distribution of soccer fans, what were the business-specific factors that primarily caused the WUSA to suspend its operations after the 2003 season had concluded?[40]

First, the league was mismanaged, in part, because it relied on the judgments of leaders who made well-intentioned but misguided and incorrect decisions. That is, the WUSA's investors and managerial staff recruited, interviewed and hired the wrong people at the highest levels of the organization. As a result, the league failed to articulate a persuasive marketing plan and the key decision makers did not execute such fundamental tasks as following up on business leads or identifying the core audience. To illustrate, in 2002 the WUSA decided to opt out of a four-year TNT agreement when its television ratings ranged from .2 to .4 or 425,000 households, and then sign a contract with the Pax Communications cable channel, which proved to be an error because the league's ratings declined to .1 or 100,000 households. Unlike TNT, Pax cable was a family oriented channel that had little prior experience with the business activities, qualities and requirements of sports broadcasting. Indeed, the WUSA allowed Pax to broadcast its teams' games in direct competition with the MLS game of the week, which was televised on ESPN. Unfortunately, those broadcasts had split the nation's soccer audience since 50 percent or more of MLS's fans were young women. With respect to the league's switch to the Pax channel, sports television executive Lydia Stephens declared, "It's very ironic in the sense the WUSA was founded and funded by major Media Systems Operators [MSOs] like Time Warner, Comcast and Cox Communications, and yet they never made TV exposure a priority." In regard to the WUSA's organization and leadership, the league's investors and managers jointly agreed to hire former Quaker Oats executive Barbara Allen to be the organization's initial chief executive officer. In hindsight, this decision was a major mistake since Allen was not very familiar with soccer operations and finances. Moreover, to execute the league's business, she had to frequently commute from Denver in Colorado to the WUSA's headquarters in New York City. For those and other reasons, Allen was an ineffective leader who left the organization after the teams played one season.

Second, the league's marketing plan had flaws, that is, it was misderived and under-budgeted at $4 million. Rather than market the sport also to soccer-obsessed dads who were involved with and attended their daughters' athletic activities, the WUSA mistakenly positioned its organization almost exclusively as an outlet for 8–12 year old girls and soccer moms. In turn, the focus on those segments of the market had alienated other customer bases such as married adult men and teenage girls, who had played soccer on their teams in schools and local programs. "There's a fundamental rule in youth marketing that you do not position yourself for the age of the children you target, but to the age that they aspire to be," commented marketing executive James Chung about the league. Besides Chung's observation, some sports analysts stated that the WUSA would need at least $10 million in its annual marketing budget to complete a regular season schedule and also receive national and some international exposure to households on television.

Third, despite being hyped in the media, this women's professional league failed, in part, because its executives did not endorse enough lucrative, long-term marketing agreements and promotional contracts with major American or foreign corporate sponsors. To illustrate, before the 2002 season began the WUSA had identified eight key sponsors who would each provide the league with $2.5 million to have their products advertised and promoted on television during regular season games. Unfortunately, the only sponsors signed by the league were two companies, Hyundai and Johnson & Johnson, who each had promised to pay the league $2 million for their products to be exposed. In short, it was partially the underperformance of the U.S. economy during the early 2000s, below-average attendances at matches, WUSA teams' annual operating deficits and increasing debts, and perhaps the immense payments spent on NBA prospects such as the $90 million endorsement package paid by Nike to high school basketball star LeBron James, that had discouraged American companies from committing more money and resources to the WUSA brand and the television exposure of its franchises. With respect to the need for sponsors and the league's potential to succeed beyond the early 2000s as an independent sports business, founder James Hendricks stated, "There has to be this critical sponsorship. It's feasible to have an independent women's professional league. But without sponsorship support, I think the sport can only survive with an existing team or organization."

Fourth, the WUSA's collapse during 2003 indicates why any new women's professional sports leagues in America or elsewhere have a relatively small chance of long-run prosperity without substantial business sponsorships, subsidies from government or payments from a men's league in the same sport. To defend and justify that hypothesis, the following three reasons are given. One, women's professional league games must compete with other types of sports and entertainment events that are broadcast on local channels and national television networks during such attractive time periods as the afternoon hours on weekends and evening hours on weekdays, when men generally control the households' selection of programs to be watched. Two, it is important that women's sports league marketing and public relation executives recognize that differences in demands and behaviors exist between the demographics of spectators and television audiences. Essentially, Neal Pilson, who served as the president of CBS Sports, emphasized this dichotomy in an interview. Pilson said, "The advertiser has a better option to reach the target audience. Women's sports are sold to advertisers who believe they will reach a women's audience, and if you go to a WNBA or WUSA game, there's a very visible high percentage of women in the target demographic. But those aren't the people that are watching women's sports on television." Besides Pilson's insights, the chairman and chief executive officer of a Denver-based sports marketing firm in 2003, Dean Bonham, had similar observations. "We do a lot of work for the

LPGA [Ladies Professional Golf Association]" stated Bonham, " . . . and one thing we've discovered in recent months is that there's more of an upside potential in marketing to the male fan than we ever thought. The short answer is, women's sports leagues, not unlike men's sports leagues, have to rely on the entire demographic spectrum." Three, a women's sports league must first uncover and target itself to a core audience such as pre-teenage girls, college-age female athletes or married heads of households, and then expand that audience into a wider market. In other words, to build and then grow a sports league in the long-term requires mass appeal to a nationwide group of fans and also, the implementation of a business model that effectively contains costs but meets the expectations of the targeted market. This relationship suggests that to increase its survival rate, an American women's soccer league may need to initially connect and collaborate with a men's sports organization like MLS or the CSA.[41]

During the middle to late months of 2003, a committee of investors was formed to study, evaluate and perhaps reestablish the eight-team WUSA sometime after 2004. To succeed as a business, the new women's soccer league would need to be better managed than its predecessor and, according to some officials, a scaled-down version of the former WUSA. While the negotiations with various potential sponsors and investors had proceeded, the committee decided to schedule a series of doubleheader soccer games and social festivals for the sports fans at the National Sports Center in Blaine, Minnesota during 17–20 June 2004 and at the Home Depot Center in Carson, California during 24–27 June 2004. Indeed, a third festival was being considered at a site for 10–13 June 2004. As such, in early 2004 the former WUSA commissioner Tony DiCicco announced the 'Keep the WUSA Dream Alive' campaign whereby fans could make pledges that might be applied to the purchase of 2005 season tickets or group sales. "Our goal is to have 2,500 clubs, organizations, [and] businesses nationwide commit to purchasing a minimum of $1,000 worth of tickets per year, for three consecutive years," said DiCicco with respect to the campaign. Besides that effort, to minimize the costs of implementing those events, the soccer players and coaches who participated would receive payments for only appearance fees and travel expenses. Some popular players that had committed to attend the festivals included the U.S. national team's Mia Hamm, Germany's Birgit Prinz, France's Marinette Pichon and Norway's Dagny Mellgren. Therefore, whether the former American women's professional soccer league, or a version of it, will be revived and launched during 2005 or thereafter depends, in part, on the revenue amounts derived from local, regional, national and international partnerships and sponsorships, the successes of the soccer games and festivals planned in 2004, any business relationships and agreements established with MLS or perhaps a foreign league, and the number, value and length of television agreements that might be concluded with one or more major sports networks. As an aside, during March of 2004 a national women's soccer team from the U.S. defeated Norway and won the Algarve Cup in southern Portugal. Indeed, the win reflected the first time that an American team had been even with Norway since the 1991 Women's World Cup final.[42]

After a discussion of the contents contained in the first four sections, European Soccer and then the WUSA were the final topics to be analyzed in Chapter 5. To consolidate and highlight, therefore, what was presented in this chapter about MLS and other American and foreign professional soccer leagues, events and programs, a Summary appears next. In turn, it is followed by the Notes, which contain the references, bibliography sources and comments about the respective topics.

Summary

In sum, Chapter 5 has revealed and incorporated, as strategics, the dominant international business alliances, events, programs, trends and other matters that have influenced the success of soccer as a sport and the development of professional soccer leagues in America, and that have involved foreign professional soccer leagues, teams and players, and especially those in European nations. To be more specific, this chapter was arranged into six parts or sections. Accordingly, each section featured an important topic and any related subtopics that applied to American and/or foreign professional soccer leagues. As sequenced in Chapter 5, the topics that were headlined included MLS International Strategies, Global Television and Media Agreements, International Soccer Competitions, MLS and International Players, European Soccer and the WUSA. Before the Notes appear to conclude this chapter, each topic and its respective subtopics are identified and briefly summarized here.

After such soccer organizations as the NASL, USA, NPSL and FIFA are mentioned, and when and how the USA and NPSL merged to become the NASL, the first portion of Chapter 5 discussed when, why and where MLS became organized and how the league has existed and changed, and to what extent it has been successful as a sports business since its formation in 1996. To examine those elements about MLS, there were interesting facts and other information presented about the league's teams' current and potential sites, quality of the soccer stadiums and the presence of soccer markets in America and abroad. During the late 1990s and early 2000s, the home attendances of teams in the U.S.-based league had gradually declined and two of its franchises had to fold their operations. Nonetheless, MLS Commissioner Don Garber remained optimistic and succeeded to convince two wealthy investors to become new owners of soccer franchises to begin play in the 2005 regular season. Indeed, one of Garber's long-term goals is to expand the league from eight to 30 or more teams before 2010.

Because professional soccer games and tournaments are not as popular or entertaining to American sports fans as the competitions of such professional sports as baseball, football and basketball, MLS teams have normally played their regular season schedules, playoff series and the Founders Cup in stadiums that were constructed for amateur and professional sports. As such, until modern, single-purpose soccer stadiums are built at sites in medium sized to large markets, where MLS and various minor league soccer teams can independently meet, practice and play their home and away games and tournaments, then the number of spectators who attend events of the U.S.-based professional league will likely remain constant or continue to decline during the early to middle 2000s. Consequently, in order to globalize the league's operations, it is predicted that before 2010 MLS will likely relocate one or more of its existing teams to, or expand the number of franchises at sites beyond the U.S. border, for example, in medium to large populated cities in southern Canada, eastern European countries and/or northern Mexico.

The relevant television network deals and other media contracts that MLS officials have negotiated and participated in since the middle to late 1990s are discussed in the second section of Chapter 5. Based on the purpose and scope of those agreements, Commissioner Garber's strategy has been for MLS teams to get more exposure of their games and thus further penetrate the North American sports markets and those in foreign nations. In short, his intent is to extend the broadcasts of the league's games and international tournaments to Latin American and Hispanic households located in U.S. southwestern States, and to soccer fans who live in the metropolitan areas of southern Canada and northern Mexico, and then to those soccer addicts in European, and Central and South American countries. To attain Garber's goal, MLS must improve the entertainment value of and competition between its teams and publicize the performances and statistics of the league's superior players on national and global cable and satellite channels and television networks, and on the Internet. In fact, besides the sport MLS must effectively market its brand, products and teams to America's Latino populations and those in foreign nations so that the league's fan base grows larger and more passionate, and especially expands for the soccer athletes, and children and young adults who enjoy American-style professional sports.

MLS teams, coaches and players who have participated in previous international soccer games and tournaments, and particularly in the World Cup competitions, is the third relevant topic examined in Chapter 5. If MLS clubs want to be respected as legitimate competitors by foreign soccer officials and federations, and by the prominent national leagues and teams that exist in European countries and other nations, it is crucial for them to increasingly play and improve their performances at those global events. Therefore, this portion of Chapter 5 provided some historical facts and insights about how MLS teams have performed in the World Cups and other international soccer tournaments. Furthermore, this section identified which foreign nations and their respective teams have excelled to win a World Cup championship, which was initially played in 1930 when the host country of Uruguay defeated Argentina by a score of four to two.

The fourth topic in Chapter 5 featured some relevant information and interesting facts about the differences, if any, that exist between U.S. and foreign professional soccer players. There are specific rules and policies, for example, which may limit the number of Americans on international teams and the number of foreigners on MLS teams. This section also revealed the advantages and disadvantages for a professional soccer team to temporarily loan one or more of its talented or inferior players to another team, since that exchange is permitted in some European leagues. After the loan policy was discussed, the section's content provided the circumstances that determined why the 14 year old American Freddy Adu had decided to join MLS's D.C. United team and not a top-notch Eastern European or South American professional soccer franchise. Although he likely negotiated a smaller base salary when he agreed to a contract with MLS than with the Premier or Spanish Leagues in Europe, apparently Adu preferred to play games on a team near his home in the State of Maryland. Or, perhaps he perceived that his future endorsements, star appeal and accomplishments in tournaments would be greater on a club in America than one in a foreign nation such as Argentina, Brazil, England, Germany, Italy, Spain or Uruguay.

The prestigious European soccer leagues and their successful high-performance teams were the next topics analyzed in Chapter 5. Because of inflated players' and teams' salaries and second, due to the decline in television revenues from sports programming during the middle to late 1990s and early 2000s, several of Europe's well-renowned clubs in such countries as Austria, France, Germany, Italy, the Netherlands, Portugal and Spain have experienced financial problems, incurred short-term operating losses and accumulated more long-term debts. To avoid bankruptcies and mergers of those organizations, European sports officials and government authorities have suggested that the professional soccer leagues must eliminate a number of teams and/or implement salary caps. Besides those issues, this section of the chapter also explained how England's Man U became a championship soccer team and why it has been successful as an international business. Finally, a table was displayed that presents the teams and transfer fees of 15 European players who were traded between 1997 and 2003.

The final topic in Chapter 5 involved the formation, three-year development and then the suspension of the WUSA in the U.S. Despite the euphoria and pride of the soccer fans who admired and supported the American women's victory at the World Cup tournament in 1999, and the implementation of a well-prepared and detailed business plan that seemed to be a reasonable model for a new soccer organization, the eight-team professional women's league suspended its operations in 2003 after three regular seasons. After the reasons for the league's failure were discussed, Chapter 5 concluded with how some investors have met to reshape and possibly reactivate that women's professional league to play again in the 2005 season or sometime thereafter.

Notes

1. For three books that discuss and/or identify various aspects of the formation, development and growth of American and/or foreign professional soccer leagues, see Kyle Rote, Jr., *Kyle Rote, Jr.'s Complete Book of Soccer* (New York, N.Y.: Simon and Schuster, 1978); Roger Allaway, Colin Rose, and David Litterer, *The Encyclopedia of American Soccer History* (Lanham, MD: Scarecrow Press Inc., 2001); Dan Woog, *The Ultimate Soccer Encyclopedia* (Chicago, IL: Lowell House, 1999). A summary of two former U.S. professional soccer leagues' histories are also contained in the "National Professional Soccer

League," at <http://www.hickoksports.com> cited 3 December 2003, and in "United Soccer Association," at <http://www.hickoksports.com> cited 3 December 2003.

2.   To read some more details about an early American professional soccer league's history, team champions, leading scorers, most valuable players and other resources, see "North American Soccer League," at <http://www.hickoksports.com> cited 3 December 2003.

3.   Besides books, there are other references that contain information about MLS' history, development and growth. Those sources include "MLS Year-by-Year Season Overview," at <http://www.mlsnet.com> cited 4 December 2003; "Major League Soccer," at <http://www. hickoksport.com> cited 3 December 2003; "MLS League History," at <http://www.mlsnet. com> cited 3 December 2003; "MLS Attendance Analysis," at <http://www.kenn.com> cited 12 April 2003; Chris Isidore, "What Does the Future Hold For Soccer in America?" at <http://www.sportsbusinessnews.com> cited 25 November 2002. Besides the contents of the previous articles, sports reporter Dean Bonham believed that MLS had a well-thought-out strategic plan. That is, it contained television contracts with ABC, ESPN, ESPN2 and Univision, long-term endorsement deals with major corporations, a salary cap and single entity financial structure, and marketing schemes tailored to appeal to Hispanic and Latin American audiences. For his views, see Dean Bonham, "Bonham on the State of Soccer," at <http://www.sportsbusinessnews.com> cited 17 December 2003. Some social aspects of competitive soccer evaluated by academics are presented in Fernando Delgado, "Major League Soccer: The Return of the Foreign Sport," *Journal of Sport and Social Issues*, Vol. 21, No. 9 (1997), 285–297; Lloyd L. Wong and Ricardo Trumper, "Global Celebrity Athletes and Nationalism: Futbol, Hockey, and the Representation of Nation," *Journal of Sport and Social Issues*, Vol. 26, No. 2 (2002), 168–194; Fernando Delgado, "Sport and Politics: Major League Soccer, Constitution, and (the) Latino Audience(s)," *Journal of Sport and Social Issues*, Vol. 23, No. 1 (1999), 41–54.

4.   See Glenn Davis, "U.S. Starting to Tune in to the Big Picture," at <http://www.houston-chronicle.com> cited 11 August 2003, and Bob Keisser, "Americans Are Getting a Kick Out of Soccer," at <http://www.presstelegram.com> cited 4 August 2003. With respect to the sport's prospects in America, Keisser declared that, "Soccer's present and future only developed because organizers allowed it to grow on its own and not force-feed consumers Euro stars or bastardize the sport (indoor soccer) for perceived American taste." Those comments aside, during early 2004 the U.S. government expressed an interest in scheduling matches with the men's national or Olympic teams of Iraq. As evidence, Iraq's Olympic Committee president Ahmed al-Samarrai planned to meet U.S. Soccer president Dr. Robert Contiguglia to discuss matches. Unfortunately, this cooperation between the two countries did not exist during Saddam Hussein's rule because Iraqi players feared being tortured for their performances by Hussein's son Uday, who then was president of the nation's Olympic committee and soccer federation. This relationship is discussed in Jack Bell, "The U.S. vs. Iraq on the (Sports) Battlefield," at <http://www.sportsbusinessnews.com> cited 13 April 2004.

5.   Those statistics were reported in the various online readings of the previous Notes in Chapter 5. Besides those sources, MLS' web site <http://www.mslnet.com> lists some current and prior articles that relate to the league's operation and business. With respect to European marketing affiliations, during 2004 the world's largest soft drink manufacturer, which is the Coca-Cola Company, agreed to sponsor England's Football League for three years. According to the contract, the League's 72 clubs will receive the same percentage they obtained from the current deal with Nationwide Building Society. The president of Coca-Cola Great Britain Charlotte Oades said about the sponsorship, "This partnership confirms our long-term commitment to football. We have been investing in the game for

over 30 years in this country." See "Coca-Cola Set to Sponsor English Soccer League," at <http://www.sportsbusinessnews.com> cited 2 March 2004.

6.   Regarding MLS exhibition games, teams' stadiums and relationships with other professional sports in Houston, Garber said, "It's the marriage between the football team, its interest in the stadium and the integration between their operation and our operation. So, specific to Robertson Stadium, if this formula doesn't work, we'll have to look at a formula that does work. We must have a [MLS] team in Houston." See David Barron, "MLS Looks to Houston as Possible Expansion Site," at <http://www.sportsbusinessnews.com> cited 13 March 2003, and "MLS Set to Expand Their Horizons," at <http://www.sportsbusinessnews.com> cited 25 November 2002.

7.   MLS officials are aware of Toronto's rich soccer heritage. However, it will cost investors about $13 million in fees to locate a franchise in that Canadian city. For the topic, see "Toronto Interested in MLS, Luke-Warm Response," at <http://www.sportsbusinessnews.com> cited 13 February 2003. Meanwhile, during late 2002 the president and co-owner of the Toronto-based computer parts giant Rusgen and Intelatech Inc., Gerry Gentile had announced the formation of the eight-team Canadian United Soccer League (CUSL). For its strategy as an international organization, the CUSL negotiated with soccer teams from Germany, Greece, Italy, Portugal and Spain to establish a relationship that would allow for the exchange and loan of players and technical staff. The plans of the CUSL are described in Peter Mallett, "The Newest Professional Canadian Sports League," at <http://www.sportsbusinessnews.com> cited 25 November 2002.

8.   See Jim Barrero, "MLS Expansion Set For 2005," at <http://www.sportsbusinessnews.com> cited 9 October 2003; Ridge Mahoney, "MLS Playing Mexican Card," at <http://sportsillustrated.cnn.com> cited 2 October 2003; Idem., "Looking For Answers as MLS Season Hits Stretch Run," at <http://si.printthis.clickability.com> cited 2 September 2003; Eric Fisher, "MLS Finding New Investors," at <http://www.sportsbusinessnews.com> cited 4 December 2003; Matthew Futterman, "Ever the Optimist, MLS Commissioner is a True Believer," at <http://www.sportsbusinessnews.com> cited 6 November 2003; Frank Del Olmo, "Commentary: Soccer is Kicking Into L.A.'s Future," *The Los Angeles Times* (3 March 2002), M5; Len Ziehm, "San Diego Likely Site For MLS Expansion in 2004," at <http://www.suntimes.com> cited 14 August 2003. Salt Lake City in Utah, San Antonio in Texas and Seattle in Washington have also been mentioned as expansion cities. See Pete Grathoff, "MLS Looking For Investors and Interested Cities," at <http://www.sportsbusinessnews.com> cited 30 January 2004.

9.   For MLS to be a first-rate professional sports league in America, its teams need to play games in soccer-only stadiums that provide amenities for spectators, and not to perform in cavernous NFL football stadiums. Commissioner Garber professed this hypothesis in Jack Bell, "Checking in on the MLS's Plans For the Future," at <http://www.sportsbusinessnews.com> cited 25 November 2003; Jack McCarthy, "MLS Now Looking to Expansion," at <http://www.sportsbusinessnews.com> cited 3 April 2003; Michelle Kaufmann, "The State of the MLS," at <http://www.sportsbusinessnews.com> cited 25 November 2002. Interestingly, Garber's commitment to the future of MLS is apparent in Steven Goff, "MLS' Commissioner Garber Signs a New Deal," at <http://www.sportsbusinessnews.com> cited 20 January 2003.

10.   There is specific information about each MLS team's stadiums at <http://www.mlsnet.com> and in a few of the online articles listed in Notes 1–9 of this chapter. During 2003, the Columbus Crew and Los Angeles Galaxy performed in their state-of-the-art soccer stadiums while the remaining MLS teams normally played in NFL football stadiums, which on average can seat more than 70,000 spectators.

11.   Ibid. For more details about the construction of the Dallas Burns' stadium in Texas, see Steve Davis, "Soccer Needs Stadiums," at <http://www.sportsbusinessnews.com> cited 20 February 2004. With respect to the stadium, the Burns' general manager Greg Elliott stated, "Profit is nice, but clearly, financial viability is the first landing spot for the sport. The stadium gives you the property to leverage into profits. But it will have a limited effect if you don't develop it properly and work at it. It's not the be all, end all solution." Interestingly, Lamar Hunt heads the group that will partially pay for the Frisco Soccer and Entertainment Center in Texas. Hunt loves soccer and has a passion for sports facilities. As a founding father of MLS, he believes that professional soccer will succeed or fail in America based on the development of stadiums. For his interest in the Center, see "Trendsetting Hunt Hopes New Stadiums Like Frisco's Kickstart MLS Growth," at <http://si.printthis.clickability.com> cited 24 February 2004.

12.   According to the U.S. national team coach Bruce Arena, the future of American soccer and the MLS are linked. That is, each depends on MLS's ability to develop youth and professional players, reach larger crowds and draw respectable television ratings. For Arena's comments, see Jere Longman, "Painstaking Progress Finally Pays Off For the U.S," *The New York Times* (25 June 2002), D3.

13.   For various aspects of MLS's games and programs on Gol TV, Sports Espanol, Telemundo and Univision, see Jeff Rusnak, "Soccer Finding Larger TV Audience," at <http://www.sportsbusinessnews.com> cited 1 December 2003.

14.   For its cable broadcasts, Gol TV charges per-subscriber fees for placement on full digital cable, sports or Latino network tiers. "Our programming is set up to have a logic or order, where the fan of a specific country's league knows when to catch the action of their favorite teams," said Gol TV's senior vice president Enzo Francesoli during early 2003. This strategy is further discussed in Simon Applebaum, "America's All-Soccer Network Ready to Take Its Shot," at <http://www.sportsbusinessnews.com> cited 20 February 2003.

15.   Fox Sports International is an international sports programming and production entity in the Fox Cable Networks Group, which is an operating unit within the Fox Entertainment Group and News Corporation. The entity's alliance with MLS is described in "MSN Signs Agreement With Fox Sports International," at <http://www.sportsbusinessnews.com> cited 3 April 2003.

16.   Yahoo!Sports is a co-sponsor of the league and Yahoo! Platinum broadcasts select MLS games online. One of Yahoo's programs at games includes targeted banner advertisements to U.S. Hispanic kids, adults and all-around soccer enthusiasts. See "MLS Signs a Spanish Sponsorship Agreement With Yahoo," at <http://www.sportsbusinessnews.com> cited 19 August 2003.

17.   During 2003, MLS's promotional slogan 'New Soccer Nation' reflected the league's strategy to attract the daughters and sons of immigrants to a familiar game. For why Hispanics are current and future soccer fans, see Jack Bell, "MLS Going After Hispanic Audience," at <http://www.sportsbusinessnews.com> cited 1 December 2003. In Bell's article, Commissioner Don Garber comments that, "For many Hispanics, the game is part of their souls—they paint their faces, they chant, they sing soccer songs. There is more on the line in the game; it is not about statistics and fantasy leagues. Ethnic fans see the game as a competition for pride."

18.   Various annual editions of *Sports Illustrated Sports Almanac* report the games and other results of World Cups and other international soccer tournaments. See, for example, pages 533–552 of *Sports Illustrated 1999 Sports Almanac* (New York, N.Y.: Little, Brown and Company, 1999). Another reference for this soccer tournament is "World Cup of Soccer," at <http://www.wldcup.com> cited 29 January 2004. As an aside, at the 2006

World Cup stadiums in Germany Anheuser-Busch will be sold, and not Bavarian beer. The switch to an American beer company occurred because of an agreement with FIFA. For the ramifications of this decision, see "Beer and Germany's 2006 Soccer World Cup," at <http://www.sportsbusinessnews.com> cited 23 April 2004.

19. For Bruce Arena's evaluation of American soccer and MLS during late 2002, see Steven Goff, "The Future of the MLS May be Linked to the World Cup," at <http://www.sportsbusinessnews.com> cited 25 November 2002, and Jerry Trecker, "U.S. Success Could Increase American Fan Base," at <http://www.sportsbusinessnews.com> cited 3 December 2002.

20. Ibid. Furthermore, see George Diaz, "World Cup Success Aside, Can the MLS Compete With European Soccer Leagues?" at <http://www.sportsbusinessnews.com> cited 3 December 2002. In Diaz's article, MLS' assistant commissioner Ivan Gazidis contends that the U.S. can retain its best players and thereby be competitive against Europe. "It's not a question of not being able to afford players, but making economically wise decisions. Before the World Cup, we signed one of the most promising [U.S.] players to a long-term contract [Josh Wolff] through 2008. [U.S. players] DaMarcus Beasley and Brian McBride also are signed on long-term contracts. We are keeping most of our best players and will continue to do that as long as it's economically rational."

21. For other readings about the sport and/or business relationships between MLS, World Cups and international soccer markets, see Greg Pesky, "World Cup '94: Shooting For Global Success," *Sporting Goods Business* (September 1993), 14A1; Eduardo Porter, "World Cup 2002: Si, Si!—Zeal of Hispanic-Americans For Soccer Finals," *Wall Street Journal* (6 May 2002), B1; Simon Kuper, "On the Eve of the World Cup, Football (Soccer) World-Wide is so Much More Then a Game," at <http://www.sportsbusinessnews.com> cited 3 December 2002; Bayan Rahman, Andrew Peaple, and Andrew Ward, "Will Soccer's World Cup be a Money Maker in the Far East?" at <http://www.sportsbusinessnews.com> cited 3 December 2002. To receive exposure in American and foreign markets, during 2004 MLS tried to schedule a high-profile international opponent for its all-star team. That is, the league spoke with officials from Real Madrid, Bayern Munich and perhaps other elite teams. For that strategy, see Steven Goff, "MLS in Search of a Home For Their All-Star and Championship Game(s)," at <http://www.sportsbusinessnews.com> cited 13 April 2004.

22. During the late 1990s and early 2000s, some experienced foreign players failed to meet MLS teams' expectations. To illustrate, Josh Wolff Matthaus pouted during one season and other players such as Adolfo Valencia, Alex Comas, Khodadad Azizi and Martin Machon were disappointments. See "Most Golden Oldies Aren't Gems," *Soccer Digest* (December 2002), 14.

23. Because of the league's system that allocates players, and due to economic reasons, MLS's MetroStars generally signed foreign players that were less talented than those who performed on other teams. To assess the team's predicament, see Alex Yannis, "MetroStars Seek a Foreign Influence," *The New York Times* (12 June 1999), 5. For rules about the allocation of players in Mexico, see "Mexican Soccer Leagues Limiting Foreign-Born Players," at <http://www.sportsbusinessnews.com> cited 19 August 2003.

24. For the choice to remain in Europe and play or return to the U.S., American professional soccer player Greg Berhalter said, "Is it a matter of dollars and cents? Yes and no. The money is important, [but] you have to have a stable life after soccer. I signed a good three-year deal. I can't take a massive pay cut to come back to the States." See Jack Bell, "European Football (Soccer) Clubs Look For Talent in the Good Old USA," at <http://www.sportsbusinessnews.com> cited 19 August 2003.

25. During 2003, England's Premier League allowed its teams to loan players to other clubs within the same division for the first time. Thus, Chelsea strikers Mikael Forssell and

Carlton Cole played for Birmingham City and Charlton Athletic, respectively. Those and other player loans appeared in Gabriele Marcotti, "Brother, Can You Spare a Star?" at <http://www.si.com> cited 11 September 2003.

26. As an experiment, in this FIFA tournament the teams were penalized for not observing the required distance of the defensive wall during free kicks. Also, the association's secretaries-general pledged that the tournament's soccer players would be less than 18 years old. See "All Eyes on Adu," at <http://cnnsi.com> cited 13 August 2003.

27. "Teen Star Adu Signs With MLS," *The Charlotte Observer* (19 November 2003), 2C; Jason La Canfora, "Looking at Why Freddy Adu Didn't Consider European Football (Soccer) Teams," at <http://www.sportsbusinessnews.com> cited 20 November 2003; Ives Galarcep, "Best Place For Adu to Land is MLS," at <http://www.northjersey.com> cited 28 August 2003; Stefan Fatsis, "Much Adu," *Wall Street Journal* (26 March 2004), W4. With respect to Adu's presence in MLS, Commissioner Garber declared, "We're not billing him as the savior of soccer, but we hope he will give our sport the recognition it deserves. We've never had the attention in the non-sports press that we've had. This stuff is unprecedented in soccer." Furthermore, see Brett Honeycutt, "Soccer's Superteen Selected 1st in Draft," *The Charlotte Observer* (17 January 2004), 3C.

28. For the managerial policies that European clubs have implemented to minimize their financial difficulties, see Gabriele Marcotti, "Shock Therapy," at <http://si.printthis.clickability.com> cited 4 December 2003, and Grahame L. Jones, "Soccer World-Wide Swimming in a Sea of Red Ink," at <http://www.sportsbusinessnews.com> cited 11 December 2002. Furthermore, many foreign professional soccer teams invaded the U.S. during 2003. See Paul Kennedy, "Too Much International Action is Damaging For MLS," at <http://www.si.printthis.clickability.com> cited 2 September 2003. Financial issues aside, security matters have also created problems for soccer organizations in Europe. To illustrate, during early 2004 Portugal announced that its police authorities would provide protection from terrorists and hooligans for those who attend the Euro 2004 soccer tournament. The tournament's security system is described in "Portugal Gives Assurances on Euro 2004 Security," at <http://si.printthis.clickability.com> cited 23 April 2004.

29. Ibid. For soccer problems experienced by leagues and/or financial remedies adopted by clubs in Italy and Spain, see Eric Sylvers, "The Business of Soccer, Not so Good in Italy," at <http://www.sportsbusinessnews.com> cited 13 November 2003; "In Italy Its Called Football and What Else it is New, It's a Big Money Game," at <http://www.sportsbusinessnews.com> cited 3 December 2002; Paul Gutierrez, "Spanish Soccer Heading For a Work Stoppage," at <http://www.sportsbusinessnews.com> cited 24 August 2003. Meanwhile, the Swiss marketing company Infront, which held the television rights to broadcast the games of German's soccer league Bundesliga, declined to sign a two-year option that would have taken affect in the Summer of 2004. According to the league's president Werner Hackmanm, "I'm confident of finding a new broadcast partner because we have a very good product to offer. The ratings are booming on all channels." See Grahame L. Jones, "German Soccer and Topsy-Turvy TV Problems," at <http://www.sportsbusinessnews.com> cited 5 January 2004.

30. See Bill Ward, "Euro Clubs Don't Want to Pay When Players Are Away For National Events," at <http://www.sportsbusinessnews.com> cited 1 December 2003, and Brian Trusdell, "European, South American Soccer Franchises Casting an Eye Towards America," at <http://www.sportsbusinessnew.com> cited 25 November 2002. With respect to the dispute with FIFA about compensation salary payments to clubs that release players for the World Cup and European championship finals, during early 2004 the G-14 filed an official complaint with Switzerland's competition commission. FIFA's president Sepp Blattner responded to the complaint when he said, "FIFA does not sit on the money generated by the

World Cup and other tournaments. It pays a grand total of $264 million to the 204 national associations and six confederations over such a period. I cannot imagine that a club would sue UEFA or FIFA." To those remarks Blattner added, "Under Swiss law, FIFA was a non-profit association unlike the billionaire clubs who have to maximize their own income . . . to absorb the ludicrously high player costs they are now lumbered with as a result of their own private but cut-throat competition to sign up the biggest stars." Meanwhile, it was reported that FIFA's total surplus is estimated to be $143.6 million during 2003–2006. By managing its costs as revenues grow, FIFA has adopted international accounting rules. As a result, Blattner has stated that, "Our [FIFA] finances are healthy in every respect. We can now celebrate the FIFA centennial safe in the knowledge that we have built upon our forefathers' legacy and done everything in our power to guarantee a successful future." For the G-14 complaint and FIFA's finances, see "Europe's Top Clubs Raise Stakes in FIFA Row," at <http://si.printthis.clickability.com> cited 13 April 2004; "FIFA is in the Big Money," at <http://www.sportsbusinessnews.com> cited 13 April 2004; "FIFA Enters Centennial Year With Sound Finances," at <http://si.printthis.clickability.com> cited 13 April 2004.

31. According to Imperial College [of] London's professor of economics Stefan Szymanski, "With American sports, you have to buy the values. It's a no brainer. It's a part of the world [Asia] with a huge population and a rising income." See Henry C. Jackson, "European Soccer Clubs Eyeing Asia," at <http://www.sportsbusinessnews.com> cited 19 August 2003.

32. Generally, the history, development and growth of Man U as a team and business were researched online at the web sites <http://www.yahoo.com>, <http://www.google.com> and <http://www.manutd.com>.

33. For Man U's championship titles, see various editions of *Sports Illustrated Sports Almanac* and Eric Fisher, "United They Stand ... to Conquer," *Insight on the News* (27 May 2002), 28–29. More information about Man U and England's prominent soccer league is in Frank Dell'Apa, "The Success and the Business of the English Premier League," at <http://www.sportsbusinessnews.com> cited 4 September 2003. Meanwhile, during early 2004 Man U's 62 year old coach Sir Alex Ferguson signed a new 12-month rolling contract to remain with the club. The deal takes affect on 30 June 2005, when Ferguson's previous three-year contract expires. See "Ferguson Signs One-Year Rolling United Contract," at <http://sportsillustrated.cnn.com> cited 30 January 2004.

34. See "Charm Offensive," at <http://www.cnnsi.com> cited 13 August 2003; Conrad De Aenlle, "ManU Making Shareholders Cheer," at <http://www.sportsbusinessnews.com> cited 2 September 2003; Stanley Holmes, Heidi Dawley, and Gerry Khermouch, "Can Man U Score in America?" *Business Week* (23 June 2003), 108–109; "Man Utd: We're on Our Way to Cracking America," at <http://cnnsi.com> cited 13 August 2003. Besides Man U, during 2004 and thereafter other elite soccer clubs will likely visit and play exhibition matches in North America. Based on an April 2004 CNN/World Soccer Top 10 poll, the highest ranked teams in the world included Italy's AC Milan and Roma, England's Arsenal and Chelsea, and Spain's Real Madrid and Valencia. For a complete list of teams and points in the poll, see "AC Milan Ousts Arsenal," at <http://sportsillustrated.cnn.com> cited 6 April 2004.

35. In part, some recent global marketing campaigns and other business deals that involved Man U are reported in "Man U's Big Sponsorship Deal of the Day," at <http://www.sportsbusinessnews.com> cited 11 December 2003; Lachian Colquhoun, "The Ever-Growing Marketing World For Man U," at <http://www.sportsbusinessnews.com> cited 20 November 2003; "Man U Headed Back Over the Pond," at <http://www.sportsbusinessnews.com> cited 13 November 2003; John Brennan, "ManU's Marketing Arm Continues Its

Reach," at <http://www.sportsbusinessnews.com> cited 5 August 2003; Paul Kelso, "A Monumental Partnership to Say the Least," at <http://www.sportsbusinessnews.com> cited 28 August 2003; Stanley Holmes, "Bend it Like—Somebody Else," *Business Week* (11 August 2003), 10.

36. For several reasons, a few wealthy investors had acquired Man U's stock during the early 2000s. To evaluate those transactions, see Jill Treanor, "Bucs Owner Invests More in Man U," at <http://www.sportsbusinessnews.com> cited 2 October 2003; Eric Portanger, "Malcolm Glazer Boosts His Stake in Soccer Club," *Wall Street Journal* (1 December 2003), C11; Dan Sabbagh, "Bucs Owner Malcolm Glazer Increasing His Man U Investment," at <http://www.sportsbusinessnews.com> cited 23 October 2003; Roger Mills, "Bucs Owners Expanding Their Horizons—Into European Soccer," at <http://www.sportsbusinessnews.com> cited 6 March 2003; Scott Barancik, "Malcolm Glazer Continues to Make His Move on Man U," at <http://www.sportsbusinessnews.com> cited 20 February 2004; "Russian Billionaire Looking at Man U," at <http://www.sportsbusinessnews.com> cited 2 January 2004. With respect to his investment in Man U, Glazer replied, "My company [Zapata Corporation] is considering possible options, which may include increasing its shareholding or decreasing it. It could also include a possible offer, or a possible sale of its shareholding." The team's investment, managerial relationship and business strategy, according to Leeds university professor of sports management Bill Gerrard implies that, "To begin with there was a high degree of mutual respect between Magnier, McManus and Ferguson, and it was good for both sides. But as they got more involved, McManus and Magnier began to have concerns about how Manchester United was run, in a sense protecting their interests in terms of their investment." Those observations were stated in Alan Cowell, "Malcolm Glazer, Man U and the Tampa Bay Bucs," at <http://www.sportsbusinessnews.com> cited 2 March 2004. Besides Man U, England's Chelsea soccer franchise has attracted international investors. For example, see Sam Walker, "Chelsea Morning," *Wall Street Journal* (1 December 2003), W3.

37. See Mike Penner, "Real Deal: It's the Marketing," *The Los Angeles Times* (18 June 2003), D1; Carlta Vitzthum and Henry C. Jackson, "Spend it Like Beckham," *Wall Street Journal* (19 June 2003), B1, B4; "AP's Big Story of the Year—Beckham," at <http://www.sportsbusinessnews.com> cited 2 January 2004. According to statistics compiled by the Companies House for Footwork Productions, during 2003 David Beckham generated $16.1 million in commercial activities such as sponsorships and advertisements. Besides a payment to him of $10.2 million, Beckham earned a dividend of $2.2 million. Indeed, Footwork Productions had been formed with its principal activity as the provision of the services of David Beckham. For the operations of the company, see Damian Reece, "Earning it Like Beckham Would be Nice," at <http://www.sportsbusinessnews.com> cited 9 March 2004. In another report, by early 2004 Beckham had expanded the value of his fortune to 65 million pounds or $117 million. That amount included his salaries from soccer teams Man U and Real Madrid, and the money from endorsing such products as Police sunglasses and Burmah Castrol lubricants. Following far behind Beckham in wealth among British athletes was Manchester City striker Robbie Fowler, Dallas Mavericks' Steve Nash who is of English parentage, Chelsea's Argentine soccer player Juan Sebastian Veron and Formula One car driver Jenson Button. In short, Beckham is the first soccer player to place in the world sport's top ten earners. See "David Beckham is One Very Rich Soccer Player," at <http://www.sportsbusinessnews.com> cited 20 April 2004.

38. For information about Chapter 5's American women's professional soccer league, see "WUSA History," at <http://www.wusa.com> cited 19 August 2003, and "Women's United Soccer Association," at <http://www.hickoksports.com> cited 3 December 2003.

39. Ibid.

40. The following articles, in part, provide various opinions and viewpoints of why, when and how the WUSA folded in 2003. For example, see Scott French, "Beginning or End—What Went Wrong in WUSA?" at <http://si.com> cited 23 October 2003; Johnette Howard, "Death of WUSA—Lack of Any Real TV Deal," at <http://www.sportsbusiness-news.com> cited 16 October 2003; Jere Longman, "The Death of the WUSA on the Eve of the Women's World Cup—It Doesn't Get Any Worse," at <http://www.sportsbusiness-news.com> cited 16 September 2003; George Vecsey, "Economically the WUSA Had to Die," at <http://www.sportsbusinessnews.com> cited 16 September 2003; Brian Straus, "The WUSA and Its Imminent Demise," at <http://www.sportsbusinessnews.com> cited 26 August 2003; Kristen Wyatt, "WUSA Folds Days Before Cup Starts," *The Charlotte Observer* (16 September 2003), 1C, 3C; Allen Barra, "A Strategic Error Doomed the WUSA to Defeat," *Wall Street Journal* (23 September 2003), D9.

41. The current and future economic climates affect the operations of women's and men's professional sports leagues. According to Randy Bernstein, the president of sports marketing firm Premier Partnerships and an architect of MLS, "Obviously, these are very challenging economic times. Still, without a doubt, there is a place today for entertaining professional men's and women's sports. You have to have a product that's exciting and creates a passion among the following. Creating controlled or realistic expectations is the most important variable out there." See Tom Timmerman, "Looking at the State of Women's Professional Sports," at <http://www.sportsbusinessnews.com> cited 25 September 2003; Eric Fisher, "Looking at Women's Professional Sports After the Death of the WUSA," at <http://www.sportsbusinessnews.com> cited 18 September 2003

42. An American women's professional soccer league may be established in or after 2004 if there is sufficient sponsorship support and a lucrative television agreement. "We're looking to keep the brand alive to benefit the women's national team as well as WUSA" said Tony DiCicco, the former national women's team coach who was the league's commissioner. For an overview of the proposals, see Ridge Mahoney, "Look For a Scaled Down Version of the WUSA in 2004," at <http://www.sportsbusinessnews.com> cited 11 December 2003; Thomas Heath, "The WUSA May Not be Dead (Yet)," at <http://www.sportsbusinessnews.com> cited 16 October 2003; Brian Straus, "Can the Women's World Cup Save the WUSA?" at <http://www.sportsbusinessnews.com> cited 18 September 2003. Regarding the two or more soccer festivals planned for 2004, the WUSA's founding players will participate along with nearly all of the league's players, although some international stars may not attend because of club and national commitments. Besides exhibition games, the festivals will include clinics, player appearances and autograph sessions. This information is revealed in "Sites Chosen For WUSA Soccer Festivals," at <http://si.printthis.clickability.com> cited 2 March 2004. The U.S. Soccer Federation, meanwhile, is evaluating a proposal in which a select team of WUSA players would serve as a training partner to prepare America's national team for the 2004 Olympic Games in Athens, Greece. For where the festivals will be held, see Kelly Whiteside, "WUSA Has Plans For 2005," at <http://www.sportsbusinessnews.com> cited 10 February 2004. Other money aspects of the festivals are reported in "WUSA Begins Ticket Drive to Fund Planned Return," at <http://sportsillustrated.cnn.com> cited 17 February 2004. With respect to the U.S. women's four to one victory in Portugal, American player Abby Wambach scored three goals and stated after the game that, "Norway is a great team, and it takes a lot to break down their defense. To be able to score two goals against Norway is a great accomplishment, never mind four." See "U.S. Women Topple Norway," *The Charlotte Observer* (21 March 2004), 5F.

Conclusion

Sports Capitalism analyzed the international strategies and business aspects of five American professional sports leagues. In sequence, those were MLB and then the NFL, NBA, NHL and MLS. The contents of this book, where appropriate, also included any relevant information and statistics, and interesting facts about professional women's sports leagues and other U.S.-based and foreign sports groups and organizations.

For each of the five leagues in *Sports Capitalism* there was a chapter, which contained several key topics and perhaps subtopics about the plans and decisions of the league's commissioner and administration, and franchise owners to market their sport in nations outside of the U.S. or beyond the borders of North America. To be more specific, the chapters' topics were primarily concerned with and highlighted the alliances, events, grassroots activities, media programs, partnerships, sponsorships and other important matters that had contributed to the worldwide exposure and success of the five sports leagues and their respective brands, images, teams and players. Indeed, the topics in Chapter 1 represented the business interests and globalization efforts of MLB, while those in Chapter 2 pertained to the NFL, Chapter 3 to the NBA, Chapter 4 to the NHL and Chapter 5 to the MLS.

Consequently, based on the topics and any subtopics as presented in each of the chapters, this book now concludes with an overview of why and how the five professional leagues have succeeded and progressed as international sports and business organizations. It is important, therefore, for those who have read *Sports Capitalism* to comprehend and remember the demographic, economic, financial, politial and social forces and trends that have caused the majority of those leagues to be very powerful entities in the global sports industry. Not to be ignored in the contents, however, are the business enterprises and local communities, and the groups of fans and government authorities in numerous foreign nations, which have been and will be affected by the prosperity and future development of the five leagues. Thus, with respect to the arrangement of the chapters about the sports leagues, in this Conclusion MLB appears first followed by the NFL, NBA, NHL and MLS.[1]

MLB

Chapter 1 began, in part, by describing how the league expanded into Canada during 1969 and 1977 when, respectively, one team nicknamed the Expos located in Montreal while the other team titled the Blue Jays settled in Toronto. After those expansions occurred, MLB officials realized that business opportunities had existed overseas to market the sport of baseball. Consequently, in 1989 the league added an organizational subunit called MLB International (MLBI) whose purpose was to extend the business of the league into foreign countries and hence generate revenue. Accordingly, that task included establishing marketing programs, grassroots activities and alliances with affiliated partners, sponsors and vendors, and furthermore initiating any other relationships that were needed to promote professional baseball in nations abroad. If the dollar amounts of revenues and cash flows have been accurately reported to and recorded by the league, then MLBI has likely benefited baseball's franchise owners because of the income earned from consumers and businesses in international markets.[2]

To learn more about MLBI and its effectiveness, and to acknowledge how extensive the worldwide popularity and growth of baseball seems to be as a leisure activity, there is a discussion in Chapter 1 about whether or not the sport thrives in ten countries besides America and Canada. Interestingly, despite the inherent differences in attributes, cultures, customs, traditions and values, baseball is admired and respected by millions of fans in various nations. That is, its' games and tournaments are more frequently played by clubs or teams who are members of leagues that are scattered throughout the urban and rural areas in Mexico, Japan and a number of the Latin American countries, than, for example, in China, Russia and eastern European nations. As a result, during the early to middle 2000s MLB officials might decide to allocate more of the league's resources and capital investments to promote the sport in several of the medium to large cities in areas of Asia and eastern Europe.[3]

In this chapter, another relevant topic discussed about MLB is when, why and how America's minor and major league baseball teams have increasingly won regular season games, division titles and World Series championships after recruiting foreign pitchers and batters who are highly skilled players, and especially those athletes that excelled in the sport from the Dominican Republic, Mexico, Puerto Rico and Venezuela. To discover, scout and sign contracts with Latinos, for example, such teams as the AL's Kansas City Royals and New York Yankees, and the NL's Chicago Cubs and Los Angeles Dodgers had decided to own or lease sport facilities, which are called baseball academies in the Latin American countries. Because of the research performed for *Sports Capitalism*, there is evidence that some MLB teams have unintentionally, or perhaps intentionally exploited international players and also overlooked the deterioration of and poor living conditions within the academies. In this portion of the chapter, one specific study is discussed that condemns teams, and the U.S. professional baseball league for its failure to maintain adequate housing standards for athletes and their families at the academies, and to upgrade their other sports structures and adjacent properties in Latin America.[4]

In addition to the mistreatment of athletes that play baseball and live in nations of Latin America, Chapter 1 provides some sports-related information about the awards and at bat statistics of the Yankees' Hideki Matsui and the Seattle Mariners' Ichiro Suzuki, who are two outstanding players that choose to emigrate from

Japan to America during the early 2000s. When such successful foreign athletes as Matsui and Suzuki leave the professional baseball teams in Japanese leagues to join clubs in MLB, the financial returns and ticket sales of those Japanese organizations are adversely affected because of fan dissatisfaction and a decline in corporate sponsorships. As a countermove, however, during early 2004 an outstanding player of the Seattle Mariners was evidently homesick so he decided to return to Japan to be with his family and play for a professional baseball club somewhere in that country.

Besides the study that reported MLB infractions overseas, and the taint and infamous publicity directed at teams about the deteriorating baseball academies in Latin American countries, there are other issues that have concerned MLB. Because of their global implications, those baseball issues that are presented for readers of *Sports Capitalism* include the problems associated with players' drug test programs, whether and when MLB should develop and implement an international draft system for its teams, when and where the league should schedule a World Cup of Baseball, and how the Canadian Baseball League (CBL) had eagerly formed and then failed within a few months. Discussed as arranged and presented in Chapter 1, the league's drug test program originally excluded many Latino players even though those athletes had represented nearly 33 percent of the rosters for the teams that existed in MLB's minor and major league system. When a newspaper article unexpectedly appeared about the widespread consumption and abuse of animal steroids and dietary supplements by athletes on teams in the Dominican Republic and Venezuela, the social pressures and complaints from foreign sports officials, organizations and governments had prompted MLB and the MLBPA to reconsider the league's policy and thus propose reforms to include those international players in the newly adopted drug test program. According to some skeptics and dissenters, since drug tests could produce inaccurate results, those players who had repeatedly flunked their tests and thereby were threatened with expulsion from the league might seek legal assistance from the MLBPA, which is the baseball players' union. If the MLBPA agrees that the tests had reported false outcomes, or that the league's standards to pass the tests were too rigid or unrealistic, then the union might request MLB to disband the drug test program or renegotiate the standards through the typical collective bargaining process. For sure, the majority of baseball fans are more interested in the teams' and players' performances than whether the drug test generates fair and accurate results. Unless there are severe penalties imposed for violations, it is questionable, therefore, whether MLB's program will significantly discourage drug usage rates or improve the long-term healthcare of the league's players.[5]

After MLB's franchise owners finally implement practical and useful policies about the academies and drug tests, then competitive balance between teams within the AL and NL might be restored when there is an international draft system that includes the amateur, semiprofessional and professional players from all nations. Rather than the league depend solely on revenue sharing and a luxury tax to transfer revenues from the high to low payroll clubs, which has not been as effective as anticipated, several controversial proposals have been recently mentioned about the types of draft policies to approve and implement. Essentially, the league and MLBPA have disagreed about the number of rounds during each draft and about the exchange values to be assigned to those players who are drafted and then immediately traded to another club. Anyway, if the league does not initiate an international draft system soon, the competitive gap might increase between such high income and wealthy teams as the NL Atlanta Braves and AL Boston Red Sox, and those clubs that decide or can only afford to pay below average salaries to players like the NL Pittsburgh Pirates and AL Tampa Bay Devil Rays. In short, although MLB and the MLBPA have occasionally discussed this topic, the gap in the competitive imbalances between large and small market teams will not significantly decrease until an efficient international draft system is approved, implemented and strictly enforced by the AL and NL franchise owners.[6]

Relative to another issue about how, where and when to further globalize the sport, MLB is prepared to sponsor a World Cup of Baseball during 2005 to be played at ballparks in medium sized to large American cities, if the tournament were held before or during baseball's Spring training period and not during the Summer months. Indeed, baseball officials have proposed several versions of a World Cup championship that would involve teams from countries in Asia, Europe and South Africa, and eventually would include one or more teams from China and Russia. Nonetheless, because the league's games have always been scheduled during months in the late Summer season, it is not likely that MLB team owners will ever approve their players to participate in a Summer Olympic Games. The primary reason is that the postponement, delay or cancellation of games during the regular season by MLB teams would cost the league's franchise owners millions of dollars, and also disrupt the AL and NL playoffs and World Series championship event, which is normally held during the month of October.[7]

Because of economic problems and other specific reasons, other American professional baseball leagues have ultimately failed such as the Union Association and Players League during the late 1800s and the Federal League and Mexican League during the early to middle 1900s. Besides those four organizations, after two months into the regular season the eight-team CBL folded its operations during July of 2003. This had occurred, in part, because of the league's ineffective marketing campaigns and the inferior quality of most of the league's teams, and below average attendances at stadiums and excessive rainfall in eastern Canada that eliminated many games, which were scheduled. Although those factors had likely doomed the CBL and caused its demise, some international investors and sports officials became optimistic when they met in late 2003 to discuss whether to start up another professional baseball organization with teams in cities somewhere in Canada.

With respect to other baseball topics from a global perspective, the final two items discussed in Chapter 1 are a table that lists five foreign cities as potential sites for a MLB expansion franchise and/or an existing relocated team, and an overview of the operations of women's baseball leagues, schedules and tournaments in America and Australia. Based on such criteria as fan bases, stadium capacities, weather conditions and populations, the cities that were evaluated in

Sports Capitalism as the best and most probable future locations for professional baseball teams included Monterrey and Mexico City in Mexico, and then San Juan in Puerto Rico, Santo Domingo in the Dominican Republic and perhaps Havana in Cuba. After the analysis of those cities is completed, the chapter concludes with a discussion about the four-team Women's Baseball League Inc., which was founded by American Justine Siegal during 1997, and also an overview of the 100 year old history of women's baseball organizations in Australia.[8]

Since the NFL was established 29 years before the NBA, and because that professional football league's games and playoffs are more popular in America and are televised in most foreign nations than those of the NHL or MLS, it follows that the NFL is the sports league featured in Chapter 2. When that chapter ended, the business decisions and international strategies of the NBA, and then the NHL and MLS were the special focus of Chapters 3–5.

NFL

In an article titled "Lessons Learned," which was published in the *Super Bowl XXXVIII Game Program*, the Columbia Broadcasting System's evening news anchor and managing editor Dan Rather restated a football metaphor that was written by a former U.S. president, Theodore Roosevelt. The metaphor Rather spoke was, "In life, as in a football game, the principle to follow is: Hit the line hard; don't foul and don't shirk, but hit the line hard." In most aspects, president Roosevelt's observation about the sport has not changed since 1902 when the first attempt to organize a professional football league in America was initiated.

Initially, Chapter 3 provided the rationale for why U.S. professional football leagues had to disband, dissolve or merge during 1926, 1937, 1941, 1949, 1969, 1975 and 1985. The reasons for those leagues' failures generally included such factors as underfunded franchises, low attendances at games because of wrong-headed decisions by coaches and poor performances by players, teams' revenue shortfalls due to the lack of regional and national television and radio contracts, disputes between team owners and players, inadequate stadium amenities and inferior team locations. Despite the presence of one or more of those factors, however, the 14-team NFL had successfully formed as a sports business organization during 1920. Since that year, the league has gradually matured and for the 2004 season, the NFL contained two 16-team conferences, which included an equal number of U.S.-based teams in the East, North, South and West divisions.[9]

Based on the previous remarks about the origin and growth of professional team football in America, this chapter consisted of four sections that represented, as a group, the primary international business operations and interests of the NFL. With respect to those sections, the topics of each were titled as the WLAF-NFLE, NFL International (NFLI), NFL Strategies by Country and Grassroots Football Programs. To provide enough contents and insights about the topics, one or more of the sections also included such subtopics as identifying the specific foreign countries that have fans who are enthusiastic about the sport of American-style football, and describing the types of NFL and NFLE grassroots activities and programs that have existed in European countries. Although different than those in MLB, and the NBA and NHL, during the 2000s each of the NFL's 32 franchises were located in America. Consequently, expansions and the movements of any NFL teams to cities in foreign nations had never occurred during the league's 84 year old history.

With respect to each topic discussed in Chapter 2, the WLAF was formed during the early 1990s and then folded after one season because of weak fan support and a national recession in America. It reemerged, however, as a six-team, European-based league in 1995. Three years later, the WLAF was renamed the National Football League Europe (NFLE). Prior to the discussion of how the WLAF and then the NFLE had operated as a sports business, in this chapter there is a table that indicates the results of the American Bowl series, which continues to be football games played each year at stadiums in European cities and elsewhere by NFL teams, since the series started in the middle of the 1980s.[10]

The worldwide exposure and prominent success as a result of the Bowl's series of games, in part, provided enough momentum for the NFL to organize and subsidize the operations of the WLAF, whose ten teams during 1991 were located in medium to large, populated American and/or European cities. To identify which of the WLAF and NFLE European teams had won World Bowl titles, another table appeared in Chapter 2 that denoted the number of seasons and average attendances of the European teams who had played in ten championship World Bowl games. In fact, the two most successful teams that won World Bowl titles were the Rhein Fire and Frankfurt Galaxy, and the least victorious were the Amsterdam Admirals and London Monarchs. In short, the American Bowl series and the WLAF and NFLE each represented how the NFL has attempted to expose and market its brand and sport in various foreign nations. Although the majority of NFLE teams have consistently incurred operating losses in the millions during regular seasons since 1998, NFL Commissioner Paul Tagliabue and the league's franchise owners have determined that there are incremental economic benefits to be earned because of the NFLE teams' presence in European cities. With respect to what the NFL realizes, those benefits from international sources include the cash inflows from football apparel, equipment and merchandise sales, and the broadcast revenues from television programs and marketing campaigns. Since it is unlikely that an existing or new NFL franchise will be located overseas during the early 2000s, it seems apparent that the NFLE is a worthwhile investment and asset to be maintained by the NFL team owners.[11]

Similar to the decision made by MLB to restructure in 1989, the NFLI was established by the league during 1996. Given its position as a subunit of NFL Enterprises, the NFLI has generated much income for the league from foreign consumers, and from various organizations that are located outside of America. Indeed, the NFLI has business relationships abroad with television broadcast networks and cable and satellite systems and operators, and with retail operations that might involve partners, sponsors, vendors and other affiliates. Furthermore, the subunit's managers have likely managed global programs such as grassroots

activities for football enthusiasts, promotion of the NFLE in each of the teams' European cities, and any international youth and semiprofessional football games, tournaments and other events. To illustrate those interests, Chapter 2 included a few examples of the NFLI's business agreements with U.S. corporations that market the brands of NFL teams in foreign nations, and those companies who promote, sell and distribute football products in nations beyond America.

Given the presence and popularity of the NFLE teams in Europe and the international business deals that have been initiated by the NFLI, which is located at the NFL's headquarters in New York City, this chapter also examined the status of professional football and the success of the league's activities and programs, if any, in six foreign nations. That is, during the 1990s the NFL had decided to open regional offices in Japan, Canada and Mexico. Because the three countries are extremely important markets to develop and nurture for the NFL, it is interesting to learn about the league's interactions with those nations' citizens and organizations, and how well the sport of American-style football is understood and respected within the six countries' cultures and societies. Since the existence and success of the Canadian Football League (CFL) has economic implications for the NFL and its teams, some business matters related to the CFL were then presented following the discussion of the NFL's office in Canada.[12]

With respect to the global presence of American football and the NFL, the three other countries that were chosen to be studied as foreign markets included England, Spain and China. Interestingly, there are large cities in each of those nations that are considered to be potentially lucrative markets for the NFL and the league's teams. Indeed, American Bowl series games were played before large crowds in London between 1986 and 1993. Barcelona, meanwhile, had hosted a series game in 1994 and was the home site of the Dragons, which was an NFLE team that won four World Bowls in 11 seasons. Even though the Dragons folded its operation as an NFLE team during 2003, Spain has tens of thousands of young people and middle age adult men who are passionate NFL fans. Regarding the third country, the appropriate government officials in China have agreed to schedule NFL exhibition and/or preseason games in the Cities of Shanghai and Beijing, which is the location of the 2008 Summer Olympic Games. Furthermore, millions of households in China increasingly watch professional football games on their television sets, which meant that the game and the NFL have become more exposed, popular and entrenched throughout that country of 1.3 billion people. In short, Chapter 2 provided some insights and facts about football in those six countries and why they are reasonably attractive markets to penetrate for the NFL, and perhaps the NFLE into the early 2000s.[13]

The fourth and final section of this chapter identified and described a few of the most well-organized and more popular grassroots football programs in America and foreign nations that have been sponsored by the NFL. The following examples, in part, illustrated how exciting those programs have become for fans and athletes, and especially for aspiring football players. During late January of 2004, which was Super Bowl Week in Houston, Texas, some competitive American high school football teams played against the national junior teams of Canada, Japan, Mexico

and Russia. To be eligible for his football team, each player who was selected from a school had compiled at least a 3.0 grade point average, which is equivalent to a B and the highest discrete letter grade below an A or 4.0 average. The tournament in January of 2004 was titled NFL Global Junior Championship VIII. Besides that event, when America Online Inc. presented the NFL Experience on 25 January 2004, the City of Houston had celebrated the Hispanic community with 'Latino Day,' which included youth clinics, cultural performances and appearances by players from the NFL's New England Patriots and Carolina Panthers who had volunteered to sign their autographs for people that attended the celebration. Meanwhile, prior to 'Latino Day' the NFL and the Association for the Advancement of Mexican Americans hosted a character education program in Houston named the 'Kids Workshop.' That program featured motivational speakers and a series of classroom and athletic activities, which were designed to teach Hispanic youngsters and their families some leadership and character development traits and skills. Rather than provide specific details about 'Latino Day' and 'Kids Workshop,' which had occurred during Super Bowl Week, this portion of the chapter primarily focused on and described such popular grassroots programs as the NFL Flag Football World Championships, European Amateur Football tournaments, and a bit more on the history of the NFL Global Junior Championship tournament.[14]

Although the NFLE teams had played their regular seasons and World Bowl championships since the late 1990s in several European cities, and even if NFL games have increasingly appeared on the television sets of households in numerous foreign countries, MLB and the NBA must be ranked moderately ahead of the NFL as international sports businesses. Based on the information presented in the Introduction and chapters of this book, that is a reasonable conclusion to derive because during the early 2000s, the statistics reveal less than 5 percent of the professional football league's players were from foreign nations and second, there is only a marginal probability that before 2010 an NFL team will be located at a site in a city outside of America. However, since the NBA had become organized as a league about 30 years after the NFL but 47 years before MLS, and given that the game of basketball is more popular among sports fans in the U.S. than ice hockey or outdoor soccer, it is the global business aspects and operations of the American professional basketball league that appear in *Sports Capitalism* after the chapters about MLB and the NFL.

NBA

Chapter 3 analyzed the activities, alliances, events, investments and programs that have projected the NBA to become the world's most dominant international basketball league, and perhaps one of the more profitable sports business and entertainment organizations in the western hemisphere. Accordingly, this chapter was divided into several interdependent sections. The specific sections were titled, respectively, as International Strategies, Global NBA Broadcasts, Foreign Players,

Global Basketball Markets and WNBA. In turn, each section presented those topics and subtopics that illustrate what is most relevant to the sport of professional basketball and the business of the NBA from a worldwide perspective.[15]

After it absorbed the National Basketball League and Basketball Association of America, the multi-team NBA had become organized to play its first season as a league in 1949. Nevertheless, as a result of the performances by inferior teams and players, fans that did not attend home games, and the financial troubles experienced by franchise owners during the 1950s and 1960s, several of the league's teams located in small and medium sized markets had to fold their operations and abandon the sport of professional basketball. Even so, between the late 1960s and 1970s many of the remaining NBA franchises had nearly bankrupted because the television ratings of professional basketball games declined in America and some of the league's players publicly abused drugs. Meanwhile, the cooperation and business relationship between the players' union and team owners seemed to deteriorate. After the late 1970s, however, the league's image, development and business environment had gradually improved. In fact, the transformation of the NBA as a business organization and its aftermath are the essential and core contents that were presented in Chapter 3.

During the 1980s and early 1990s, the characteristics of the basketball executives and players, and events that rejuvenated the NBA from an international perspective were Commissioner David Stern's vision and leadership in promoting the league in markets overseas, and also the exciting play and showmanship of the Chicago Bull's Michael Jordan, Scotty Pippen and Dennis Rodman, the competitiveness of other superstars like the Boston Celtics' Larry Bird, Los Angeles Lakers' Magic Johnson and Utah Jazz's Karl Malone, and the publicity from the U.S. Dream Team's championship in 1992 at the Summer Olympic Games in Barcelona, Spain. Consequently, as the league and the sport of basketball became more popular and dispersed abroad throughout the 1990s, two new NBA franchises had joined the 1995 season in Canada as the Toronto Raptors and Vancouver Grizzlies. Meanwhile, the exposure of the league's games, teams and players seemed to increase on foreign television and radio networks, and articles appeared about the NBA in newspapers and sports magazines that were distributed to citizens in various countries of Africa, Asia, Europe, and Latin and South America. As their exposure globally expanded, the NBA teams vigorously competed with each other to scout, recruit, draft, and sign contracts with outstanding basketball athletes from many foreign nations, who then excelled as players in the league. In short, the actions, events and strategies as portrayed in Chapter 3 indicate that between the early 1980s and late 1990s the NBA had developed into an international sports and business organization that was recognized and adored by millions of basketball enthusiasts, players and other sports fans from cities in Australia to China and areas in Argentina to Sweden.[16]

Given those historical facts and opportunities, there are other developments that partially explained why the sport of basketball and the NBA had grown in popularity worldwide since the early 1980s. The league, for example, decided to establish mutual affiliations with television broadcast networks and cable systems, and with American and foreign companies who then joined with the league to serve as partners, sponsors and vendors. Beside those successful marketing endeavors and relationships, during the 1990s and early 2000s the league's teams had played exhibition games in cities of the Dominican Republic, France, Israel, Italy, Mexico, Puerto Rico and Spain, and regular season games in areas of Japan and Mexico. For the international basketball fans who for some reason could not attend those exhibition and regular season competitions, the league launched its web site identified as NBA.com. That online service primarily provided basketball game highlights, sports shows and news programs about the league. In turn, the Internet also created an array of options for how the league could advertise, sell and distribute its professional basketball equipment, and the teams' merchandise and players' apparel and shoes. Those commercial activities and operations are more thoroughly explored in the section of Chapter 2 that is titled, Global NBA Broadcasts.[17]

Another strategic aspect of the league's globalization policy is reflected by the NBA teams' increased use of and dependence on foreign players. Although a relatively small proportion of those athletes had played in the league before the 1990s, it was the success of foreign country's national teams at international tournaments and in the Olympic Games that ultimately inspired NBA franchise owners to confidently pursue and hire such outstanding players as Serbia-Montenegro's Vlade Divac, Nigeria's Hakeem Olajuwon, Germany's Detlef Schrempf, Spain's Pau Gasol and Croatia's Tony Kukoc. Moreover, after the 1980s the culture of sports in America had fundamentally changed. That is, native U.S. athletes who were physical, athletic and skilled seemed to become greedier, self-centered, individualistic and less team-oriented, but more inclined to experiment with illegal drugs during their leisure time, and at games displayed rowdy and discourteous behavior toward their opponents and referees and occasionally toward those fans in attendance at the arenas. Meanwhile, for various reasons the supply of talented and experienced foreign basketball players had increased in the labor markets, which meant that more of them were qualified and willing to perform at the professional level for the NBA teams in North America or for national and professional clubs overseas.

Besides discussing those issues that involve American and foreign basketball athletes, there were two specific subtopics in this part of the chapter. Those are, respectively, some interesting facts and pertinent information about the emigration of European players that have joined eastern and western conference teams in the NBA, and about the entry into the U.S. of China's Yao Ming and how he has influenced the fans' image of the Houston Rockets, and impacted the global marketing and power of the league. Because of Ming's charisma and demeanor as a celebrity with his team in the midwest division of the western conference, and China's goal to eventually become a world power in basketball, it is likely that each NBA franchise owner will devote additional resources to recruit and draft preferably tall, and perhaps medium sized players from the national and company teams in Asian countries.[18]

To reveal the presence and quality of junior, semiprofessional and professional basketball programs abroad, and to determine whether there are any business relationships between the NBA and sports organizations in China, Mexico and a few African countries, the fourth part of Chapter 3 was presented. The readers of *Sports Capitalism*, for example, learned how embedded basketball is in China's culture and society, and that there are three professional leagues in Mexico's Basketball Federation. In part, it is because of the Dallas Mavericks' Eduardo Najera, who was born in Mexico and plays as a backup center on the team, that the sport has increasingly appealed to the Latinos who reside in America's southwestern and western States, and to the passionate sports fans that live in areas of northern Mexico. Interestingly, as a result of Najera and other Spanish-speaking players in the league, during the early 2000s the NBA had intensified its efforts to arrange the broadcasts of professional basketball games and tournaments to Latinos in those markets. Similarly, the league had become more popular for and attracted fans in African nations when Commissioner Stern, and some of the NBA's coaches and players appeared and spoke or performed at clinics for young athletes from Kenya, Zaire and South Africa. Besides being taught some fundamental basketball skills and also how to out compete their opponents during games, at the clinics African children were informed about education and social programs. In short, those sessions exposed the children to the advantages of books and computers, and how the quality of their lives could be improved by technology and participating in leadership and reading programs, and by conscientiously following health care guidelines in order to avoid communicable diseases and lifetime illnesses.[19]

Indeed, since basketball is a global sport and hence played by athletes in many foreign nations, a table appeared in Chapter 3 that presented some population statistics to justify why the five most attractive cities beyond North America to locate one or more NBA teams during the early to middle 2000s would be first, Mexico City in Mexico, and then Berlin in Germany, Barcelona in Spain, Beijing in China and San Juan in Puerto Rico. Nevertheless, although the metropolitan area populations of those cities are each at least two million, and that fan bases likely exist in the areas to support an American professional basketball team, those cities' infrastructures and stadiums surely need to be modernized before a team relocation or league expansion could occur at the sites. Besides the five locations, other well-qualified places for the NBA to consider as potential sites include such cities and nations as Bologna in Italy, Frankfurt in Germany, London in England, Madrid in Spain, Monterrey in Mexico, Paris in France and Tel Aviv in Israel.

The international aspects of the WNBA, which has been America's premier professional women's basketball league since the late 1990s, were the final contents about the sport that are discussed in Chapter 3. Although the majority of the league's operations are actually subsidized by payments from the NBA team owners, the WNBA had the foresight to gradually increase its employment of foreign players from fewer than ten in 1997 to 30 or more in 2004. Furthermore, as explained in the chapter, a large portion of the WNBA's regular season games have been televised in nearly 200 countries and the league expanded its broadcast agreements with media companies during the early 2000s, and especially with respect to markets in Africa and the Middle East. Even so, because of the organization's need to become financially stable in the long-term and perhaps less dependent on the NBA, the WNBA will not be expected to expand into one or more cities outside of America before 2006 or 2007.[20]

In short, Chapter 3 included the most interesting and relevant topics and subtopics about the NBA's activities and programs in various nations across the globe. As a group, the topics and subtopics in that chapter reflected the entertainment value of the game of basketball and therefore, represented the league's history, operation and progress as an international sport and business organization.

The final two U.S.-based sports leagues that are discussed next in this Conclusion are the NHL and MLS. As examined before with respect to MLB, and the NFL and NBA, what are the business strategies and international topics that relate to and involve each of these prominent American ice hockey and outdoor soccer leagues?

NHL

As indicated in the beginning paragraphs of Chapter 4, for various economic and sport-specific reasons American professional ice hockey associations had failed during 1916, 1925 and 1979. Nonetheless, three years before the NFL had organized as a league in 1920, the NHL, which was originally composed of four Canadian teams, formed its business venture in Montreal, Canada. Between 1942 and 1967, however, the league consisted of Canadian ice hockey teams in Montreal and Toronto, and American clubs in the large markets of Boston, Chicago, Detroit and New York City. Then, the NHL expanded by six franchises in the 1960s, ten in the 1970s and finally eight in the 1990s. Interestingly, 17 of those expansions occurred in medium sized to large U.S. cities and the other seven in Canadian cities. Since 1967, therefore, the league has significantly increased its presence and exposure, and the sport of ice hockey in North America.[21]

Besides a discussion of when and where there was franchise expansion, this chapter primarily focused on such topics as the NHLI, Global NHL-Media Business, NHL International Players, Alternative Ice Hockey Leagues, and the World Cup of Hockey and other worldwide tournaments that have featured teams in the sport. In total, those topics determine how, why and to what extent the sport and league have progressed globally from 1917 to the early 2000s. Chapter 4, therefore, incorporated the activities, alliances, events, grassroots programs and business relationships that have affected the NHL and its teams and players, international tournaments, and if appropriate, any foreign ice hockey leagues, federations and other sport-related organizations.

Similar to the respective organizational units or subunits established in MLB, and the NFL and NBA, during 1993 the NHLI was organized to concentrate efforts and resources on expanding the international business and markets of the NHL. That is, the NHLI controls and manages the league's marketing campaigns and commitments abroad such as any relationships and contracts with foreign broadcast networks, media affiliates and partners, sponsors, vendors and licensees. Besides those tasks and responsibilities, the NHLI likely arranges and assists with the development and implementation of grassroots ice hockey programs overseas, monitors any teams and tournaments that involve foreign leagues, and conducts promotional activities as necessary in countries beyond the U.S. and Canada. As such, the NHLI is involved with numerous ice hockey events that include the NHL's All-Star games and Stanley Cup championships, and the Winter Olympic Games, World Cup of Hockey competitions, NHL Mall, Challenge Series and Million Dollar Challenge, and such attractions as the NHL Slapshot and Rapid Fire. The NHLI, therefore, will play a key role in the league's quest to expand the sport of professional ice hockey and place franchises in regions outside of North America.

To ensure that the league's games, promotions and products are recognized abroad and receive more exposure on the Internet and on television and cable networks in foreign nations, during the early 2000s the NHL successfully negotiated agreements with companies that included Ignite Media, Sun Microsystems and GlobeCast North America. Those three companies, as a group, provided the software, technology and communication systems for the league to deliver its games and programs almost everywhere in the world. As a result, the sports fans that lived in China, Russia and many eastern and western European countries were able to watch the league's athletes vigorously skate and perform during their games in stadiums, and then those fans could purchase apparel, merchandise and ice hockey equipment on the teams' web sites and on NHL.com. During 2003, for example, a portion of the league's regular season games were broadcast from ice hockey rinks in America and Canada, and then transmitted on cable and satellite networks to the television sets of sports consumers in the Czech Republic, Hungary, Japan and Spain. Indeed, because ice hockey enthusiasts frequently use online services and are known to be extremely computer-savvy, Internet programming services will probably be a growing source of revenue for the NHL teams during the early 2000s.[22]

Because of what the NHLI has accomplished for the sport, and how the worldwide popularity of ice hockey and the NHL have expanded, the league's international players increased relatively from 2 percent in 1975 to nearly 25 percent in 1999. Those athletes were primarily natives of America and Canada. Nonetheless, during the middle to late 1990s many Russian and European players had decided to join the league. That is, although most ice hockey experts consider Canadians Wayne Gretzky, Mario Lemieux, Gordie Howe, Bobby Hull, Bobby Orr and Henri Richard to be the sport's six all-time greatest professional players based on points per game, league scoring titles and participation on Stanley Cup championship teams, such Russians as Sergei Fedorov and Pavel Bure, and Europeans as Jaromir Jagr and Peter Forsberg also became dominant NHL players. In this section of Chapter 4, a table was displayed that listed the distribution of NHL players for six U.S.- and Canadian-based teams during the 2003–2004 season. That distribution, in part, denoted that on average the highest proportion of players on the 12 teams tended to be from Canada, and then from Europe, America, Russia and such foreign nations as Brazil, Latvia and Slovakia.[23]

An interesting and relevant subtopic in this chapter was the current differences that exist between the language, interpretation and enforceability of contracts endorsed by NHL players and the employment agreements signed by ice hockey athletes who had performed on national and professional teams in their respective countries. As such, it appears that foreign nations have specific legal rules and enforcement policies and procedures with respect to athletes' contracts that somewhat conflict with those for NHL players in North America. To illustrate what the differences are, four cases were presented about how the compensation and condition of employment of U.S. and foreign players with contracts have affected NHL teams and/or certain clubs in the IIHF. In short, it is evident that American and international ice hockey officials must discuss, develop and disclose a system to ensure that ice hockey players' contracts are written in a format, language and style that is unambiguous, concise and not contradictory with respect to the treatment of salaries, incentives and other fringe benefits. Indeed, when the disputes about the contract issues are resolved, then professional ice hockey players will have more opportunity and freedom to move from one team to another within a league, and perhaps between the NHL and international leagues, especially those that exist in Eastern and Western European countries.[24]

The fourth part of this chapter first examined the organizations and plans of the FHL and WHA, which are projected to be two new professional ice hockey leagues, and then the part contained a review of the history and rationale for why the second-tier IHL was forced to fold its operations in 2001. The FHL and WHA might succeed, at least in the short-run, if a total work stoppage occurs in the NHL during the Fall or Winter of 2004. That is, the new leagues' teams might thrive because they generally will play in small to medium sized cities in North America that are not the home sites of an existing NHL club, except for the Canadiens in Montreal, Oilers in Edmonton and the Canucks in Vancouver of Canada. Interestingly, neither the FHL nor WHA had identified in their press releases any potential sites in cities outside of North America. So, even if a union strike or management lockout does occur in the NHL during 2004, the teams in the two new leagues will likely struggle to attract ice hockey fans to their games and to receive regional, national and international exposure on television and the Internet. Indeed, an NHL shutdown of any portion of its season would upset sports fans, which in turn is detrimental to teams' home site attendances. Moreover, if the new leagues' teams play mediocre or inferior ice hockey in their rinks, that would probably mean less media coverage of those teams' games. As previously stated, besides reading about the expectations for the FHL and WHA, this section also explained why the IHL collapsed as a sports league during 2001 after 56 years of operations. In short, after the league had decided to expand into several cities across North America, a number of the small market teams ceased to exist rather than operate as franchises at a financial loss and hence accumulate excessive short- and long-term debts. Meanwhile, during the expansion phase many of the IHL's medium and large market teams spent generous amounts of money to sign and retain their players and travel to games. As a result, most of the teams in the IHL had to fold their organizations although a few of the league's teams restructured their organizations and joined the American Hockey League in time to play the following season.[25]

The fifth part of Chapter 4 highlighted a few of the popular international hockey tournaments that had occurred during the 1970s, 1980s and 1990s, and discussed the composition of the World Cup of Hockey championship that is scheduled in 2004. Interestingly, there are a number of NHL players who are natives of countries in Europe. Undoubtedly, most of those athletes will qualify and perform for their national ice hockey teams in the World Cup tournament. This com- petition, as expected, should provide more global exposure for the NHL, and an opportunity for the league to further penetrate the world's sports markets, especially in European countries. Indeed, if the U.S. national team wins or at least reaches the semifinals in the tournament, the sport of ice hockey will become even more popular in America. In turn, this might create a larger fan base for the NHL's teams and perhaps encourage more high school, college and semiprofessional athletes to participate in the sport as players.[26]

After a discussion of those tournaments, in this chapter's part, three options were presented that offer solutions about how the NHL might have to operate once the NHLPA and the league's officials agree to and sign a new collective bargaining agreement during 2004 or 2005. In general, some of the league's franchise owners could decide to merge their teams while other owners may fold their organization in the NHL rather than to operate at a deficit and incur financial liabilities. Nonetheless, the growth in the players' compensation of each franchise must be curtailed if the league expects to exploit markets abroad during the 21st century. In short, for more detailed information about the topics and subtopics that were discussed in Chapter 4, the reader should consult the chapter's Notes, which include specific readings and sources that supplement the contents with respect to ice hockey and the NHL.

MLS

In America, the USA and NPSL had merged to form the 17-team NASL during 1968. Seven years later, the NASL decided to terminate its operations because of the teams' low attendances at games and the failure of the league to negotiate a long-term national broadcast or international television network contract. Despite the NASL's demise in 1975, it was the success of the U.S. women's soccer team in the 1999 World Cup and the men's team in 1994 that provided the inspiration for the formation of MLS in 1996. To examine the international business activities, events and programs, and other global aspects and relationships of that American men's professional soccer organization, Chapter 5 included such topics as MLS International Strategies, Global Television and Media Agreements, International Soccer Competitions, MLS and International Players, European Soccer and the WUSA.[27]

Although most of the teams' attendances at games had been disappointing during the regular seasons of the late 1990s and early 2000s, MLS Commissioner Don Garber has expressed his optimism about and plans for the league's future development. That is, for local and international exposure and market penetration, Garber has stated that the league must expand by 20 or more teams before 2010. Besides Houston in Texas and Cleveland in Ohio, there are medium and large cities in Canada and Mexico which are potential sites for a relocated MLS team or an expansion franchise. Indeed, during 2004 or 2005 a Mexican entrepreneur will likely move his soccer team from Mexico to a city in southern California in order to join and compete in MLS. According to Garber, the construction of new single-purpose soccer stadiums, and not baseball or football facilities, are also needed so that the league's teams have permanent places to practice, play their home games and earn more revenues at those stadiums from ticket sales, television broadcasts, parking, concessions and spectator purchases of the home teams' soccer apparel, merchandise and equipment. For sure, the capital investments in soccer projects will require millions of dollars from sponsors and team owners, and from local investors and/or municipal taxpayers.

Several spokespersons that represent various U.S. cities have expressed an interest in hosting a MLS franchise once a stadium proposal is negotiated and a local fan base has been identified for the team. Meanwhile, Commissioner Garber and other soccer officials foresee a large growth during the early 2000s in the number of American athletes who want to play on a semiprofessional or profess-ional soccer team as a sports career. That growth will occur when more youth in the U.S. participate in soccer programs at the elementary, high school and college levels, which means new semiprofessional and minor leagues will gradually develop that provide the training and experience for athletes who value performing for a club in MLS.[28]

As described in Chapter 5, the FSN and ESPN networks in America and the Telemundo and Univision networks in Mexico have each committed to broadcast MLS games and other soccer events on their television channels. Furthermore, the league has negotiated contracts with various media companies so that its games and international tournaments are transmitted to soccer fans in Central and South America. Moreover, MLS has endorsed an integrated marketing and content agreement with Yahoo, who will provide the coverage of teams' and players' participation in soccer All-Star games, international exhibitions and World Cup competitions. Meanwhile, there is a Spanish version of those events that are broad-casted on Yahoo! en espanol. In short, during the early 2000s MLS has succeeded to contract with a number of U.S.-based and foreign media networks and other communication companies so that the league's brand, and its games and programs are advertised and promoted in several countries of North, Latin and South Amer-ica, and eventually in some nations of Asia and Europe.[29]

Other topics that are included in Chapter 5 involve MLS players and their participation on national teams that compete in international tournaments. Gener-ally, U.S.-born players and American-based soccer teams have moderately pro-gressed to become more competitive against well-respected foreign players and teams, particularly since 1996 when MLS was founded. Regarded as the best competitors in the sport, some of the countries that have succeeded in World Cup tournaments are identified with respect to this topic because of the championships they had won with outstanding coaches, teams and players. Those nations with one or more World Cup titles include Argentina, Brazil, England, France, Germany, Italy, Uruguay and West Germany. Consequently, for America to become an international threat or superpower in outdoor soccer tournaments the U.S. needs an effective developmental system for youngsters to assemble in organized groups, and then practice and compete while enjoying the sport. From such a system, gifted athletes will eventually emerge who want to play on teams in MLS or perhaps for the league's professional clubs in a minor league organization rather than struggle to perform on teams in amateur, semiprofessional and professional baseball, football, basketball or ice hockey leagues.

If a passion to be the best country in soccer becomes a goal in American culture, then MLS will seek to globalize its operations and evaluate whether to place one or more of its teams in Canada, nations of Europe and/or Latin and South America. As described in this portion of Chapter 5, when 14 year old American Freddy Adu signed a multiyear contract during 2003 to play with D.C. United and not a foreign team, Adu's decision might imply that MLS has an opportunity to grow and develop, and eventually prosper as a competitive international sport and business league.[30]

With respect to professional soccer games being played across the globe, the powerful teams are predominately located in European countries and to a lesser extent, in the nations of Africa and South America. Thus, the operations of European soccer leagues and a portion of their fabulous clubs such as Arsenal, AS Roma, Barcelona, Juventus, Inter Milan, Leeds United and Real Madrid are represented in this chapter as the premier soccer organizations in Europe. Besides those great teams, there are some historical facts and interesting business matters about Manchester United, which is considered to be the most valuable sports franchise on earth. To illustrate the relative salaries of professional soccer athletes who excel for European clubs, a table lists 15 transfers of players from one team to another that had occurred between 1997 and 2003. In spite of those prominent leagues and clubs that have been successful in the sport, some European soccer teams in Austria, France, the Netherlands and Portugal have experienced short-term financial difficulties. As explained in this section of Chapter 5, those problems might unfortunately trigger the implementation of salary caps or even the dissolution or merger of some European clubs in the countries.[31]

Besides the information presented about MLS and a few of the European soccer leagues, teams and players, a women's professional soccer league named the Women's United Soccer Association (WUSA) had existed in America from 2001 to 2003. That league entered its first season with the enthusiasm and high expectations of Commissioner Don Garber and the league's team owners, coaches and players, and with the support of various partners, sponsors and investors, and female soccer fans. The WUSA had failed, however, because the organization's business plan and pro forma financial statements were based on overoptimistic forecasts of the teams' regular season attendances and cash flow balances, and because the plan had evidently contained inflated revenue estimates derived from national and local television broadcasts, and from the marketing agreements and promotional contracts with sponsors, partners and other affiliates. Furthermore, some of the league's executives were not competent as decision makers about the soccer business. Moreover, those managers did not develop a schedule of games and other events that were realistic and consistent with respect to the demand for women's professional soccer in the teams' markets across America.

Although the WUSA had collapsed in 2003, some sports groups and wealthy investors have met to revive the eight-team league but on a smaller scale of operations. During June of 2004, for example, two or more weekend soccer festivals, with doubleheaders and clinics for kids at sites in several U.S. cites, had been planned to promote the sport to American soccer fans. If those events succeed, then the league will likely return as a restructured organization sometime during 2005. Accordingly, the WUSA is the final topic about professional soccer that is discussed in Chapter 5.[32]

Given the topics about each of the leagues as depicted and analyzed in Chapters 1–5 of *Sports Capitalism*, during the early 2000s it was MLB and the NBA, followed by the NFL, NHL and MLS that rank in order as the most successful globalized professional sports organizations, which were based in America. To be more specific, the rank order was determined by each of the leagues' international and business affiliations, alliances, events, grassroots programs and any other activities and relationships that had exposed the sport's games and tournaments, and the professional teams and players to populations in foreign nations. That is, in those countries beyond the geographic borders of America for the NFL and MLS, and outside of North America for MLB, and the NBA and NHL.[33]

With respect to globalization and the specific leagues, during 2004 there were two MLB clubs located in Canada, foreign-born players comprised nearly 30 percent of the teams' rosters, several of the teams' baseball academies existed in some cities of Latin America and MLB anticipated hosting a World Cup of Baseball tournament in 2005. Furthermore, a league office opened in Tokyo and a broadcast agreement was signed that tripled MLB's television revenues from Japan. Finally, the MLBI office had created marketing campaigns and developed grassroots programs and events for baseball fans and other sports enthusiasts in countries beyond North America.

Meanwhile, an NBA team nicknamed the Raptors had played games at its home site in Toronto, Canada since 1995, the league planned for an expansion franchise to be located in a city of Europe or elsewhere before the early 2010s, 73 international players appeared on the NBA teams' rosters during the 2003–2004 regular season, and foreigners purchased approximately 20 percent, which amounted to $600 million of the league's merchandise. Also, more than 20,000 fans attended the league's opening game that was played in Japan during the Fall of 2003, nearly 50 percent of the visits to NBA.com originated from outside America, and

Commissioner David Stern had vigorously promoted the league in China, Russia and Latin American countries.

During the early 2000s, the NFL operated its European league that was labeled the NFLE, the NFLI office established television contracts with foreign broadcast networks and marketing deals with sponsors and partners overseas, regional league offices existed in Canada, Mexico and Japan, and various teams in the NFL participated in the American Bowl series. Furthermore, some grassroots clinics were sponsored and placed by the league in European nations, and the NFL's annual Super Bowl games were generally rated as one of the top television sports programs in North America and perhaps the world.

Regarding the NHL, the NHLI office has provided marketing opportunities for the league to expand its business in foreign nations, the league's televised games appeared as entertainment events to thrill ice hockey fans who live in China, Russia and in eastern and western European countries, and a growing proportion of the NHL players had emigrated to America and Canada from European cities. Lastly, the World Cup of Hockey and other international tournaments have exposed the sport and professional ice hockey teams and players to sports fans within and outside of North America.

Since the late 1990s, more of the MLS teams have played their games in soccer-only stadiums while the league has attempted to promote its brand and the sport to Hispanic populations in nations of North, Latin and South America. Furthermore, MLS players enthusiastically participated in the World Cup of Soccer tournaments and Olympic Games, and the league encouraged the visits of prestigious European soccer clubs such as Manchester United and some teams from Mexico and South America to play exhibition games in the U.S. Then, during 2003 the league signed Freddy Adu, a teenage American soccer player to a lucrative, multiyear contract. His leadership qualities and performances for the D.C. United, which is based in America's capital city of Washington, D.C., are expected to provide international exposure, prestige and market power for MLS.

In the Appendix, Table A.11 indicated where 131 professional sports franchises were located in North America during 2004. Based on the population statistics and ranks in Table A.11, some of the prominent U.S. metropolitan areas for a future MLB team are Portland in Oregon, Sacramento in California and Orlando in Florida; for an NFL club are Los Angeles-Anaheim in California, Portland in Oregon and Sacramento in California; for an NBA team are San Diego in California, St. Louis in Missouri and Tampa Bay-St. Petersburg in Florida; for an NHL franchise are Houston-Galveston in Texas, Seattle-Tacoma in Washington and Cleveland in Ohio; for a MLS club are Philadelphia in Pennsylvania, Detroit in Michigan and Houston-Galveston in Texas. However, one or more of those sites may or may not be selected by the leagues. For example, an NBA expansion team was awarded to Black Entertainment Television owner Robert Johnson, who decided to place his team in Charlotte, North Carolina to begin the 2004–2005 season in November of 2004. Furthermore, some league officials have discussed Indianapolis in Indiana and San Antonio in Texas to be prime areas for a MLB team. With respect to the populations of international sports sites, in the Appendix is Table A.12, which showed that attractive areas for a relocation or expansion team include Tokyo in Japan and Mexico City and Monterrey in Mexico for MLB; Berlin, Hamburg and Frankfurt in Germany for the NFL; Shanghai and Beijing in China and Madrid in Spain for the NBA; Amsterdam in the Netherlands, Prague in the Czech Republic and Dublin in Ireland for the NHL; and Sao Paulo in Brazil, London in England and Santo Domingo in the Dominican Republic for MLS. Indeed, before 2015 there might be teams from the American-based professional sports leagues based in one or more of those international metropolitan areas.

In sum, those were the salient topics and global business matters about the five U.S.-based professional team sports leagues that conclude *Sports Capitalism*.[34]

Notes

1.   The Notes in the Conclusion of *Sports Capitalism* contain the most insightful, interesting and relevant articles, books and Internet sources in the literature with respect to those topics as presented in the content of the chapters. That is, each Note represents the best readings about a topic that relate to one or more aspects of the short- and long-term business, operations and strategies of the sports leagues, which were identified in sequence as MLB and then as the NFL, NBA, NHL and MLS. Besides those five organizations, the Notes also include the most important readings about such other professional sports leagues as the CBL, CFL, WNBA, WHA and the English Premier League. In short, the readers of *Sports Capitalism* should review the materials in the Conclusion's Notes to learn about the business matters of the global sports industry.

2.   To determine the relocation of professional baseball teams and MLB expansions, see Frank P. Jozsa, Jr. and John J. Guthrie, Jr., *Relocating Teams and Expanding Leagues in Professional Sports: How the Major Leagues Respond to Market Conditions* (Westport, CT: Quorum Books, 1999); Frank P. Jozsa, Jr., *American Sports Empire: How the Leagues Breed Success* (Westport, CT: Praeger Publishers, 2003); James Quirk and Rodney D. Fort, *Pay Dirt: The Business of Professional Team Sports* (Princeton, N.J.: Princeton University Press, 1992); Neil J. Sullivan, *The Dodgers Move West: The Transfer of the Brooklyn Baseball Franchise to Los Angeles* (New York, N.Y.: Oxford University Press, 1987). Furthermore, the internationalization of MLB is expected to continue at least throughout the early portion of the 21st century. For why, when, where and how this previously had occurred, that is, with the formation of MLBI and particularly since the early 1990s, see Terry Lefton, "Global Grand Slam," *Brandweek* (18 October 1999), 20–22; Dennis W. Organ, "Baseball and Global Capitalism," *Business Horizons* (September/October 2002), 1; Claire Smith, "The Game Looks to Foreign Fields," *The New York Times* (27 October 1992), B9, B12; Mike Hiserman, "The Growing Globalization of MLB," at <http://www.sportsbusinessnews.com> cited 25 November 2002; Larry Eichel, "MLB's 'Vision' of a Global Game," at <http://www.sportsbusinessnews.com> cited 23 October 2003.

3.   Based on the research, since the middle of the 1990s MLB games, teams and players have become more popular worldwide because of the league's television agreements and marketing campaigns and promotions. For a sample of those business strategies, see Stefan Fatsis and Suzanne Vranica, "Major League Baseball Agrees to $275 Million Deal in Japan," *Wall Street Journal* (31 October 2003), B4; Kelly Grimes, "Global Access Sends Major League Baseball Overseas," *Business Wire* (30 April 1996), 43; Paul Dykewicz, "Spotlight: Baseball's All-Star Game Goes Global," *Satellite News* (21 July 2003), 1;

"MLB.com to Video Stream MLB Playoffs to Overseas Markets," at <http://www.sports-businessnews.com> cited 25 November 2002.

4. Various officials have criticized MLB teams' treatment of their academies in Latin America. In part, this exposure has likely damaged the league's image and has thwarted its' efforts to expand operations into such nations as the Dominican Republic, Puerto Rico and Venezuela. Some detailed information about those baseball academies is contained in Arturo J. Marcano and David P. Fidler, *Stealing Lives: The Globalization of Baseball and the Tragic Story of Alexis Quiroz* (Bloomington, IN: Indiana University Press, 2003). Besides that book, the academies are discussed in Jim Souhan, "Latin American Academies Becoming the Norm," at <http://www.sportsbusinessnews.com> cited 14 January 2003, and Gary Marx, "An Expose on Baseball Training Facilities in Latin America," at <http://www.sportsbusinessnews.com> cited 19 August 2003. For the environment and condition of workers in the Costa Rican factories that produce baseballs for the league, see Tim Weiner, "Costa Ricans Sweat Details For Major-League Baseballs," *The Charlotte Observer* (25 January 2004), 10A.

5. During early 2004, some newspaper reports revealed that a California firm had possibly distributed steroids and other drugs to prominent players on teams in MLB. Even so, the MLBPA has resisted that players be randomly tested for drugs during the off-season and more frequently during the regular season. In fact, the players' union is not obligated to bargain with the league until the current collective bargaining agreement expires in December of 2006. Yet, minor league baseball players, who increasingly are athletes from foreign countries, are subjected to more strict policies with respect to illegal drugs than major league players. Various aspects of MLB's drug test program are discussed in "Baseball to Start Testing Latin American Players," at <http://www.cnn.com> cited 4 September 2003; Steve Fainaru, "MLB to Consider Drug Testing For Foreign Players," at <http://www.sportsbusinessnews.com> cited 19 August 2003; John Donovan, "As Steroid Use Goes, Baseball's Numbers Just Don't Add Up," at <http://www.sportsillustrated.cnn.com> cited 20 November 2003. Indeed, President George Bush and the U.S. Congress have publicized their concerns about the use of illegal drugs in professional baseball and the need for MLB and the MLBPA to implement policies that reduce the incentives for players to consume performance-enhancing substances.

6. If the MLBPA cooperates, *Sports Capitalism* predicts that MLB will implement an international player draft system before 2006. The teams' owners generally support a system whereby all American and foreign players, if eligible, are included in a draft. Certainly, the league and union have discussed various proposals and plans. To become knowledgeable about the composition of baseball's future draft system, see Tom Singer, "MLB.com Looks at the Concept of a World-Wide Baseball Draft," at <http://www.sportsbusinessnews.com> cited 3 December 2002; Thomas Harding, "MLB and MLBPA Still Working on World-Wide Draft Plan," at <http://www.sportsbusinessnews.com> cited 25 November 2002; Gary Klein, "Global Draft," *Los Angeles Times* (3 June 2003), D6; Kevin Kelley, "Worldwide Draft Caps Wealthy Teams' Monopoly," at <http://www.sportsbusinessnews.com> cited 19 August 2003. However, some problems with a global baseball draft system are expressed in Dave Sheinin, "A World-Wide Baseball Draft Could be a Logistical Nightmare," at <http://www.sportsbusinessnews.com> cited 19 August 2003.

7. Based on interviews and the announcements of MLB Commissioner Bud Selig, league executives and team owners, a World Cup of Baseball tournament will be organized soon. The tournament's scheduled time period and sites, and the number of teams and player's compensation are problems to be resolved before the competition is held. For facts about this international event, see George Gross, "Former MLB President Paul Beeston Wants a Baseball World Cup by 2005," at <http://www.sportsbusinessnews.com> cited 25 Nov-

ember 2002; Murray Chass, "A World Event Could Solve All-Star Blahs," *The New York Times* (9 July 2002), D3; Barry M. Bloom, "MLB Looking at World Cup in 2005," at <http://www.sportsbusinessnews.com> cited 1 August 2003; Mike Bauman, "Bud Believing in a Baseball World Cup," at <http://www.sportsbusinessnews.com> cited 13 November 2003. Some obstacles that require resolution with respect to this tournament are documented in Murray Chass, "Problems With Proposed MLB 2005 World Cup," at <http://www.sports-businessnews.com> cited 10 February 2004.

8.   Several articles depict the status of baseball and/or MLB as represented in various Asian, Latin American and European countries. That is, the sport is popular or has gained market share in many nations of those areas. For an evaluation of baseball's prospects in foreign nations, see such articles as Calvin Sims, "Japanese Leagues Worry About Being Overshadowed," *The New York Times* (30 March 2000), 3; Ken Belson, "Baseball in the Land of the Rising Sun," at <http://www.sportsbusinessnews.com> cited 3 April 2003; Rob Evans, "U.S. Baseball Expects Big Hit in Mexico," *Amusement Business* (8 July 1996), 19–20; Justin Martin, "Can Baseball Make it in Mexico?" *Fortune* (30 September 1996), 32–33; "Baseball Has Been Very, Very Good to the Dominican," at <http://www.sports-businessnews.com> cited 19 August 2003; Kathleen O'Brien, "In the Dominican is Baseball a Ticket to Paradise?" at <http: //www.sportsbusinessnews.com> cited 24 February 2004; Steve Cummings, "Baseball and Cuba," at <http://www.sportsbusinessnews.com> cited 19 August 2003; John Vinocur, "Baseball in Europe," at <http://www.sportsbusinessnews.com> cited 19 August 2003; Gordon Edes, "MLB in Europe in 2005?" at <http://www.sportsbusinessnews.com> cited 22 September 2003; Michael A. Lev, "Baseball in the People's Republic," at <http://www.sportsbusinessnews.com> cited 21 August 2003; Barry M. Bloom, "MLB and China Sign a Working Agreement," at <http://www.sportsbusiness-news.com> cited 1 December 2003; Kim Palchikoff, "Youth Baseball in Russia," at <http: //www.sportsbusinessnews.com> cited 19 August 2003.

9.   During the 1900s, there were professional football leagues that had organized and failed in America. For some history about those organizations, see such books as David S. Neft and Richard M. Cohen, *The Sports Encyclopedia: Pro Football*, 5th ed. (New York, N.Y.: St. Martin's Press, 1997); Robert W. Peterson, *Pigskin: The Early Years of Pro Football* (New York, N.Y. and London, England: Oxford University Press, 1996); Eric M. Leifer, *Making the Majors: The Transformation of Team Sports in America* (Cambridge, MA: Harvard University Press, 1996); Frank P. Jozsa, Jr. and John J. Guthrie, Jr., *Relocating Teams and Expanding Leagues in Professional Sports*, 27–32; Frank P. Jozsa, Jr., *American Sports Empire*, 19–25.

10.   During the early 1990s, the NFL initiated a risky venture when the league organized the WLAF. For the development, formation, operation and failure of the WLAF, see "Rozelle Looks to Europe," *The New York Times* (21 March 1989), B13; Gerald Eskenazi, "Global N.F.L. Game Plan: Springtime Play Overseas," (20 July 1989), A1; "1990 Opener is a Global Enterprise," *The New York Times* (2 August 1990), B11; "World Football League Quick History," at <http://wflfootball.tripod.com> cited 6 October 2003; "WFL Europe," at <http://www.wfl.com> cited 13 October 2003; Ariel Simon, "Touchdown!" *Harvard International Review* (Winter 2001), 12–13.

11.   The American Bowl series, NFLE and the World Bowl, which is the 'Super Bowl' of the NFLE, are each important elements of the NFL's international strategies. That is, the American Bowl series of games have been played in an international city since the middle of the 1980s, the NFLE exists for football fans in Europe, and the World Bowl games are a popular event throughout Europe. In part, those elements are discussed on such web site articles as in "American Bowl Results (1986–2000)," at <http://www.tinfl.com> cited 9

October 2003; "American Bowl Series," at <http://www.nfl.com> cited 9 October 2003; "National Football League Europe," at <http://www.nfleurope.com> cited 13 October 2003; "N.F.L. Europe Loses $20 Million," at <http://www.sportsbusinessnews.com> cited 3 December 2002; Ivan Carter, "Is the End Near For NFL Europe?" at <http://www.sportsbus-inessnews.com> cited 19 August 2003; "NFL Owners Will Keep Europe Alive," at <http: //www.sportsbusinessnews.com> cited 18 September 2003; Scott Miller, "Paul Tagliabue on the Importance of the NFL in Europe," at <http://www.sportsbusinessnews. com> cited 25 November 2002.

12.   The NFLI is an increasingly important organizational unit of the NFL. With regional offices located in Europe, and in Canada, Japan and Mexico, the NFL depends on the NFLI for its international exposure and the sales of teams' apparel and equipment. In short, during the early 2000s the NFLI will continue to expand its operations and responsibilities across the globe, and especially in specific Asian and European countries. To become more in-formed about the NFLI and the league's regional offices, see the booklet *NFL International* (New York, N.Y.: National Football League, 2002), and Don Garber, "NFL Sets Up Unit to Plot Overseas Pitch," *Brandweek* (14 October 1996), 14; "NFL International is a Success," at <http://ww2.nfl.com> cited 25 November 2002; "NFL Opens Office in Japan," at <http: //ww2.nfl.com> cited 25 November 2002; "NFL International Historical Results," at <http: //ww2.nfl.com> cited 25 November 2002; Wayne Washington, "Craig Lands NFL Monday Night Football Rights," *The America's Intelligence Wire* (9 May 2003), 1; William Houston, "NFL Network in the Frozen North," at <http://www.sportsbusinessnews.com> cited 19 August 2003. With respect to the operations and status of the CFL during the early 2000s, and the league's relationship with the NFL, see "Canadian Football League Looks at Expansion," at <http://www.sportsbusinessnews.com> cited 3 December 2002; "CFL En-joying a Renaissance of Sorts," at <http://www.sportsbusinessnews.com> cited 20 Nov-ember 2003; Mark Harding, "These Are Heady Days For the Canadian Football League," at <http://www.sportsbusinessnews.com> cited 3 December 2002; "CFL Happy With NFL Partnership," at <http://www.sportsbusinessnews.com> cited 3 December 2002; "CFL Extends NFL Agreement," at <http://www.sportsbusinessnews.com> cited 4 December 2003; "Cost of Business in the CFL Way Up!!" at <http://www.sportsbusinessnews.com> cited 26 August 2003.

13.   During the early 2000s, the NFL has promoted professional football and marketed its teams' merchandise and equipment in England, Spain and China. The highest-valued market opportunities exist, however, in China because of the country's enormous population, above average economic growth and efforts to reform its infrastructure and adopt new sports activities. Accordingly, the NFL's presence in each nation is reflected in Daniel Thomas, "American Football to Launch $5m UK Push, *Marketing Week* (15 May 2003), 10; "NFL Finalizes Deal With F.C. Barcelona," at <http://ww2.nfl.com> cited 3 December 2002; George Solomon, "FC Barcelona (Football Club) and the NFL Team Up," at <http://www. sportsbusinessnews.com> cited 3 December 2002; Curtis Eichelberger, "NFL Considering Heading to China For Pre-Season Games," at <http://www.sportsbusinessnews.com> cited 2 January 2003; "NFL Looks to China as Next Stop," *The Los Angeles Times* (1 January 2003), D4; Thomas Heath, "NFL Has Ambitions For China," *The Washington Post* (1 August 2002), D1; "NFL Coverage Spans the Globe—Agreements Bring Football to Japan, China," at <http://www.nfl.com> cited 4 December 2003.

14.   The NFL and NFLI have sponsored a variety of grassroots activities and programs in various nations. As such, the league attempts to provide football as an entertainment option for children and teenagers who have generally been lifelong soccer and ice hockey fans and/or players. Besides organizing and funding international tournaments and championship series, the league operates camps and clinics, and supervises games, which might feature

football coaches and players as instructors. Furthermore, some of the league's programs involve the development of the kids' academic and social skills. Consequently, those programs benefit the participants and likewise, motivate them to play the sport of football and thereby become future NFL fans. For a selection of the grassroots events, see "History of the Global Junior Championships 1997–2002," at <http://www.nfleurope.com> cited 12 October 2003; "Mexico Crowned Flag Football Champs," at <http://www.nfleurope.com> cited 12 October 2003; "European Junior Championship Lineups Unveiled," at <http://www.nfleurope.com> cited 12 October 2003; "Russians Keen to Prove Worth," at <http://www.nfleurope.com> cited 13 October 2003; "Berlin Welcomes YOU and the NFLX," at <http://www.nfleurope.com> cited 9 October 2003; "NFL Experience Rolls on Through Europe," at <http://www.nfleurope.com> cited 12 October 2003.

15. For the organization and development of the NBA with respect to *Sports Capitalism*, the reader is encouraged to research such books as Frank P. Jozsa, Jr. and John J. Guthrie, Jr., *Relocating Teams and Expanding Leagues in Professional Sports*, 33–38; Frank P. Jozsa, Jr., *American Sports Empire*, 12–19; Andrew D. Bernstein, *NBA Hoop Shots: Classic Moments From a Super Era* (San Francisco, CA: Woodford Press, 1996); Walter LaFeber, *Michael Jordan and the New Global Capitalism* (New York, N.Y. and London, England: W.W. Norton & Company, 1999); Alexander Wolff, *Big Game, Small World: A Basketball Adventure* (New York, N.Y.: Warner Books, 2002); Martin Tarango, *Basketball Biographies* (Jefferson, N.C. and London, England: McFarland & Company, 1991); Roger G. Noll and Andrew Zimbalist, eds., *Sports, Jobs and Taxes: The Economic Impact of Sports Teams and Stadiums* (Washington, D.C.: Brookings Institution Press, 1997).

16. During the 1980s, 1990s and early 2000s, NBA Commissioner David Stern had applied his marketing skills to promote and expand the business of the league into numerous nations. To learn about various aspects and results of Stern's globalization strategies, see Jack McCallum, "Tomorrow the World," *Sports Illustrated* (7 November 1988), 58–63; Jeffrey A. Trachtenberg, "Playing the Global Game," *Forbes* (23 January 1989), 90–91; Linda Deckard, "Global Expansion Next Step For NBA?" *Amusement Business* (22 April 1991), 35–36; Carl Desens, "The NBA's Fast Break Overseas," *Business Week* (5 December 1994), 94; Greg Pesky, "Spanning the Globe," *Sporting Goods Business* (November 1993), 36; Ross Siler, "Is the NBA Really Looking at Global Expansion?" at <http://www.sportsbusinessnews.com> cited 10 February 2004; George Diaz, "NBA Going Global," at <http://www.sportsbusinessnews.com> cited 20 February 2004; Daniel Eisenberg, "The NBA's Global Game Plan," *Time* (17 March 2003), 59–60; "Stern and Granik Get Ready For a New NBA Season," at <http://www.sportsbusinessnews.com> cited 23 October 2003; "David Stern Still Looking to Globalize the Game," at <http://www.sportsbusinessnews.com> cited 6 November 2003; Frank Lawlor, "NBA Czar Reaches Out to the World," *International Herald Tribune* (4 February 1999), 17.

17. Besides more affiliations with partners and sponsors, during 2002 and 2003 the NBA had increased its global presence with the broadcasts of basketball games and shows on television. For an overview of those marketing strategies, see "The NBA, WNBA and Yahoo! Announce Groundbreaking Global Agreement," *Business Wire* (11 September 2000), 9–19; "Gatorade and NBA Enter Global Partnership," *AsiaPulse News* (8 November 2002), 49; "Anheuser-Busch & NBA Extend Global Partnership," *PR Newswire* (10 December 2002), 4; "NBA Renews International Television Agreements," at <http://www.sportsbusinessnews.com> cited 25 November 2002; Eric Fisher, "The NBA Continues to Use TV to Drive Its Product Internationally," at <http://www.sportsbusinessnews.com> cited 25 November 2002; "NBA Renews International TV Deals," at <http://www.nba.

com> cited 21 May 2003; "NBA Blankets Germany With TV Agreements," at <http://www. nba.com> cited 21 May 2003.

18.   Because they are experienced, skilled and well trained in the fundamentals of the sport, basketball athletes from European countries have joined NBA teams and performed as excellent role players. In part, their presence and impact on the league is described in David Shields and Phil Poynter, "Foreign Guys Can Shoot: That's Why the N.B.A. is in the Import Business," *The New York Times Magazine* (3 March 2002), 56; Chad Ford, "European NBA Talent—Pay Later, Develop Now," at <http://www.sportsbusinessnews.com> cited 3 December 2002; Peter Gwin, "Transatlantic: How Europe is Shaping US Basketball Hoops," *Europe* (June 1997), 33–35; Mike Fish, "European Invasion Has Prep Stars Focusing on Fundamentals," at <http://sportsillustrated.cnn.com> cited 17 July 2003; Alexander Wolff, "Foreign Intrigue," at <http://cnnsi.printthis.clickability.com> cited 28 June 2003. Interestingly, the entry of China's Yao Ming into the NBA has improved the attendance and performance of the Houston Rockets. Indeed, Ming has become an all-star player in the league's Western Conference and challenges the Los Angeles Lakers' Shaquille O'Neal as the best center in the sport. Consequently, the NBA games have become more appealing and entertaining to basketball fans, especially in Asian countries. For the exposure, publicity and business that has been generated since Ming joined the league, see Stefan Fatsis, Peter Wonacott, and Maureen Tkacik, "A Basketball Star From Shanghai is Big Business," *Wall Street Journal* (22 October 2002), A1, A10; Jill Painter, "This Just in ... Yao Ming Big Business," at <http://www.sportsbusinessnews.com> cited 20 February 2003; Scott Soshnick, "Yao Ming and One Billion Chinese Basketball Fans," at <http://www.sportsbusinessnews.com> cited 3 December 2002; "The Global Marketing of Yao Ming," at <http://www.sportsbusinessnews.com> cited 22 January 2003.

19.   In specific nations such as China and Mexico, NBA games and programs have become more popular leisure activities among sports fans. As a result, the league has increased its marketing campaigns and promotions in those countries. To expose some facts about the implementation and affect of the NBA's strategy in China and Mexico, see Jackie MacMullan, "The Sport and a Quarter of the World's Population," at <http://www.sportsbusinessnews.com> cited 27 February 2003; Jeff Coplon, "Basketball in the World's Most Populated Country," at <http://www.sportsbusinessnews.com> cited 1 December 2003; Eric Fisher, "Selling U.S. Professional Sports in China," at <http://www.sportsbusinessnews.com> cited 20 January 2004; Craig S. Smith, "How China Intends to Benefit From the NBA or China's Version of Democracy," at <http://www.sportsbusinessnews.com> cited 3 December 2002; Art Garcia, "Basketball's Popularity Growing in Mexico," at <http://www.sportsbusinessnews.com> cited 9 October 2003; Magaly Morales, "Telemundo Set to Begin Their NBA Coverage," at <http://www.sportsbusinessnews.com> cited 25 November 2002; Eddie Sefko, "Mavericks—Jazz Play Preseason Game in Mexico," at <http://www.sportsbusinessnews.com> cited 9 October 2003. Besides China and Mexico, the NBA has established grassroots basketball events and social programs in some African nations. Indeed, team coaches and players operate camps and clinics, organize games and lecture African children about healthcare issues to prevent the spread of short- and long-term communicable diseases and illnesses. The NBA in Africa is discussed in Ashley McGeachy Fox, "NBA Continues to Expand Horizons," at <http://www.sportsbusinessnews.com> cited 9 October 2003; Alexander Wolff, "International Hoops," *The New York Times* (31 May 2002), A23; "NBA Players Unite For Africa 100 Camp," at <http://www.nba.com> cited 15 August 2003.

20.   Before the WNBA considers placing a team in Canada or Mexico, or in a European city, the league must increase its popularity abroad. Because of the international television

broadcasts of WNBA games and playoffs, teams' employment of foreign players, and Americans who play on national basketball clubs in Europe and elsewhere, the WNBA has gradually received more attention in the media across the globe. The WNBA's operation and exposure is discussed in "WNBA Players From Around the World: 2003 Season," at <http://www.wnba.com> cited 21 October 2003; "2003 WNBA Season to be Broadcast in 183 Countries," at <http://www.wnba.com> cited 21 October 2003; Lorraine A. Woellert, "For the WNBA, It's No Easy Layup," *Business Week* (1 May 2000), 102, 106; Chris Isidore, "WNBA: Lovable Money Loser," at <http://www.si.com> cited 17 August 2001; Frank P. Jozsa, Jr. and John J. Guthrie, Jr., *Relocating Teams and Expanding League in Professional Sports*, 11, 158–162; Frank P. Jozsa, Jr., *American Sports Empire*, 18, 128.

21. With respect to *Sports Capitalism*, several books discuss amateur and professional ice hockey leagues and various aspects about the sport's origin and development during the 20th century. For example, see Andrew Podnieks and Sheila Wawanash, *Kings of the Ice: A History of World Hockey* (Richmond Hill, Ontario, Canada: NDE Publishers, 2002); M.R. Carrroll, Andrew Podnieks, and Michael Harling, *The Concise Encyclopedia of Hockey* (Vancouver, Canada: Greystone Books, 2001); Ken Dryden, *The Game* (New York, N.Y.: John Wiley & Sons, Inc., 2003); Patrick Houda and Joe Pelletier, *The World Cup of Hockey* (Toronto, Canada: Warwick Publishing Inc., 2002); Jeff Z. Klein and Karl-Eric Reif, *The Death of Hockey* (Toronto, Canada: Macmillan Canada, 1998); Frank P. Jozsa, Jr., *American Sports Empire*, 26–30.

22. The NHLI is involved with the global exposure, marketing and operation of the league. As such, business relationships have been established with television networks and other communication companies to broadcast the NHL's games and programs beyond North America. For the readers of *Sports Capitalism*, and especially for ice hockey fans who are interested in how the league markets itself overseas, see "NHL International," at <http://www.nhl.com> cited 8 March 2003; "NHL Selects GlobeCast to Offer Hockey in Europe," *Communications Today* (25 October 2002), 1; "Sun Microsystems, NHL Form Strategic Relationship," *Presswire* (24 January 2002), 1; Hilary Cassidy, "Power Play: NHL Nets Broadcast Partners For Overseas Promos," *Brandweek* (11 December 2000), 9; Rich Thomaselli, "NHL Markets Web Site, *Advertising Age* (20 August 2001), 14; Michael Russo, "NHL Offers International Flair," Broadcasts Game in Russia," at <http://www.sportsbusinessnews.com> cited 6 November 2003.

23. During the 1900s, the nationalities and types of players in the NHL gradually changed as proportionately more European and Russian athletes joined teams and scored goals in the regular season games, playoffs and Stanley Cups. Although NHL teams primarily consist of Canadians players, foreign nations in Western Europe have development systems and youth ice hockey leagues that produce world-class players who are prepared to compete for NHL teams. Relative to *Sports* Capitalism, there are interesting features about international ice hockey players contained in Elliott Teaford and Jim Hodges, "Sports Extra/NHL Preview," *The Los Angeles Times* (30 September 1999), 1; Terry Frei, "NHL and NBA Choosing Different Marketing Strategies," at <http://www.sportsbusinessnews.com> cited 13 November 2003; "Alien Invaders Altering Look of the NBA," *Toronto Star* (17 October 2000), 6; Larry Wigge, "Global Ice Rink," *The Sporting News* (14 February 2000), 42; Idem., "A World of Difference," *The Sporting News* (21 February 1994), 48–49. For the profiles of players who are on the rosters of specific teams such as the Montreal Canadiens and Vancouver Canucks, see "Roster," at <http://www.canadiens.com> cited 2 December 2003, and "Roster: Player Bios," at <http://www.canucks.com> cited 2 December 2003. Furthermore, the rosters of NHL players are reported at two web sites, that is, <http://www.nhl.com> and <http://sports.espn.go.com>.

24.   Before there is more interaction and business between the NHL and international ice hockey federations, leagues and players, the conflicts that exist between the NHL and those groups regarding buyouts, contracts, transfer fees and collective bargaining issues must be discussed and resolved. Otherwise, the free movement of players among countries will be blocked, in part, because of differences in nations' labor laws and rules. Various aspects of those problems are highlighted in Barry M. Bloom, "The NHL and the World Hockey Federation Make Friends," at <http://www.sportsbusinessnews.com> cited 3 December 2002; "International Hockey Leader Upset With the NHL," at <http://www.sportsbusiness-news.com> cited 3 December 2002; Chris Foster, "Is the Russian Ice Hockey Federation Withholding Players From the NHL?" at <http://www.sportsbusinessnews.com> cited 3 December 2002; Karo Yorio, "Russia, Defections, the NHL and Money," at <http://www. sportsbusinessnews.com> cited 15 December 2003; Matthew Fisher, "European Hockey Official Look to Squeeze NHL For More Money," at <http://www.sportsbusinessnews. com> cited 13 February 2003.

25.   Besides the NHL, Chapter 4 in *Sports Capitalism* analyzed other professional ice hockey businesses such as the FHL, WHA and IHL. Those leagues were studied because of their unique organizations, operations and teams' sites in Canada or the U.S. If the NHL declines in power and prestige during the early 2000s because of management and union issues, then another ice hockey league might emerge to compete with the NHL in the North American market. Some information about the three alternative leagues is presented in "New Canadian Pro Hockey League," at <http://www.federalhockeyleague.ca> cited 12 November 2003; "A New Hockey League in Canada," at <http://www.sportsbusinessnews.com> cited 19 August 2003; "World Hockey Association," at <http://www.worldhockeyassociation.net> cited 25 November 2003; Rod Beaton, "The New WHA Could Capitalize on NHL Labor Woes," at <http://www.worldhockeyassociation.net> cited 25 November 2003; "A Look Back at the International Hockey League," at <http://www.sportsbusinessnews.com> cited 3 December 2002; "International Hockey League to Cease Operations," at <http://www.allsports.com> cited 25 November 2003.

26.   The World Cup of Hockey is a well-regarded international tournament that involves competition between the national teams from various nations. Although the Stanley Cup is an annual event, there are foreign players on NHL teams who, if qualified, have represented their respective countries in World Cup tournaments. To read about the significance and interest in the World Cup, see "World Cup of Hockey Information," at <http://sportsillus-trated.cnn.com> cited 30 January 2004; "World Cup of Hockey to Return," at <http://www. upi.com> cited 26 November 2003; "Details Revealed For 2004 World Cup of Hockey," *Europe Intelligence Wire* (3 April 2003), 1; Terry Jones, "World Cup of Hockey to Return in 2004," at <http://www.sportsbusinessnews.com> cited 25 November 2002.

27.   For *Sports Capitalism*, the three books that were primarily researched on soccer and/or MLS included Kyle Rote, Jr., *Kyle Root, Jr.'s Complete Book of Soccer* (New York, N.Y.: Simon and Schuster, 1978); Roger Allaway, Colin Jose, and David Litterer, *The Encyclopedia of American Soccer History* (Lanham, MD: Scarecrow Press Inc., 2001); Dan Woog, *The Ultimate Soccer Encyclopedia* (Chicago, IL: Lowell House, 1999). The operations of three former U.S.-based professional soccer leagues are reported in "National Professional Soccer League," at <http://www.hickoksports.com> cited 3 December 2003; "United Soccer Association," <http://www.hickoksports.com> cited 3 December 2003; "North American Soccer League," at <http://www.hickoksports.com> cited 3 December 2003.

28.   As discussed in Chapter 5, there appears to be growing support for professional men's soccer teams from fans, cities and investors in America. Since the sport and MLS are expected to attract a larger fan base and market during the early 2000s, the financial condition of the league will likely improve and thereby provide the funds to promote MLS

in European and Latin American nations. Indeed, several articles reflect the anticipated success about the future business of MLS in North America and elsewhere. For example, see "MLS Set to Expand Their Horizons," at <http://www.sportsbusinessnews.com> cited 25 November 2002; Eric Fisher, "MLS Finding New Investors," at <http://www.sportsbusinessnews.com> cited 4 December 2003; Matthew Futterman, "Ever the Optimist, MLS Commissioner Don Garber is a True Believer," at <http://www.sportsbusinessnews.com> cited 6 November 2003; Pete Grathoff, "MLS Looking For Investors and Interested Cities," at <http://www.sportsbusinessnews.com> cited 30 January 2004; Jack McCarthy, "MLS Now Looking to Expansion," at <http://www.sportsbusinessnews.com> cited 3 April 2003; Jere Longman, "Painstaking Progress Finally Pays Off For the US," *The New York Times* (25 June 2002), D3; Jeff Rusnak, "Soccer Finding Larger TV Audience," at <http://www.sportsbusinessnews.com> cited 1 December 2003.

29.   For MLS to prosper globally, more television exposure and publicity from the local media are vital, especially in those nations where soccer is a national pastime. Because the league realizes the importance of communicating with its fans, new alliances have been established with cable networks, and corporate partners and sponsors. To illustrate those business relationships, see Simon Applebaum, "America's All-Soccer Network Ready to Take Its Shot," at <http://www.sportsbusinessnews.com> cited 20 February 2003; "MSN Signs Agreement With Fox Sports International," at <http://www.sportsbusinessnews.com> cited 3 April 2003; "MLS Signs a Spanish Sponsorship Agreement With Yahoo," at <http://www.sportsbusinessnews.com> cited 19 August 2003.

30.   In his first professional game with D.C. United during March of 2004, 14 year old Freddy Adu scored a goal in eleven minutes. For when, why and how Adu joined a team in MLS, read "All Eyes on Adu," at <http://cnnsi.com> cited 13 August 2003; "Teen Star Adu Signs With MLS," *The Charlotte Observer* (19 November 2003), 2C; Jason La Canfora, "Looking at Why Freddy Adu Didn't Consider European Football (Soccer) Teams," at <http://www.sportsbusinessnews.com> cited 20 November 2003; Brett Honeycutt, "Soccer's Superteen Selected 1st in Draft," *The Charlotte Observer* (17 January 2004), 3C; Ives Galarcep, "Best Place For Adu to Land is MLS," at <http://www.northjersey.com> cited 28 August 2003.

31.   As depicted in *Sports Capitalism*, historically European soccer federations, leagues, teams and players have been important with respect to the international development and growth of professional soccer as a sport and business. In the future, MLS will interact more frequently with European soccer officials and organizations to schedule exhibition games, programs and tournaments, and to compete for and sign the world's best players. Those activities are indicated in Jack Bell, "European Football (Soccer) Clubs Look For Talent in the Good Old USA," at <http://www.sportsbusinessnews.com> cited 19 August 2003; Brian Trusdell, "European, South American Soccer Franchises Casting an Eye Towards America," at <http://www.sportsbusinessnews.com> cited 25 November 2002; Alex Yannis, Metro-Stars Seek a Foreign Influence," *The New York Times* (12 June 1999), 5. Furthermore, great European teams such as Manchester United and Real Madrid will gradually become more respected by American soccer fans as the sport achieves a larger market share in North America relative to baseball, football, basketball and ice hockey. For some facts and insights about the fame, fortune and power of Manchester United, see Conrad De Aenlle, "ManU Making Shareholders Cheer," at <http://www.sportsbusinessnews.com> cited 2 September 2003; "ManU's Big Sponsorship Deal of the Day," at <http://www.sportsbusinessnews.com> cited 11 December 2003; Lachian Colquhoun, "The Ever-Growing Marketing World For Man U," at <http://www.sportsbusinessnews.com> cited 20 November 2003; John Brennan, "ManU's Marketing Arm Continues Its Reach," at <http://www.sportsbusinessnews.

com> cited 5 August 2003; "Charm Offensive," at <http://www.cnnsi.com> cited 13 August 2003.

32.   Soccer analysts and officials have different views about why the WUSA failed as a league during 2003. Those reasons are given in Scott French, "Beginning or End—What Went Wrong in WUSA?" at <http://si.com> cited 23 October 2003; Johnette Howard, "Death of WUSA—Lack of Any Real TV Deal," at <http://www.sportsbusinessnews.com> cited 16 October 2003; George Vecsey, "Economically the WUSA Had to Die," at <http://www.sportsbusinessnews.com> cited 16 September 2003; Brian Straus, "The WUSA and Its Imminent Demise," at <http://www.sportsbusinessnews.com> cited 26 August 2003; Allen Barra, "A Strategic Error Doomed the WUSA to Defeat," *Wall Street Journal* (23 September 2003), D9.

33.   On 31 March 2004, the author of *Sports, Inc.: 100 Years of Sports Business* (Amherst, N.Y.: Prometheus Books, 2004) mailed me his rankings of the most successful global American sports leagues to be the NBA, and then MLB, NHL, NFL and MLS. According to author Phil Schaaf, the NBA ranks first because the league's teams include many European players, and due to the presence of China's Yao Ming on the Houston Rockets, interest of sports fans in remote countries who watch professional basketball games and shows on television, and the passion for basketball by the people in such nations as Brazil and Tunisia. MLB ranked second since foreign players are a moderately high proportion of teams' rosters. In Schaaf's view, "Between the Latin Americans and Asians, and the excellent things they [MLB] are doing on the web, look to baseball as having exceptional growth in foreign markets . . . they will have a tough time in Europe, but they will do well in 3 other very important continents." After the NBA and MLB, Schaaf ranked the NHL third. That is, the league's teams include many European players and the sport is popular throughout Europe but not in nations as the equator is approached. Even though fans in many cities and metropolitan areas of the U.S. support the games of NHL teams, ice hockey has not established a large fan base in America as a national sport. The NFL, meanwhile, struggles globally since the game is not familiar to people outside of North America. Furthermore, the NFLE is unstable and football players have difficulty getting visibility in Europe as Wayne Gretzky did in the U.S. during the early 1980s. As Schaaf states about the league, "I just don't see how the NFL can create a legitimate, profitable toe-hold in the next 10–15 years [in Europe]. If they keep the league over there, it might catch on by 2020, but it will be hard pressed to do it without tremendous resources." Besides those observations, Schaaf thinks that the NFL will have a tough time to penetrate foreign markets and generate revenue potential because there are not many Asians, Latinos and Europeans who play professional football. Yet, if the NFL teams decide to use more foreign athletes and the NFLE becomes popular in European nations, the league will then create a larger fan base and its profits from ancillary markets will increase. This scenario, however, may take another 10–20 years of development, dedication and purpose. Finally, Schaaf ranked MLS below the other four U.S.-based leagues because of its brief existence [founded in 1996] and inferior quality. Although soccer is the top sport in the world, MLS is not considered to be a legitimate league by the truest of soccer fans. But, MLS's recognition and success may change in the next 25 years if its players emerge as great athletes from a competitive perspective. In sum, Schaaf comments about the leagues' rankings that, "I don't have the financials handy, but in pondering the issue, think about the above brands' abilities to access a variety of markets with effective promotion (meaning: results). I think if you approach the question with that in mind, you will arrive at the same conclusion." For another expert's opinion about which of America's professional sports leagues were the most and least internationalized, Mount Union College's professor of sport management and the author of *Sport Governance in the*

Global Community James E. Thoma wrote in an email that, "I would place the NBA as number 1. Although baseball has been international and many MLB players are from outside the U.S.A., the NBA has been global longer and to a greater extent. Now [NBA Commissioner] David Stern has committed to having four teams in Europe by 2010, if the arenas are built." With respect to their worldwide exposure and market penetration as sports leagues, after the NBA Thoma ranked MLB, and then the NFL, NHL and MLS.

34.   Besides the focus on international business and global strategies, there have been an impressive number of articles published about various social aspects of professional sports and globalization from diverse theoretical and disciplinary perspectives. For example, in the Selected Bibliography of *Sports Capitalism* see C. Roger Rees, "Race and Sport in Global Perspective," *Journal of Sport and Social Issues*, Vol. 20, No. 1 (1996), 22–32; Toby Miller, "How Founding the United Nations Professionalized Sport," *Journal of Sport and Social Issues*, Vol. 22, No. 2 (1998), 123–126; Deborah Stevenson, "Women, Sport, and Globalization: Competing Discourses of Sexuality and Nation," *Journal of Sport and Social Issues*, Vol. 26, No. 2 (2002), 209–225; Peter Donnelly, "The Local and the Global: Globalization in the Sociology of Sport," *Journal of Sport and Social Issues*, Vol. 20, No. 3 (1996), 239–257; Jean Harvey, Genevieve Rail, and Lucie Thibault, "Globalization and Sport: Sketching a Theoretical Model For Empirical Analyses," *Journal of Sport and Social Issues*, Vol. 20, No. 3 (1996), 258–277; Robert V. Bellamy, Jr., "Issues in the Internationalization of the U.S. Sports Media: The Emerging European Marketplace," *Journal of Sport and Social Issues*, Vol. 17, No. 3 (1993), 168–180. For books that discuss and reveal sports and/or sports organizations from a global perspective, see Douglas M. Turco, *The Wide World of Sport Programming* (Champaign, IL: Stipes Publishing L.L.C., 1996); Carlos Pestana Barros, Muradali Ibrahimo, and Stefan Szymanski, *Transatlantic Sport: The Comparative Economics of North American and European Sports* (Cheltenham, UK: Edward Elgar Publishing Limited, 2002); James E. Thoma and Laurence Chalip, *Sport Governance in the Global Community* (Morgantown, WV: Fitness Information Technology, Inc., 1996; Trevor Slack, *Understanding Sport Organizations* (Champaign, IL: Human Kinetics, 1997).

Appendix

Table A.1 Distribution of MLB Team Rosters, by Nationality of Players, March 2004

Team	American	Latin American	Other
Anaheim Angels	24	10	1
Arizona Diamondbacks	20	8	1
Atlanta Braves	23	6	1
Baltimore Orioles	17	12	3
Boston Red Sox	29	6	1
Chicago Cubs	25	6	1
Chicago White Sox	20	10	1
Cincinnati Reds	23	6	1
Cleveland Indians	27	6	0
Colorado Rockies	22	4	3
Detroit Tigers	24	9	0
Florida Marlins	17	9	2
Houston Astros	25	6	0
Kansas City Royals	27	6	2
Los Angeles Dodgers	15	10	6
Milwaukee Brewers	26	3	0
Minnesota Twins	19	8	5
Montreal Expos	19	10	3
New York Mets	27	5	2
New York Yankees	17	10	2
Oakland Athletics	29	4	1
Philadelphia Phillies	23	9	1
Pittsburgh Pirates	22	7	1
San Diego Padres	26	5	1
San Francisco Giants	29	7	0
Seattle Mariners	23	6	2
St. Louis Cardinals	26	5	1
Tampa Bay Devil Rays	23	8	1
Texas Rangers	24	8	2
Toronto Blue Jays	29	5	0

Notes: The Other column includes non-U.S. and non-Latin American players.

Source: "MLB Team Rosters," at <http://sports.espn.go.com> cited 16 March 2004.

Sports Capitalism

Table A.2 Distribution of Non-U.S. MLB Players, by Team and Position, March 2004

Team	Catcher	Infielder	Outfielder	Pitcher
Anaheim Angels	3	1	2	5
Arizona Diamondbacks	0	3	2	4
Atlanta Braves	1	2	2	2
Baltimore Orioles	2	3	3	7
Boston Red Sox	0	0	2	5
Chicago Cubs	0	1	2	4
Chicago White Sox	3	2	3	3
Cincinnati Reds	0	4	1	2
Cleveland Indians	1	2	1	2
Colorado Rockies	0	3	2	2
Detroit Tigers	1	3	1	4
Florida Marlins	1	5	2	3
Houston Astros	1	1	2	2
Kansas City Royals	1	1	4	2
Los Angeles Dodgers	0	4	4	8
Milwaukee Brewers	0	0	0	3
Minnesota Twins	1	3	1	8
Montreal Expos	0	4	2	7
New York Mets	0	2	3	2
New York Yankees	1	2	3	6
Oakland Athletics	0	2	1	2
Philadelphia Phillies	0	3	2	5
Pittsburgh Pirates	1	3	2	2
San Diego Padres	2	1	0	3
San Francisco Giants	2	3	1	1
Seattle Mariners	0	2	1	5
St. Louis Cardinals	0	1	2	3
Tampa Bay Devil Rays	0	2	1	6
Texas Rangers	1	1	1	7
Toronto Blue Jays	1	1	0	3

Notes: To start a game, each team must use one catcher, four infielders, three outfielders and one pitcher.

Source: "MLB Team Rosters," at <http://sports.espn.go.com> cited 16 March 2004.

Table A.3 NFLE International Players, by Team, March 2004

Team	Players	Country
Amsterdam Admirals	11	Austria/France/Japan(4)/Mexico(3)/ Netherlands(2)
Berlin Thunder	11	Denmark/England/Finland(2)/ France(2)/Germany(3)/Mexico/ Switzerland
Cologne Centurions	11	France/Germany(3)/Japan(5)/ Mexico/Sweden
Frankfurt Galaxy	10	France/Germany(6)/Mexico(2)/ Turkey
Rhein Fire	10	Austria/France(2)/Germany(6)/ Switzerland
Scottish Claymores	11	England(5)/France/Scotland(3)/ Sweden(2)

Notes: On each team roster, there is listed an international player's number, name, position, height, weight, college and how acquired, which is designated as national/country. There are approximately 60–65 total players on each of the rosters.

Source: "NFL Europe Team Rosters," <http://www.nfleurope.com> cited 23 March 2004.

Table A.4 NFL International Players, Totals Ranked by Team, March 2002

Team	Number of Players	Country
Jacksonville Jaguars	7	Barbados/Canada (3)/ Germany (2)/VI
Minnesota Vikings	7	Canada/Jamaica/NZ (2)/ Nigeria/SA/Uganda
San Diego Chargers	5	Australia/Canada (2)/ Jamaica/Zaire
Buffalo Bills	3	Canada/Norway/Philippines
Carolina Panthers	3	AS/Canada/Zaire
New York Giants	3	Canada (3)
Oakland Raiders	3	AS/Iran/Poland
Philadelphia Eagles	3	Germany (3)
San Francisco 49ers	3	El Salvador/Guyana/Nigeria
Arizona Cardinals	2	Argentina/Sierra Leone
Chicago Bears	2	Germany/Russia
Cincinnati Bengals	2	Japan/Mexico
Dallas Cowboys	2	Ghana/Germany
Denver Broncos	2	Germany/Holland
Indianapolis Colts	2	Canada/SA
Pittsburgh Steelers	2	Canada/Ivory Coast
Seattle Seahawks	2	Canada/Jamaica
St. Louis Rams	2	Jamaica/Mexico
Tennessee Titans	2	AS/Germany
Atlanta Falcons	1	Jamaica
Cleveland Browns	1	Cameroon
Green Bay Packers	1	Liberia
Kansas City Chiefs	1	Zaire
Miami Dolphins	1	Jamaica
New England Patriots	1	Uganda
New Orleans Saints	1	Jamaica
New York Jets	1	Germany
Tampa Bay Buccaneers	1	Argentina

Notes: VI is Virgin Islands, NZ New Zealand, SA South Africa and AS American Samoa. In March of 2002, there were no international players on the rosters of the Baltimore Ravens, Detroit Lions, Houston Texans and Washington Redskins.

Source: "Foreign-Born Players in the NFL," at <http://www.nfl.com> cited 9 March 2004.

Table A.5 NBA International Players, Totals Ranked by Team, March 2004

Team	Number of Players	Countries
San Antonio Spurs	6	Argentina/Brazil/France/ Slovenia/Turkey/VI
Utah Jazz	6	Croatia/Puerto Rico/Russia/ S-M/Spain/VI
Dallas Mavericks	5	Canada/France/Mexico/ Germany/Iceland
Cleveland Cavaliers	3	Cameroon/Lithuania/Senegal
Los Angeles Clippers	3	Nigeria/S-M (2)
Phoenix Suns	3	Brazil/Poland/S-M
Toronto Raptors	3	Belize/France/Scotland
Atlanta Hawks	2	Senegal/S-M
Denver Nuggets	2	Brazil/Georgia
Golden State Warriors	2	France/Grenadines
Houston Rockets	2	China/Slovenia
Los Angeles Lakers	2	Canada/Ukraine
Memphis Grizzlies	2	Greece/Spain
Miami Heat	2	China/Georgia
Milwaukee Bucks	2	Croatia/Netherlands
New York Knicks	2	Congo/Poland
Philadelphia 76ers	2	Canada/Haiti
Sacramento Kings	2	S-M (2)
Seattle Supersonics	2	S-M/Ukraine
Boston Celtics	1	Czech Republic
Detroit Pistons	1	Turkey
Indiana Pacers	1	Slovenia
Minnesota Timberwolves	1	Slovenia
New Jersey Nets	1	Bosnia-Herzegovina
New Orleans Hornets	1	Canada
Orlando Magic	1	Georgia
Portland Trailblazers	1	Georgia

Notes: The (2) indicates two players on the team. S-M is Serbia-Montenegro and VI is the Virgin Islands. Although there is an NBA franchise in Toronto, Canadian-born players are considered to be International in Table A.5. On 8 March of 2004, there were no international players on the rosters of the Chicago Bulls and Washington Wizards.

Source: "International Players in the NBA," at <http://www.nba.com> cited 8 March 2004.

Table A.6 NBA International Players, Team Totals by Position, March 2004

Team	Center	Forward	Guard
San Antonio Spurs	2	1	3
Utah Jazz	0	4	2
Dallas Mavericks	2	1	2
Cleveland Cavaliers	2	1	0
Los Angeles Clippers	2	0	1
Phoenix Suns	0	2	1
Toronto Raptors	0	2	1
Atlanta Hawks	2	0	0
Denver Nuggets	0	2	0
Golden State Warriors	1	0	1
Houston Rockets	1	1	0
Los Angeles Lakers	0	2	0
Memphis Grizzlies	1	1	0
Miami Heat	2	0	0
Milwaukee Bucks	1	1	0
New York Knicks	2	0	0
Philadelphia 76ers	2	0	0
Sacramento Kings	1	1	0
Seattle Supersonics	1	1	0
Boston Celtics	0	1	0
Detroit Pistons	1	0	0
Indiana Pacers	0	1	0
Minnesota Timberwolves	1	0	0
New Jersey Nets	0	0	1
New Orleans Hornets	1	0	0
Orlando Magic	0	1	0
Portland Trailblazers	1	0	0

Notes: A starting basketball team consists of one center, two forwards and two guards. Most teams' rosters listed approximately 12 players. Those players listed on rosters with two pos- itions such as Center-Forward, were reported in Table A.6 by the first position. On 8 March 2004, there were no international players on the rosters of the Chicago Bulls and Washing- ton Wizards.

Source: "International Players in the NBA," at <http://www.nba.com> cited 8 March 2004.

Table A.7 Distribution of NHL Team Rosters, by Nationality of Players, March 2004

Team	American	Canadian	European	Russian	Other
Anaheim Mighty Ducks	1	11	9	2	0
Atlanta Thrashers	3	15	10	2	0
Boston Bruins	7	15	4	2	0
Buffalo Sabres	6	12	7	2	0
Calgary Flames	2	19	6	1	1
Carolina Hurricanes	5	10	6	0	1
Chicago Blackhawks	4	13	1	2	0
Colorado Avalanche	6	9	6	2	0
Columbus Blue Jackets	4	16	5	1	0
Dallas Stars	3	16	3	1	0
Detroit Red Wings	4	12	8	1	0
Edmonton Oilers	3	15	4	2	0
Florida Panthers	1	13	9	0	0
Los Angeles Kings	5	15	9	1	0
Minnesota Wild	1	15	4	1	1
Montreal Canadiens	3	18	2	2	0
Nashville Predators	5	12	9	1	0
New Jersey Devils	9	10	3	3	0
New York Islanders	5	9	8	2	0
New York Rangers	6	15	5	3	0
Ottawa Senators	3	15	8	1	0
Philadelphia Flyers	5	10	8	3	0
Phoenix Coyotes	7	11	3	2	0
Pittsburgh Penguins	5	14	7	1	0
San Jose Sharks	4	14	4	1	1
St. Louis Blues	4	18	5	1	0
Tampa Bay Lightning	3	14	4	2	0
Toronto Maple Leafs	3	12	8	1	1
Vancouver Canucks	0	15	10	2	0
Washington Capitals	7	11	3	1	0

Notes: The Other column includes players from such nations as Brazil, Brunei, Kazakhstan, and South Korea. During early March of 2004, the rosters ranged from 20 for the Chicago Blackhawks to 30 for the Atlanta Thrashers and Los Angeles Kings.

Source: The rosters of each team are posted at <http://www.nhl.com>.

Table A.8 Distribution of Non-North American NHL Players, by Team and Position, March 2004

Team	Center	Defenseman	Goaltender	Wing
Anaheim Mighty Ducks	3	5	1	2
Atlanta Thrashers	1	4	3	4
Boston Bruins	1	2	0	3
Buffalo Sabres	0	3	1	5
Calgary Flames	0	2	2	4
Carolina Hurricanes	1	1	1	4
Chicago Blackhawks	2	0	0	1
Colorado Avalanche	2	2	2	2
Columbus Blue Jackets	1	3	0	2
Dallas Stars	1	2	0	1
Detroit Red Wings	2	3	1	3
Edmonton Oilers	0	2	1	3
Florida Panthers	2	3	0	4
Los Angeles Kings	2	3	2	3
Minnesota Wild	1	2	0	3
Montreal Canadiens	1	1	0	2
Nashville Predators	2	4	1	3
New Jersey Devils	5	1	0	0
New York Islanders	1	6	0	3
New York Rangers	1	4	0	3
Ottawa Senators	1	2	1	5
Philadelphia Flyers	2	6	0	3
Phoenix Coyotes	0	1	0	4
Pittsburgh Penguins	1	4	0	3
San Jose Sharks	0	1	2	3
St. Louis Blues	2	2	1	1
Tampa Bay Lightning	1	1	1	3
Toronto Maple Leafs	3	3	0	4
Vancouver Canucks	4	3	1	4
Washington Capitals	0	1	1	2

Notes: Table A.6 excludes NHL players born in America and Canada.

Source: The rosters of each team are posted at <http://www.nhl.com>.

Table A.9 MLS International Players, Totals Ranked by Team, March 2004

Team	Number of Players	Country
Los Angeles Galaxy	11	Caicos/Columbia/Guatemala/ Honduras/Jamaica/Mexico(3) NZ/South Korea/Venezuela
Dallas Burn	9	Columbia/El Salvador/Germany/ Jamaica/Liberia/Ireland/ Northern Ireland/South Africa/ Uganda
Colorado Rapids	8	Argentina/Canada/England/ France/Jamaica/Liberia/Mexico/ Scotland
New England Revolution	8	Argentina/Columbia/Grenada/ Jamaica(2)/Mali(2)/Uruguay
Columbus Crew	7	Brazil/Costa Rica/Ecuador/ England/Guatemala/Jamaica/NZ
D.C. United	7	Brazil/Bolivia/El Salvador/Mali/ Netherlands/NZ/Ukraine
MetroStars	6	Angola/Argentina (2)/Bolivia/ Ghana/Honduras/
Kansas City Wizards	5	Columbia/England/Romania/ Russia/Yugoslavia
San Jose Earthquakes	5	Brazil/Canada (2)/Denmark/ Switzerland
Chicago Fire	4	Botswana/Canada/Jamaica/ South Korea

Notes: The (2) and (3) indicate two and three players from those nations on the team. NZ is New Zealand. The teams' active rosters varied from 20 for the New England Revolution to 29 each for the Columbus Crew Crew, Los Angeles Galaxy and San Jose Earthquakes.

Source: "Major League Soccer Teams," at <http://www.mlsnet.com> cited 9 March 2004.

Table A.10 Distribution of MLS International Players, by Team and Position, March 2004

Team	Defender	Forward	Goalkeeper	Midfielder
Chicago Fire	0	2	1	1
Colorado Rapids	2	2	0	4
Columbus Crew	2	1	0	4
Dallas Burn	4	2	0	3
D.C. United	1	3	1	2
Kansas City Wizards	1	1	0	3
Los Angeles Galaxy	2	4	0	5
MetroStars	3	0	0	3
New England Revolution	2	2	0	4
San Jose Earthquakes	1	2	1	1

Notes: Because of injuries and trades, the rosters and numbers of international players per team generally change during a season.

Source: "Major League Soccer Teams," at <http://www.mlsnet.com> cited 9 March 2004.

Table A.11 Distribution of Major League Sports Teams in North American Metropolitan Areas, Ranked by Population, March 2004

Area	MAPOP	MLB	NFL	NBA	NHL	MLS
America						
New York-New Jersey	21.2	2	2	2	3	1
Los Angeles-Anaheim	16.3	2	0	2	2	1
Chicago	9.2	2	1	1	1	1
Washington-Baltimore	7.6	1	2	1	1	1
San Francisco-Oakland	7.0	2	2	1	1	1
Philadelphia	6.2	1	1	1	1	0
Boston	5.8	1	1	1	1	1
Detroit	5.5	1	1	1	1	0
Dallas-Fort Worth	5.2	1	1	1	1	1
Houston-Galveston	4.7	1	1	1	0	0
Atlanta	4.1	1	1	1	1	0
Miami	3.9	1	1	1	1	0
Seattle-Tacoma	3.6	1	1	1	0	0
Phoenix	3.3	1	1	1	1	0
Minneapolis-St. Paul	3.0	1	1	1	1	0
Cleveland	2.9	1	1	1	0	0
San Diego	2.8	1	1	0	0	0
St. Louis	2.6	1	1	0	1	0
Denver-Boulder	2.5	1	1	1	1	1
Tampa Bay-St. Petersburg	2.4	1	1	0	1	0
Pittsburgh	2.3	1	1	0	1	0
Portland	2.2	0	0	1	0	0
Cincinnati	2.1	1	1	0	0	0
Kansas City	1.9	1	1	0	0	1
Sacramento	1.8	0	0	1	0	0
Milwaukee	1.7	1	0	1	0	0
Orlando	1.7	0	0	1	0	0
Indianapolis	1.6	0	1	1	0	0
San Antonio	1.6	0	0	1	0	0
Columbus	1.5	0	0	0	1	1
Charlotte	1.5	0	1	0	0	0
New Orleans	1.4	0	1	1	0	0
Salt Lake City	1.3	0	0	1	0	0
Nashville	1.2	0	1	0	1	0
Raleigh-Durham	1.2	0	0	0	1	0
Buffalo	1.2	0	1	0	1	0
Memphis	1.1	0	0	1	0	0

Table A.11 Continued

Area	MAPOP	MLB	NFL	NBA	NHL	MLS
Jacksonville	1.1	0	1	0	0	0
Green Bay	.3	0	1	0	0	0
Canada						
Toronto	6.7	1	0	1	1	0
Montreal	3.6	1	0	0	1	0
Vancouver	2.0	0	0	0	1	0
Calgary	1.0	0	0	0	1	0
Edmonton	.9	0	0	0	1	0
Ottawa	.9	0	0	0	1	0

Notes: Area is the metropolitan area. MAPOP is the total population in the metropolitan area in millions. Due to rounding, some areas tied in population but were ranked as obtained from the sources. There are 30 MLB, 32 NFL, 29 NBA, 30 NHL and ten MLS teams listed in Table A.11.

Source: "Ranking Tables For Metropolitan Areas," at <http://www.census.gov> cited 30 March 2004, and "List of Metropolitan Areas by Population," <http://en.wikipedia.org> cited 30 March 2004.

Table A.12 Selected International Sports Cities, Ranked by Metropolitan Area Population, March 2004

Country	City	MAPOP
Japan	Tokyo	33.7
Mexico	Mexico City	21.8
Korea	Seoul	21.7
Brazil	Sao Paulo	20.2
Russia	Moscow	15.3
China	Shanghai	12.5
England	London	11.9
China	Beijing	9.9
France	Paris	9.8
China	Tianjin	5.5
Spain	Madrid	5.2
China	Guangdong	4.8
Venezuela	Caracas	4.5
Australia	Sydney	4.2
Germany	Berlin	4.2
Spain	Barcelona	3.8
Mexico	Monterrey	3.8
Italy	Rome	3.3
Israel	Tel Aviv	3.0
Dominican Republic	Santo Domingo	2.8
Germany	Hamburg	2.6
Cuba	Havana	2.7
Puerto Rico	San Juan	2.4
Netherlands	Amsterdam	2.1
Germany	Frankfurt	2.0
Germany	Cologne	1.9
Germany	Munich	1.9
Czech Republic	Prague	1.4
Germany	Düsseldorf	1.4
Mexico	Tijuana	1.3
Ireland	Dublin	1.1
Sweden	Goteborg	.8
Scotland	Edinburgh	.5

Notes: The 33 cities were mentioned in the Introduction or in one or more chapters of *Sports Capitalism*. Country and City are self-explanatory. MAPOP is the metropolitan area popul- ation in millions with respect to the City.

Source: "List of Metropolitan Areas by Population," at <http://en.wikipedia.org> cited 30 March 2004, and "City and Area Population," at <http://www.world-gazetteer.com> cited 30 March 2004.

Glossary

accounting profit The total amount of money received by a business from sales less the dollar cost of producing goods and/or services.

All-American The men and women intercollegiate players who, because of their outstanding abilities and performances, have been selected to be members of the top team in a sport for the year.

All-star game This game features the best college or professional players who were voted by fans to represent their clubs at the various team positions.

American Basketball Association Formed in 1967, this U.S.-based professional basketball league survived until 1976, when four of its teams entered the NBA. A new version of this association was organized in America with seven teams during 2003.

American Football League This U.S.-based professional football organization existed between 1960 and 1969. Because of economic reasons, in 1970 the league merged with the NFL and several of its teams joined the American Football Conference of the NFL.

American Hockey League (AHL) Established in 1936 with eight teams, this U.S.-based minor league has been one of the prime feeder systems for the NHL through direct affiliation with the NHL teams.

American West Hockey League Founded in 1992 as the American Frontier Hockey League, this group is a junior A ice hockey league that competes for the Gold Cup championship.

antitrust legislation U.S. federal government laws that aim to preserve free and unfettered competition in the product and resource markets.

arbitration The hearing and determining of a dispute between parties, such as a team representative and player agent, by a person or persons chosen and accepted by the parties.

Arena Football League An American indoor professional football league that serves as a feeder system for the NFL and NFLE.

bankruptcy A legal mechanism that allows creditors to assume control when the decline in a firm's assets triggers a default. It is a result, and not the cause, of a decline in a firm's value.

barriers to entry The demographic, economic, political and social factors that make it difficult or costly for professional sports leagues and franchises to enter a foreign market.

baseball academies These consist of rookie and minor league training facilities and summer league camps, clinics and programs that are operated by MLB teams in Latin American countries.

Basketball Without Borders An NBA grassroots program in which coaches and players participate in and present camps, clinics and seminars to young athletes in nations of Africa, Europe and South America.

Board of Governors A select group of NBA or NHL team owners, for example, who are involved with and participate in specific league actions with respect to expansion, relocation, rule changes and other matters.

brand A name, term, sign, symbol and design, or a combination of them, which are intended to identify the goods or services of a team or league and to differentiate the goods or services from those of other teams or leagues.

brand extension This occurs when a sports business uses its strong brand name to launch new products.

brand loyalty A consistent preference for, or the repeat purchase of one sports brand over other sports brands in a product category.

brand recognition A measure of the awareness of sports fans and other consumers to identify or recognize the products and services of professional teams and leagues.

branding Any combination of name, design and symbol that a sports organization uses to differentiate its product from those of competitors.

business alliance Normally, an agreement established between a professional sports franchise or league and a company whereby the company commits to promote and distribute sports products and/or services to consumers in the marketplace.

business model This term refers to the mission, purpose, type of organization, structure and function of a representative professional sports franchise or league.

buyout A clause in a player's contract that authorizes the team to purchase the remaining years of the contract. In ice hockey, the player becomes an unrestricted free agent once bought out.

Canadian Assistance Program A subsidy paid by the Canadian government to one or more of the six NHL franchises to compensate those clubs for the weak Canadian dollar. The total amount of the subsidy has been approximately $20 million per year.

Canadian Baseball League (CBL) An eight-team professional baseball organization that had formed in, and then suspended operations during 2003 because of attendance and stadium problems and poor weather conditions in Canada.

Canadian Football League (CFL) This group was first introduced in North America during the late 1800s and then adopted its current title in 1958. There are teams in nine Canadian cities that compete for the Grey Cup championship. The league is the only professional sports organization that operates entirely in Canada.

Canadian Hockey League (CHL) This is an umbrella organization for other minor ice hockey leagues in Canada. It is one of the most important leagues for NHL teams to recruit their future players.

Canadian Soccer Association (CSA) This governing body is responsible for, and oversees all soccer organizations and programs in Canada.

capital investment The decisions made by professional sports leagues and teams to invest funds in programs and ventures, and in new and renovated facilities and other structures.

capitalism An economic system in which the means of production and distribution are for the most part privately owned and operated for private profit.

cartel A type of oligopoly market structure in which a few firms have market power and attempt to impose a collusive (monopolistic) set of price-output decisions.

catcher A baseball defensive player or fielder who takes the position behind home base. This athlete normally provides hand signals to the pitcher and catches balls thrown by the pitcher to strike out the batter.

center The basketball player who plays near the basket on defense and offense. This player is usually the team's tallest player and best rebounder, and perhaps top scorer. In ice hockey, the center plays on the forward line, usually leads the attacks to score a goal, takes part in most face offs, controls the puck and either tries to score or pass the puck to a teammate in better position to score.

Central Hockey League A multi-team minor league ice hockey group, with headquarters in the midwest of America, that began operations during 1992–1993.

centralization The concentration of power in a central group or institution.

Champions League An annual European soccer tournament that involves more than 30 club teams including league champions and a few runner-ups.

Code of Conduct A document that provides specific policies, rules, penalties and enforcement procedures for those MLB teams that operate baseball academies in Latin American countries and in other developing nations.

collective bargaining agreement A legal contract negotiated between professional sports league owners and a players association. It determines the wages, hours, rules and working conditions of the players based on the time period that is established in the agreement.

commissioner The top administrative official who is appointed collectively by the franchise owners to represent their interests in all activities and matters that relate to a professional sports league.

compensation This dollar amount includes the total income earned by players in a sport. It includes money received from salaries, bonuses, endorsement, incentives and postseason performances.

competitive balance A concept that reflects the relative strength between the rosters of teams with respect to a division, conference or league.

Confederation of North and Central American and Caribbean Football (CONCACAF) Founded in 1961, this is one of FIFA's confederations. It monitors and organizes international competitions and includes approximately 38 soccer-playing nations.

Confederations Cup This is an international soccer tournament that schedules the FIFA confederation champions against each other.

conferences In the NFL, the American and National Football Conferences each consist of four divisions and each division includes four teams. The winners of the conferences meet in the Super Bowl after the regular season and playoffs conclude.

conglomerate A company that consists of a number of subsidiary companies or divisions in a variety of unrelated industries, usually as a result of merger or acquisition.

contraction This occurs when a professional sports league, for various reasons, decides to reduce the number of member teams in the organization.

cultural imperialism To change by imposition, or the policy of extending the rule, authority or power of an empire or nation over foreign countries.

debt security A financial document, such as a bond, that represents an offer made by a borrower to an investor to provide a series of fixed interest payments during the security's life, along with a fixed payment of principal when it matures.

defender The soccer player whose primary job is to prevent offensive penetration, win the ball and initiate an attack. Also called fullback, the position includes outside or flank defender, central defender, stopper and sweeper. The majority of professional soccer teams play with three or four defenders.

defensemen The two ice hockey players who are usually stationed near the defensive zone to help the goalie guard against an attack. These players sometimes lead attacks and cover the left and right sides of the rink.

democracy A political system, exercised directly or through elected representatives, in which government is by the people.

demographic environment Refers to a market's size and growth rate of population, age distribution, ethnic mix, educational levels, household patterns and regional characteristics and movements.

deregulation The elimination of government restrictions and other requirements with respect to the conduct of a professional sports business or industry.

developmental league This professional sports organization exists to train athletes who have the potential to become players on a major league team. Normally, a major league or team subsidizes it.

draft system A selection process operated by the professional sports leagues to acquire amateur athletes who are eligible to become players for teams.

Dream Team The U.S. national basketball team that consisted of elite NBA players and amateurs who excelled to win a gold medal at the 1992 Olympic Games in Barcelona, Spain.

drug test This is issued by professional sports teams to determine the amount and type of illegal substances consumed by players during a specified time period.

East Coast Hockey League An American minor league established in 1988- 1989. Although its quality is below the AHL, the NHL scouts this league for talent.

economic benefit Any income, revenue and appreciation in value that was derived from an investment or expenditure in a sports activity, event or asset.

economic profit The difference between total revenue and the total opportunity cost of producing a firm's goods and/or services.

economic resource Anything that is used to produce a good or service in order to achieve a goal. Labor, land, capital and managerial talent are each a resource.

economic value The perceived benefits of a sports product or service, or what the product or service does for the user based on its intangible and tangible features.

efficient market A sports labor or product market whose prices reflect all available information.

elite players Those athletes who have excellent skills and superior performances for teams in professional baseball, football, basketball, ice hockey and soccer.

English League The biggest professional soccer league in the world. Its top division is Premier followed by the First, Second and Third Divisions.

Entertainment Sports Program Network (ESPN) A television and radio media organization that broadcasts sports games, programs and shows across the globe.

entertainment value The implicit amount of enjoyment or pleasure experienced by an individual or group from observing or participating in a sports activity or event.

Euroleague Formed under the auspices of the Union of European Basketball League in 2000 when it had separated from the FIBA, this professional basketball organization consists of 24 teams assembled in four groups that compete to be league champion.

European Union (EU) A form of regional economic integration among countries in Europe that involves a free trade area, a customs union and the free mobility of factors of production, and that is moving toward economic and political integration.

exporting players The voluntary outflow or free movement of athletes from their home countries to other countries in order to join and play for a team in a professional sports league.

external forces Those U.S. and foreign demographic, economic, political and social circumstances and events that are outside the control of a professional sports league and team.

fan base The number of consumers in a market who are dedicated to and support a team or teams that exist in one or more professional sports leagues.

fan identification The personal commitment and emotional involvement customers have with one or sports organizations.

Federal Hockey League (FHL) A professional, multi-team Canadian league organized during 2003 and incorporated in the province of British Columbia. Its goal is to provide sports entertainment for kids, families and the average individual at an affordable price.

Federation Internationale de Football Association (FIFA) As the international governing body of soccer, this organization governs the rules, transfers, international competitions, referee standards, sports medicine and development with respect to its multiple confederations.

Federation of International Basketball Association (FIBA) Formed during the early 1900s to promote basketball across the world, this group contains more than 200 member basketball federations located in five geographic zones.

Flag Football This is the NFL's core international grassroots program. It is designed to help children learn the basics of American football and teach them how to play and enjoy the game.

Forbes A successful Amerian business magazine that features articles about U.S. and foreign firms in various industries including professional sports.

Foreign direct investment The direct expenditures by professional sports leagues and teams in the business operations in foreign nations.

foreign nation A country that is outside of North America with respect to MLB and the NBA and NHL, and beyond the U.S. borders regarding the NFL and MLS. The three former leagues have teams based in America and Canada, while the two latter leagues have teams located only in the U.S.

forward Soccer player on offensive line whose primary job is to score and assist on goals. The position is also called striker. Most forwards win balls from defenders in the offensive one-third of the field. In basketball, the two forwards on a team are usually smaller than the center but taller than the guards. These athletes are generally leading scorers on offense and good rebounders. They play closer to the basket than the guards but not as near as the center.

Founders Cup This is the name of the trophy awarded to the WUSA team that wins the championship match as decided by the regular season games and playoffs.

Fox Sports Network (FSN) The U.S.-based 24-hour sports television network, which is a broadcasting unit within the News Corporation.

free agent Those professional players who are free to negotiate with other teams. If unrestricted, there is no compensation to teams losing a player. If restricted, the current team has the right to match any offer, which is called the right of first refusal.

futbol The Spanish word for football, which is what soccer is called in many parts of the world.

game attendance This is the actual number of spectators who attended a game rather than those who purchased a ticket but failed to attend the game.

general manager An important sports franchise administrator or executive who usually supervises the team coach or club manager, and makes decisions regarding budgets, player contracts and other operations of the business.

global exposure The extent and frequency to which a sports league team, game or show appears in the broadcast and print media to consumers located across the world.

globalization The broadening interdependences and deepening relationships that exist between and among people and organizations from different nations.

goalkeeper Soccer player whose main job is to keep the ball out of the goal and to initiate an attack after a save or back pass. Also called a goalie or keeper, a goalkeeper is allowed to use her or his hands in the penalty area and may roam far outside the box to play an offensive role on the squad.

Godzilla The nickname that has been assigned to Hideki Matsui, who plays as an outfielder for MLB's New York Yankees baseball team. In Japanese films, Godzilla is a giant monster, popular hero and movie star who battles other monsters and invades cities after leaving a place in the ocean.

governance system The method by which a professional sports league exercises authority, manages and controls its organization, and represents the interests of all stakeholders with respect to a sport.

grassroots activities These are the various types of events and programs that are funded and operated by professional teams and leagues for the children and other youth in America and foreign nations.

guard A basketball player who is usually the smallest on the court. Besides scoring points, this athlete sets up the plays on offense and attempts to pass the ball to teammates who are closer to the basket. There are two guard positions on a five-person team.

G-14 An organization of 14 leading soccer clubs in Europe. Its goals are to improve and promote the sport, strengthen the missions of the clubs in an environment dominated by federations, and cooperate with the FIFA, JEFA and other sporting institutions.

Hall of Fame The professional sports players who are recognized for their abilities and performances as the all-time greatest athletes in a specific sport.

harmonization The state of being in agreement in action, feeling or sense.

hegemony The leadership, supremacy or predominate influence especially when exercised by one state over others.

hip-hop A popular urban youth culture that is closely associated with rap music and with the styles and fashions of African American inner-city residents.

Hockey Night in Canada Launched in 1937, this weekly sports program about ice hockey has been produced by a public network named the Canadian Broadcasting Corporation. Its commentators include Don Cherry, who provides a lively discussion of various aspects of the game and international players.

home country The source country for foreign direct investment.

host country The receipient country of inward investment by a foreign professional sports organization.

implementation A decision in sports marketing such as who will provide the organization's plans, and why and when the plans will be executed.

infielder A defensive baseball player or fielder who occupies a position in the infield as a first, second or third baseman, or shortstop. This player attempts to catch balls hit in the air or on the ground so that the batter will record an out.

inflation A general increase in prices as measured by an index, and/or an increase in costs that are unmatched by productivity gains.

infrastructure The fundamental underpinnings of an economy or society and includes such things as a nation's communication systems, energy supplies, highways, railroads, schools and water supply.

international business This term represents all commercial transactions and deals that involve America's professional sports leagues and/or teams, and any individuals, private companies and governments in foreign countries.

International Hockey League (IHL) This minor professional ice hockey league was formed during 1945 in Detroit, Michigan. Despite growth in the 1980s and 1990s, some chronic financial problems forced the IHL to collapse in 2001.

International Ice Hockey Federation (IIHF) Headquartered in Zurich, Switzerland, this organization was formed in 1908 to oversee all international ice hockey tournaments that involve the national representation of players from countries around the world.

international strategy The ways that professional sports leagues and teams make choices about obtaining and applying scarce resources to achieve their global objectives.

internationalization theory To earn a higher return on investment, a professional sports league transfers its superior knowledge to a foreign entity or affiliate.

interpreter Those individuals or organizations that are hired by professional sports teams to teach their foreign players the English language and how to interpret American customs, values and traditions.

investment risk The exposure to financial losses by professional sports leagues and teams when they make investments in assets, resources and operations in America and foreign countries.

joint venture A direct investment in which two or more companies cooperate and share the ownership of a project that exists either for a limited or longstanding duration.

Koshien The name of the stadium that hosts the most prestigious national high school baseball tournament in Japan.

labor union The organization that represents professional sports players in their collective bargaining with one or more leagues.

lanqiu The word used to define basketball in China.

Latino An American or foreign citizen or resident of Latin American or Spanish-speaking descent.

league expansion The decision by professional sports leagues to approve, identify and locate one or more new franchises at sites in America or foreign nations.

lease A contractual agreement that commits a professional sports team as the lessee to rent a facility from the owner or the lessor. The transaction involves a series of fixed payments by the team during a specific time period.

less developed countries Those nations with low per capita incomes and levels of industrialization, high illiteracy rates and usually political instability.

licensing A contractual arrangement in which one firm grants the access to its patents, technologies or trademarks to another firm for a fee or royalty.

lockout The right exercised by a professional sports league to ban the teams' players from participating in practices or playing games in the sport.

luxury tax A percentage levied by a league on the portion of a team's payroll that exceeds a predetermined dollar value. A league allocates the tax from high to low payroll teams as a means of revenue sharing.

Major League Baseball (MLB) This has been the premier professional baseball organization in the world since the early 1900s. It consists of multiple sports teams in the American and National leagues.

Major League Baseball Players Association (MLBPA) This labor union exists for the purpose, in whole or in part, of dealing with MLB concerning grievances, labor disputes, wages, rates of pay, hours of employment, or conditions of work. It also represents professional baseball players during collective bargaining with MLB.

Major League Soccer (MLS) Organized as a group in 1996 with ten teams and headquartered in New York City, this is the top men's professional outdoor soccer league in America.

market penetration strategy The ways that commercial and professional sports firms or groups increase the market shares of their products and services in current and new markets.

market power The ability of professional sports leagues and franchises to exercise control over prices or outputs.

market promotion This includes all forms of communication between a professional sports league or team and the consumers in their respective local, national and international markets.

market share The overall proportion or percentage of consumers in a market who primarily are fans with respect to one or more professional sports, sport teams, or leagues.

market value The final dollar amount or worth of a sports enterprise or asset when it is sold to a buyer in a market transaction.

marketing strategy These are the types of methods, tactics and techniques that professional sports franchises and leagues select and apply to achieve their business goals.

media An element in the communications process by which the message is transmitted to the audience. The major types of mediums include the Internet, direct mail, magazines, newspapers, outdoor displays, radio and television.

merchandise The numerous products sold by sports leagues and teams besides apparel, equipment and food.

metropolitan area This is the space or surface land occupied by a city and its surrounding region.

Mexican Basketball Federation The organization that influences, promotes and supports the majority of minor and professional basketball leagues and teams in Mexico.

midfielder The soccer player who controls the direction and pace of the attack generally from the middle of the field and acts as a link between defenders and strikers. The position includes outside or flank and central midfielders.

MLB International (MLBI) This organizational unit is involved with establishing international marketing campaigns and generating revenues for MLB and the league's teams primarily in foreign nations.

MLS Cup The trophy awarded to the professional soccer team that wins the MLS championship game.

monopoly An economic structure in which a local sports franchise has the exclusive right to be the sole producer of a professional sport in the relevant market.

Montreal Expos The professional baseball team based in Montreal, Canada that is controlled and owned by MLB until new ownership of the franchise has been approved and transferred.

Most Valuable Player (MVP) This prestigious award is granted by teams and leagues to the player or players who contributed the most to their organization's success that season or year.

NAFTA The North American Free Trade Agreement that will establish a free trade area between Canada, Mexico and the United States.

National Basketball Association (NBA) Since the late 1940s, this has been the premier professional basketball league in the world.

National Basketball Players Association (NBPA) The labor union that repre- sents professional basketball players in regard to the relevant employment issues with the NBA.

National Collegiate Athletic Association (NCAA) Established in 1905 as the Intercollegiate Athletic Association of the United States, this organization assumed its current name in 1910 and since has become the primary governing body for collegiate athletic programs in America.

National Football League (NFL) Since 1922, this has been the top professional sports league in the world with respect to American football.

National Football League Players Association (NFLPA) This labor union represents professional football players regarding employment conditions in the NFL.

National Hockey League (NHL) Established during 1917 in Montreal, Canada, this is ice hockey's premier professional league in North America. During 2004, it consisted of 24 teams based in the U.S. and six in Canada.

National Hockey League International (NHLI) This division of NHL Enterpris- es is responsible for the development of international competition, corporate sponsorships, marketing, broadcasting, new media, licensing and other NHL business activities conducted outside of North America.

National Hockey League Players Association (NHLPA) The labor union that was created during 1967 to represent professional ice hockey players in collective bargaining with the league.

National Professional Soccer League (NPSL) This indoor league, whose season operates from October through April, was founded as the American Indoor Soccer Association in 1984. It became the NPSL during 1990.

nationalism A strong attachment to and the support of a country by individuals and groups.

NBA Finals The best of a seven-game series played between the top team from the Eastern and Western Conferences to determine the league championship.

NCAA Division I This category includes the large American colleges and universities that operate big time athletic programs.

NFL International (NFLI) As a component of the NFL Enterprises, this division seeks to promote the NFL internationally and establish business relationships with foreign companies, consumers and governments.
North American Soccer League (NASL) This U.S.-based soccer league was formed in 1967. After rapid expansion to 24 teams, it folded during 1985 because of high salaries and the failure to negotiate a national television contract.

oligopoly A market structure in which a few or limited number of firms produce a large portion of the output such as in professional sports.
operating cash flow The cash generated by a franchise from normal business operations such as broadcasting rights, concessions, gate receipts and the sales of team apparel, equipment, food and merchandise.
organizational culture The shared values between the members of a sports team or league. The values identify and establish preferred behaviors by the team or league.
outfielder A baseball defensive player or fielder who occupies a position in the outfield, which is the area of the playing field most distant from home base. The three outfielders on a baseball team attempt to catch balls in the air and on the ground that are hit by batters.

Pan American Games The sports event held every four years during the summer preceding the Olympic Games. It includes competition between the countries in Central, North and South America.
partnership A type of business arrangement that establishes a joint relationship between two or more individuals and/or groups.
Pele Considered the greatest male soccer player ever, he led Brazil to three World Cup championships. Then, after setting virtually every scoring record, he decided to retire for a second time in 1977.
pesos The basic currency that is used for business transactions in Mexico.
pitcher A baseball defensive player or fielder who is designated to throw the ball to the batter. This player throws various types of pitches and attempts to get the batter to swing and miss the pitch or hit it to the other fielders for an out.
player contract An agreement negotiated with a team that contains all aspects of the working conditions and obligations of a professional sports player with respect to employment.
player market This economic concept refers to the demand and supply of amateur and professional U.S. and foreign athletes who each play baseball, Ameri- can football, basketball, ice hockey or soccer.
policy This is a standing plan that sets broad guidelines for a professional sports organization.
political economy The study of how political forces influences the functioning of an economic system.
political risk The probability that political forces will cause dramatic changes in a nation's business environment that will adversely affect the goals of sports organizations.

product differentiation　To modify the conformance, design, durability, feature, performance, reliability, repairability and/or style of one or more sports products.

product quality　The degree to which sports goods meet and exceed consumers' needs.

quarterback　The American football offensive team position occupied by a player who takes snaps from the center and either runs the ball, hands the ball off to a running back or throws the ball. Also, the quarterback communicates each play to the team and is usually the leader of the team and a playmaker. Each team fields at least one quarterback during a game.

quota　A restriction on the number of foreign players from one or more countries on the roster of a team.

rationalization　The process of ascribing acts or opinions to causes that seem valid but actually are not the true, possibly unconscious causes.

referees　The men or women who are officially in charge of a professional sports game or match. Their primary duty and responsibility are to ensure that each team adheres to the sport's rules during the competition.

regular season　The schedule of teams' games that has been established by each of the respective professional sports leagues.

revenue sharing　A league-approved system to reallocate specific types of revenues from one or more clubs to another club or clubs in the group to increase competitive balance.

rights fee　An amount of money provided by the professional sports leagues and teams to individuals or groups that supply products and/or perform services for the leagues and teams.

royalties　The remuneration that is paid to professional sports leagues and teams by others for the use of patents, technology and trade names.

Russian Baseball Federation　This group cooperates and coordinates with leagues to promote and support national and local baseball teams and other baseball events in the nation.

salary caps　Implemented during the 1980s in the NBA, these are the maximum and minimum amounts a team can pay its players.

scout　Normally a sports team employee who evaluates the skills and performances of amateur and professional ballplayers on clubs in America and other nations.

secularism　The view that public education and other matters of civil policy should be conducted without the introduction of a religious element.

shareholder　A person and/or group that owns one or more shares of common and/or preferred stock in a company or other business enterprise or venture.

site　The exact place within a city or metropolitan area where an arena, ball field, ice rink or sports stadium is located.

skaters　As listed on some NHL team rosters, these are the ice hockey players other than the goalies, that is, the group of centers, defensemen and wings.

soccer festival A special soccer event hosted during 2004 by investors and sports officials to generate national interest and support for the revival of the WUSA.

Soccer United Marketing A joint venture of MLS, AEG and the Japanese advertising agency Dentsu that, during 2002, purchased the rights to the Mexican national soccer team.

specialization The act of pursuing some special line of study or work.

spectators The consumers who acquire benefits by observing a game or other type of event performed by a professional sports team.

sponsors In professional sports, these are the individuals, organizations and other groups that finance, in part, the activities and operations of specific leagues and teams.

sponsorship The element in the promotional mix that uses investment in such a sports entity as an athlete, event, league or team to support the organization's objectives, marketing goals and promotional strategies.

sport franchise A person or group that is awarded a license to serve the league's fans and to play league games in a prescribed geographic area. The license permits the ownership and operation of a sports team as a member of a league.

sports agent This is a person or group that is empowered to conduct business for a professional sports player. The legal relationship between the player and agent is generally specified in a written contract, which is governed by contract and agency law. A sports agent is called *buscones* or a finder in Latin American countries.

sports culture Based on attitudes, beliefs and values, this is the learned norms of a society with respect to sports and the sports business and industry.

sports environment The local, national and international conditions and forces that influence and surround the development and success of a professional sports franchise and league.

sports executives The sports league or team decision makers who are at the highest level of the organization. This group includes the league commissioner and staff, and teams' presidents, vice presidents and general managers.

sports market This represents the economic relationships and interactions that exist between consumers and teams with respect to the provision of a sport in a territory.

sports product A good, service or a combination of them that is designed to provide economic and social benefits to a sports participant, spectator or sponsor.

sportsbusinessnews.com The American-based web site that provided daily articles about the professional sports business, industry and events, leagues, teams and players.

stakeholders These groups include one or more persons, businesses, sports team owners, fans, investors, the media, politicians, professional players, unions and national, regional and local governments.

Stanley Cup This is North America's oldest championship trophy for professional sports. Since the NHL gained control of the Cup in 1926, it has been awarded each year to the professional ice hockey team that wins the series played between the Eastern and Western Conference champions.

strategic alliance An agreement between a professional sports league and team and one or more companies that is essential or vital to the short- and long-term operation and success of the league or team.

strategic planning process A disciplined and well-defined organizational effort and approach directed at a league or a team's strategy and the assignment of responsibilities to execute it.

strategic sports marketing process A series of actions that involve planning, implementing and controlling marketing efforts to meet an organization's objectives and satisfy consumers' needs.

strategy This is a fundamental framework through which a league or team asserts its vital continuity, while, at the same time, it forcefully facilitates its adaptation to a changing environment.

subsidiary A company owned by another company, which is referred to as the parent company.

subsidy An explicit or implicit payment made by taxpayers and governments to professional sports teams for the cost of facilities or operations, or by sports leagues to teams for the same reasons.

Super Bowl The game played between the top team from each of the American and National Football Conferences. It determines the NFL championship.

superstar A player who excels or performs as an outstanding athlete on offense and/or defense for a team during one or more seasons.

takeover target This term refers to a sports organization that is vulnerable and a candidate to be acquired by one or more businesses in the same or another industry.

target marketing The selection of a segment(s) that permits a sports entity to efficiently and effectively attain its marketing goals.

team active duty roster A team's players, listed by name and position that are currently available and authorized for scheduled games. This list excludes a club's injured and nonroster players and those on the taxi squad.

Team China The name assigned to the group of women hockey players who are the national team in China.

team logo This is a symbol or other indicator that distinctly identifies the source of a product. It is classified as a trademark, whose owner may seek legal recourse against others when its use gives rise to a likelihood of confusion in the market.

team relocation A league-approved movement by a team from one city or area to another because of demographic, economic, financial or social factors.

Telemundo A subsidiary of NBC, which is owned by the General Electric Corporation, this is a Spanish-language television network and the rights holder to the NBA telecasts of regular season games.

Title IX A law passed in 1972 by the U.S. Congress, it provides equal educational opportunities and bans discrimination in American schools with respect to academic and athletic programs. The law focuses on women to have equal opportunities as a group and not on an individual basis. The law covers, in part, athletic financial assistance, accommodation of athletic interests and abilities, and other program areas.

trade barrier Any obstacle(s) imposed by foreign governments, or the presence of cultural differences between nations, that serve to restrict or prevent a professional sports league or team from entry to a market.

trademark An identifier that indicates a sports organization has legally registered its brand name or mark. This prevents other organizations from using it.

transfer fee A payment of hundreds of thousands of dollars made by the NHL to the IIHF in exchange for the services of one or more foreign hockey players.

trend analysis model A statistical technique whereby successive observations of a variable, at regular time intervals, are analyzed to determine patterns and estimates of future values.

Union of European Football Associations (UEFA) This FIFA confederation includes all soccer-playing European nations.

United Soccer Association (USA) Organized in America during 1967, that year this professional league merged with the NPSL to form the NASL.

Univision Communications Inc. The Spanish language television network that provides news stories, health and fitness programs, weather, sports shows and other events at the local, national and international levels. The network is based in Los Angeles, California and committed to soccer broadcasts.

U.S. Soccer Federation Also called U.S. Soccer, this affiliate of FIFA is the national governing body for soccer in America. Based in Chicago, Illinois, its mission is to make soccer, in all forms, the preeminent sport in the U.S.

U-17 World Championship This soccer tournament is restricted to players who are less than 17 years old.

values Any abstract ideas about what a society believes to be desirable, good and right.

venue The arena, ball field, rink or stadium where a sports game, match or other event is held.

wa A Japanese expression that means a harmonious relationship exists.

West Coast Hockey League Based in the western U.S., this is a low rung minor ice hockey league that consists of teams located in several states.

wing The two ice hockey players who flank the center on the left and right sides and with the center, comprise the attacking unit or forward line.

Women's Baseball League Inc. (WBL) Formed in America during 1997, its mission is to enhance awareness and provide an opportunity for female athletes to participate in baseball and to promote the qualities and standards of the sport.

Women's National Basketball Association (WNBA) Since 1997, this has been the premier professional basketball league for women in America. To provide a regular season schedule of games, the NBA has subsidized the league's operations.

Women's United Soccer Association (WUSA) Organized in 2001, this Ameri-can-based professional women's soccer league folded during 2003 because of poor attendance at games and the lack of financial support from sponsors and television.

work ethic A belief in the moral benefit and importance of work and its inherent ability to strengthen character.

World Championships In soccer, these are the U-17 and U-20 tournaments that are scheduled every two years.

World Cup First played in 1930 and about every four years thereafter, this is the most prestigious soccer tournament in the world. Brazil, Italy and Germany have been the most successful World Cup teams.

World Football League (WFL) A U.S.-based professional league that was established during 1973. Two years later, it folded because of poor attendances, minimal television exposure and inferior performances by teams and players.

World Games An international multi-sport event that is hosted by the International World Games Association under the patronage of the International Olympic Committee. The event is held every four years during the year following a summer Olympics.

World Hockey Association (WHA) This is an alternative professional ice hockey league that is scheduled to open its first season in various North American cities during 2004 or 2005. If the NHL avoids a strike or lockout, this league may not be viable.

World League of American Football (WLAF) Organized by the NFL in 1991, this league had teams located in America and Europe. It suspended operations after the 1992 season but reemerged in 1995. Three years later, it was renamed the NFL Europe.

World Series The final best of seven-game baseball series that is played between the top team from each of the American and National Leagues to determine the MLB championship. Normally the Series is played each October.

YES Network Established during 2002, it is the New York Yankees' cable channel that broadcasts the games of the Yankees, New Jersey Nets and Manchester United, and those of selected colleges and universities. The channel has approximately three million subscribers who are located in at least four U.S. states.

yuan The Chinese currency that is pegged at about 8.2 to the U.S. dollar.

Selected Bibliography

Articles

"A League of Tim's Own." *Cablevision* (27 March 2000): 18.

"A New Face at the NHL: Litner Seeks to Heighten Hockey's Global Profile." *Brandweek* (29 November 1999): 18.

"Alien Invaders Altering Look of the NBA." *Toronto Star* (17 October 2000): 6.

Allen, K. "NHL's Bettman Won't Let Go of Dream." *USA Today* (18 February 1994): E11.

"All-Stars and Others International Influx." *The Charlotte Observer* (31 March 2003): 7C.

"Anheuser-Busch & NBA Extend Global Partnership." *PR Newswire* (10 December 2002): 4.

Aron, Jaime. "2 Owners Like Vegas For Expansion Team." *The Charlotte Observer* (23 January 2004): 4C.

Atkin, Ross. "Mexico in the Super Bowl? Hmmm . . . " *The Christian Science Monitor* (22 January 1997): 1.

Baker, Geoff. "Backers Pitch Merits of New League." *Toronto Star* (21 November 2002): D5.

Balfour, Frederick. "It's Time For a New Playbook." *Business Week* (15 September 2003): 56.

Ballinger, Jeff. "Nike's Voice Looms Large." *Social Policy* (Fall 2001): 34–37.

Barra, Allen. "A Strategic Error Doomed the WUSA to Defeat." *Wall Street Journal* (23 September 2003): D9.

———. "An International Game." *Wall Street Journal* (13 July 2001): W6.

———. "Reality Check For the NHL." *Wall Street Journal* (1 March 2002): W7.

"Baseball Hits Home Run in Europe, Latin America." *Video Age International* (October-November 1991): 44.

"Baseball Hot on Mexico." *The Charlotte Observer* (17 July 1998): 4B.

"Baseball: 18 Teams to Start April 5; Season Opener in Japan." *The Charlotte Observer* (25 January 2004): 14F.

"Basketball's Yao Ming Sues Coke For a Yuan." *Wall Street Journal* (27 May 2003): B4.

Beaton, R. "Braves Strike Unique Mexican Deal." *USA Today* (17 February 1995): C12.

Bellamy Jr., Robert V. "Issues in the Internationalization of the U.S. Sports Media: The Emerging European Marketplace." *Journal of Sport and Social Issues*. Vol. 17, No. 3 (1993): 168–180.

Benson, Mitchel. "Sacramento Kings Count on a Troika in the NBA Playoffs." *Wall Street Journal* (19 April 2002): A1, A8.

Berlage, Gai Ingham. "Women's Professional Baseball Gets a New Look: On Film and in Print." *Journal of Sport and Social Issues*. Vol. 16, No. 2 (1992): 149–152.

Black, James T. "Nashville's Dream Team." *Southern Living Magazine* (August 2001): 64, 66–69.

Blenkinsopp, Alexander. "Asian Invasion: Baseball's Ambassadors." *Harvard International Review* (Spring 2002): 12–13.

Blum, Ronald. "Offenses Thunder During Spring Games in Mexico." *The Charlotte Observer* (17 March 2003): 5C.

Bonnell, Rick. "Charlotte's Return Comes at a Time NBA Looks Overseas to Fill Skills Gap." *The Charlotte Observer* (20 April 2003): 1F, 4F.

———. "Gone Global." *The Charlotte Observer* (20 April 2003): 1F, 4F.

———. "Tapscott Hits Europe in Bobcats GM Search." *The Charlotte Observer* (9 October 2003): 1C.

———. "Tapscott Says Italian is Serious GM Candidate." *The Charlotte Observer* (10 October 2003): 2C.

———. "Yao's Arrival a Smooth One." *The Charlotte Observer* (20 April 2003): 4F.

Borrelli, Tom. "Quick Sticks." *Sport* (January 1998): 91–92.

Brewer, Jerry. "NBA Embraces International Flavor." *Knight Ridder/Tribune Star News Service* (22 June 2002): 19.

Broussard, Chris. "Americans Top Rookie Class." *The Charlotte Observer* (30 November 2003): 4F.

———. "Ilgauskas Living Up to Potential." *The Charlotte Observer* (21 March 2004): 4F.

Caldera, Pete. "Matsui Home Run Thrills Fans in Japan." *The Charlotte Observer* (29 March 2003): 9C.

———. "Players to Consider Testing For Cup." *The Charlotte Observer* (29 March 2004): 9C.

Campbell, Ken. "Toronto to be Major World Cup of Hockey Site." *Toronto Star* (20 September 2002): F2.

Caple, Jim. "America's Game Takes on World Flavor With Growth of International Talent." *Baseball Digest* (September 2001): 48.

Cassidy, Hilary. "Power Play: NHL Nets Broadcast Partners For Overseas Promos." *Brandweek* (11 December 2000): 9.

Caudwell, Jayne. "Women's Football in the United Kingdom: Theorizing Gender and Unpacking the Butch Lesbian Image." *Journal of Sport and Social Issues.* Vol. 23, No. 4 (1999): 399–402.

Chass, Murray. "A World Event Could Solve All-Star Blahs." *The New York Times* (9 July 2002): D3.

———. "A World of Opportunity For America's Pastime." *The New York Times* (28 March 2002): D1.

———. "Mexico is Now in Picture For Possible Expansion." *The New York Times* (10 June 1994): B17.

Chen, Albert. "Inside Baseball." *Sports Illustrated* (28 April 2003): 66.

Chezzi, Derek. "What's Old is New: Lacrosse." *Maclean's* (27 August 2001): 46.

Clarey, Christopher. "France's Newest Passion: The N.B.A." *The New York Times* (16 June 1993): B9.

Clough, Michael. "The (Multi) National Pastime: As Professional Sports Go Global, Will Local Communities be Shunted Aside?" *The Los Angeles Times* (31 March 1996): M1.

Copetas, A. Craig. "Europe is U.S. Sports' New Classroom." *Wall Street Journal* (29 November 1996): B7.

———. "Soccer Teams Study Stadium Branding." *Wall Street Journal* (24 April 2000): A11C.

Craig, Susanne. "Canadians Skate to Hockey's Roots." *Wall Street Journal* (16 April 2003): B4A.

Cummins, Chip. "On the Rebound: Iraqi Basketball Needs to Recover, Too." *Wall Street Journal* (20 May 2003): A1, A13.

Cyphers, Luke. "NBA Shoots Toward the Pacific Rim as Part of Global Marketing." *The Asian Wall Street Journal Weekly* (6 April 1992): 2.

Deckard, Linda. "Global Expansion Next Step For NBA?" *Amusement Business* (22 April 1991): 35–36.

Delgado, Fernando. "Major League Soccer: The Return of the Foreign Sport." *Journal of Sport and Social Issues*. Vol. 21, No. 9 (1997): 285–297.

———. "Sport and Politics: Major League Soccer, Constitution, and (the) Latino Audience(s)." *Journal of Sport and Social Issues*. Vol. 23, No. 1 (1999): 41–54.

Desens, Carl. "The NBA's Fast Break Overseas." *Business Week* (5 December 1994): 94.

"Details Revealed For 2004 World Cup of Hockey." *Europe Intelligence Wire* (3 April 2003): 1.

Donnelly, P. "The Local and the Global: Globalization in the Sociology of Sport." *Journal of Sport and Social Issues*. Vol. 20, No. 3 (1996): 239–257.

Donohue, Steve. "Rebranding Key to NFL Europe." *Electronic Media* (23 March 1998): 36.

Dykewicz, Paul. "Spotlight: Baseball's All-Star Game Goes Global." *Satellite News* (21 July 2003): 1.

Eisenberg, Daniel. "The NBA's Global Game Plan." *Time* (17 March 2003): 59–60.

Eskenazi, Gerald. "Global N.F.L. Game Plan: Springtime Play Overseas." *The New York Times* (20 July 1989): A1.

———. "Pro Leagues in America Eye the Globe." *The New York Times* (9 April 1989): 19.

Evans, Rob. "U.S. Baseball Expects Big Hit in Mexico." *Amusement Business* (8 July 1996): 19–20.

Ewing, Jack. "Let the Games Begin—On Time." *Business Week* (15 December 2003): 109–110.

"Expos to Begin Play in San Juan Today." *The Charlotte Observer* (11 April 2003): 4C.

Fackler, Martin. "Baseball Players Are the Latest Casualty of Japan's Slump." *Wall Street Journal* (7 January 2004): A1–A2.

Fatsis, Stefan. "A Global Network of Scouts and Spies Hunts For NBA Gold." *Wall Street Journal* (26 June 2003): A1, A6.

———. "Can New $220 Million NFL Deal Appease Restive Owners?" *Wall Street Journal* (16 December 2003): B1, B11.

———. "Cuba Si, Stardom, No." *Wall Street Journal* (17 August 2001): W4.

———. "Disney Nears Sale of Baseball Team to Businessman." *Wall Street Journal* (14 April 2003): B5.

———. "For Love of the Game." *Wall Street Journal* (23 April 2003): B1, B4.

———. "Gatorade—NFL Deal Douses Firestorm Over Halftime Show." *Wall Street Journal* (23 February 2004): B6.

———. "Montreal Expos: No Place to Call Home Plate." *Wall Street Journal* (7 August 2003): B1.

———. "Much Adu." *Wall Street Journal* (26 March 2004): W4.

———. "NHL Says Players' Salaries Put League in Financial Peril." *Wall Street Journal* (19 September 2003): B1, B3.

———. "Salaries, Promos and Flying Solo." *Wall Street Journal* (9 February 2004): R4, R10.

Fatsis, Stefan, and Suzanne Vranica. "Major League Baseball Agrees to $275 Million Deal in Japan." *Wall Street Journal* (31 October 2003): B4.

Fatsis, Stefan, Peter Wonacott, and Maureen Tkacik. "A Basketball Star From Shanghai is Big Business." *Wall Street Journal* (22 October 2002): A1, A10.

Ferraro, Tom. "Globalization of Sports Can Enlighten Athletes." *Long Island Business News* (14 April 2000): 54A.

Fisher, Eric. "United They Stand . . . to Conquer." *Insight on the News* (27 May 2002): 28–29.

Flagg, Michael. "U.S. Sports Teams Seek Larger Piece of Asian Markets." *Wall Street Journal* (30 October 2000): B11E.

———. "U.S. Sports Teams Look to Asia For a Cheerleader." *Wall Street Journal* (30 October 2000): C13A.

Flynn, Michael A., and Richard J. Gilbert. "The Analysis of Professional Sports Leagues as Joint Ventures." *Economic Journal* (February 2001): F27.

Gammons, Peter. "International Pastime." *Boston Globe* (27 March 1998): F2.

Garber, Don. "NFL Sets Up Unit to Plot Overseas Pitch." *Brandweek* (14 October 1996): 14.

"Gatorade and NBA Enter Global Partnership." *AsiaPulse News* (8 November 2002): 49.

Gergen, Joe. "Is Global Expansion the Wave of the Future?" *The Sporting News* (28 August 1989): 9.

Gloede, B., and C. L. Smith Muniz. "NBA Goes Global." *Sports Inc.* (16 November 1987): 29–30.

Goldsmith, Charles, and Vanessa O'Connell. "Is Europe Ready For Some Football?" *Wall Street Journal* (15 January 2003): B4.

Gonzalez, G. Leticia. "The Stacking of Latinos in Major League Baseball." *Journal of Sport and Social Issues*. Vol. 20, No. 2 (1996): 134–160.

Gould IV, William B. "Baseball and Globalization: The Game Played and Heard and Watched 'Round the World.'" *Indiana Journal of Global Legal Studies*, Vol. 8:85 (Fall 2000): 85–120.

Grandstaff, Chris. "Orosco: Baseball's Pitching Ironman." *The Charlotte Observer* (6 April 2003): 7F.

Granitsas, Alkman. "China Sees Dawn of Big-Money Sports TV." *Wall Street Journal* (31 May 2002): B4.

Grimes, Kelly. "Global Access Sends Major League Baseball Overseas." *Business Wire* (30 April 1996): 43.

Grover, Ronald. "Is This an End Run by the NFL?" *Business Week* (27 October 2003): 86.

Gunther, Marc. "They All Want to be Like Mike." *Fortune* (21 July 1997): 51–53.

Gwin, Peter. "Transatlantic: How Europe is Shaping US Basketball Hoops." *Europe* (June 1997): 33–35.

Hall, Kevin. "Mexico's 'Little Giants' Flex Major Muscles." *The Charlotte Observer* (9 November 2003): 18A.

"Hard Pills to Swallow." *Time* (17 August 1992): 16.

Harrop, JoAnne Klimovich. "SupHer Bowl Puts on Good Show." *Pittsburgh Tribune-Review* (28 July 2002): C1.

Harvey, Jean, Genevieve Rail, and Lucie Thibault. "Globalization and Sport: Sketching a Theoretical Model For Empirical Analyses." *Journal of Sport and Social Issues*. Vol. 20, No. 3 (1996): 258–277.

Hauser, Susan G. "Japanese Baseball Stars Turn Seattle Radio Bilingual." *Wall Street Journal* (10 July 2001): A16.

Heath, Thomas. "NFL Has Ambitions For China." *The Washington Post* (1 August 2002): D1.

Hiserman, Mike. "World Series." *The Los Angeles Times* (23 October 2003): U1.

Hodges, Jim. "League of Nations: As the Number of European Players Continues to Grow, The NHL Reaches New Levels of Talent." *The Los Angeles Times* (30 September 1999): 1.

Hoffer, H. "South of the Border." *Sports Illustrated* (12 July 1993): 38–41.

Holmes, Stanley. "Bend it Like—Somebody Else." *Business Week* (11 August 2003): 10.

Holmes, Stanley, Heidi Dawley, and Gerry Khermouch. "Can ManU Score in America?" *Business Week* (23 June 2003): 108–109.

Honeycutt, Brett. "Soccer's Superteen Selected 1st in Draft." *The Charlotte Observer* (17 January 2004): 3C.

Hunter, Paul. "Maple Leaf Hype Fails to Score." *Toronto Star* (11 September 2003): 1.

Hyman, Mark. "Sports." *Business Week* (12 January 1998): 124.

———. "Where *Beisbol* is the Stuff of Revolution." *Business Week* (15 May 2000): 28, 30.

"Intelsat Beams Baseball Worldwide Via Fiber, Uplinks." *Fiber Optics News* (4 August 2003): 1.

"International Influx." *The Charlotte Observer* (31 March 2003): 7C.

Johnson, Hillary. "Just Give Us the Damn Ball." *The New York Times* (22 October 2000): 80–88.

Jones, Grahame L. "The Inside Track: Q & A With Don Garber." *The Los Angeles Times* (6 June 2003): D2.

Kahn, Gabriel. "Yo, Yao: What's Up With Chinese Ads in Texas?" *Wall Street Journal* (7 February 2003): B1, B4.

Kim, Lucian. "Football's Drive to Gain Yardage in Europe." *The Christian Science Monitor* (17 May 1999): 1.

Klein, Frederick C. "On Sports: Gridiron Broadcasts Behind the Great Wall." *Wall Street Journal* (20 January 1987): 1.

———. "The International Pastime?" *Wall Street Journal* (23 October 1992): A12.

Klein, Gary. "Global Draft." *The Los Angeles Times* (3 June 2003): D6.

Koppett, Leonard. "The Globalization of Baseball: Reflections of a Sports Writer." *Indiana Journal of Global Legal Studies*, Vol. 8:8 (Fall 2000): 81–84.

Krich, John. "Asian Sportscasters, Stumped by 'Airball,' Opt For 'Bread Roll.' *Wall Street Journal* (27 April 2004): A1, A14.

———. "Show Me the Yuan." *Wall Street Journal* (5 September 2003): B1, B4.

Kruczek, Steven. "A Worldly Game." *Harvard International Review* (Fall 1998): 12–13.

"Latino Day." *Super Bowl XXXVIII Game Program* (2004): 30.

Lawlor, Frank. "NBA Czar Reaches Out to World." *International Herald Tribune* (4 February 1999): 17.

Lefton, Terry. "Adidas Hits Road With MLB Abroad." *Brandweek* (2 November 1998): 16.

———. "Global Grand Slam." *Brandweek* (18 October 1999): 20–22.

Lefton, Terry, and Matthew Grimm. "Labatt in Seven-Figure NFLI Deal For Budweiser North of the Border." *Brandweek* (4 January 1999): 10.

Leifer, Eric M. "The Ultimate Expansion: Internationalizing Sports." *Across the Board* (June 1999): 20–24.

Lentze, Gregory. "The Legal Concept of Professional Sports Leagues: The Commissioner and an Alternative Approach From a Corporate Perspective." *Marquette Sports Law Journal* (Fall 1995): 65–94.

Lewis, Adrienne. "Foreign Imports." *USA TODAY* (4 June 2003): 3C.

Lidz, Franz. "Achtung! Football Does a Flip-Flop." *Sports Illustrated* (24 June 2002): 56–57.

Lilly, J. "Russian Revolution." *Sports Illustrated* (10 January 1994): 56–61.

Longman, Jere. "Painstaking Progress Finally Pays Off For the U.S." *The New York Times* (25 June 2002): D3.

Lott, John. "Baseball North." *National Post* (22 February 2003): B10.

MacDonald, Jason. "Sports Looking to Global Arena." *Marketing Magazine* (19 February 2001): 6–8.

Mandese, Joe. "How Fox Deal Aids NFL Global Aim." *Advertising Age* (3 January 1994): 4–5.

———. "Murdoch Adds Football to List of Global Ambitions." *Advertising Age* (13 June 1994): 66–67.

Martin, Justin. "Can Baseball Make it in Mexico?" *Fortune* (30 September 1996): 32–33.

McCallum, Jack. "Tomorrow the World." *Sports Illustrated* (7 November 1988): 58–63.

Miller, D. W. "Scholars Call a Foul on Pro Sports Leagues." *The Chronicle of Higher Education* (13 October 2000): A28–29.

Miller, Toby. "How Founding the United Nations Professionalized Sport." *Journal of Sport and Social Issues*. Vol. 22, No. 2 (1998): 123–126.

Millman, Joel. "Diamondbacks Look to Mexico to Fill More Seats." *Wall Street Journal* (27 July 2002): B1.

———. "Young Maverick Sits on Sidelines But Stars in Ads." *Wall Street Journal* (27 February 2002): B1, B3.

"MLB.com Launches Online 2003 All-Star Game Ballots in Japanese and Spanish For the Second Consecutive Year." *PR Newswire* (21 May 2003): 12.

Moore, David. "Pistons Coach Blasts Dallas Owner Cuban." *The Charlotte Observer* (9 February 2004): 4C.

"More Matsui Mania." *The Charlotte Observer* (7 April 2004): 6C.

"Most Golden Oldies Aren't Gems." *Soccer Digest* (December 2002): 14.

Muret, Don. "Demise of International Hockey League Leaves Several Scrambling For Dates." *Amusement Business* (11 June 2001): 8.

———. "With CBA in Mexico City, Can NBA be Far Behind?" *Amusement Business* (6 June 1994): 13.

Neuharth, A. "Next: Letting World in on World Series." *USA Today* (16 October 1992): A9.

"NFL Flag Football." *Super Bowl XXXVIII Game Program* (2004): 157.

"NFL Global Junior Championship." *Super Bowl XXXVIII Game Program* (2004): 28.

"NFL Looks to China as Next Stop." *The Los Angeles Times* (1 January 2003): D4.

"NHL Selects GlobeCast to Offer Hockey in Europe." *Communications Today* (25 October 2002): 1.

"1990 Opener is a Global Enterprise." *The New York Times* (2 August 1990): B11.

Norton, E. "Baseball Hopes to be Big Hit in Europe." *Wall Street Journal* (11 June 1993: B1.

Olmo Del, Frank. "Commentary: Soccer is Kicking Into L.A.'s Future." *The Los Angeles Times* (3 March 2002): M5.

Organ, Dennis W. "Baseball and Global Capitalism." *Business Horizons* (September/October 2002): 1.

Peng, T.C. "From Unknown to Stardom." *Chinese American Forum* (April 2003): 2–3.

Penner, Mike. "Real Deal: It's the Marketing." *The Los Angeles Times* (18 June 2003): D1.

Pesky, Greg. "Global Game Plans." *Sporting Goods Business* (September 1998): 12A–13A.

———. "Spanning the Globe." *Sporting Goods Business* (November 1993): 36.

———. "World Cup '94: Shooting For Global Success." *Sporting Goods Business* (September 1993): 14A1.

Petrecca, Laura. "A Whole New Ball Game: Fitness Guru Steinfeld Places Bet on Lacrosse League." *Advertising Age* (9 October 2000): 38.

Portanger, Erik. "Malcolm Glazer Boosts His Stake in Soccer Club." *Wall Street Journal* (1 December 2003): C11.

Porter, Eduardo. "World Cup 2002: Si, Si!—Zeal of Hispanic-Americans For Soccer Finals." *Wall Street Journal* (6 May 2002): B1.

Posnanski, Joe. "Fans From U.S. Are Often Ignorant." *The Charlotte Observer* (6 April 2003): 7F.

Prager, Joshua Harris. "Managing Cultural Diversity—On the Pitcher's Mound." *Wall Street Journal* (30 September 1998): B10.

Protzman, Ferdinand. "N.F.L. a Big Hit in West Germany." *The New York Times* (12 August 1990): 29.

Pursell, Chris. "Fields of Competition: American Pastimes Going For O'seas Gold." *Variety* (29 June 1998): 27–28.

Quirk, James, and Mohamed A. El-Hodiri. "An Economic Model of a Professional Sports League." *Journal of Political Economy 79* (March/April 1975): 1302–1319.

Rees, C. Roger. "Race and Sport in Global Perspective." *Journal of Sport and Social Issues.* Vol. 20, No. 1 (1996): 22–32.

Reilly, Jim. "The In (Door) Crowd." *Soccer Jr.* (September 2002): 24–25.

Repak, Chaz. "The Meaning of Ichiro." *Wall Street Journal* (Ecstasy in the Ballpark): W6.

"Report Pegs Losses at \$272 Million For League." *The Charlotte Observer* (13 February 2004): 4C.

Reynolds, Mike. "Full Global Press." *Inside Media* (1 February 1995): 22.

Richards, Donald R. "A (Utopian?) Socialist Proposal For the Reform of Major League Baseball." *Journal of Sport and Social Issues.* Vol. 27, No. 3 (2003): 308–324.

Richardson, Karen. "Full-Court Press: Promoter Envisions NCAA in China." *Wall Street Journal* (22 April 2004): A1, A16.

Robichaux, Mark. "International Basketball League Shoots For a Following—WBL, in Its Third Year, Hopes to Cash in on Growing Popularity of Sport." *Wall Street Journal* (25 January 1990): B2.

"Rookie Honors Awarded." *The Charlotte Observer* (11 November 2003): 2C.

Rosentraub, Mark S. "Governing Sports in the Global Era: A Political Economy of Major League Baseball and Its Stakeholders." *Indiana Journal of Global Legal Studies,* Vol. 8:12 (Fall 2000): 121–144.

"Rozelle Looks to Europe." *The New York Times* (21 March 1989): B13.

Rozin, Skip. "Godzilla to the Rescue?" *Business Week* (3 March 2003): 95.

"Scoring Drive." *Business Mexico* (October 1998): 12–15.

Shields, David, and Phil Poynter. "Foreign Guys Can Shoot: That's Why the N.B.A. is in the Import Business." *The New York Times* (3 March 2002): 56.

Shipley, Amy. "Baseball's International Stage." *The Washington Post* (21 May 2003): D1.

Shropshire, Kenneth. "Thoughts on International Professional Sports Leagues and the Application of United States Antitrust Laws." *Denver University Law Review,* Vol. 67:2 (Winter 1990): 193–212.

Simon, Ariel. "Touchdown!" *Harvard International Review* (Winter 2001): 12–13.

Sims, Calvin. "Japanese Leagues Worry About Being Overshadowed." *The New York Times* (30 March 2000): 3.

"16 Teams to Participate in Baseball World Cup in Cuba." *Xinhua News Agency* (14 February 2003): 1.

"Slam Dunk." *Wall Street Journal* (9 January 2003): B5.

Slater, Joanna. "One Man's Drive Helps Make Cricket a Big-Money Sport." *Wall Street Journal* (27 February 2003): A1–A2.

Smith, Claire. "The Game Looks to Foreign Fields." *The New York Times* (27 October 1992): B9, B12.

"Soccer League Set For Launch by Next Year." *Toronto Star* (3 May 2001): SP11.

"So What if NHL Shuts Down, World Cup is Coming to T.O." *Toronto Star* (2 April 2003): E1.

"Spitballing the Minors." *Wall Street Journal* (22 April 2004): A18.

Stevenson, Deborah. "Women, Sport, and Globalization: Competing Discourses of Sexuality and Nation." *Journal of Sport and Social Issues*. Vol. 26, No. 2 (2002): 209–225.

Stewart, Larry. "It's Not Futbol, But NBA's Global Appeal is Growing." *The Los Angeles Times* (8 June 2002): W6.

Stoddart, Brian. "Convergence." *Journal of Sport and Social Issues*. Vol. 21, No. 1 (1997): 93–102.

"Sun Microsystems, NHL Form Strategic Relationship." *Presswire* (24 January 2002): 1.

Suzuki, Ichiro. "Going Global: Major League Sports Poised to Expand to Overseas." *The Washington Times* (5 January 2003): A1.

Teaford, Elliott, and Jim Hodges. "Sports Extra/NHL Preview." *The Los Angeles Times* (30 September 1999): 1.

"Teen Star Adu Signs With MLS." *The Charlotte Observer* (19 November 2003): 2C.

"The NBA Needs to do Some Globetrotting." *Business Week* (19 July 1999): 19.

"The NBA, WNBA and Yahoo! Announce Groundbreaking Global Agreement." *Business Wire* (11 September 2000): 9–19.

"The NFL Experience." *Super Bowl XXXVIII Game Program* (2004): 30.

Thomas, Daniel. "American Football to Launch $5m UK Push." *Marketing Week* (15 May 2003): 10.

Thomaselli, Rich. "NHL Markets Web Site." *Advertising Age* (20 August 2001): 14.

Tkacik, Maureen. "High Court May Decide to Hear Whether Nike's PR Statements to Media, Others Are Protected." *Wall Street Journal* (10 January 2003): B1, B3.

Trachtenberg, Jeffrey A. "Playing the Global Game." *Forbes* (23 January 1989): 90–91.

"U.S. Women Topple Norway." *The Charlotte Observer* (21 March 2004): 5F.

Varadarajan, Tunku. "India vs. Pakistan: Cricket's Tribal Intensity." *Wall Street Journal* (27 February 2003): D8.

"Visa International Becomes the Official and Preferred Payment Card." *PR Newswire* (22 October 1998): 1.

"Visa, NFL Join in Deal For Foreign Marketing." *American Banker* (16 November 1998): 1.

Vitzthum, Carlta, and Henry C. Jackson. "Spend it Like Beckham." *Wall Street Journal* (19 June 2003): B1, B4.

Vrooman, John. "A General Theory of Sports Leagues." *Southern Economic Journal* (1 April 1995): 971–990.

Walker, Monique. "A Powerful Draw." *Pensacola News Journal* (26 May 2001): 1D–5D.

Walker, Sam. "Adios, NFL!" *Wall Street Journal* (5 December 2003): W4.

———. "Catch Yao Later." *Wall Street Journal* (7 February 2003): W4.

———. "Chelsea Morning." *Wall Street Journal* (1 December 2003): W3.

———. "Lost in Transition." *Wall Street Journal* (24 October 2003): W9.

———. "Not Necessarily the NFL." *Wall Street Journal* (10 January 2003): W4.

Washington, Wayne. "Craig Lands NFL Monday Night Football Rights." *The America's Intelligence Wire* (9 May 2003): 1.

Weiner, Tim. "Costa Ricans Sweat Details For Major-League Baseballs." *The Charlotte Observer* (25 January 2004): 10A.

Weingarten, Marc. "Site by Site, N.B.A. Takes on the World." *The New York Times* (14 November 2002): G2.

Weinstein, Elizabeth. "Eurotel Brings First Pro Cheerleaders to Eastern Europe." *Wall Street Journal* (15 November 2002): B1, B6.

Weir, T. "Basketball's Appeal is International." *USA Today* (18–20 June 1993): A1–A2.

White, Erin. "Is Europe Ready For Some Football?" *Wall Street Journal* (15 January 2003): B4.

Wigge, Larry. "A World of Difference." *The Sporting News* (21 February 1994): 48–49.

———. "Global Ice Rink." *The Sporting News* (14 February 2000): 42.

Wilbon, Michael. "Basketball's New World Order." *The Washington Post* (6 September 2002): D1.

Wilstein, Steve. "Shadow on the Game." *The Charlotte Observer* (1 April 2004): 1C, 3C.

Woellert, Lorraine A. "For the WNBA, It's No Easy Layup." *Business Week* (1 May 2000): 102, 106.

Wolff, Alexander. "International Hoops." *The New York Times* (31 May 2002): A23.

Wolverton, Brad. "Does Major League Soccer Have Legs?" *Business Week* (23 March 1998): 68, 70.

Wonacott, Peter, and Betsy McKay. "Yao is a Pitchman Torn Between Two Colas." *Wall Street Journal* (16 May 2003): B1, B4.

Wong, Lloyd L., and Ricardo Trumper. "Global Celebrity Athletes and Nationalism: Futbol, Hockey, and the Representation of Nation." *Journal of Sport and Social Issues*. Vol. 26, No. 2 (2002): 168–194.

Wright, Allison. "Play Ball." *Business Mexico* (April 2000): 44–48.

Wright, George. "The Impact of Globalisation." *New Political Economy* (July 1999): 268–274.

Wyatt, Kristen. "WUSA Folds Days Before Cup Start." *The Charlotte Observer* (16 September 2003): 1C, 3C.

Yannis, Alex. "MetroStars Seek a Foreign Influence." *The New York Times* (12 June 1999): 5.

"Yanqui Doodle Dandy." *Wall Street Journal* (20 February 2004): W11.

Yomiuri, Shimbun. "NHL Short Sighted in Drive For Global Expansion." *The Daily Yomiuri* (5 September 2000): 1.

Books

Allaway, Roger, Colin Jose, and David Litterer. *The Encyclopedia of American Soccer History.* Lanham, MD: Scarecrow Press Inc., 2001.

Bairner, Alan. *Sport, Nationalism, and Globalization: European and North American Perspectives.* Albany, N.Y.: State University of New York Press, 2001.

Ball, Donald A., Wendell H. McCulloch, Jr., Paul L. Frantz, J. Michael Geringer, and Michael S. Minor. *International Business.* New York, N.Y.: McGraw-Hill/Irwin, 2004.

Barros, Carlos Pestana, Muradali Ibrahimo, and Stefan Szymanski. *Transatlantic Sport: The Comparative Economics of North American and European Sports.* Cheltenham, UK: Edward Elgar Publishing Limited, 2002.

Baye, Michael R. *Managerial Economics and Business Strategy.* 4th ed. New York, N.Y.: McGraw-Hill, 2003.

Bernstein, Andrew D. *NBA Hoop Shots: Classic Moments From a Super Era*. San Francisco, CA: Woodford Press, 1996.

Bidini, Dave. *Tropic of Hockey: My Search For the Game in Unlikely Places*. Toronto, Canada: McClelland & Stewart, 2002.

Bougheas, Spiros, and Paul Downward. *The Economics of Professional Sports Leagues: A Bargaining Approach*. Nottingham, England: University of Nottingham, 2000.

Caiger, Andrew, and Simon Gardiner. eds. *Professional Sport in the European Union: Regulation and Reregulation*. Cambridge, U.K.: Cambridge University Press, 2001.

Carroll, M.R., Andrew Podnieks, and Michael Harling. *The Concise Encyclopedia of Hockey*. Vancouver, Canada: Greystone Books, 2001.

Corrado, Charles J., and Bradford D. Jordan. *Fundamentals of Investments: Valuation and Management*. 3rd ed. New York, N.Y.: McGraw-Hill/Irwin, 2005.

Cruise, David, and Alison Griffiths. *Net Worth: Exploding the Myths of Hockey*. New York, N.Y.: Viking Press, 1991.

Daniels, John D., Lee H. Radebaugh, and Daniel P. Sullivan. *Globalization and Business*. Upper Saddle River, N.J.: Prentice Hall, 2002.

Davidson, John, and John Steinbreder. *Hockey For Dummies*. 2nd ed. Foster City, CA: IDG Books Worldwide Inc., 2000.

Demmert, Henry G. *The Economics of Professional Team Sports*. Lexington, MA: D.C. Heath and Company, 1973.

Downward, Paul, and Alistair Dawson. *The Economics of Professional Team Sports*. London, England and New York, N.Y.: Routledge, 2000.

Dryden, Ken. *The Game*. New York, N.Y.: John Wiley & Sons, Inc., 2003.

Echevarria, Roberto Gonzalez. *The Pride of Havana: A History of Cuban Baseball*. New York, N.Y.: Oxford University Press, 1999.

Elicksen, Debbie. *Inside the NHL Dream*. Calgary, Canada: Freelance Communications, 2002.

Euchner, Charles C. *Playing the Field: Why Sports Teams Move and Cities Fight to Keep Them*. Baltimore, MD: Johns Hopkins Press, 1993.

Fort, Rodney, and John Fizel. *International Sports Economics Comparisons*. Westport, CT: Praeger Publishers, 2004.

Guttman, Allen. *Games and Empires: Modern Sports and Cultural Imperialism*. Chapel Hill, N.C.: Columbia University Press, 1994.

———. *Sports Spectators*. New York, N.Y.: Columbia University Press, 1986.

Hax, Arnoldo C., and Nicolas S. Majluf. *The Strategic Concept and Process: A Pragmatic Approach*. Englewood Cliffs, N.J.: Prentice Hall, 1991.

Hill, Charles W.L. *International Business*. 3rd ed. New York, N.Y.: McGraw-Hill/Irwin, 2002.

Hollander, Zander, ed. *The Modern Encyclopedia of Basketball*. Old Tappan, N.J.: Four Winds Press, 1969.

Holzman, Morey, and Joseph Nieforth. *Deceptions and Doublecross: How the NHL Conquered Hockey*. Toronto, Canada: Dundurn Press, Ltd., 2002.

Houda, Patrick, and Joe Pelletier. *The World Cup of Hockey*. Toronto, Canada: Warwick Publishing Inc., 2002.

Jamail, Milton H., and Larry Dierker. *Full Count: Inside Cuban Baseball*. Carbondale, IL: Southern Illinois University Press, 2000.

Jones, Michael E. *Sports Law*. Upper Saddle River, N.J.: Prentice Hall, 1999.

Jozsa, Frank P., Jr. *American Sports Empire: How the Leagues Breed Success*. Westport, CT: Praeger Publishers, 2003.

Jozsa, Frank P., Jr., and John J. Guthrie, Jr. *Relocating Teams and Expanding Leagues in Professional Sports: How the Major Leagues Respond to Market Conditions.* Westport, CT: Quorum Books, 1999.

Kiggundu, Moses N. *Managing Globalization in Developing Countries and Transition Economies.* Westport, CT: Praeger Publishers, 2002.

Klein, Alan M. *Sugarball: The American Game, the Dominican Dream.* New Haven, CT: Yale University Press, 1991.

Klein, Jeff Z., and Karl-Eric Reif. *The Death of Hockey.* Toronto, Canada: Macmillan Canada, 1998.

Koppett, Leonard. *Sports Illusion, Sports Reality: A Reporter's View of Sports, Journalism, and Society.* 2nd ed. Urbana and Chicago, IL: University of Illinois Press, 1994.

Kotler, Philip. *Marketing Management: Analysis, Planning, Implementation, and Control.* 8th ed. Upper Saddle River, N.J.: Prentice Hall, 1994.

LaFeber, Walter. *Michael Jordan and the New Global Capitalism.* New York, N.Y. and London, England: W.W. Norton & Company, 1999.

Lawrence, Paul R. *Unsportsmanlike Conduct: The National Collegiate Athletic Association and the Business of College Football.* Westport, CT: Praeger Publishers, 1987.

Leifer, Eric M. *Making the Majors: The Transformation of Team Sports in America.* Cambridge, MA: Harvard University Press, 1996.

Littlewood, Mary L. *Women's Fastpitch Softball—The Path to the Gold: An Historical Look at Women's Fastpitch in the United States.* Columbia, MO: National Fastpitch Coaches Association, 1998.

Marcano, Arturo J., and David P. Fidler. *Stealing Lives: The Globalization of Baseball and the Tragic Story of Alexis Quiroz.* Bloomington, IN: Indiana University Press, 2003.

Menke, Frank G. *The Encyclopedia of Sports.* 5th ed. Cranbury, N.J.: A.S. Barnes and Company, 1975.

Miller, Marvin. *A Whole Different Ballgame: The Sport and Business of Baseball.* New York, N.Y.: Birch Lane Press, 1991.

Miller, Toby, Geoffrey Lawrence, Jim McKay, and David Rowe. *Globalization and Sport: Playing the World.* Thousand Oaks, CA: Sage Publications, 2001.

Mooy, M. de. *Global Marketing and Advertising: Understanding Cultural Paradoxes.* Thousand Oaks, CA: Sage Publications, 1998.

Neft, David S., and Richard M. Cohen. *The Sports Encyclopedia: Pro Football.* 5th ed. New York, N.Y.: St. Martin's Press, 1997.

Noll, Roger G. ed. *Government and the Sports Business.* Washington, D.C.: The Brookings Institution, 1974.

Noll, Roger G., and Andrew Zimbalist. eds. *Sports, Jobs and Taxes: The Economic Impact of Sports Teams and Stadiums.* Washington, D.C.: Brookings Institution Press, 1997.

Peterson, Robert W. *Pigskin: The Early Years of Pro Football.* New York, N.Y. and London, England: Oxford University Press, 1996.

Pluto, Terry. *Loose Balls: The Short, Wild Life of the American Basketball Association—As Told by the Players, Coaches, and Movers and Shakers Who Made It.* New York, N.Y.: Simon & Schuster, 1990.

Podnieks, Andrew, and Sheila Wawanash. *Kings of the Ice: A History of World Hockey.* Richmond Hill, Ontario, Canada: NDE Publishers, 2002.

Price, S. L. *Pitching Around Fidel: A Journey Into the Heart of Cuban Sports.* Hopewell, N.J.: Ecco Press, 2000.

Quirk, James, and Rodney D. Fort. *Pay Dirt: The Business of Professional Team Sports.* Princeton, N.J.: Princeton University Press, 1992.

Radnedge, Keir. *The Complete Encyclopedia of Soccer: The Bible of World Soccer*. London, England: Carlton, 2000.

Robidoux, Michael A. *Men at Play: A Working Understanding of Professional Hockey*. Montreal, Canada: McGill-Queens University Press, 2001.

Rosentraub, Mark S. *Major League Losers: The Real Costs of Sports and Who's Paying For It*. New York, N.Y.: Basic Books, 1997.

Rote, Jr., Kyle. *Kyle Rote, Jr.'s Complete Book of Soccer*. New York, N.Y.: Simon and Schuster, 1978.

Sanful, John. *Russian Revolution: Exodus to the NHL*. Worcestershire, England: Malvern Publishing Company, 1999.

Schaaf, Phil. *Sports, Inc.: 100 Years of Sports Business*. Amherst, N.Y.: Prometheus Books, 2004.

Seavoy, Ronald E. *Origins and Growth of the Global Economy*. Westport, CT: Praeger Publishers, 2003.

Seymour, Harold. *Baseball: The Golden Age*. 2nd ed. New York, N.Y.: Oxford University Press, 1989.

Shank, Matthew D. *Sports Marketing: A Strategic Perspective*. 2nd ed. Upper Saddle River, N.J.: Prentice Hall, 2002.

Shropshire, Kenneth L. *The Sports Franchise Game: Cities in Pursuit of Sports Franchises, Events, Stadiums, and Arenas*. Philadelphia, PA: University of Pennsylvania Press, 1995.

Slack, Trevor. *Understanding Sport Organizations*. Champaign, IL: Human Kinetics, 1997.

Smith, Doug, and Adam Frattasio. *Goon: The True Story of an Unlikely Journey Into Minor League Hockey*. Fredrick, MD: PublishAmerica, Inc., 2002.

Smith, Ron, Ira Winderman, and Mary Schmitt Boyer. *The Complete Encyclopedia of Basketball*. London, England: Carlton, 2001.

Sports Encyclopedia. New York, N.Y.: Ottenheimer Publishers Inc., 1976.

Sports Illustrated 1999 Sports Almanac. New York, N.Y.: Little Brown and Company, 1999.

Staudohar, Paul D., and James A. Mangan, eds. *The Business of Professional Sports*. Champaign, IL: University of Illinois Press, 1991.

Sullivan, Neil J. *The Dodgers Move West: The Transfer of the Brooklyn Baseball Franchise to Los Angeles*. New York, N.Y.: Oxford University Press, 1987.

Tarango, Martin. *Basketball Biographies*. Jefferson, N.C. and London, England: McFarland & Company, 1991.

Terpstra, V., and K. David. *The Cultural Environment of International Business*. 3rd ed. Cincinnati, OH: South-Western, 1991.

The World Almanac and Book of Facts. Mahwah, N.J.: World Almanac Books, 1950–2002.

Thoma, James E., and Laurence Chalip. *Sport Governance in the Global Community*. Morgantown, WV: Fitness Information Technology, Inc., 1996.

Turco, Douglas M. *The Wide World of Sport Programming*. Champaign, IL: Stipes Publishing L.L.C., 1996.

Westerbeek, Hans, and Aaron Smith. *Sport Business in the Global Marketplace*. New York, N.Y.: Palgrave Macmillan, 2003.

Whiting, Robert. *The Meaning of Ichiro*. Boston, MA: Warner Books, 2004.

———. *You Gotta Have Wa*. Lincolnshire, IL: Vintage Publishing, 1989.

Wise, A. N., and B. S. Meyer, eds. *International Sports Law & Business*. Ardsley, N.Y.: Transnational Publishers, 1997.

Wolff, Alexander. *Big Game, Small World: A Basketball Adventure*. New York, N.Y.: Warner Books, 2002.

Woog, Dan. *The Ultimate Soccer Encyclopedia.* Chicago, IL: Lowell House, 1999.

Dissertations

Dobbs, Michael E. "The Organization of Professional Sports Leagues: Mortality and Founding Rates, 1871–1997." Ph.D. diss., University of Texas at Dallas, 1999.
Grice, James J. "The Monopolistic Market Structure of Professional Sports Leagues." Senior Thesis diss., Colorado College, 1987.
Jozsa, Frank P., Jr. "An Economic Analysis of Franchise Relocation and League Expansion in Professional Team Sports, 1950–1975." Ph.D. diss., Georgia State University, 1977.
Kammer, David John. "Take Me Out to the Ballgame: American Cultural Values as Reflected in the Architectural Evolution and Criticism of the Modern Baseball Stadium." Ph.D. diss., University of New Mexico, 1982.
Rascher, Daniel A. "Organization and Outcomes: A Study of Professional Sports Leagues." Ph.D. diss., University of California at Berkeley, 1997.

Internet Sources

"A Look Back at the International Hockey League." <http://www.sportsbusinessnews.com> cited 3 December 2002.
"A New Hockey League in Canada." <http://www.sportsbusinessnews.com> cited 19 August 2003.
"ABA: Fourteen and Still Counting—Jacksonville Florida in!" <http://www.abalive.com> cited 13 April 2004.
"ABA: Franchise Information." <http://www.abalive.com> cited 13 April 2004.
"ABA: League Office." <http://www.abalive.com> cited 13 April 2004.
"ABA: Standings." <http://www.abalive.com> cited 13 April 2004.
"ABA: The Players." <http://www.abalive.com> cited 13 April 2004.
"ABA: 2004–2005 Expansion Teams." <http://www.abalive.com> cited 13 April 2004.
"About Eurobasket." <http://www.eurobasket.com> cited 27 October 2003.
"About the American Hockey League." <http://www.monarchshockey.com> cited 29 November 2001.
"AC Milan Ousts Arsenal." <http://sportsillustrated.cnn.com> cited 6 April 2004.
Adams, Alan. "Canada Thirsts For Six-Pack." <http://www.nhl.com> cited 30 March 2004.
———. "Recruiting Task Tough For Team USA." <http://www.nhl.com> cited 23 April 2004.
Aenlle, Conrad De. "ManU Making Shareholders Cheer." <http://www.sportsbusinessnews.com> cited 2 September 2003.
Allen, Percy. "David Stern Still Looking to Globalize the Game." <http://www.sportsbusinessnews.com> cited 6 November 2003.
———. "NBA Tips Off in Japan." <http://www.sportsbusinessnews.com> cited 30 October 2003.
"All Eyes on Adu." <http://cnnsi.com> cited 13 August 2003.
"All-Star Game Ratings We're Talking Japan." <http://www.sportsbusinessnews.com> cited 19 August 2003.

Alm, Richard. "Japanese Players and Baseball Cards." <http://www.sportsbusinessnews. com> cited 3 December 2002.

———. "The Globalization of Sports." <http://www.sportsbusinessnews.com> cited 25 November 2002.

"American Bowl Results (1986–2000)." <http://www.tinfl.com> cited 9 October 2003.

"American Bowl Series." <http://www.nfl.com> cited 9 October 2003.

"American Women's Baseball." <http://womensbaseball.com> cited 1 December 2003.

"Anniversary Party: Best European Player to be Revealed at UEFA Congress." <http://si. printthis.clickability.com> cited 23 April 2004.

Applebaum, Simon. "America's All-Soccer Network Ready to Take Its Shot." <http://www. sportsbusinessnews.com> cited 20 February 2003.

"AP's Big Story of the Year—Beckham." <http://www.sportsbusinessnews.com> cited 2 January 2004.

"A's Return to Spanish Radio." <http://www.sportsbusinessnews.com> cited 19 August 2003.

Asher, Mark. "Viva, Monterrey, Mexico and Los Expos." <http://www.sportsbusinessnews. com> cited 19 August 2003.

Baines, Tim. "City of Ottawa—Not a Baseball Town." <http://www.sportsbusinessnews. com> cited 23 March 2004.

"Ballparks." <http://www.ballparks.com> cited 31 December 2003.

Baker, Geoff. "Backers Pitch Merits of New League." <http://mail.pfeiffer.edu> cited 8 April 2003.

Baker, Kent. "Professional Playing Opportunities For Non-Playing NBA Basketball Players." <http://www.sportsbusinessnews.com> cited 19 August 2003.

Barancik, Scott. "Malcolm Glazer Continues to Make His Move on Man U." <http://www. sportsbusinessnews.com> cited 20 February 2004.

Barker, Barbara. "The Internationalization of the NBA." <http://www.sportsbusinessnews. com> cited 25 November 2002.

Barrero, Jim. "MLS Expansion Set For 2005." <http://www.sportsbusinessnews. com> cited 9 October 2003.

Barron, David. "MLS Looks to Houston as Possible Expansion Site." <http://www.sports-businessnews.com> cited 13 March 2003.

"Baseball Has Been Very, Very Good to the Dominican." <http://www.sportsbusinessnews. com> cited 19 August 2003.

"Baseball to Start Testing Latin American Players." <http://www.cnnsi.com> cited 4 September 2003.

"Baseball World Cup Could Get Green Light Soon." <http://www.sportsillustrated.cnn. com> cited 13 November 2003.

"Basketball Without Borders: Fact Sheet." <http://www.nba.com> cited 13 August 2003.

"Basketball Without Borders 2003 Fact Sheet." <http://www.nba.com> cited 13 August 2003.

Bauman, Mike. "Bud Believing in a Baseball World Cup." <http://www.sportsbusiness-news.com> cited 13 November 2003.

Baxter, Kevin. "A Not so Glorious Ending For MLB's Weekend in Mexico." <http://www. sportsbusinessnews.com> cited 16 March 2004.

———. "Los Expos in Puerto Rico." <http://www.sportsbusinessnews.com> cited 6 March 2003.

Beaton, Rod. "The New WHA Could Capitalize on NHL Labor Woes." <http://www.world-hockeyassociation.net> cited 25 November 2003.

"Beer and Germany's 2006 World Cup." <http://www.sportsbusinessnews.com> cited 23 April 2004.

"Beginners Guide to Football." <http://www.nfleurope.com> cited 9 October 2003.

Bell, Jack. "Are Soccer's Cosmos on the Way Back." <http://www.sportsbusinessnews. com> cited 20 February 2003.

———. "Checking in on the MLS's Plans For the Future." <http://www.sportsbusiness-news.com> cited 25 November 2002.

———. "European Football (Soccer) Clubs Look For Talent in the Good Old USA." <http: //www.sportsbusinessnews.com> cited 19 August 2003.

———. "Man U Heading Back Over the Pond." <http://www.sportsbusinessnews.com> cited 23 March 2004.

———. "MLS Going After Hispanic Audience." <http://www.sportsbusinessnews.com> cited 1 December 2003.

———. "The Art of Trying to Host the World Cup In." <http://www.sportsbusinessnews. com> cited 27 April 2004.

———. "The U.S. vs. Iraq on the (Sports) Battlefield." <http://www.sportsbusinessnews. com> cited 13 April 2004.

Bellman, Eric. "Trying to Leverage Success in Japanese Baseball." <http://www.sports-businessnews.com> cited 19 August 2003.

Belson, Ken. "Baseball in the Land of the Rising Sun." <http://www.sportsbusinessnews. com> cited 3 April 2003.

———. "Building a Ballpark in the Land of the Rising Sun." <http://www.sportsbusiness-news.com> cited 4 December 2003.

———. "High School Baseball . . . in Japan." <http://www.sportsbusinessnews.com> cited 26 August 2003.

———. "More Japanese Baseball Stars Heading to America." <http://www.sportsbusiness-news.com> cited 3 December 2002.

———. "NFL Continues to Market Itself in Japan." <http://www.sportsbusinessnews.com> cited 19 August 2003.

———. "The NBA is Talking Japanese." <http://www.sportsbusinessnews.com> cited 30 October 2003.

Berendt, Johannes. "Kickin' Style." <http://www.nba.com> cited 20 April 2004.

"Berlin Welcomes YOU and the NFLX." <http://www.nfleurope.com> cited 9 October 2003.

"Big Game, Small World: A Basketball Adventure." <http://www.amazon.com> cited 10 July 2003.

Blackistone, Kevin B. "David Stern on Basketball's Global Game." <http://www.sportsbus-inessnews.com> cited 25 November 2002.

Blair, Jeff. "Are Los Expos Done in Puerto Rico For 2004?" <http://www.sportsbusiness-news.com> cited 2 September 2003.

———. "In Canada, Women's Sport Channel Axed." <http://www.sportsbusinessnews. com> cited 2 September 2003.

Bloom, Barry M. "Baseball World Cup Being Planned For 2005." <http://www.sports-businessnews.com> cited 13 November 2003.

———. "Bud a Baseball World Cup and Drug Testing." <http://www.sportsbusinessnews. com> cited 29 March 2003.

———. "Diversity Producing Key Leaders." <http://www.mlb.com> cited 15 May 2003.

———. "MLB and China Sign a Working Agreement." <http://www.sportsbusinessnews. com> cited 1 December 2003.

————. "MLB Looking at World Cup in 2005." <http://www.sportsbusinessnews.com> cited 1 August 2003.

————. "Playoff Atmosphere in Tokyo." <http://mlb.mlb.com> cited 30 March 2004.

————. "The NHL and the World Hockey Federation Make Friends." <http://www.sports-businessnews.com> cited 3 December 2002.

Bonham, Dean. "Bonham on the State of Soccer." <http://www.sportsbusinessnews.com> cited 17 December 2003.

————. "Book Takes a Look at the History of Sports as a Business." <http://www.sports-businessnews.com> cited 2 March 2004.

"Brazil Denies U.S. Once Again." <http://cnnsi.printthis.clickability.com> cited 13 August 2003.

Brennan, John. "ManU's Marketing Arm Continues Its Reach." <http://www.sportsbusin-essnews.com> cited 5 August 2003.

"British Youngsters Battle." <http://www.nfleurope.com> cited 13 July 2003.

"Brother, Can You Spare a Star?" <http://www.si.com> cited 11 September 2003.

Broussard, Chris. "The NBA and the Never Ending Search For Talent." <http://www.sports-businessnews.com> cited 16 September 2003.

"Bucs' Owner Increases Man Utd Shares Again." <http://si.printthis.clickability.com> cited 27 April 2004.

Buteau, Michael, and Barry M. Bloom. "The NHL and the World Hockey Federation Make Friends." <http://www.sportsbusinessnews.com> cited 3 December 2002.

"Canadian Baseball League Moving Forward." <http://www.sportsbusinessnews.com> cited 25 November 2002.

"Canadian Baseball League to Conclude Inaugural Season After All-Star Game." <http://www.canadianbaseballleague.com> cited 6 September 2003.

"Canadian Football League Looks at Expansion." <http://www.sportsbusinessnews.com> cited 3 December 2002.

Canfora, Jason La. "Looking at the State of Hockey in Russia." <http://www.sportsbusin-essnews.com> cited 27 April 2004.

————. "Looking at Why Freddy Adu Didn't Consider European Football (Soccer) Teams." <http://www.sportsbusinessnews.com> cited 20 November 2003.

Cannizzaro, Mark. "Godzilla (Matsui) is Missed." <http://www.sportsbusinessnews.com> cited 19 August 2003.

Caplan, Jeff. "Is the NBA Operating a Sweatshop?" <http://www.sportsbusinessnews.com> cited 17 February 2004.

Capozzi, Joe. "MLB in Mexico, is Italy Next?" <http://www.sportsbusinessnews.com> cited 16 March 2004.

Carley, Jim. "Hispanic Players in the NFL." <http://www.sportsbusinessnews.com> cited 19 August 2003.

Carpenter, Les. "MLB Ready For Another Japanese Star." <http://www.sportsbusinessnews.com> cited 6 November 2003.

Carter, Ivan. "Is the End Near For NFL Europe?" <http://www.sportsbusinessnews.com> cited 19 August 2003.

Case, Brendan M. "The NFL Heads to Mexico City." <http://www.sportsbusinessinessnews.com> cited 3 December 2002.

"CFL Enjoying a Renaissance of Sorts." <http://www.sportsbusinessnews.com> cited 20 November 2003.

"CFL Extends NFL Agreement." <http://www.sportsbusinessnews.com> cited 4 December 2003.

"CFL Happy With NFL Partnership." <http://www.sportsbusinessnews.com> cited 3 December 2002.

"Charm Offensive." <http://www.cnnsi.com> cited 13 August 2003.

Chass, Murray. "Deal All But Done, Expos Set to Play 20 Games in San Juan." <http://www.sportsbusinessnews.com> cited 25 November 2002.

———. "Problems With Proposed MLB 2005 World Cup." <http://www.sportsbusinessnews.com> cited 10 February 2004.

———. "Time to Move Forward With Baseball World Cup." <http://www.sportsbusinessnews.com> cited 27 April 2004.

"China Holds First NFL Flag Football Clinic." <http://www.nfl.com> cited 4 December 2003.

"City and Area Population." <http://www.world-gazetteer.com> cited 30 March 2004.

"Coaches Clinic." <http://www.nfleurope.com> cited 9 October 2003.

"Coca-Cola NBA Jam Session Debuts in China." <http://www.nba.com> cited 25 September 2003.

"Coca-Cola Set to Sponsor English Soccer League." <http://www.sportsbusinessnews.com> cited 2 March 2004.

Coleman, Joseph. "NBA Commissioner Sees More Globalization For Basketball." <http://www.yahoo.com> cited 11 November 1999.

Colquhoun, Lachian. "The Ever-Growing Marketing World For Man U." <http://www.sportsbusinessnews.com> cited 20 November 2003.

Cook, John. "Professional Women's Hockey League Looking to Turn the Corner." <http://www.sportsbusinessnews.com> cited 30 March 2004.

Coplon, Jeff. "Basketball in the World's Most Populated Country." <http://www.sportsbusinessnews.com> cited 1 December 2003.

"Cost of Business in the CFL Way Up!!" <http://www.sportsbusinessnews.com> cited 26 August 2003.

Cowell, Alan. "Malcolm Glazer, Man U and the Tampa Bay Bucs." <http://www.sportsbusinessnews.com> cited 2 March 2004.

Crasnick, Jerry. "Baseball May [be] Headed to the Caribbean." <http://www.sportsbusinessnews.com> cited 3 December 2002.

Cressman, Jim. "London Argonauts Are a Possibility." <http://www.sportsbusinessnews.com> cited 19 August 2003.

Cummings, Steve. "Baseball and Cuba." <http://www.sportsbusinessnews.com> cited 19 August 2003.

Dahlburg, John-Thor. "Looking Beyond Ball and Bat to See What Baseball Really Stands For in Puerto Rico." <http://www.sportsbusinessnews.com> cited 19 August 2003.

"David Beckham is One Very Rich Soccer Player." <http://www.sportsbusinessnews.com> cited 20 April 2004.

"David Stern Still Looking to Globalize the Game." <http://www.sportsbusinessnews.com> cited 6 November 2003.

Davidi, Shi. "Canadian Baseball League Counting on Communities." <http://www.sportsbusinessnews.com> cited 18 May 2003.

Davis, Glenn. "U.S. Starting to Tune in to the Big Picture." <http://www.houstonchronicle.com> cited 11 August 2003.

Davis, Steve. "Soccer Needs Stadiums." <http://www.sportsbusinessnews.com> cited 20 February 2004.

Dell'Apa, Frank. "The Success and the Business of the English Premier League." <http://www.sportsbusinessnews.com> cited 4 September 2003.

Dellios, Hugh. "Monterrey Wants the Expos." <http://www.sportsbusinessnews.com> cited 10 February 2004.

"Devils Center Igor Larionov Announces Retirement." <http://nhl.com> cited 20 April 2004.

Diaz, George. "NBA Going Global." <http://www.sportsbusinessnews.com> cited 20 February 2004.

———. "World Cup Success Aside, Can the MLS Compete With European Soccer Leagues?" <http://www.sportsbusinessnews.com> cited 3 December 2002.

Donovan, John. "A New Game Face." <http://www.cnnsi.com> cited 17 July 2003.

———. "As Steroid Use Goes, Baseball's Numbers Just Don't Add Up." <http://sports-illustrated.cnn.com> cited 20 November 2003.

———. "Game Face." <http://sportsillustrated.cnn.com> cited 13 April 2004.

———. "Globalization of the Grand Old Game Hits All-Time High." <http://cnnsi.com> cited 17 July 2003.

Doyle, Paul. "At Least One Group Hoping NHL Armageddon 2004 Becomes Reality." <http://www.sportsbusinessnews.com> cited 10 October 2003.

Duhatschek, Eric. "International Ice Hockey President Not a Fan of Girls Playing With Boys." <http://www.sportsbusinessnews.com> cited 20 February 2003.

———. "What Makes European Professional Hockey Work?" <http://www.sportsbusiness-news.com> cited 14 January 2004.

Dutton, Bob. "Royals Have Shifted Direction in Latin America But Still Trying to Catch Up." <http://www.kansascity.com> cited 8 April 2003.

Edes, Gordon. "Making it Sound so Easy For MLB to Play Games in Europe." <http://www.sportsbusinessnews.com> cited 27 March 2003.

———. "MLB in Europe in 2005?" <http://www.sportsbusinessnews.com> cited 22 September 2003.

Eichel, Larry. "MLB's 'Vision' of a Global Game." <http://www.sportsbusinessnews.com> cited 23 October 2003.

Eichelberger, Curtis. "NFL Considering Heading to China For Pre-Season Games." <http://www.sportsbusinessnews.com> cited 2 January 2003.

"EJC Qualification Begins." <http://www.nfleurope.com> cited 12 October 2003.

Eliot, Darren. "The Euro Conversion Rate." <http://www.cnnsi.com> cited 8 January 2003.

"Euro Football (Soccer) Teams Want to See the Money." <http://www.sportsbusinessnews.com> cited 20 November 2003.

"European Junior Championship Lineups Unveiled." <http://www.nfleurope.com> cited 12 October 2003.

"Europe's Top Clubs Raise Stakes in FIFA Row." <http://si.printthis.clickability.com> cited 13 April 2004.

"Expos Complete Successful San Juan Homestand." <http://www.mlb.com> cited 21 April 2003.

Fainaru, Steve. "MLB May be Looking to Regulate Dominican Agents." <http://www.sportsbusinessnews.com> cited 18 September 2003.

———. "MLB to Consider Drug Testing For Foreign Players." <http://www.sportsbusin-essnews.com> cited 19 August 2003.

———. "The Big Business of Latin American Baseball Players." <http://www.sportsbusin-essnews.com> cited 3 December 2002.

Fatsis, Stefan. "The Continued Globalization of the NBA." <http://www.sportsbusiness-news.com> cited 19 August 2003."

Ferguson, Carrie. "Founder and CEO of a Dream." <http://www.tennessean.com> cited 9 June 2003.

"Ferguson Signs One-Year Rolling United Contract." <http://sportsillustrated.cnn.com> cited 30 January 2004.

"FHL Finalizes Cities in Canada." <http://www.federalhockeyleague.ca> cited 12 November 2003.

"FHL: Free Agent Evaluation Camp." <http://www.federalhockeyleague.ca> cited 12 November 2003.

"FHL: General Information." <http://www.federalhockeyleague.ca> cited 12 November 2003.

"FHL: Investment Opportunities." <http://www.federalhockeyleague.ca> cited 12 November 2003.

"FHL: League Updates." <http://www.federalhockeyleague.ca> cited 12 November 2003.

"FHL: Teams." <http://www.federalhockeyleague.ca> cited 12 November 2003.

"FIFA Enters Centennial Year With Sound Finances." <http://si.printthis.clickability.com> cited 13 April 2004.

"FIFA is in the Big Money." <http://www.sportsbusinessnews.com> cited 13 April 2004.

Finnigan, Bob. "Mariners Not Expected to Open 2004 Season in Japan." <http://www.sportsbusinessnews.com> cited 13 November 2003.

———. "Presenting the International Entity Known as MLB." <http://www.sportsbusinessnews.com> cited 25 November 2002.

"First Drop in Seven Years." <http://si.printthis.clickability.com> cited 13 April 2004.

Fish, Mike. "Basics Training." <http://sportsillustrated.cnn.com> cited 17 July 2003.

———. "European Invasion Has Prep Stars Focusing on Fundamentals." <http://sportsillustrated.cnn.com> cited 17 July 2003.

Fisher, Eric. "Hoping Les Becomes Los Expos For 2004." <http://www.sportsbusinessnews.com> cited 22 August 2003.

———. "Looking at Women's Professional Sports After the Death of the WUSA." <http://www.sportsbusinessnews.com> cited 18 September 2003.

———. "Los Expos Not as Popular the Second Time Around." <http://www.sportsbusinessnews.com> cited 27 April 2004.

———. "MLB Finally Taking Notice of Far East." <http://www.sportsbusinessnews.com> cited 19 August 2003.

———. "MLS Finding New Investors." <http://www.sportsbusinessnews.com> cited 4 December 2003.

———. "NFL Owners Will Keep NFL Europe Alive." <http://www.sportsbusinessnews.com> cited 18 September 2003.

———. "Selling U.S. Professional Sports in China." <http://www.sportsbusinessnews.com> cited 20 January 2004.

———. "The NBA Continues to Use TV to Drive Its Product Internationally." <http://www.sportsbusinessnews.com> cited 25 November 2002.

Fisher, Matthew. "European Hockey Official Look to Squeeze NHL For More Money." <http://www.sportsbusinessnews.com> cited 13 February 2003.

Fitz-Gerald, Sean. "All is as Well as Can be Expected When it Comes to the Canadian Football League." <http://www.sportsbusinessnews.com> cited 3 December 2002.

———. "CFL Makes it Official: They Now Control Another Franchise." <http://www.sportsbusinessnews.com> cited 19 August 2003.

"Flag and Tackle Summer Camps Announced." <http://www.nfleurope.com> cited 12 October 2003.

"Flag Qualifying Tournaments Begin." <http://www.nfleurope.com> cited 12 October 2003.

"Forbes Magazine's 2003 NFL Franchise Valuation." <http://www.sportsbusinessnews. com> cited 2 September 2003.

Ford, Chad. "European NBA Talent—Pay Later, Develop Now." <http://www.sportsbusin- essnews.com> cited 3 December 2002.

———. "NBA Scouting Becomes a World-Wide Experience." <http://www.sportsbusiness- news.com> cited 3 December 2002.

"Foreign-Born Players in the NFL." <http://ww2.nfl.com> cited 25 November 2002.

"Foreign-Born Players in the NFL." <http://www.nfl.com> cited 9 March 2004.

"Foreign Legions." <http://sportsillustrated.com> cited 4 April 2001.

Foster, Chris. "Is the Russian Ice Hockey Federation Withholding Players From the NHL?" <http://www.sportsbusinessnews.com> cited 3 December 2002.

Fox, Ashley McGeachy. "NBA Continues to Expand Horizons." <http://www.sportsbusin- essnews.com> cited 9 October 2003.

Frei, Terry. "NHL and NBA Choosing Different Marketing Strategies." <http://www. sportsbusinessnews.com> cited 13 November 2003.

———. "World Cup a Tease of Global Proportions." <http://sports.espn.go.com> cited 26 November 2003.

French, Scott. "Beginning or End—What Went Wrong in WUSA?" <http://si.com> cited 23 October 2003.

Futterman, Matthew. "Ever the Optimist, MLS Commissioner Don Garber is a True Believ- er." <http://www.sportsbusinessnews.com> cited 6 November 2003.

Gaddis, Carter. "Baseball and Japan." <http://www.sportsbusinessnews.com> cited 30 March 2004.

Galarcep, Ives. "Best Place For Adu to Land is MLS." <http://www.northjersey.com> cited 28 August 2003.

Galehouse, Maggie. "Word Play: Translators Help Foreigners in NBA." <http://www.nba. com> cited 30 March 2004.

"Games and Empires: Modern Sports and Cultural Imperialism." <http://www.amazon. com> cited 13 September 2003.

Garcia, Art. "Basketball's Popularity Growing in Mexico." <http://www.sportsbusiness- news.com> cited 9 October 2003.

"Girl Power." <http://www.nfleurope.com> cited 9 October 2003.

"Global Mailbox: Andrei Kirilenko." <http://www.nba.com> cited 20 April 2004.

"Global Mailbox: Jamaal Magloire." <http://www.nba.com> cited 20 April 2004.

"Globalization and Sport: Playing the World." <http://www.amazon.com> cited 31 March 2003.

"Globalization of the Grand Old Game Hits All-Time High." <http://cnnsi.com> cited 17 July 2003.

Goff, Steven. "MLS' Commissioner Garber Signs a New Deal." <http://www.sportsbusin- essnews.com> cited 20 January 2003.

———, "MLS in Search of a Home For Their All-Star and Championship Game(s)." <http://www.sportsbusinessnews.com> cited 13 April 2004.

———. "Running a Soccer Empire." <http://www.sportsbusinessnews.com> cited 25 Nov- ember 2002.

———. "The Future of the MLS May be Linked to the World Cup." <http://www.sports- businessnews.com> cited 25 November 2002.

Goodnight, Lisa. "Columbian Soccer Comes to America." <http://www.sportsbusinessnews. com> cited 3 December 2002.

Grange, Michael. "The Ever-Expanding National Lacrosse League." <http://www.sports-businessnews.com> cited 3 December 2002.

Grathoff, Pete. "MLS Looking For Investors and Interested Cities." <http://www.sports-businessnews.com> cited 30 January 2004.

Griffith, Bill. "Red Sox Adding Spanish Broadcasts This Year." <http://www.sportsbusin-essnews.com> cited 27 March 2003.

Gross, George. "Former MLB President Paul Beeston Wants a Baseball World Cup by 2005." <http://www.sportsbusinessnews.com> cited 25 November 2002.

"Growing Number of Major Leaguer's Born Outside the USA." <http://www.sportsbusin-essnews.com> cited 3 December 2002.

Gutierrez, Paul. "Fifa Boss Thanks US on Hosting World Cup Again." <http://www.sports-businessnews.com> cited 9 October 2003.

———. "Spanish Soccer Heading For a Work Stoppage." <http://www.sportsbusinessnews.com> cited 24 August 2003.

Handle, Judy Van. "NWBL Alive and Growing." <http://www.sportsbusinessnews.com> cited 3 February 2004.

Harding, Mark. "These Are Heady Days For the Canadian Football League." <http://www.sportsbusinessnews.com> cited 3 December 2002.

Harding, Thomas. "MLB and MLBPA Still Working on World-Wide Draft Plan." <http://www.sportsbusinessnews.com> cited 25 November 2002.

Harris, Stephen. "Clouded Future Remains For WHA." <http://www.sportsbusinessnews.com> cited 11 December 2003.

Harrow, Rick. "Sneaker Companies Broadening Their Horizons." <http://www.sportsbusin-essnews.com> cited 25 November 2002.

———. "Some MLB Business Issues to Examine." <http://www.sportsbusinessnews.com> cited 9 March 2004.

Heath, Thomas. "Is the NFL Considering Playing a Pre-Season Game in China?" <http://www.sportsbusinessnews.com> cited 25 November 2002.

———. "The WUSA May Not be Dead (Yet)." <http://www.sportsbusinessnews.com> cited 16 October 2003.

Henning, Lynn. "Challenges Faced From Baseball's Expanding International Horizons." <http://www.sportsbusinessnews.com> cited 25 November 2002.

Hermoso, Rafael. "With Los Expos a Success, MLB Looking at Further Expanded Horizons." <http://www.sportsbusinessnews.com> cited 22 August 2003.

"He's No. 1: Zidane Edges Beckenbauer as Europe's Top Player of the Past 50 Years." <http://si.printthis.clickability.com> cited 23 April 2004.

Hinton, Ed. "Is NASCAR Looking Beyond Its Current Borders." <http://www.sportsbusin-essnews.com> cited 4 October 2003.

Hiserman, Mike. "The Growing Globalization of MLB." <http://www.sportsbusinessnews.com> cited 25 November 2002.

"History of Australian Women's Baseball." <http://womensbaseball.com> cited 1 December 2003.

"History of the Global Junior Championships 1997–2002." <http://www.nfleurope.com> cited 12 October 2003.

Hoag, Christina. "Spanish Language Sports Broadcast Have Their Own Unique Style." <http://www.sportsbusinessnews.com> cited 25 November 2002.

———. "Sports Focusing More of Their Efforts on the Hispanic Market." <http://www.sportsbusinessnews.com> cited 25 November 2002.

Houston, William. "Don Cherry and HNIC." <http://www.sportsbusinessnews.com> cited 30 January 2004.

———. "NFL Network in the Frozen North." <http://www.sportsbusinessnews.com> cited 19 August 2003.

———. "Stanley Cup Ratings Continue to Deliver in Canada." <http://www.sportsbusinessnews.com> cited 20 April 2004.

Howard, Johnette. "Death of WUSA—Lack of Any Real TV Deal." <http://www.sportsbusinessnews.com> cited 16 October 2003.

Hughes, Frank. "NBA Not Strongly Embraced in Japan." <http://www.sportsbusinessnews.com> cited 30 October 2003.

"IBL's Slam Appears on Verge of Closing Its Doors." <http://www.sportsbusinessnews.com> cited 3 December 2002.

Ihejirika, Maudlyne. "Japanese Fans and the Chicago White Sox." <http://www.sportsbusinessnews.com> cited 30 January 2004.

"IIHF: History of Ice Hockey." <http://iihf.com> cited 12 November 2003.

"IIHF: No NHLers at Olympics if League Shut Down." <http://si.printthis.clickability.com> cited 27 April 2004.

"IIHF Pres Says Players Should Compete in World Champs as Payback." <http://www.sportsbusinessnews.com> cited 20 November 2003.

"Improved Stadium Awaits Expos in Puerto Rico." <http://si.printthis.clickability.com> cited 13 April 2004.

"In Italy Its Called Football and What Else it is New, It's a Big Money Game." <http://www.sportsbusinessnews.com> cited 3 December 2002.

"International Hockey Leader Upset With the NHL." <http://www.sportsbusinessnews.com> cited 3 December 2002.

"International Hockey League to Cease Operations." <http://www.allsports.com> cited 25 November 2003.

"International Players Head to Training Camp." <http://www.nfl.com> cited 18 July 2003.

"International Players in the NBA." <http://www.nba.com> cited 21 May 2003.

"International Players in the NBA." <http://www.nba.com> cited 8 March 2004.

"Introduction to Mexican Basketball." <http://www.latinbasket.com> cited 27 October 2003.

Isidore, Chris. "By All Appearances, Japan is Loving MLB TV." <http://www.sportsbusinessnews.com> cited 13 November 2003.

———. "Coming to America From the Land of the Rising Sun . . . Baseball Star's." <http://www.sportsbusinessnews.com> cited 3 December 2002.

———. "Skating on Thin Ice." <http://cnnmoney.com> cited 16 October 2003.

———. "The International Pastime." <http://cnnmoney.printthis.clickability.com> cited 13 April 2004.

———. "What Does the Future Hold For Soccer in America?" <http://www.sportsbusinessnews.com> cited 25 November 2002.

———. "WNBA: Lovable Money Loser." <http://www.si.com> cited 17 August 2001.

"Its Official—Les/Los Expos Return For 2004." <http://www.sportsbusinessnews.com> cited 11 December 2003.

Jackson, Barry. "World Hockey Association 'Awards' Franchise to Arena Set to be Demolished." <http://www.sportsbusinessnews.com> cited 27 April 2004.

Jackson, Henry. "European Soccer Clubs Eyeing Asia." <http://www.sportsbusinessnews.com> cited 19 August 2003.

Jacobs, Jeff. "A Look Back at the International Hockey League." <http://www.sportsbusinessnews.com> cited 3 December 2002.

Janoff, Barry. "NFL Heads to Mexico to Market the League." <http://www.sportsbusinessnews.com> cited 25 November 2002.

"Japanese Players and Baseball Cards." <http://www.sportsbusinessnews.com> cited 3 December 2002.

Johnson, Roy S. "The Vote is in." <http://sportsillustrated.cnn.com> cited 4 July 2003.

Jones, Grahame L. "Galaxy Making Some Lucrative International Stops." <http://www.sportsbusinessnews.com> cited 6 February 2003.

———. "German Soccer and Topsy-Turvy TV Problems." <http://www.sportsbusinessnews.com> cited 5 January 2004.

———. "Soccer World-Wide Swimming in a Sea of Red Ink." <http://www.sportsbusinessnews.com> cited 11 December 2002.

Jones, Terry. "World Cup of Hockey to Return in 2004." <http://www.sportsbusinessnews.com> cited 25 November 2002.

Jordan, Mary. "Mexico and Les/Los Expos." <http://www.sportsbusinessnews.com> cited 2 October 2003.

"Just How Much of an Effect Will a Higher Canadian Dollar Have on the Maple Leafs." <http://www.sportsbusinessnews.com> cited 6 November 2003.

Kaegel, Dick. "Baseball Has Become America's Game." <http://www.kansascity.com> cited 8 April 2003.

———. "Baseball May Not be King in All Mexico, But it is in Hermosillo." <http://www.kansascity.com> cited 8 April 2003.

Kaufmann, Michelle. "The State of the MLS." <http://www.sportsbusinessnews.com> cited 25 November 2002.

Keisser, Bob. "Americans Are Getting a Kick Out of Soccer." <http://www.presstelegram.com> cited 4 August 2003.

Kelly, Kevin. "Worldwide Draft Caps Wealthy Teams' Monopoly." <http://www.sportsbusinessnews.com> cited 19 August 2003.

Kelso, Paul. "A Monumental Partnership to Say the Least." <http://www.sportsbusinessnews.com> cited 28 August 2003.

Kennedy, Paul. "Too Much International Action is Damaging For MLS." <http://si.printthis.clickability.com> cited 2 September 2003.

Kepner, Tyler. "Yankees Expanding Their International Horizons." <http://www.sportsbusinessnews.com> cited 25 November 2002.

Kim, Randy. "Tall Tales: Catching Up With Gheorghe Muresan." <http://www.nba.com> cited 20 April 2004.

King, David. "Baseball—The Global Game." <http://www.sportsbusinessnews.com> cited 25 November 2002.

———. "How About Dueling Permanent Homes For Les/Los Expos." <http://www.sportsbusinessnews.com> cited 17 December 2003.

Knight, Dana. "Marketing the World Basketball Championships." <http://www.sportsbusinessnews.com> cited 3 December 2002.

Koreen, Mike. "The Strange Tale of the National Lacrosse League Final Continues." <http://www.sportsbusinessnews.com> cited 3 December 2002.

Kubatko, Roch. "Orioles Move Their Triple-A Franchise to Ottawa, is Anyone Happy." <http://www.sportsbusinessnews.com> cited 3 December 2002.

Kuper, Simon. "On the Eve of the World Cup, Football (Soccer) World-Wide is so Much More Then a Game." <http://www.sportsbusinessnews.com> cited 3 December 2002.

Lev, Michael A. "Baseball in the People's Republic." <http://www.sportsbusinessnews.com> cited 21 August 2003.

"List of Metropolitan Areas by Population." <http://en.wikipedia.org> cited 30 March 2004.

Longman, Jere. "The Death of the WUSA on the Eve of the Women's World Cup—It Doesn't Get Any Worse." <http://www.sportsbusinessnews.com> cited 16 September 2003.

Lubin, Marshall. "Women's Professional Football Hits Long Island." <http://www.sportsbusinessnews.com> cited 13 April 2004.

Luecking, Dave. "The Future of Hockey in Canada." <http://www.sportsbusinessnews.com> cited 3 December 2002.

MacLeod, Robert. "Raptors, NBA Not Heading Overseas." <http://www.sportsbusinessnews.com> cited 25 November 2003.

———. "Toronto Raptors Looking to Take Control of NBA Canada." <http://www.sportsbusinessnews.com> cited 24 February 2004.

MacMullan, Jackie. "The Sport and a Quarter of the World's Population." <http://www.sportsbusinessnews.com> cited 27 February 2003.

———. "Yao Ming and the History of Basketball in China." <http://www.sportsbusinessnews.com> cited 27 February 2003.

Mahoney, Ridge. "Look For a Scaled Down Version of the WUSA in 2004." <http://www.sportsbusinessnews.com> cited 11 December 2003.

———. "Looking For Answers as MLS Season Hits Stretch Run." <http://si.printthis.clickability.com> cited 2 September 2003.

———. "MLS Playing Mexican Card." <http://sportsillustrated.cnn.com> cited 2 October 2003.

"Major League Soccer." <http://www.hickoksports.com> cited 3 December 2003.

"Major League Soccer Teams." <http://www.mlsnet.com> cited 9 March 2004.

"Making the Majors: The Transformation of Team Sports in America." <http://www.amazon.com> cited 31 March 2003.

Malkin, Elisabeth. "The Mexican Billionaire in Search of the American Dream." <http://www.sportsbusinessnews.com> cited 25 November 2002.

Mallett, Peter. "The Newest Professional Canadian Sports League." <http://www.sportsbusinessnews.com> cited 25 November 2002.

Manfull, Megan, and Jonathan Feigen. "Rockets New Arena May Have International Appeal." <http://www.sportsbusinessnews.com> cited 19 August 2003.

"Man U Headed Back Over the Pond." <http://www.sportsbusinessnews.com> cited 13 November 2003.

"Man U's Big Sponsorship Deal of the Day." <http://www.sportsbusinessnews.com> cited 11 December 2003.

"Man Utd: We're on Our Way to Cracking America." <http://cnnsi.com> cited 13 August 2003.

Marcano, Arturo J., and David P. Fidler. "Memorandum." <http://www.sportinsociety.org> cited 2 October 2003.

Marcotti, Gabriele. "Brother, Can You Spare a Star?" <http://www.si.com> cited 11 September 2003.

———. "Shock Therapy." <http://si.printthis.clickability.com> cited 4 December 2003.

"Mariners Announce Working Agreement With Japanese Team." <http://baseball.yahoo.com> cited 18 February 1998.

Marx, Gary. "An Expose on Baseball Training Facilities in Latin America." <http://www.sportsbusinessnews.com> cited 19 August 2003.

Maske, Mark. "NFL Opening Their Doors to Foreign Players." <http://www.sportsbusinessnews.com> cited 11 March 2004.

McCalvy, Adam. "Select Brewers Games to be Broadcast in Spanish." <http://www.sportsbusinessnews.com> cited 13 February 2003.

McCarthy, Jack. "MLS Now Looking to Expansion." <http://www.sportsbusinessnew.com> cited 3 April 2003.

McDermott, Mark. "MLB Set to Support New Women's Professional Softball League." <http://www.sportsbusinessnews.com> cited 23 March 2004.

McElheran, Graeme. "Goodbye Canadian Baseball League." <http://www.sportsbusinessnews.com> cited 19 August 2003.

McKee, Sandra. "Maryland's Indoor Soccer Team Making Some Money." <http://www.sportsbusinessnews.com> cited 2 January 2004.

"McKeon, Pena Easy Manager of the Year Winners." <http://sportsillustrated.cnn.com> cited 13 November 2003.

"Meet the Leafs." <http://www.torontomapleleafs.com> cited 2 December 2003.

"Mexican-American Football HOF Makes Presentation in Canton." <http://www.profootballhof.com> cited 6 August 2003.

"Mexican Soccer Leagues Limiting Foreign-Born Players." <http://www.sportsbusinessnews.com> cited 19 August 2003.

"Mexico Crowned Flag Football Champs." <http://www.nfleurope.com> cited 12 October 2003.

"Michael Jordan and the New Global Capitalism." <http://www.amazon.com> cited 31 March 2003.

Miller, Scott. "Paul Tagliabue on the Importance of the NFL in Europe." <http://www.sportsbusinessnews.com> cited 25 November 2002.

Mills, Roger. "Bucs Owners Expanding Their Horizons—Into European Soccer." <http://www.sportsbusinessnews.com> cited 6 March 2003.

"MLB Announces New Licensing Agreements." <http://www.sportsbusinessnews.com> cited 5 August 2003.

"MLB.com to Video Stream MLB Playoffs to Overseas Markets." <http://www.sportsbusinessnews.com> cited 25 November 2002.

"MLB Drug World Cup Testing Agreement in Place." <http://www.sportsbusinessnews.com> cited 27 April 2004.

"MLB Team Rosters." <http://sports.espn.go.com> cited 16 March 2004.

"MLS Attendance Analysis." <http://www.kenn.com> cited 12 April 2003.

"MLS League History." <http://www.mlsnet.com> cited 3 December 2003.

"MLS Set to Expand Their Horizons." <http://www.sportsbusinessnews.com> cited 25 November 2002.

"MLS Signs a Spanish Sponsorship Agreement With Yahoo." <http://www.sportsbusinessnews.com> cited 19 August 2003.

"MLS Signs Agreement With Fox Sports International." <http://www.sportsbusinessnews.com> cited 3 April 2003.

"MLS Year-by-Year Season Overview." <http://www.mlsnet.com> cited 4 December 2003.

Morales, Magaly. "Telemundo Set to Begin Their NBA Coverage." <http://www.sportsbusinessnews.com> cited 25 November 2002.

Moreno, Jenalia. "NFL Boosts Mexican Economy." <http://www.sportsbusinessnews.com> cited 19 August 2003.

———. "NFL Not Quite Ready For That Mexican—Cowboys/Texans Pre-Season Game." <http://www.sportsbusinessnews.com> cited 25 November 2002.

Morrissey, Michael. "Will MLB be Holding Exhibition Games in Mexico City This Year?" <http://www.sportsbusinessnews.com> cited 20 February 2003.

"MSN Signs Agreement With Fox Sports International." <http://www.sportsbusinessnews.com> cited 3 April 2003.

Mullen, Maureen. "Small World at Women's Series." <http://www.sportsbusinessnews.com> cited 19 August 2003.

Myles, Stephanie. "Los Expos Set to Return to San Juan." <http://www.sportsbusinessnews.com> cited 4 December 2003.

———. "Montreal Reaction to Likely Return to San Juan." <http://www.sportsbusinessnews.com> cited 23 October 2003.

"National Football League Europe." <http://www.nfleurope.com> cited 13 October 2003.

"National Pro Fastpitch." <http://profastpitch.com> cited 23 March 2004.

"National Professional Soccer League." <http://www.hickoksports.com> cited 3 December 2003.

"National Women's Hockey League." <http://www.dgp.utoronto.ca> cited 14 January 2004.

Naylor, David. "Canadian Football League and Debts Unpaid." <http://www.sportsbusinessnews.com> cited 3 December 2002.

———. "In the Canadian Football League, When a Salary Cap Isn't a Salary Cap." <http://www.sportsbusinessnews.com> cited 3 December 2002.

"NBA Announces International Preseason Schedule." <http://www.nba.com> cited 4 August 2003.

"NBA Back in Africa For Basketball Without Borders." <http://www.nba.com> cited 6 April 2004.

"NBA Blankets Germany With TV Agreements." <http://www.nba.com> cited 21 May 2003.

"NBA Board of Governors Report." <http://www.sportsbusinessnews.com> cited 16 October 2003.

"NBA Heading to China For Pre-Season Games." <http://www.sportsbusinessnews.com> cited 17 February 2004.

"NBA Mulls Regular-Season Games in China." <http://si.printthis.clickability.com> cited 2 October 2003.

"NBA Players Unite For Africa 100 Camp." <http://www.nba.com> cited 15 August 2003.

"NBA Renews International Television Agreements." <http://www.sportsbusinessnews.com> cited 25 November 2002.

"NBA Renews International TV Deals." <http://www.nba.com> cited 21 May 2003.

"NBA Stars Return to Europe to Educate Youth." <http://www.nba.com> cited 6 April 2004.

"NBA Wants to Turn Yao Admirers Into Team Fans." <http://sportsillustrated.cnn.com> cited 6 April 2004.

"New Canadian Pro Hockey League." <http://www.federalhockeyleague.ca> cited 12 November 2003.

"NFL and Hispanic Fans." <http://www.sportsbusinessnews.com> cited 3 February 2004.

"NFL Coverage Spans the Globe—Agreements Bring Football to Japan, China." <http://www.nfl.com> cited 4 December 2003.

"N.F.L. Europe Loses $20 Million." <http://www.sportsbusinessnews.com> cited 3 December 2002.

"NFL Europe Team Rosters." <http://www.nfleurope.com> cited 23 March 2004.

"NFL Expanding Their Broadcast Horizons." <http://www.sportsbusinessnews.com> cited 4 September 2003.

"NFL Experience Gears Up For New Season of Fun." <http://www.nfleurope.com> cited 12 October 2003.

"NFL Experience Rolls on Through Europe." <http://www.nfleurope.com> cited 12 October 2003.

"NFL Finalizes Deal With F.C. Barcelona." <http://ww2.nfl.com> cited 3 December 2002.

"NFL Football Heads to Japanese TV." <http://www.sportsbusinessnews.com> cited 25 November 2002.

"NFL International Historical Results." <http://ww2.nfl.com> cited 25 November 2002.

"NFL International is a Success." <http://ww2.nfl.com> cited 25 November 2002.

"NFL International Signs Outside Licensing Deal." <http://ww2.nfl.com> cited 25 November 2002.

"NFL Opens Office in Japan." <http://ww2.nfl.com> cited 25 November 2002.

"NFL Owners Will Keep Europe Alive." <http://www.sportsbusinessnews.com> cited 18 September 2003.

"NHL Board of Governors Approve Agreement With World Hockey Federation." <http://www.yahoo.com> cited 19 June 2001.

"NHL International." <http://www.nhl.com> cited 8 March 2003.

"NHL on Tour Visits Sweden." <http://www.nhl.com> cited 26 September 2003.

"North American Soccer League." <http://www.hickoksports.com> cited 3 December 2003.

O'Brien, Kathleen. "In the Dominican is Baseball a Ticket to Paradise?" <http://www.sportsbusinessnews.com> cited 24 February 2004.

O'Neil, Danny. "The Marketing of Yao Ming, a Work in Progress." <http://www.sportsbusinessnews.com> cited 3 December 2002.

"One-Sided Rivalry." <http://sportsillustrated.cnn.com> cited 13 April 2004.

Ortiz, Jose De Jesus. "Mexicans Far From Believers in MLB Dream." <http://www.sportsbusinessnews.com> cited 16 March 2004.

Painter, Jill. "This Just in . . . Yao Ming is Big Business." <http://www.sportsbusinessnews.com> cited 20 February 2003.

Palchikoff, Kim. "Youth Baseball in Russia." <http://www.sportsbusinessnews.com> cited 19 August 2003.

Pennington, Bill. "Canadian Minor Hockey Fiasco(s) Makes it to the New York Times." <http://www.sportsbusinessnews.com> cited 3 December 2002.

Perkins, Dave. "Merger of Toronto Sports Properties Could Happen." <http://www.sportsbusinessnews.com> cited 11 July 2003.

Peterson, Rob. "Fabulous Foreign Freshmen." <http://www.nba.com> cited 13 April 2004.

Peterson, Rob. "Q&A With Mavs Assistant Del Harris." <http://www.nba.com> cited 6 April 2004.

Peticca, Mike. "WNBA Not Concerned About Drop in Attendance." <http://www.sportsbusinessnews.com> cited 16 October 2003.

Pitoniak, Scott. "The Golden Jet on His New Hockey Dream." <http://www.sportsbusinessnews.com> cited 23 April 2004.

"Portugal Gives Assurances on Euro 2004 Security." <http://si.printthis.clickability.com> cited 23 April 2004.

Posnanski, Joe. "Few Baseball Dreams Realized But Many Dashed in Dominican Republic." <http://www.kansascity.com> cited 8 April 2003.

―――. "Spanish Lessons." <http://www.kansascity.com> cited 8 April 2003.

Preston, Mike. "Outdoor Pro Lacrosse League Anything But a Success Story." <http://www.sportsbusinessnews.com> cited 3 December 2002.

"Program to Encompass Three Continents in 2004." <http://www.nba.com> cited 6 April 2004.

"QB Hutchinson Among 229 NFL Europe Invitees." <http://www.sportsillustrated.cnn.com> cited 10 February 2004.

Rahman, Bayan, Andrew Peaple, and Andrew Ward. "Will Soccer's World Cup be a Money Maker in the Far East?" <http://www.sportsbusinessnews.com> cited 3 December 2002.

"Ranking Tables For Metropolitan Areas." <http://www.census.gov> cited 30 March 2004.

Reece, Damian. "Earning it Like Beckham Would be Nice." <http://www.sportsbusinessnews.com> cited 9 March 2004.

Rhoden, William C. "MLB and Japanese Baseball." <http://www.sportsbusinessnews.com> cited 3 December 2002.

Richman, Howard. "MISL Has Big Plans." <http://www.sportsbusinessnews.com> cited 3 December 2002.

―――. "MISL Wanting to Head to That Next Level." <http://www.sportsbusinessnews.com> cited 3 December 2002.

Roarke, Shawn P. "Stars' Prospects Jump at European Assignment." <http://www.nhl.com> cited 13 August 2003.

―――. "Trophies: NHL Announces Awards Finalists." <http://www.nhl.com> cited 23 April 2004.

Romaniuk, Ross. "What About an NHL Facility in Winnipeg." <http://www.sportsbusinessnews.com> cited 5 January 2004.

―――. "Winnipeg Interested in Getting the Pittsburgh Penguins." <http://www.sportsbusinessnews.com> cited 5 January 2004.

"Roster." <http://www.canadiens.com> cited 2 December 2003.

"Roster: Player Bios." <http://www.canucks.com> cited 2 December 2003.

Rothbauer, Kevin. "Goodbye Canadian Baseball League." <http://www.sportsbusinessnews.com> cited 19 August 2003.

Rovell, Darren. "Drafting European Players, Its Buyer Beware." <http://www.sportsbusinessnews.com> cited 3 December 2002.

―――. "Is Reebok About to Sign Yao Ming?" <http://www.sportsbusinessnews.com> cited 25 September 2003.

―――. "Other, Hidden Costs of the NBA's Internationalization." <http://www.sportsbusinessnews.com> cited 25 November 2002.

―――. "Sports Business Trends to Look For in 2003." <http://www.sportsbusinessnews.com> cited 8 January 2003.

―――. "Yao Ming is Loving McDonald's." <http://www.sportsbusinessnews.com> cited 20 February 2004.

Rusnak, Jeff. "Soccer Finding Larger TV Audience." <http://www.sportsbusinessnews.com> cited 1 December 2003.

"Russia Are Champions." <http://www.nfleurope.com> cited 9 October 2003.

"Russia Beats United States 3–2 For Under-18 Title." <http://si.printthis.clickability.com> cited 20 April 2004.

"Russian Billionaire Looking at Man U." <http://www.sportsbusinessnews.com> cited 2 January 2004.

"Russians Keen to Prove Worth." <http://www.nfleurope.com> cited 13 October 2003.

Russo, Michael. "NHL Offers International Flair, Broadcasts Game in Russia." <http://www.sportsbusinessnews.com> cited 6 November 2003.

Sabbagh, Dan. "Bucs Owner Malcolm Glazer Increasing His Man U Investment." <http://www.sportsbusinessnews.com> cited 23 October 2003.

Sandomir, Richard. "Its Good For MLB to Open Their Season in Japan." <http://www.sportsbusinessnews.com> cited 16 March 2004.

———. YES Network Will Focus on Yankees in Japan." <http://www.sportsbusinessnews.com> cited 30 March 2004.

Scanlan, Wayne. "Chinese Women Hockey Team Overcoming Odds." <http://www.sportsbusinessnews.com> cited 1 December 2003.

Schmuck, Peter. "Angelos Spurring the Game of Baseball Abroad (Athens Awaits)." <http://www.sportsbusinessnews.com> cited 19 August 2003.

Sefko, Eddie. "Mavericks—Jazz Play Preseason Game in Mexico." <http://www.sportsbusinessnews.com> cited 9 October 2003.

———. "Mav's Coach Nelson Doesn't See the Value in a Global Market For the NBA." <http://www.sportsbusinessnews.com> cited 16 October 2003.

Shaikin, Bill. "Arte Moreno's Angels Spending Spree May Not be Done." <http://www.sportsbusinessnews.com> cited 14 January 2004.

Shapiro, Leonard. "The Commish (Paul Tagliabue) on NFL Europe." <http://www.sportsbusinessnews.com> cited 3 December 2002.

Shea, John. "The City by the Bay's Connection to Japanese Baseball." <http://www.sportsbusinessnews.com> cited 3 December 2002.

Sheinin, Dave. "A World-Wide Baseball Draft Could be a Logistical Nightmare." <http://www.sportsbusinessnews.com> cited 19 August 2003.

Sherman, Joel. "Rationale Behind the Yankees Joining the MLB Japanese Tour." <http://www.sportsbusinessnews.com> cited 3 December 2002.

Sherwin, Bob. "The Globalization of Baseball Scouting." <http://www.sportsbusinessnews.com> cited 25 November 2002.

Shipley, Amy. "Baseball Looking to Internationalize." <http://www.sportsbusinessnews.com> cited 19 August 2003.

Shoalts, David. "NHL in Europe—Not Anytime Soon." <http://www.sportsbusinessnews.com> cited 24 September 2003.

Siler, Ross. "Is the NBA Really Looking at Global Expansion?" <http://www.sportsbusinessnews.com> cited 10 February 2004.

Simpson, Gordon. "*Inter*national Basketball Association." <http://www.insidehoops.com> cited 30 June 2003.

Singer, Tom. "MLB.com Looks at the Concept of a World-Wide Baseball Draft." <http://www.sportsbusinessnews.com> cited 3 December 2002.

"Sites Chosen For WUSA Soccer Festival." <http://si.printthis.clickability.com> cited 2 March 2004.

Smith, Craig S. "How China Intends to Benefit From the NBA or China's Version of Democracy." <http://www.sportsbusinessnews.com> cited 3 December 2002.

Smith, Sekou. "David Stern Expects to See the NBA in Europe." <http://www.sportsbusinessnews.com> cited 30 March 2004.

"Soccer League Set For Launch by Next Year." <http://mail.pfeiffer.edu> cited 8 April 2003.

Solomon, George. "FC Barcelona (Football Club) and the NFL Team Up." <http://www.sportsbusinessnews.com> cited 3 December 2002.

Soshnick, Scott. "NBA's Mexican Born Player and Endorsement Opportunities." <http://www.sportsbusinessnews.com> cited 3 December 2002.

———. "NBA Makes it Official—No Teams Heading to Europe or Far East." <http://www.sportsbusinessnews.com> cited 25 November 2003.

———. "Yao Ming and One Billion Chinese Basketball Fans." <http://www.sportsbusinessnews.com> cited 3 December 2002.

Souhan, Jim. "Baseball in Latin America, as Colorful as the Countries." <http://www.sportsbusinessnews.com> cited 20 January 2003.

———. "Latin American Academies Becoming the Norm." <http://www.sportsbusinessnews.com> cited 14 January 2003.

"Sport Business in the Global Marketplace." <http://www.amazon.com> cited 31 March 2003.

"Sport, Nationalism, and Globalization: European and North American Perspectives." <http://www.amazon.com> cited 31 March 2003.

"Stars of GJC VII Sign National Letters of Intent." <http://www.nfleurope.com> cited 9 October 2003.

"Stealing Lives: The Globalization of Baseball and the Tragic Story of Alexis Quiroz." <http://www.amazon.com> cited 31 March 2003.

"Stern and Granik Get Ready For a New NBA Season." <http://www.sportsbusinessnews.com> cited 23 October 2003.

Stier, Kit. "Jets Hope to Break Into Japanese Market." <http://www.sportsbusinessnews.com> cited 19 August 2003.

Stone, Larry. "Selig Discusses Cancellation of Overseas Opener." <http://www.sportsbusinessnews.com> cited 27 March 2003.

Straus, Brian. "Can the Women's World Cup Save the WUSA?" <http://www.sportsbusinessnews.com> cited 18 September 2003.

———. "The WUSA and Its Imminent Demise." <http://www.sportsbusinessnews.com> cited 26 August 2003.

Struck, Doug. "Japanese Appreciative of Their Exports." <http://www.sportsbusinessnews.com> cited 19 August 2003.

"Summer Lovin' For Youngsters." <http://www.nfleurope.com> cited 12 October 2003.

"Super Bowl to Focus on Hispanic Market." <http://www.sportsbusinessnews.com> cited 30 October 2003.

Sylvers, Eric. "The Business of Soccer, Not so Good in Italy." <http://www.sportsbusinessnews.com> cited 13 November 2003.

Talalay, Sarah. "Miami Heat Continue Their Hispanic Marketing Efforts." <http://www.sportsbusinessnews.com> cited 3 December 2002.

———. "NFL Looking to Grow Latin Fan Base." <http://www.sportsbusinessnews.com> cited 13 November 2003.

———. "The Internationalization of the NBA Continues." <http://www.sportsbusinessnews.com> cited 2 January 2004.

"Tampa Bay Lightning Roster and Printable Player Cards." <http://www.tampabaylightning.com> cited 2 December 2003.

Taylor, Phil. "Global Game." <http://sportsillustrated.com> cited 2 July 2003.

———. "Will Foreign-Born Players Bring the U.S. Fans Back to the NBA?" <http://www.sportsillustrated.com> cited 2 July 2003.

"The Global Marketing of Yao Ming." <http://www.sportsbusinessnews.com> cited 22 January 2003.

"The World Cup of Baseball." <http://www.sportsbusinessnews.com> cited 25 November 2002.

"The World Gazetteer." <http://www.world-gazetteer.com> cited 1 November 2003.

"The World Hockey Association Concludes Two Days of Meetings in Toronto." <http://www.worldhockeyassociation.net> cited 22 January 2004.

Thompson, Wright. "Cuban Ballplayers Have More Than Most, But Still Not Enough." <http://www.kansascity.com> cited 8 April 2003.

———. "Some Baseball Scouts in Cuba, But the Risks Are High." <http://www.kansascity.com> cited 8 April 2003.

"Time on Yao's Side." <http://www.nba.com> cited 27 April 2004.

Timmermann, Tom. "Looking at the State of Women's Professional Sports." <http://www.sportsbusinessnews.com> cited 25 September 2003.

Timmons, Heather. "An Important European Television Football (Soccer) Deal." <http://www.sportsbusinessnews.com> cited 2 January 2004.

Topkin, Marc. "Making MLB Heading to Japan—Feel Comfortable." <http://www.sports-businessnews.com> cited 23 March 2004.

———. "Yankees International MVP Readies For Media Circus." <http://www.sports-businessnews.com> cited 6 February 2003.

"Toronto Interested in MLS, Luke-Warm Response." <http://www.sportsbusinessnews.com> cited 13 February 2003.

Treanor, Jill. "Bucs Owner Invests More in Man U." <http://www.sportsbusinessnews.com> cited 2 October 2003.

Trecker, Jerry. "U.S. Success Could Increase American Fan Base." <http://www.sportsbusinessnews.com> cited 3 December 2002.

"Trendsetting Hunt Hopes New Stadiums Like Frisco's Kickstart MLS Growth." <http://si.printthis.clickability.com> cited 24 February 2004.

Trusdell, Brian. "European, South American Soccer Franchises Casting an Eye Towards America." <http://www.sportsbusinessnews.com> cited 25 November 2002.

"TV Azteca and the NBA Extend Broadcast Partnership." <http://www.nba.com> cited 29 August 1998.

"2004 Mock Draft." <http://www.nbadraft.net> cited 13 April 2004.

"2004 World Cup of Hockey Information." <http://sportsillustrated.cnn.com> cited 30 January 2004.

"2004 World Cup of Hockey Schedule." <http://www.si.com> cited 17 April 2003.

"2003 WNBA Season to be Broadcast in 183 Countries." <http://www.wnba.com> cited 21 October 2003.

"2003 Women's World Series." <http://www.wibba.com> cited 1 December 2003.

"2003–2004 Edmonton Oilers." <http://www.edmontonoilers.com> cited 2 December 2003.

"UEFA: Birth of UEFA." <http://www.uefa.com> cited 26 November 2003.

"UEFA: Champions League." <http://www.uefa.com> cited 26 November 2003.

"UEFA: Overview." <http://www.uefa.com> cited 26 November 2003.

Umstead, R. Thomas. "Women's Network Unsure of Their Commitment to WNBA." <http://www.sportsbusinessnews.com> cited 26 August 2003.

"United Soccer Association." <http://www.hickoksports.com> cited 3 December 2003.

"U.S. to Face Lithuania in Olympic Basketball." <http://sportsillustrated.cnn.com> cited 13 November 2003.

"USA World Champions." <http://www.nfleurope.com> cited 12 October 2003.

Vecsey, George. "Economically the WUSA Had to Die." <http://www.sportsbusinessnews.com> cited 16 September 2003.

"Venezuelan Baseball League." <http://www.geocities.com> cited 2 October 2003.

Verducci, Tom. "The African-American Baseball Player is Vanishing. Does He Have a Future?" <http://sportsillustrated.cnn.com> cited 17 July 2003.

Vinocur, John. "Baseball in Europe." <http://www.sportsbusinessnews.com> cited 19 August 2003.

Waldie, Paul. "NHL Armageddon 2004—the Bank(s) Are Calling." <http://www.sportsbusinessnews.com> cited 20 February 2004.

Walker, Sam. "The (Non) Internationalization of the NFL." <http://www.sportsbusinessnews.com> cited 11 December 2003.

Wang, Gene. "Is Yao Ming Bridging the Gap Between China and the United States?" <http://www.sportsbusinessnews.com> cited 6 March 2003.

Ward, Andrew. "Will Soccer's World Cup be a Money Maker in the Far East?" <http://www.sportsbusinessnews.com> cited 3 December 2002.

Ward, Bill. "Euro Clubs Don't Want to Pay When Players Are Away For National Events." <http://www.sportsbusinessnews.com> cited 1 December 2003.

Warren, Ken. "The Death of the IHL." <http://www.sportsbusinessness.com> cited 3 December 2002.

Warren, Tim. "After the Pillage, European Basketball is Not Happy With the NBA Style of B-Ball." <http://www.sportsbusinessnews.com> cited 16 September 2003.

Weber, Bruce. "Did Baseball Originate in Egypt?" <http://www.sportsbusinessnews.com> cited 3 September 2003.

Westhead, Rick. "NHL Expanding European Revenue Generation Potential." <http://www.sportsbusinessnews.com> cited 25 November 2002.

"WFL Europe." <http://www.wfl.com> cited 13 October 2003.

Whincup, Tony. "Britain Braces For Athlete Influx." <http://cnn.allpolitics.printthis.clickability.com> cited 27 April 2004.

Whiteside, Kelly. "WUSA Has Plans For 2005." <http://www.sportsbusinessnews.com> cited 10 February 2004.

Wilson, Peter, and Nick Benequista. "Not a Great Season For the Venezuela's Professional Baseball League." <http://www.sportsbusinessnews.com> cited 20 January 2003.

Windhorst, Brian. "Yao is a Big Star." <http://www.sportsbusinessnews.com> cited 20 February 2004.

Wise, Mike. "The Globalization of the NBA." <http://www.sportsbusinessnews.com> cited 25 November 2002.

———. "World Basketball Championships a Non Success (Off the Court)." <http://www.sportsbusinessnews.com> cited 3 December 2002.

Wise, Mike, and Craig S. Smith. "How China Intends to Benefit From the NBA or China's Version of Democracy." <http://www.sportsbusinessnews.com> cited 3 December 2002.

"WNBA Extends Their Season." <http://www.sportsbusinessnews.com> cited 16 October 2003.

"WNBA Players From Around the World: 2003 Season." <http://www.wnba.com> cited 21 October 2003.

Wolff, Alexander. "A Truly Global Game." <http://sportsillustrated.cnn.com> cited 26 June 2003.

———. "Basketball in a Post-9/11 World." <http://www.twbookmark.com> cited 25 June 2003.

———. "Expanding to Europe Could be in the Cards For the NBA." <http://sportsillustrated.cnn.com> cited 26 June 2003.

———. "Foreign Intrigue." <http://cnnsi.printthis.clickability.com> cited 28 June 2003.

————. "International Basketball Association?" <http://sportsillustrated.cnn.com> cited 26 June 2003.

————. "The Decline of U.S. Dominance." <http://sportsillustrated.cnn.com> cited 25 June 2003.

————. "The Rest of the World Nearly Has Caught Up to the U.S." <http://sportsillustrated.cnn.com> cited 26 June 2003.

"Women's Baseball League Inc." <http://baseballglory.com> cited 1 December 2003.

"Women's Football Getting Ready to do the Ickey Shuffle." <http://www.sportsbusinessnews.com> cited 23 March 2004.

"Women's United Soccer Association." <http://www.hickoksports.com> cited 3 December 2003.

Wood, Sean. "Rangers Target Hispanic Fans . . . Again." <http://www.sportsbusinessnews.com> cited 27 March 2003.

"World Cup of Hockey Information." <http://sportsillustrated.cnn.com> cited 30 January 2004.

"World Cup of Hockey to Return." <http://www.upi.com> cited 26 November 2003.

"World Cup of Soccer." <http://www.wldcup.com> cited 29 January 2004.

"World Football League Quick History." <http://wflfootball.tripod.com> cited 6 October 2003.

"World Hockey Association." <http://www.worldhockeyassociation.net> cited 25 November 2003.

"World League Renamed NFL Europe." <http://www.nfl.com> cited 11 March 1998.

"WUSA Begins Ticket Drive to Fund Planned Return." <http://sportsillustrated.cnn.com> cited 17 February 2004.

"WUSA History." <http://www.wusa.com> cited 19 August 2003.

"Yankees International MVP Readies For Media Circus." <http://www.sportsbusinessnews.com> cited 6 February 2003.

"Yao Has the Answers." <http://www.nba.com> cited 20 April 2004.

Yorio, Karo. "Russia, Defections, the NHL and Money." <http://www.sportsbusinessnews.com> cited 15 December 2003.

York, Geoffrey. "Live From China—the Legend of Yao Ming." <http://www.sportsbusinessnews.com> cited 8 January 2003.

Zelkovich, Chris. "Blue Jays May be Headed to Global." <http://www.sportsbusinessnews.com> cited 25 November 2002.

————. "Selling Canadian Sports Programming on American Sports Television." <http://www.sportsbusinessnews.com> cited 15 December 2003.

Ziehm, Len. "San Diego Likely Site For MLS Expansion in 2004." <http://www.suntimes.com> cited 14 August 2003.

Media Guides

Hurricane Watch. Issue 3, Volume 5 (Raleigh, N.C.: Carolina Hurricanes Hockey Club, 2001).

NFL International (New York, N.Y.: National Football League, 2002).

NFL 2001 Record & Fact Book (New York, N.Y.: National Football League, 2001).

Sports Media & Technology (New York, N.Y.: Street & Smith's Sports Business Journal, 2002).

Super Bowl XXXVIII Game Program (Houston, TX: National Football League, 2004).

2002 SupHer Bowl (Pittsburgh, PA: National Women's Football League, 2002).

2003 Championship (Nashville, TN: National Women's Football Association, 2003).
2004 Media Guide (Nashville, TN: National Women's Football Association, 2004).
World Congress of Sports (New York, N.Y.: Street & Smith's Sports Business Journal, 2003).

Reports

Lapchick, Richard E. *2003 Racial and Gender Report Card* (Orlando, FL: University of Central Florida, 2003).

Index